A HYMNAL:
The Controversial Arts

William F. Buckley, Jr.

A HYMNAL:

The Controversial Arts

G. P. Putnam's Sons
New York

SBN:399-12227-3

Library of Congress Cataloging in Publication Data

Buckley, William Frank, 1925-
    A hymnal

    Includes index.
I. Title.
AC8.B733   1978   081   78-18892

Printed in the United States of America

Fifth Impression

Acknowledgments
My thanks to the proprietors of the following where this material originally appeared: *The American Spectator, Commentary,* the *Daily* and *Sunday Telegraph* (London), *Esquire, Flying,* Gateway Editions, *National Review,* the New York *Times, The New Yorker, Vogue,* and the Washington Star Syndicate. My thanks to Joseph Isola for his fine copyreading, and to Frances Bronson and Robin Wu for help of every kind.

For Pitts, with love

Contents

Introduction   15

I. *The Struggle*

After Ten Years: A Toast on the 10th Anniversary of
    The American Spectator, 1977   23
Socialism and Freedom   25
Vietnam   28
    On the collapse of Saigon   28
    No breast-beating?   30
    What happened?   32
    Lest we forget   34
Human Rights   36
    Mr. Carter's discovery   36
    Pravda's concern   39
    A dupe's progress   41
    What happened to the Genocide Convention? 43
    Cambodia   45
Détente   47
    Crisis on Soyuz-Apollo   47
    On refusing to greet Solzhenitsyn   49
    Kissinger as historical pessimist   51
    American businessmen in the Soviet Union 53

When is a nation "Marxist"?   57
Can Carter mean what he says?   59
The CIA   63
   The stigma of having been one   63
   The scandals   65
   The FBI and Martin Luther King   67
   The new Intelligence Committee   69
   How Robert Redford saved us from the CIA   71

II. *Politics*

Richard Reeves on President Ford   77
Enter Carter   80
   What are they doing to him?   80
   Carter invincible?   82
   New boy in town   84
The Conventions   86
   The Democratic Platform, 1976   86
   Carter adieu   89
   Naming Schweiker: the afterbirth   91
   Enter Buckley   93
   The sights and the smells   95
   The GOP triumphant   97
   Closing night   99
The Campaign   102
   Presidents and cherry trees   102
   Earl Butz's joke   104
   The Polish joke   106
   Buckley on Buckley   108
   Citizen Brown?   110
   Al Smith night   112

III. *The Long Reach of Watergate*

John Ehrlichman's Testament   117
Approaching the Anniversary   121
Nixon as the Last Picture Show   124

Nixon on Nixon   126
  Frost: 1, 2, 3   126
Arthur Schlesinger, Jr. at Camelot   132

IV. *People, Characters*

The Long War Against McCarthyism   139
  Lillian Hellman: Who is the ugliest of them all?   139
  Tail Gunner Joe   152
  I remember Paul Hughes   157
  Commemorating Paul Robeson   159
  Honoring Linus Pauling   161
A Tory's Tribute to Hubert Humphrey   163
Senator Buckley *vs.* New York?   174
Eric Sevareid's Disillusionment   176
The Vindication of Sacco and Vanzetti   179
Chou En-lai, RIP   181
Venezuela's CAP   183
Ferdinand Marcos: The Bloody Beginning   186
The Rogues and Heroes of John Greenway   188
David Niven Recreates Hollywood   190
James Jackson Kilpatrick Celebrates Scrabble, Va.   194

V. *Reforms*

Social Security: The Inside Story   199
Inflation: Senator Kennedy's Funny Money   201
Resignation: The Neglected Alternative   203
The Libel Laws: Desolation   205
Gun Control: It Won't Work   207
Federal Subsidies: Civil War   210
Federal Wage Increase Reform: *Mea Culpa*   212
The Law: Malpractice   214
A National I.D.?: Yes   216
Three-Martini Lunch?   218
For the Inflationists: Mug Shots   220
Energy: Keeping the Issues in Sight   222
The Duty to Vote: Passing the Torch   224

VI. *Abroad*

The Panama Canal: An Opening Statement, Debate with
  Ronald Reagan   229
On Hating America from Abroad   235
The United Nations   237
  Experiencing Carter   237
  Experiencing Andy Young   240
So What *Is* Wrong with Great Britain?   242
London Notes: 1975, 1976, 1977   245
A Day in Israel   250
A Light on Darkest Africa   252
General Franco's Executions   255
Revisiting the Soviet Union   257
  Russia *contra naturam*   257
  Sunday in Leningrad   259
  Restoration in Russia   261
An Evening with Fidel Castro   264
Terror in Argentina   266
South African Impasse   270
The Beauty of Chinese Shadows   272
The Chastened Dollar   274
Airline Update   276

VII. *Manners, Morals, Mannerists*

Abortion as a Campaign Issue   281
Auction Time at the ACLU   283
The Trials of Christianity   285
His New Prayer   287
The Quinlan Case   290
Feminism: Unsex Me Now   293
Personal   295
  Does anyone know Elton John?   295
  Up from misery: Kenneth and AA   298
  Mrs. Ford on chastity   300

Your ethos is slipping   303
Please don't eat the daisies   305
Just call me Bill   307
Reflections on gift-giving   310
Sex scandal in Mormonland   312
Pity Harry Reems?   314
Even little gulls do it   316
Do you know Barney's?   318
The selling of your own books: a bill of rights   320

VIII. *Notes & Asides*

IX. *Crime and Punishment*

Crime in America   385
Chicago Is Not the Worst   387
Death for Gilmore?   389
The Electric Chair and the Mayoral Campaign   391
Thinking about Crime   393
The Return of Edgar Smith   395
Edgar Smith, Act III   397

X. *At Home*

The House   403
The Cook   406
The American Look   409

XI. *Education*

God and Man at Yale: Twenty-five Years Later   415

XII. *Sport*

We Learned to Ski   451
Learning to Fly   454
At Sea   462

Index   503

Introduction

THIS IS THE SIXTH volume in which I collect some of my writings on the assumption, so far happily justified by experience, that some of them weather at least the shorter seasons. To be sure, this is primarily an economic assumption, by which I mean that this book would not be published except on the expectation by the publisher that it will, manfully, shoulder its capital burden. That it will do so does not of course say anything about it beyond that exactly: that there is a market for it. What its prospects are in the long, critical term one cannot know. That statement is not merely a ritual gesture to modesty. After all, it is altogether possible that the future will welcome that which is inferior, rejecting that which is virtuous, witty, eloquent and wise. Who knows? All an author can say is what I have said before, namely that it follows that the views expressed herein are—in the author's judgment at least—illuminating, at best sublime: else why not present different views which *are* that? There is no reason to advance these positions except on the assumption that they are the very best in current circulation. That is why, in an age where even the most sacred objects permit themselves to be used as metaphor, I call this book: *A Hymnal.* And subtitle it, "The Controversial Arts." Controversial because for almost everything that is said here, there is an opposite, if intellectually unequal, reaction set down somewhere. This is of course a pity but on the other hand I have not expected to bring around the world by acclamation.

Correspondence provoked by previous volumes suggests

15

that there are a few questions, some of them mechanical, concerning which there is considerable curiosity. Those that I can answer, I take this opportunity to do, adding a point or two of possible interest.

How much editing is done by an author bringing together a collection? I don't know about the generality of collections. In my own case very little, unless you count as editing the process of selection. In the course of a typical year, I compose 150 newspaper columns, a dozen longer articles or reviews, eight or ten speeches, fifty introductions for television, the editorial arrangements of twenty-five columns for *National Review*, and a book. Times three ends you up with a vast amount of material from which to pluck out a volume of this size. In that sense there is editing. Here and there I shorten a piece, and occasionally I run two columns as a single article, adjusting the transition. And—rarely—I substitute a different word, or phrase, for what was in the original.

I have discovered, in sixteen years of writing columns, that there is no observable difference in the quality of that which is written at very great speed (twenty minutes, say), and that which takes three or four times as long. Perversely, it is sometimes otherwise, which is to say that pieces that take longer to write sometimes, on revisiting them, move along grumpily. This could mean that they had been interrupted, from paragraph to paragraph, to introduce intricate figures or analysis. Or it could mean nothing at all. I make the point only because a number of correspondents express curiosity about it.

While on the general subject, I note that the preparation of these volumes requires, for me, more time than the writing of a brand new book. Between assembling my previous collection and this one, I wrote two novels and a book about sailing, each one of which I completed in fewer working hours than were consumed by this hymnal. That is in part because I read very slowly, and the sheer bulk of the material I need to go through consumes a great deal of time. Subsequent parings, and groupings, also take time, with the added disadvantage that when you put aside such a book as this to resume work on it the next day, only after doing your routine work, having lunch, and skiing (this always precedes work on my books), it is harder to pick up the story line. In assembling collections, I find it difficult at first to remember where I had put all the straws on which I had concentrated so heavily the night before and, inevitably, work is repeated.

A note or two about items in *Hymnal*. It contains two pieces commissioned by the New York *Times* but never published there. The first is called "A Tory's Tribute to Hubert Horatio Humphrey." It was known in October 1977 that the senator would not live for many more weeks and the editor of the New York *Times Magazine* thought it would be arresting to publish an essay on the senator by a member of the political opposition. I thought the whole notion risky, but I was dealing with an editor of great and communicable personal conviction who persuaded me to take on the assignment. I did, composing the piece while flying to Tokyo and telephoning it in from there to meet a deadline. A few days later, reaching Honolulu, I got word that the piece was deemed "too savage" to run about a dying man. So I published it in *National Review*, and then sent it to Senator Humphrey. I cherish a note from his assistant, written shortly after the senator's death, that Mr. Humphrey had enjoyed the piece and would have acknowledged it save for his diminished energy. None of this is to reproach the editors of the *Times*, who by the way instantly and uncomplainingly paid over the proffered fee. It is difficult exactly to recapture the emotions of a transient national mood, and conceivably such a piece as this, critical of the senator's positions and of his intellectual habits, would have outraged the *Times*'s readers appearing at a time when the senator was terminally ill. Still, it will be interesting to know how it is received at this point.

It was I who proposed to the editor of the New York *Times Book Review* that I review a volume by John Greenway. The idea approved, I did so: and the months went by. Pressuring an editor to publish a review which editor holds life and death power over your own books is a temptation authors even brasher than I know how to modulate. I expressed my pique by declining several proffered reviews over a period of a year, but managed a reconciliation in plenty of time to cure relations before the appearance of my novel, *Stained Glass*. I mention this because it is the only piece in this book that has not previously appeared in print, and readers may wish to speculate why. The easiest explanation, of course, is that it contains an obscenity; but I tend to think this insufficient.

A word or two, finally, about the two final selections. The first is an introduction, written in the fall of 1977, to the reissuance of my first book, *God and Man at Yale*. This appeared, in drastic truncation, in *Harper's* Magazine, and although it was skillfully edited, it did not, in that form, communicate what I wished to communicate. The essay is long but I think spicy and in its way convincing. It gave me a sense of consummation twenty-five years of silence had, I discovered, denied me. As is so often the case, a controversy that reaches rabid proportions (I think of all that whirled about the head of Senator Joseph McCarthy) is sometimes more interesting as experience than as disagreement. It is hard to believe, in the uproar over *God and Man at Yale*, how some people behaved as recently as twenty-five years ago; but they did, they did, and now that activity is preserved in amber. I did not edit out the page numbers appearing in the essay because I found them, for reasons difficult to describe exactly, integral to the rhythmic effect of the essay.

Very few people who pick up this book will have seen the essay in question, as the reissue of *God and Man at Yale* was intended for a very small audience interested in historical curios. This is not so of the final essay in this book. That essay is on sailing, and is drawn from my book *Airborne*. The editorial condensation was done by the editors of *The New Yorker* magazine. I reproduce it here because it is the only thing I have ever written that everyone liked. I exaggerate. In this case it is fair to say that comments about it were in a number of cases ecstatic. I really don't know exactly why, surmising that it must be because so many sailors have had similar experiences and were inspirited by the knowledge that others had suffered the same vexations. But, strangely, many who wrote have never ridden in a sailboat, and they too were caught up in this essay. So here it is, to be read fresh by those who missed it and are curious; to be available for those who wish to read it again. I was disappointed when my friend Mr. Walter Minton, the president of Putnam's, told me that my obduracy in including the two long essays on Yale and sailing meant that this book would be priced at more than twelve dollars, but I have learned to live with disappointments, and continue to hope that the extra dollar or two will, at least by a few, be spent without undue resentment. If it worked out that that extra dollar came to me, I'd gladly refund it to those who wrote to express their chagrin. Alas, the miserable authors have to get along with only 15 percent. If, in return for a dollar taken from the consumer, I returned him fifteen cents, I would be made to feel like the Federal Government and that, as so much of this volume attests, would be intolerable.

—WFB

Stamford, Connecticut
May 1, 1978

I.

The Struggle

1*

After Ten Years: A Toast on the 10th Anniversary of *The American Spectator*

November 1977

GEORGE NASH has done the best that could be done to chronicle the development of a movement. Several times in his book (*The Conservative Intellectual Movement in America since 1945*) he stresses that it is a *movement* he is talking about, and then, drawing copiously on his gifts for summary and contraction, he tells us what went into the mix: quite a gallimaufry, including economic distillations inspired by the Alpine air at Mont Pèlerin, a prayerful re-examination of the Declaration of Independence and the Constitution, searching questions about the responsibility of Socrates for his own elimination, the revival of the great tradition by Leo Strauss, empirical studies of the work of regulatory commissions, high colonic examinations of the internal cancer of the West, lyrical tributes to the good life as, for instance, by Richard Weaver, swashbuckling marches through the tortured ranks of our stuttering social scientists, the reassertion of form and the rejection of formalism by T. S. Eliot: all of this happened, and suddenly—little by little—we felt that there was—a brotherhood. Not quite so cohesive as that which grew up in response to the excesses of Orwell's Big Brother, or one whose members were bound to each other as men and women are bound who knew Gulag. But something of a brotherhood, and that is one of the principal differences between the struggle, then and now.

There was, even before *The American Spectator* was founded, way back in 1950 a "conservative" alliance. It was a legacy of inertial ideology from turn-of-the-century America. It was lubricated by profitable—and exploitative—relations—between business and its clients, between farmers and the state, between whites and racial supremacy. It had a certain sense of obligation to the old virtues, but it was, as we think back on it, highly unexplicated. The reasons for encouraging

23

a private sector were wonderfully well known and advertised in the same classics to which we continue now to defer. But the new wave—a kind of secular modernism—was sweeping it all away, mostly in the classrooms of America, where the struggle was seen if not exactly in Marxist terms (Marxist rigor was never appealing to Americans at large), at least in neo-Marxist terms—the catalyst of my book, *God and Man at Yale*. Conservatives had a quintessential representative: Senator Robert A. Taft, whose strength derived from his integrity, his nimble (if less than profound) mind; and a considerable political agility. There was formal and even spontaneous enthusiasm for Senator Taft, even among young people: but never any sense of romance. Probably because conservatism was thought of, even by its friends, as something of a desiccated competitor in lusty ideological wars that had dominated the century: lacking in system, unlike fascism; in eschatology, unlike Communism; and in idealistic passion, unlike liberalism. Back in those days Whittaker Chambers wrote to me to warn that the hordes would not be stopped by fresh transcripts by Russell Kirk of the vaticinations of Edmund Burke.

There is no reason to suppose that the hordes will be stopped now, but every reason to suppose that the forces that stop them, if ever they mobilize to do so, will have been touched by that unbought grace of which the exegetes of Burke have reminded us. Could it be that the distinctive difference in the struggle, then and now, is that in the interim it has acquired grace? Is it not *grace*—most spectacularly celebrated in the final episode of Malraux's *La Condition Humaine*, when the older of the condemned men passes out his suicide pill to his two younger, frailer associates—that is the distinctive attribute of the movement now, as compared to then? In those days there was *1984*, but it was fantasy. Today, we have *The Gulag Archipelago*, and *One Day in the Life of Ivan Denisovich*; and *First Circle*—and by them we are annealed into a brotherhood, with a sense of mission marked by that grace which reminds us that, ultimately, we owe each other everything—even our private resources of self-destruction, of release. To read these books is to undergo a sacramental experience. I feel differently in the company of

men who have read Solzhenitsyn. Solzhenitsyn was the sol-
vent. He vested all that came before, all that George Nash
wrote about, with a kind of unity which defined the struggle,
even if it did not make self-evident the means of pursuing it.

On the tenth anniversary of this journal there are grounds
for rejoicing. It is a journal of joy, reminding us in every issue of the reasons to celebrate the zest of combat, the joy of
right thinking, the pleasure of language. I join this happy
company in paying tribute to you.

Socialism and Freedom

April 1978

WHEN I WAS a boy at Yale, along about the time they were su-
perannuating God, they were enshrining something called
economic democracy. Many of my classmates, by the time
they had gone through the typical ration of introductory
courses in economics and allied fields, were ready to live and
die, if necessary, to bring economic democracy to America.
In those days anything attached to democracy was osmotically desirable, democracy having been postulated as the highest civic good. We had, then, not only economic democracy
as a social desideratum, but its cousin, industrial democracy.
Educational democracy enjoyed morganatic privileges, and
of course social democracy was tantamount to eudaemonia.
Henry Wallace could not give a speech without a dozen references to economic democracy, and of course it transpired
that what was meant by the term was a progressive socialization of the economy. That which was capitalistic in form was
disparaged quite consistently, especially by those who
thought themselves progressive, as in the Progressive Party
which fielded Henry Wallace as its candidate during my
sophomore year.

But like executive supremacy, which was good when exercised by FDR and Truman, bad when attempted by Richard

Nixon, the term democracy began to suffer and, *pari passu,* economic democracy. I like to think that the bubble burst when some scholar, who flogged himself through John Dewey's *Democracy and Education,* carefully annotated twenty-two distinct uses to which Mr. Dewey had put the words democracy and democratic. There was, of course, the postwar confusion caused by the establishment of such states as the German Democratic Republic, and the endless encomiums in the Communist and fellow-traveling press to the democratic arrangements in Stalin's Russia, which of course was what the Webbs and Harold Laski had hailed as the fountainhead of economic democracy. There were the noble dissenters—I think Sidney Hook was the most vociferous, not to say encephalophonic—who kept stressing the differences between true economic democracy and the kind of thing practiced in Russia. But doubts had begun to set in, reinforced during the 1960's by the advent of democracy in Africa. Democracy had been used, along with "independence," as an antonym for colonialism. And when it became clear that the expulsion of the colonizers in Africa would bring not democracy but merely an end to white rule, many Americans, rather than sort out their frustrations, simply stopped reading about Africa, even as one stops counting Bolivian coups. And I think it correct to say that the term economic democracy tiptoed out of the workaday rhetoric of progressive politicians who although generally the last group to recognize the uselessness of shibboleths, are sensitive to public ennui. Economic democracy was increasingly understood to be the progressive transfer of power from the private to the public sector. There is continuing enthusiasm for this, but it tends to be inertial and dogmatic. Looking again for symbols, I think of Peter F. Drucker who in his *The Age of Discontinuity* dropped the line that modern experience has demonstrated that the only thing the state can do better than society is inflate the currency and wage war. The experience of Vietnam brings one of those two claims for the state into question.

With the demythologization of the state as the agent of universal well-being came also a revived curiosity about what it is in democracy that is desirable. Begin by admitting that

the democracy that brought us Perón and Hitler is an imperfect cathedral in which to worship, and you have come a long
way. If democracy can substantially diminish human freedom, it is only casually interesting that that diminution of
freedom was effected by political due process. Which
brought to the attention of the curious, particularly among
libertarians, the startling insight that it is altogether conceivable that in a given situation one might be faced with freedom and democracy as mutually exclusive alternatives. Not
entirely so, because if you surrender democracy on the
grounds that democracy is heading you toward a totalitarian
abyss, you have indeed given up something. But that something which you give up is not necessarily more valuable than
that which by giving it up you stand to retain. Burke said it
most simply when he remarked that the end of political freedom is human freedom.

It is best, I think, to ruminate on these matters by reasoning *a posteriori*. Freedom *can* be quantified. Freedom is not, in
an imperfect world, indefeasible. If, let us say, a society ac-
knowledges (1) the freedom to write, (2) the freedom to own
property, and (3) the freedom to practice one's religion, it is
a better state than the state that grants only two of those freedoms. But the state that grants two of those freedoms is better than the state that grants only one of them. By extension,
the republic with a vigorous public sector that protects the
right of property and the attendant right of economic enterprise is one which understands democracy as primarily a
procedural commitment—instructing us how to make such
changes in public policy as are desired by the majority, but
warning us that the use of that procedural authority for the
purpose of limiting substantial freedoms is intolerable. It is
plain that an increasing number of intellectuals, dismayed by
contemporary experience, have stopped superordinating
democracy to all other specified and specifiable freedoms.
Having done that, it is easier to arrive at the conclusion that a
vigorous private sector is necessary for the validation of democracy. Democratic socialism, as the venerable insight tells
us, is all about A meeting with B for the purpose of deciding
what C will give to X. To say that democratic socialism

"works" in Scandinavia is merely to say that the individual who makes that statement would rather exchange those freedoms absent in Scandinavia for those social perquisites offered in Scandinavia. If democracy is to be the servant of human freedom rather than the instrument by which to afflict the minority, then it must acknowledge the great self-denying ordinances which reasonably limit all other freedoms.

Alert intellectuals are in increasing numbers interested by what the lawyers anxious to preserve constitutional guarantees call the "slippery-slope" theory, the generic statement of which is, Give them an inch and they'll take a mile. The appetite of the socialist to govern tends to insatiability. Thus Freedom House, in the latest of its annual tables of political rights and civil rights, is instructive. The nations of the world are divided into three categories: the capitalist, the mixed, and the socialist. Only a single state is both socialist and politically free. For those interested in purple cows, that state is Guyana.

Vietnam

On the collapse of Saigon

April 5, 1975

THERE ISN'T anything we can do, at this point, to reverse the situation in South Vietnam. What we *could* do is stop talking about the causes of the South Vietnamese defeat in all those nice formulations whose common denominator is that it wasn't our fault. In preference to taking any such pledge, the columnists for the New York *Times* would prefer atom-bombing Hanoi.

It won't help in the case of South Vietnam, but the following points should be made, for future reference:

1. The so-called will to resist is a hugely exaggerated factor in assessing a nation's disposition to resist aggression. I assume, for instance, that the metropolitan population of New York City deeply desires to resist the city's murderers, rapists, robbers, and muggers, but every year the statistics show with great plainness that the underworld is in more or less effective charge. By this I mean that every year the odds improve for those who desire to murder, rob, rape, or mug.

2. The principal question to ask isn't whether a population has the will to resist its marauders, but whether it has the means and the organization. There is no more eloquent testimony than the lengths the refugees have gone to avoid coexistence with the enemy from the North on the point of what the South Vietnamese population *desires*. It desires to keep the enemy away. We all took it for granted that the people who inhabited the Lowlands, and the Republic of France, had the "will" to resist the armies of Adolf Hitler. But they contained Hitler less successfully, over a shorter period of time, than South Vietnam contained North Vietnam. And if, say in the summer of 1941, the United States had decided to end all aid to England and the Soviet Union, there is every reason to suppose that Hitler would have occupied London and Moscow. Thieu never had the means to carry the offensive into North Vietnam. We do not know how it would have gone if he had had those means. It may well be that the South Vietnamese people, being a pacific breed, would have fought poorly that far away from home. This is a commendable, not disdainful, national trait.

3. The best organization of a military machine is done by the leader who is without human scruple. The history books are ever so fond of talking about the "corruption" that surrounded Chiang Kai-shek. There is no doubt that it did, as there is no doubt that he cavilled at certain means of eliminating corruption.

The courts of New York City could exhibit their will to reduce the criminal element in New York quite readily. All it requires is that you shoot everybody you catch stealing. It is quite literally that simple. Thieu's toleration of corruption has earned him the contempt of many American peacocks of civic righteousness. One wonders whether they would have admired him more if he dealt with corruption the way they deal with it in North Vietnam, or China. A country that loses a war against an enemy that fights like Genghis Khan deserves something closer to sympathy than contempt.

4. The combination of ruthlessness and audacity is powerful. Cortés brought with him to Mexico 508 soldiers, 100 seamen, sixteen horses, ten bronze guns, four falconettes, and thirteen shotguns, and conquered an empire of brave, but easygoing people. The North Vietnamese, day by day, developed an arms edge over the South Vietnamese and calmly constructed great superhighways down which to parade the unlimited supply of tanks showered on them by Moscow and Peking even as Congress slowly closed the faucet.

For every observable sin committed by Thieu, the leaders of the Third Republic in France committed a dozen. But it takes a special sort of callousness to say that a failure to develop the characteristics appropriate to resisting Genghis Khan merit life under Hitler, which is the kind of life toward which the South Vietnamese are now headed.

5. We are entitled to conclude that the North Vietnamese did indeed fight as bravely and as tenaciously as Hitler's soldiers.

No breast-beating?

April 22, 1975

THE CLICHÉ of the day is "stop the recriminations!" That is one of several inflections, another being "stop the breast-beating!"—which is the title of a sermon by George W. Ball in the current issue of *Newsweek*, wherein he gives us a lesson on how to stop the breast-beating. You begin by ignoring treaties made by the United States, ignoring any responsibility by the United States for living up to the terms of the treaties. You add a long list of complaints against the sloth and mismanagement of any Oriental who was ever dumb enough to be on our side in opposing Communism in Asia, and before you know it, you not only have stopped breast-beating, you are looking around the hall expecting the adulation of all the peoples of the world.

Mr. Ball, who was Under Secretary of State under JFK and LBJ and who took us into the Southeast Asian mess without giving any thought to the consequences of fighting it the way they chose to fight it, was not quite so talkative back when he was the second man in the State Department. Now he writes from his seat in Lehman Brothers that "once we withdrew our soldiers and our bombers, it was inevitable that the house of cards [in Vietnam] would come tumbling down." I don't remember his saying that at the time, and I wonder why not. Was he on a mission for Lehman Brothers that gagged him? Was he out of communication with *Newsweek* magazine? Clairvoyants should practice their gift while it is still useful, rather than discover it retrospectively. The alternative is to expect a certain amount of breast-beating and recrimination.

We are all being asked to believe that there was something on the order of manifest destiny working for the North Vietnamese. That they really "owned" South Vietnam, in the same sense that the early Americans owned California. To get California we had to claw our way past a few Indians, and snooker the Mexicans into one of the great land grabs of the nineteenth century. But what was hardest about acquiring California was things like scaling mountains and crossing deserts and laying railroad lines.

What was hard about taking South Vietnam was—people. About 16 million people who were 80 percent opposed to living under the rule of the North. Eighty percent is slightly better than the number of Americans who sided with George Washington in the Revolutionary War. The will to resist was there, and for all the talk of South Vietnamese pusillanimity and disorganization and graft, you will find that a far higher percentage of them died or were wounded in the war than Frenchmen defending themselves against Hitler. The military mistakes of General Thieu cannot have been worse than those of the succession of generals appointed by President Lincoln until he happened upon a Ulysses Grant. The notion that Abraham Lincoln was more successful than Thieu in bringing the political opposition into his tent is chauvinism of the worst sort: it is ignorance. If George Washington, leaning as he did on critical help from the French, had been dealt with as we finally dealt with the South Vietnamese, we would have lost that war, General Washington would have been hanged, and George Ball would now be giving us his instructions in an English accent.

If it was so obvious to Ball—one of the two or three most conspicuous Democratic mouthpieces in matters of foreign policy—that the Treaty of Paris was a phony, he should there and then have denounced it. It was certainly a mistake of President Nixon not to have insisted that Congress there and then either accept or reject responsibility for enforcing the terms of the Treaty, which Henry Kissinger would never have initialed had he anticipated the flight in Congress from the implicit responsibility of the principal sponsor of that accord—the United States. We talk about how the South Vietnamese have run. At least they did so under the pressure of Russian tanks. Congress ran under the pressure of moral fatigue. I'd sooner, fighting for my life, do so in the company of fifteen South Vietnamese soldiers, than of the fifteen members of the Senate Foreign Relations Committee.

What happened?

April 26, 1975

THIS MUCH at least should be said in behalf of Henry Kissinger:

The treaty he initialed he would not have initialed if he had had any intimation that Congress would, in the months ahead, pull back from discharging its implicit obligations.

It should be recalled that in January 1973, Richard Nixon was triumphant. He had won the largest political victory in the history of the United States. The Congress, duly chastened by the successes of the Christmas bombing, was at his feet. Vietnamization was in effect. Our prisoners of war were returning. Who can doubt that if, instead of presenting the

Paris Accords along with their implicit obligations, the President had asked the Congress to bind itself by them, they would have sailed through both houses?

Kissinger did not doubt it, and he gave an assurance to Thieu in good faith. Thieu accepted that assurance, and this was his tragic mistake. Chiefs of State cannot afford to make such mistakes. But who could have anticipated Watergate?

A recent issue of *New York* magazine features a close analysis of the behavior of Richard Nixon during 1973 and 1974 by John Osborne. He is the well-respected writer, associated with *The New Republic*, who developed a feature that became famous called "The Nixon Watch." Osborne concludes, in words of one syllable, that Richard Nixon, some time early in 1973, went—nuts.

This analysis sounds cruel, said about anybody. It is hard to understand why, when said about Richard Nixon. Is there a more charitable explanation for his behavior during 1973 and 1974 when Watergate closed in than that he was not in possession of his faculties? If, during those eighteen months, he had been hypnotized by Tom Wicker, making statements and reaching decisions calculated to ensure the destruction of his Presidency, could he have acted more brilliantly to achieve that end? Why should conservatives shrink from reaching a conclusion merely because it has been advanced by a political liberal? John Osborne could very easily be correct, and if he is, the judgment of Nixon, far from becoming more severe, becomes more charitable. One does not expect responsible conduct from people who have lost effective control of their faculties.

All of which reminds us that for all we know about Watergate, in fact the great story has not been told. It is this: What would Nixon, under Kissinger's prodding, have done, if his reactions had been healthy, when only a few weeks after the Paris Accords were executed, the North began its blatant disregard of them?

My own information is that it was planned, some time in April, to pulverize Hanoi and Haiphong. If that had been done, not only would the North Vietnamese juggernaut have disintegrated, an entirely new meaning would have attached to the concept of détente. Remember, we are talking about a treaty that was initialed by the other two great superpowers, China and Russia, and that was broken only as a result of their active collaboration. Thus to have acted decisively would have had the effect not only of saving South Vietnam, but of warning the Soviet Union and China that detente is what we have always insisted it is: an invitation to our two principal antagonists to cooperate with us. Not an invitation to them to fish in troubled waters, to repeat the phrase President Ford used thumpingly when last he addressed Congress. When he uttered those words, they were bereft of meaning. What Russian general or Chinese theorist has any reason, at this point, to believe that détente is in fact anything other than that—an invitation to profiteer from America's unilateral attachment to a will-o'-the-wisp?

This does not bring South Vietnam back to life. But it gives one an idea of the incredible reaches of Watergate. It very probably drove Nixon out of his mind, and the result is a disequilibrium in world politics. There is nothing here to explain the strange, perverse failure of Congress, or to lessen the pain our allies must feel. But if Henry Kissinger is ever free to tell it all, we can hope that he would say something on this order. And that he will remember that Congress must not ever again be taken for granted.

Lest we forget

July 3, 1975

THERE IS a priceless institution in America called John Lofton. He is a youngish man who used to edit the Republican Party's official newsletter *Monday*, wherein he took licentious pleasure in reproducing statements by prominent American liberals exactly contradicting their present positions. He is now a syndicated columnist, and not since the days of Westbrook Pegler has anyone felt as free—indeed, as duty-bound—to telephone public figures to ask them, so to speak face-to-face, just exactly what did they mean by saying so-and-so.

Take, for instance, the lovely Shana Alexander, a cultural delight who used to write a column for *Newsweek*. When there is a liberal zephyr in the air, Shana will rustle. And sure enough, just a few weeks ago she found herself saying, apropos of her disapproval of the South Vietnamese refugee problem, "If we know one thing about the government founded by Ho Chi Minh, it is that his social services are excellent: good health care, day care, and educational programs abound, especially for the poor."

Now you and I and three and one-half million people who read *Newsweek* would pass over that asseveration without applying our automatic brakes. Not Lofton. Moreover, he proceeds to put in a call to Shana Alexander. He doesn't know her, but that doesn't matter—Miss Alexander, a professional journalist, has put in heaps of calls to people she doesn't know. Journalists understand that they have responsibilities to fellow journalists.

How, Lofton asked over the telephone, does Miss Alexander *know* this about North Vietnam? Well, she said snippily, she was "busy typing" just then, and didn't care to discuss "this thing"; Lofton should call her research assistant. So he did. She genially confessed she didn't know exactly where Miss Alexander had got her facts. So he called others: the International Red Cross, the UN's World Health Organization, the State Department. None of them had the foggiest. So he called Vietnam expert Douglas Pike, who called Miss Alexander's assertion "absurd, really," and added that with a per capita income of $85 per year North Vietnam could hardly afford special services for anyone, as North Vietnamese documents themselves admit.

A few days later, Lofton found himself on television facing Sander Vanocur and Gloria Emerson, who were crowing over the North Vietnamese victory. I find it almost unfair to quote Miss Emerson, since on the subject of Vietnam she is, quite simply, unbalanced: but after all, she did feed it out, day after day, in the columns of the New York *Times* for three and a half years, where she ran the longest serialized atrocity story in American history. Here (it wasn't hard) Lofton *forced* Miss Emerson to fly her banner. She was "very glad" the North Vietnamese won. She thought the North Vietnamese would, to be sure, run "a very austere, well-ordered, regimented society which in the long run will profit a vast majority of the Vietnamese." (That's the kind of society Adolf Hitler ran.) John Lofton demurred, and the lady replied with an expletive deleted. Finally Lofton gave the lady one more absolutely straightforward chance:

JL: "What did the North Vietnamese ever do in the war in Indochina that you disapprove of? Anything they ever did. *Anything*. Say *anything* bad about them. Did they do *anything* bad *anywhere?*"

GE: "In the south?"

JL:"Anywhere in Indochina. Have the Communists done *anything* bad?"

GE: "Yes they have done things that I don't approve of."

JL: "What? What? Name one [thing]."

GE: "I'm sorry that they put American prisoners of war under enormous duress. But I'm also sorry about the way the Americans treated the South Vietnamese . . . "

It is a complicated formulation, but there is no simpler way to put it: critics of the critics of the war in Vietnam have been profoundly right all those years they claimed that, in their hearts, the leaders of the antiwar movement were pro-North Vietnamese. John Lofton has done a fine job of teasing this admission out of one of their spokesmen.

Human Rights

Mr. Carter's discovery

March 10, 1977

London—MR. CARTER's references to human rights are causing quite a commotion in these parts. It is not really expect-

ed, by working statesmen, that anything more will be done
about human rights than to mention them genially from time
to time. Sir Alec Douglas-Home, who was keynoter at the
Helsinki Conference that eventually brought forth the Declaration, stressed in 1972 that this time around the West
would not settle for mere talk. That is the diplomatic way of
saying, "This time around the West will again settle for mere
talk." It is the diplomatic equivalent of the vernacular use of
the word "literally." "Literally" is used to mean "not-literal-
ly": as in, "I called you literally a hundred times over the
weekend." When on a subsequent occasion, after it became
quite clear that the Soviet Union was *not* intending to do anything about human rights and Sir Alec was asked what the
West was going to do about it, he said, literally, nothing. That
tends to be the preferred way of doing things about human
rights, where the Soviet Union is concerned. Ask anyone
who has labored in the United Nations on the subject of human rights. He—I mean he or she—will tell you.

That is why Mr. Carter's behavior, which one would not
really have thought so extraordinary, is causing such
upheavals here. President Giscard d'Estaing is positively
truculent on the subject. Human rights, he passed the word
to the noble Amalrik, who sought vainly to interview him, are
not to be discussed with mere Soviet martyrs. They are to be
negotiated through channels, which is the same institution
through which we negotiated the fate of Eastern Europe.
Chancellor Schmidt of West Germany has flatly refused to
see Amalrik, consigning him to as subordinate a secretary in
the foreign ministry as he could find.

Another interesting argument has been raised against Mr.
Carter's behavior, this time from the right. Mr. Peregrine
Worsthorne of the *Daily Telegraph*, who specializes in saying
interesting things, makes this point: America is way behind
in the business of keeping up militarily with the Soviet Union. And the only reason we exert ourselves as we do is that
we sense how awful Soviet life is. Now, if we continue to put
pressure on the Soviet Union, what is likely to happen is that
the Kremlin will give free speech to all of the two hundred
Russians who desire it, then will smile toothily at us, and we
will fall over ourselves with appreciation, disbanding the
army, the navy, the air force, and the Boy Scouts.

There is a subtle point here. It is related to our current eagerness to make love, not war, with Vietnam. All Vietnam has to do is allow three Red Cross workers into the country to prove Vietnam is not holding eight hundred Americans Missing in Action. Even if it transpires that the reason they are not being detained is that they were all tortured to death, the Senate Foreign Relations Committee would hail this act of creative statesmanship as reason to proceed to recognize— or, as we put it these days, "normalize" relations with—Vietnam. It is true that if Bukovsky were given tenure at the University of Moscow, half the Eastern liberal Establishment would announce that the world crisis was over.

What actually has President Carter done? And how can the Soviet Union respond?

Mr. Carter has with utter dignity done just a little more than talk abstractly about human rights. He has recognized the existence of real heroes, genuine victims of systematic persecution. He has mentioned a few by name. He has, albeit as discreetly as if he had arranged to see a peep-show, actually visited with one. In terms of policy, he has used no sanctions against the Soviet Union—only against relatively impotent Latin American nations. In the course of doing so—of ruling, e.g., against Uruguay but not against the Philippines—Carter stressed quite candidly the necessity of superordinating the national interest. Translated, that means the Philippines can hit back at us, Uruguay can't.

The Soviet Union would not be motivated to strike or not to strike by our behavior toward the Bukovskys. But a crystallization of world opinion against the tormentors of the Bukovskys is something the Soviet Union clearly does not want—and may not be able to afford. In a melancholy way, the European statesmen here make a certain amount of sense. Are we willing to see through to the implications of our challenge to the Soviet Union to civilize itself? It means, among other things, giving them no acceptable alternative. And that means rearmament, and all those grim and costly things.

Pravda's concern

March 17, 1977

IT IS, AS of today, official. The Soviet Union has confirmed what some critics of President Carter have been saying, for the most part surreptitiously. Official United States concern for human rights endangers détente and demilitarization. To use the words of *Pravda*, we must reject the "illogic of the argument" that we can simultaneously pursue human rights in the Soviet Union, plus détente. "Détente and the normal conduct of talks presuppose the establishment of trust between the negotiating partners and respect for the laws and traditions of each other, while attempts to exert pressure on us and to bargain for concessions of principles are bringing about an atmosphere of distrust."

Concerning which, a few observations:

1. The United States through President Carter has been bringing pressure on the Soviet Union to observe *its own laws and commitments*. This point cannot be overstressed. The Soviet Constitution of 1936, the United Nations Covenants ratified by the Soviet Union in 1973, and the Helsinki Agreement of 1975 are explicit statements of Soviet commitments to principles. There is nothing Mr. Carter has urged upon the Soviet Union in any way different from what the Soviet Union freely undertook.

Consider now the bearing of all this. For the Soviet Union to say that we are now asking it to make "concessions of principles" can only mean that its "principle" is to make a public commitment and then to flout it. There is no other meaning, in the circumstances, that can be attached to their objection.

Now this being so, the bearing on SALT II is quite direct. The Soviet Union would appear to be saying that it is a matter of principle for the Soviet Union to make a commitment with one hand, while rejecting it with another. With its right hand, it signs the Helsinki Agreement guaranteeing, e.g., freedom of emigration for dissidents, while with its left hand it turns the lock on the prison door. The relevance to arms control is obvious: the Soviet Union is suggesting that, as a

matter of principle, it will promise to disarm *pari passu* with
the United States, meanwhile pursuing its policy of military
expansionism. Is there another understanding?

2. Is it indeed "illogical" to pursue both disarmament and
human rights? One would not suppose so normally. That is
to say, disarmament and civil rights don't get in the way of
each other for ontological reasons. It isn't like saying that you
cannot simultaneously paint your barn black and also white.
In recent times we have seen disarmament and human rights
go together hand in hand in Japan and West Germany.

No, the peculiar meaning of the disjunction as given by
Pravda is alarming precisely because it harmonizes with its
point about concessions of principle. Human rights get in the
way not of disarmament, but of simulated disarmament. We
know that the Soviet Union has cheated on SALT I. Philadelphia lawyers would insist on fine tuning that statement by
saying that the Soviet Union had taken every ambiguity in
SALT I and run with it. But there will always be ambiguities
in arms control agreements whose enforcement provisions
are in effect limited to the vision of peeping Tom satellites
flying fifty miles above Soviet silos.

The thing about human rights is that they include the
right of a free press. A free press means a sanctuary for an
inquisitive eye. How can the Soviet Union simultaneously a)
permit a free press; and b) cheat on arms control? Therein
the illogic of which *Pravda* complains.

There are those who believe it illogical to proceed to make
any agreement with the Soviet Union which is other than
self-policing. And such agreements are extremely difficult to
sculpt. We are interested in human rights because we are involved in mankind. Beyond that there is the pragmatic argument. Human rights are a precondition to effective arms
control.

A dupe's progress

March 16, 1976

London—ANY STUDENT of his career would have to acknowledge that Representative Edward Koch of Manhattan is,
whatever his ideological failings, a man of principle, and a
first-class public servant.

The story begins with an organization called "U.S. Committee for Justice to Latin-American Political Prisoners." A
connoisseur, running his tongue over such a name, would acknowledge the high probability that it is a Committee for Immunity for any Latin-American Leftist. The signers of the
Committee's recent petition in behalf of Hugo Blanco,
identified as "author, internationally known Peruvian peas-
ant-union leader, and refugee of the Chile coup," include
such as Richard Fagan of Stanford, Richard Falk of Princeton, Congressman Michael Harrington, Tom Hayden late of
the SDS, and Sidney Lens. The only person missing from *that*
list is Kropotkin, and then only because he is dead.

But Edward Koch, to whom the Committee wrote asking
him to intercede with the State Department to get a visa for
Hugo Blanco, reaches no premature conclusions. So the long
correspondence began.

1. Dr. Benjamin Spock (the baby doctor) to Koch. "Dear
Ed: I feel indignant about the State Department's denying
admission to a speaker whom many want to hear, presumably because he will testify to the brutality of the repression
in Chile, and to our government's complicity in bringing it
into power. Kissinger has all the instincts of a thug, coated
over with professional pomposity. Sincerely, Benjamin
Spock, MD."

2. Koch to Kissinger. Why aren't you giving a visa to Hugo
Blanco?

3. McCloskey of the Department of State to Koch. "Mr.
Blanco, a Peruvian citizen presently residing in Sweden, is
ineligible for a visa under section 212 (a) (28) (F) of the Immigration and Nationality Act. A decision as to whether to

recommend a waiver of his ineligibility to the Attorney General is receiving active consideration."

4. Koch to Spock ("Dear Ben"). Says he has written to Kissinger. And gives his own rules on the matter. "I take the position that with the exception of terrorists who publicly advocate murder in pursuit of their goals, those who want to have a full and free discussion of ideas should not be impeded in coming to this country for that purpose."

5. Koch to McCloskey. Why isn't the State Department recommending a waiver to let Blanco come in?

6. McCloskey to Koch. Because Blanco's "previous terrorist activities" led the State Department to "conclude it would not be in the public interest to authorize his temporary admission into the United States."

7. Koch to McCloskey. Hey, what exactly do you mean by Blanco's "previous terrorist activities"?

8. McCloskey to Koch. We're not allowed to divulge classified information.

9. Koch to McCloskey. That's a hell of a note. You aren't allowed to divulge secret information, but you go ahead and act on it. "I urge you to reconsider this matter."

10. McCloskey to Koch. We can't give you much of the information we have on Blanco, which is classified. However, "a part of the public record is his declaration that he took full and sole responsibility for the murders of three policemen which occurred during a raid he and his followers made on a police station in Peru during 1962. The *Congressional Record* of December 19, 1975, contains further information about his affiliation with the Fourth International and other groups, as well as quotations from his writings in which he has advocated the use of violence." Under the law, he simply cannot be given a visa.

11. Koch to Spock. Summarizes McCloskey's letter. And adds: "In your original letter to me your reference to Henry Kissinger was, 'has all the instincts of a thug, coated over with professional pomposity.' My question is, how would you now characterize Hugo Blanco?"

12. Spock to Koch. "Thank you for looking into the Hugo Blanco issue. I have no idea where the truth lies. The plea for his entry came from a responsible organization."

13. WFB to Koch. Nice going.

14. WFB to Spock. "Dear Ben: You are the incarnation of the dupe. And since you talk a lot of the time about justice, you will presumably be sending an apology to Henry Kissinger. I'd appreciate receiving a copy. Best, Bill."

What happened to the Genocide Convention?

March 3, 1977

NOW IT IS SAID by refugees that General Amin has given orders to liquidate two Ugandan tribes, an undertaking which if consummated would perhaps double, even quadruple, the number of Ugandans slaughtered by General Amin since he took power. Everyone believes something should be done about it. Given the incidental and systematic cruelties in the world, why Uganda?

A book recently published in West Germany explores the Nuremberg trial and reaches two conclusions. The first is that the trial was legitimate, that the conventional objections to it, based on *ex post facto* law and the impurity of a tribunal that included a Soviet judge, cannot be sustained against all the arguments that can be marshaled in favor of the trial. The second conclusion is that the Nuremberg trial was a strategic failure. The reason it was so adjudged is not that it resulted in the hanging of a dozen Nazis who deserved that fate, but that it failed in its ultimate purpose.

This purpose was most explicitly in the minds of the prosecutors and most of the judges at the trial. It was to elevate genocide to special consideration in the community of nations. There was nothing to be done to bring back six million Jews who died in the holocaust. Only one significant tribute could be paid to them: the assurance that such a thing would not happen again. Accordingly, the Convention on the Prevention and Punishment of the Crime of Genocide.

This Convention, to which most countries and all African countries are signatories, has been in force since January 12,

1951. It can be said to be moribund in the same sense that Connecticut's anti-sodomy statute is moribund. Any Convention never invoked, notwithstanding that it prohibits activity that is current, is dead letter law, though its revivification is not excluded.

Not since the holocaust has genocide been carried to such lengths as in Cambodia by the Khmer Rouge during 1976. Before that, one thinks of Rwanda and Burundi, and Tibet. The North Vietnamese, whose victory would, it was widely predicted, bring a bloodbath, held their fire. But what is going on now? Vietnam's Communists have banished three-quarters of a million Saigonese to "new economic zones." More than 50,000 people who served in the Thieu government are now in "re-education" camps. What exactly is a re-education camp? Was Auschwitz one? We do not know, and are not likely to find out.

No less a figure than Ramsey Clark, former Attorney General of the United States—whose solicitude for open-mindedness went so far as to bring him to broadcast from Hanoi that our prisoners of war were being well treated, even as they suffered torture—has been rebuffed. Along with other anti-war activists he requested the government of North Vietnam to observe the civil rights of the South Vietnamese, and for his pain has been called by Hanoi a "barbarian" and a "U.S. imperialist." The mandate of Nuremberg is unheeded.

So what can be done about the mad Amin, before he takes another 50,000 or 100,000 lives? Above all it is necessary that the black African states take the initiative. In the absence of concerted action by them, action by others appears to be interventionist, and condescending. One can imagine how the world would react if Vorster of South Africa announced that he would undertake beginning soon the liquidation of a tribe of 50,000 troublemakers. Joan Baez would be calling for nuclear war. But if it is only blacks who are to be slaughtered...? The community of nations should rouse itself to this point.

The key non-African figure is Andrew Young. He is perfectly situated to take the initiative against Amin. The Security Council should take up the Ugandan question immediately, with highest priority. Sanctions should be voted, the country isolated. Somebody's CIA—not ours, as we do not wish to give offense, you know—should take the initiative internally. Amin is making gestures so wild as to be grotesque. We are sitting about with an international Convention in our law libraries which threatens now to be meaningless. It is a bizarre thing to say, but it is true, that if Amin is not stopped, the Jews of Europe died in vain.

Cambodia

September 10, 1977

I AM QUITE serious: Why doesn't Congress authorize the money to finance an international military force to overrun Cambodia? That force should comprise primarily Asians— Thais, notably, but also Malaysians, Filipinos, Taiwanese, Japanese. Detachments from North Vietnam and China should be permitted, and token representatives from voluntary units of other countries that are signatories to the Genocide Convention and to the various protocols on human rights. Our inactivity in respect of Cambodia is a sin as heinous as our inactivity to save the Jews from the holocaust. Worse, actually; because we did mobilize eventually to destroy Hitler. We are doing nothing to save the Cambodians. What is happening in Cambodia mocks every speech made by every politician in the United Nations and elsewhere about our common devotion to human rights.

The idea, in Cambodia, isn't to go there and set up a democratic state. It is to go there and take power away from one, two, three, perhaps as many as a half-dozen sadistic madmen who have brought on their country the worst suffering, the worst conditions brought on any country in this bloody century.

Father François Ponchaud, who lived in Cambodia from 1965 to 1975, estimates that 800,000 Cambodians have died since the Khmer Rouge took over two years ago. And *he* is thought to be inaccurate on the low side. Richard Holbrooke, our Assistant Secretary of State for East Asian Affairs, puts the figure as high as 1.2 million.

Hundreds of thousands of these were executions. The balance was worse: death, mostly by starvation. We finally mustered the judicial energy to execute Gary Gilmore last January. We could not have found one American, short possibly of the Son of Sam, who would have voted to starve him to death. Others die of malaria and other diseases. The Khmer Rouge disdains to accept medical aid from the West, or food.

As for the death figures, what do they mean to those for whom human life means nothing? Mr. Stéphane Groueff, of *France Soir*, went to within a dozen kilometers of Cambodia recently, talking to hundreds of refugees. It is the deepest mystery what actually is the constitution of that evil leadership, as no correspondent has been there in two years, and the eight diplomatic legations (seven Communist, plus Egypt) are house-bound, and denied permission to speak to any Cambodians. There is speculation that the energumen running the show is a forty-six-year-old French-educated Khieu Samphan, the head of the Presidium.

When you ask the refugees who is the authority behind the Khmer Rouge, they will tell you, presumably in whispers, "Angkar." What is Khieu Samphan to Angkar? What is the role of the Prime Minister Pol Pot? Or of Ieng Sari, the Hanoi intellectual whose real name is Nguyen Sao Levy? Or the Communist Party Secretary General, Saloth Sar? Mr. Groueff reports that there is only one known interview with Samphan. It was given to an Italian journalist at last summer's Colombo conference.

"'In five years of war,' Khieu Samphan told him, 'more than a million Cambodians died. The present population of the country is five million. Before the war it was seven million.'

"'What happened to the other million?' the journalist asked. Samphan was annoyed.

"'It's incredible,' he said, 'the way you Westerners worry about war criminals.'"

Two out of seven Cambodians already dead. That is the equivalent of 57 million Americans killed. Even Stalin might have shrunk from genocide on such a scale. And what are we doing about it? Wait for Rolf Hochhuth to write a play? Is there no *practical* idealism left in this world? Only that endless talk, which desecrates the language, and atrophies the soul?

Détente

Crisis on Soyuz-Apollo

July 19, 1975

THIS IS WALTER CRONKITE, and we are continuing our coverage of the historic link-up between our own Apollo V missile and the Soviet Soyuz missile, which have been linked in space for almost three days now, and are preparing now for separation, and re-entry: the Soyuz will come down directly into the heart of Russia, and the Apollo will come down, as is the American practice, in the Pacific. Yes? Yes? Come in, Dan.

Rather. There's something going on here in Houston, Walter. Can't quite make it out. The routine communication with Tom Stafford which we have been monitoring has suddenly gone into code.

Walter. Gone into what, Dan?

Dan. Gone into code. There is active radio communication between Stafford and Houston Control, but we can't discern what they are saying. I'm flashing over to Mike, who has collared Dr. Thornton at the communications center. Let's see what he has to say. Mike?

Wallace. I have Dr. Thornton here. Dr. Thornton, what is the reason for the transmissions in code?

Thornton. Well, Mike, our rockets are, er, equipped with, er, scrambling devices in case it should be necessary to communicate confidentially to Houston Control.

Wallace. What would be the nature of such confidential communications?

Thornton. I'm sure I don't know, Mike, but I suppose if Stafford wants to communicate privately to Houston, that means he doesn't want what he says to be broadcast live on CBS television.

Wallace. You don't suppose he's reading from the Bible, and figures he won't antagonize the Supreme Court if he reads it in code?

Thornton. We are not encouraged to speculate, Mike.

Cronkite (cutting in). We have something from Dan Schorr at the White House. Come in, Dan.

Schorr. There's a lot of excitement here, Walter. The President is reported to be in direct communication with Houston Control, and maybe even with Stafford. Secretary of State Kissinger came in from the State Department with a police escort, and James Schlesinger of the Defense Department has joined the huddle. There's something going on, Walter, but we haven't got the...

Cronkite. Excuse me, Dan, but Roger Mudd has just located Dan Ellsberg at Santa Barbara, and he has something here for us. Roger?

Mudd. Dr. Ellsberg, you have a code transcriber in your rumpus room, I understand, and you've been listening in on the communications from the Soyuz-Apollo mission. Can you tell us what's going on?

Ellsberg. Well, Roger, as you are aware, I believe in the people's right to know, and the Supreme Court upheld, 7-2, the publication of the papers I gave to the New York *Times* in 1971...

Mudd. Yes yes, Dr. Ellsberg. But could you tell us what in fact is going on right now?

Ellsberg. Well, Roger, the Astronaut Stafford reports that the Cosmonaut Leonov says that he and the Cosmonaut Kubasov demand political asylum, and refuse to release the linking module and land back in the Soviet Union. The cosmonauts want to land jointly with the Americans in the Pacific. They insist on being flown back to the United States. Wait a minute...they're saying something else.

Mudd. Yes! Yes!

Ellsberg. They say that it's the only way they can ever get to meet Solzhenitsyn.

Mudd. Well what is the White House saying?

Ellsberg. President Ford is negotiating. He's asking Houston Control whether the Apollo-Soyuz mission could arrange to land in the Mediterranean somewhere if we can get Solzhenitsyn to agree to fly back to Europe.

Mudd. What is Houston saying?

Ellsberg. Something about our fleet in the Mediterranean is not big enough to cope with the situa . . .

Cronkite. Roger? Roger! We seem to be having some, er, technical difficulties, ladies and gentlemen. Please stand by. I'm sure we'll be able to clear all this up in just a . . .

Screen goes blank. Shows only Apollo-Soyuz Project shield, with Russian-American handclasp.

On refusing to greet Solzhenitsyn

July 12, 1975

THE VERY WORST part of it is that Gerald Ford has a certain reputation for spontaneous goodwill. There probably isn't a bureaucracy surrounding any leader anywhere in the free world who would recommend to a chief of state that he give an audience to anybody whose ties to politics are closer than Charlie Brown's, But Ford struck us as someone powerful enough to wrest his leg up through the cobwebs of the Lilliputians to do the natural thing. Perhaps it was all those months without a swimming pool that made him flaccid. For a horrible moment one was tempted to wonder whether Mr. Ford knew who Aleksandr Solzhenitsyn was.

Don't laugh. You cannot, for one thing, know who Solzhenitsyn is unless you read Solzhenitsyn. Otherwise he is merely another adamant freedom fighter—but there are a lot of these, and we certainly do not write our foreign policy around the compunction to a) give them aid, or even b) celebrate their existence. Solzhenitsyn, if one has not read *One Day in the Life of Ivan Denisovich*, or *The First Circle*, or *Gulag*, is like Shakespeare if one hasn't read *King Lear* or *Hamlet*: a mere evocation. I earnestly hope and pray that Gerald Ford has never read a work by Solzhenitsyn. If it were confided to me that he had done so, and even so refused to greet Solzhenitsyn in the White House and count that moment his most intimate contact with the divine circuitry of the human spirit, he should be ever after despised as a philistine. No: he could not have read Solzhenitsyn.

I remember a testimonial dinner three years ago in honor of the sixtieth birthday of the self-effacing publisher-intellectual who founded the Henry Regnery Company in Chicago just after the war. Henry Regnery had known Nixon for years, had contributed to his political campaigns, and had, almost singlehandedly, published during the bleak Forties and Fifties books of conservative tendency that challenged the orthodoxy of Eastern Seaboard Liberalism and were admired by Nixon. The toastmaster wrote to the President and asked if he would be so kind as to send a message to be read at the banquet. A bureaucrat in the White House replied that the President does not send messages "to commemorate commercial occasions" (it was the sixtieth birthday of Regnery, not of his company); that the toastmaster should apply to the Secretary of Commerce for a message. One of the reasons given out why President Ford did not greet Solzhenitsyn while he was in Washington was that Solzhenitsyn was in America in connection with the promotion of his new book. This happens not to be true. But at least President Ford didn't direct his Secretary of Commerce to invite Solzhenitsyn in for a talk.

How clearly, every day that we log the activities of the free nations of the world in juxtaposition with those of the enemy, their moral—yes, *moral*—superiority strikes us. There is a genuine integrity in people like Mao Tse-tung, and even such bureaucratic imitations as Leonid Brezhnev. It would not matter in the least to Mao or Brezhnev if a celebrity was renowned primarily for the number of women and children he had killed: if he was a voluble and famous apologist for Communism, he would be received at court. When I was last in the Soviet Union, the United States Information Agency

Exhibit at Donetsk opened pursuant to a treaty between the Soviet Union and the United States—to foster international understanding. The entire publicity given in the press to our exhibit consisted of two sentences. A huge portion of the press for that day was given over to Angela Davis, who was touring the Soviet Union to denounce the United States.

I cannot think of a single person of international stature who would be denied access to Leonid Brezhnev on the grounds that seeing him would offend American official or public opinion (save possibly an American conservative). Brezhnev can without flinching be hearty, even effusive, in greeting American senators, and talk about international peace and understanding. He would not hesitate to schedule the following hour with Bobby Seale or William Kunstler, to mourn together American fascism.

The episode ennobles Solzhenitsyn. If added strength were needed to communicate his message, Ford has given it. The only good Russian is the lockstep Communist. On this Brezhnev and Ford are agreed. We call it détente.

Kissinger as historical pessimist

April 10, 1975

THE TIME DEVOTED to an inquiry into what Henry Kissinger truly believes is the fate of the United States is an exercise in morbidity except insofar as it is assumed that someone who believes himself fated to lose is incapable of making the struggle. It simply isn't true that Henry Kissinger does not desire to make the struggle. It is an open question whether, to the extent he is convinced that our civilization is ending, he generates the kind of power you need to shed the mortal coil, and breathe again.

We must remember that pessimism about the prospects for the United States is hardly the distinguishing stigmata of jaded American liberalism. When Abraham Lincoln asked at Gettysburg whether government by the people, of the people and for the people would endure, he meant precisely to be asking a question: i.e., he was not sure of the answer. American conservatives venerate the awful vision of Orwell: he sought to tell us what it would be like to be alive in 1984— if we pursued policies he was analyzing back in the days when Solzhenitsyn was proud of the West.

Whittaker Chambers believed that he was leaving the winning side in order to join the losing side, and over a decade in the 1950's he wrote the most moving, but nonetheless lugubrious, prose ever composed predicting the end of the West: a most eloquent passage of which was recalled by Ronald Reagan the same week he launched his campaign. James Burnham's classic, *Suicide of the West*, was published almost fifteen years ago. There is a blueprint for the loss of the world. There isn't anything gone wrong in the world today which mught not have been averted by acting on that volume, and its comprehensive analysis of the causes of our faltering policies.

Walker Percy, in his novel, *Love in the Ruins*, gives us an American version of 1984. What one might call Free Enterprise Dissolution. His vision of a future isn't that of Americans become Mao Men, as Orwell saw us; but of society atomized: without order, without services, without loyalties, institutions, conventions, prescriptions.

These, I repeat, are men whose vision of the future is itself testimony to their fear of that future; implicitly, it is their way of attempting to rouse the community to resistance to that future. What Ronald Reagan seems to be saying is that the private vision of Henry Kissinger incapacitates him from rendering effective service to avoid that vision. I do not think that this follows. Though at the same time, I do not think we have had effective leadership. I assign the blame for that principally to Richard Nixon.

Effective leadership in a free society is, at the margin, exercised over the public. It is the President who speaks to the public. His Secretary of State is a technician. He does, to be sure, speak directly to the people's representatives. But they are taking, in the absence of redirection from thcir constituencies, the thoughtless, factionalist, unconcerted, disoriented actions predicted by Burnham as issuing from a clouded vision and anemic will; and, by Chambers, as issuing out of a spiritual torpor. Either way, we lose: whether our Secretary of State is Henry Kissinger or Theodore Roosevelt.

Kissinger, who defended every tough action we took in Vietnam, is hardly the dove of recent myth. It was Kissinger who associated himself with efforts to frustrate Allende's taking power. Who spoke warnings about Portugal. Who has begged Congress not to throw away Turkey and Greece and Egypt; who railed against the aggression on Angola; who now predicts that if the Communists are invited into the governments of Western Europe, NATO will die. His are neither the words nor the deeds of a man who welcomes the day when his dark, private vision will be realized.

That leaves us with the point: can the pessimist triumph? And, put in another way, can the leader who, convinced that history has spoken its sullen and irreversible judgment, understand himself to be capable of something other than merely stalling? Is that how best to characterize our foreign policy during the Kissinger years? And is there an alternative?

The trouble—and listen carefully—is this. There is an alternative. But it is a measure of our malady that it cannot be spoken by anyone who desires to be President.

American businessmen in the Soviet Union

January 9, 1977

ONE OF THE matters concerning which the new Administration ought to express itself is the credit being extended to the Soviet Union for the purpose of, (choose one) a) reorienting its economy to peacetime pursuits; or b) burying us. The capitalist community in America isn't quite sure which of the two it will be, but, exercising its inclination to economic prudence, it appears to be betting on a).

The other day, in Nabvrezhnye Chelny, USSR, they opened up a trucking plant built, substantially, by United States technology and United States capital. A little perspective is in order. In 1970, the Russians invited Henry Ford to Moscow where he was treated like Marco Polo, and if anyone during the banquets held in his honor uttered a whispering word of derogation of the capitalist system, the offender was no doubt sent off to Gulag for ten years. But it did not work: on returning to the United States, Mr. Ford announced that his company would not build a truck plant for the Soviet Union. No doubt he was in part motivated by the flow of Russian truck traffic from North Vietnam to South Vietnam carrying ammunition for use against American soldiers. Capitalists aren't dumb: the more American soldiers killed in Vietnam, you see, the fewer potential buyers of Ford cars.

The Russians blasted the decision of Henry Ford—all that hospitality wasted—and said that, after all, all they needed to do was bestow their commercial favors elsewhere. However, the months went by and no other company stepped forward, presumably because Europeans didn't have the right combination of technology and credit.

But American companies in due course came in. A combine of the Pullman Company, IBM, Westinghouse, Ingersoll-Rand, and others stepped forward and, $4 billion later, the curtains were drawn on the Kama River plant. Listen to the report from Mr. David Shipler of the New York *Times*:

" . . . the whole effort is already being hailed by both sides as a huge monument to the power of Soviet and American economic cooperation. The Kama River plant embodies the Soviet passion for bigness and the American aptitude for automation. By its sheer size, the huge complex, which covers more than thirty-eight square miles and will employ 90,000 workers, is as bold as the thunder of a propaganda poster, embodying the industrial might and heroism that constitute much of the Soviet definition of socialism and patriotism."

Now it isn't as though we and our brothers in the Kremlin had had a perfect time of it. Something happened along the way, namely the Jackson Amendment, the terms of which deny to the Soviet Union the economic benefits of Most Favored Nation until the Soviet Union permits its nationals the right to emigrate guaranteed under the Soviet Constitution and the United Nations Declaration on Human Rights.

* * *

There are interesting arguments to the effect that the Jackson Amendment is the wrong kind of pressure to use in foreign affairs; but it is hard to marshal emotional arguments against it. Such feelings are not entertained at the Kama River plant by Communist officials, needless to say; but not by Americans, either. Listen.

"Foreign Trade Minister Nikolai Patolichev said in a speech that without some change soon, Moscow would turn more of its attention to trade with other countries.... At a dinner here, American executives rose one after another to toast their Soviet hosts and to denounce the law; one even thanked the Russians for being so 'patient' with the United States."

The American capitalist who is so embarrassed by American obstructionism in our relations with the Soviet Union is well known in Soviet mythology. He is the proverbial capitalist who will sell the Communists the rope with which to hang the last capitalist. He may not be exactly typical of American capitalists. But he is the quintessential capitalist as seen by the dissidents within the Soviet Union—the man Solzhenitsyn talked about when he addressed the AFL-CIO Convention in Washington in 1975. How should these capitalists abroad be regarded by Americans in general?

Let us attempt a couple of fundamental distinctions. At one end of the trade spectrum are the instruments of war or of torture. Solzhenitsyn, addressing the AFL-CIO and deploring the activities of many American capitalists, made a direct reference to a recent exhibit in the Soviet Union of United States anti-criminal technology: an exhibit that so engrossed the Russians they put in orders for the lot, cash on the barrelhead. The problem, Solzhenitsyn pointed out, being that we were selling our scientific paraphernalia not to the law-abiding for use against criminals, but—given the constitution of Soviet authority—to criminals (the people who run Russia) for use against those who would abide by the law (the dissenters, who wish to implement the provisions of the Soviet Constitution and the United Nations Declaration of Human Rights). It was rather like inventing the guillotine for the purpose of slaughtering cattle, and then selling it to

Robespierre in full knowledge of the uses to which he intended to put it.

At the other end of the spectrum is, let us say, wheat. Wheat is not thought of as grist either for Russia's torture mills or for its war machine. To be sure, if one were persuaded to think of wheat as, say, the ecologists think of the least of the effluents, as the nutritionists think of beef fatteners, as the conservationists think of the bald eagle, we would be arguing that wheat was an indispensable and indistinguishable part of the whole—of the entire imperialistic Soviet enterprise; and of course it is. No wheat, no guns. Still, the soritical leap from bread to nuclear missiles gives time for the easing of the capitalist conscience.

In between the two is such hardware as the Kama plant will produce, and such hardware as went into the development of the Kama plant. And always there is the question of credit. It is estimated that the Soviet Union now owes Western banks $40 billion. The rule of thumb of international bankers is that a nation's debt service (i.e., yearly interest plus amortization) ought not to exceed 15 percent of its hard-currency earnings. But the Soviet figure has risen to 25 percent, and this in a nation that devotes more than twice as large a share of its GNP to the military as we do. In the past five years, the West has increased by ten times goods exported to the Soviet Union. The reciprocal figure is four times. The differential is, essentially, Western credit.

The significance of this analysis is that Soviet economic threats against the United States ("We will take our business elsewhere!") are largely empty. It is a grand version of the indigent, refused credit at the bar, announcing he will patronize a competitor. And the significance of this datum is that the residual problem is really a political problem. Will the governments of the West use the leverage they have over the Soviet Union to force it to retrench? What will Mr. Carter and his people say on the subject? Will the threat to "détente" prove to be the intimidating instrument the Soviet Union so greatly desires it to be? Capitalist enterprises aren't, when all is said and done, foreign-policy makers. And the behavior of the American capitalist who toasted Soviet patience at Kama is no more offensive than some of Richard Nixon's toasts in China. But American business enterprise needs to know whether it is participating in a corporate act: the defense of America, and the concentration of pressures on the Soviet Union to devote its own resources to its extramilitary industrial plant. Failure to think the problem through renders us vulnerable to the haunting observations of Solzhenitsyn . . .

"This is something which is almost incomprehensible to the human mind, that burning greed for profit that goes beyond all reason, all self-control, all conscience." Greed can be the lubricant of material progress, even as ambition is often the lubricant of public service. What is missing today is an elaborated doctrine that unites economic and public policy. Carter, as chief foreign-policy maker, should accept the responsibility for attempting to formulate a coherent doctrine.

When is a nation "Marxist"?

February 18, 1977

THE LEARNED professor made withering sport, after dinner, of the lady who professed her fear that a particular country in Africa might turn Communist. There being no scorn more withering than that of John Kenneth Galbraith, the lady felt the agonies of annihilation. Actually, she shouldn't have. The point nicely illustrates the difference between the paradigm and the existential.

Professor Galbraith's point is that you cannot have a Marxist-Communist state without going through the antecedent stages. These are: feudalism, capitalism, and (in most cases), imperialism. A state that is not industrialized cannot, so the argument goes, proceed through the necessary metamorphosis. Marxism foresees the struggle between the property-owners and the workers, resulting in the ascendancy of the workers, the socialization of property and of the means of production, distribution, and exchange, a great historical period during which there is a dissipation of those tensions that mounted under the old order; followed by the disappearance of the state.

Under this definition, rigorously applied, there is no Communist state anywhere. China was barely industrialized in 1949, and in any event it was peasants, not industrial workers, who made up the legions finally commanded by Mao Tse-tung. The Soviet Union depends increasingly on a price system, has created a new class of governors who enjoy every one of the perquisites of the old capitalist class, plus the indescribable pleasures of being able to torment and torture people they don't like; and, after sixty years of power, enjoys a state apparatus that makes Nicholas II look like the czar of Monaco.

Solzhenitsyn informs us that he doubts that there is anybody at all—not one individual—living in Russia who believes in Marxism. And he may be right. But whether he is right or wrong, it is impossible to say about the Soviet Union that it is a Marxist state in the theoretical sense. Accordingly, we must reason not *a priori*, from the general to the particular, as Mr. Galbraith is forever doing, but *a posteriori*, from the particular to the general, in search of the modern meaning of a Marxist-Leninist state. I tend to the conclusion that being a Marxist-Leninist state is something like being a Jew: the accepted definition of a Jew is somebody who believes he is a Jew. Who will say him nay?

Consider Angola, now. Hardly an industrial state. Hardly a state that has passed through Marx's transitional stages. But recently its leader in a state speech described it as a "Marxist-Leninist republic." This brought a great guffaw from the distinguished British journalist Lord Chalfont, who commented that that designation was presumably in honor of those two celebrated African tribal philosophers." But, actually, if we survey history since the first Communist coup d'état in search of the attributes of states that consider themselves Marxist-Leninist, we find, after a short exercise in reductionism, that they are uniform in: (1) hostility to private property; (2) hostility to other human freedoms; (3) hostility to religion; (4) hostility to countries that do not share these hostilities. That is really all it takes. What country dares call itself a Marxist country with total doctrinal fidelity? As many countries as would dare call themselves Christian countries if it were supposed that these are countries whose people and governors practice the doctrines of Christ.

This morning brings the news that the Soviet Union's U.S.A. Institute, whose leader the day before reassured President Carter that the Soviet Union harbored no hostility against us, gave an honorary degree to the U.S. Communist leader Henry Winston. Mr. Winston's citation is a classic statement of Marxist eschatology, which is now Soviet cant. Listen: Winston is cited for "his outstanding contribution to the scientific analysis of the practical aspects of the revolutionary struggle of the working class, of all the progressive forces of America against racism and for a democratic and social reformation of society." And they made fun of people who wondered how many angels could stand on the head of a pin.

Can Carter mean what he says?

May 27, 1977

AFTER MR. Carter delivered the ritual Presidential speech to the United Nations in March, I speculated that his speechwriters, in retaliation against the loss of their limousines, were engaged in what we in America call a slow-down. The speech was a chaotic venture in half-thoughts, expressed in language appropriate to them. The same speechwriters wrote the President's message as delivered on Commencement Day at Notre Dame, in South Bend, Indiana, on May 22. It was a speech which for good reasons disturbs our allies, who are entitled to wonder whether President Carter is capable of consistent thought.

"Being confident of our own future," he said, "we are now free of that inordinate fear of Communism which once led us to embrace any dictator who joined us in our fear."

To borrow from Fowler, the American people are divided, in respect of the matter of our confidence in our own future, between those who don't care, those who don't know, those who care and know, those who don't care and don't know; and those who distinguish. Those who know best are frankly and publicly worried about the Soviet build-up and the incommensurate United States effort, particularly at the tactical level.

Though thought of as the author of detente, and bard of self-satisfaction, it was Henry Kissinger himself who used such terms as "catastrophic" and "intolerable" to describe geopolitical advances by the enemy in Southeast Asia and in Africa during his own term of office. Every important official associated with the Pentagon worries greatly about America's ability to cope with the Soviet Union. Those dictators we "joined" in resisting Communist imperialism—the reference is clearly to Franco and Salazar—would be interested to know that their fear of Communism was inordinate, Franco having experienced Communists during a civil war that convulsed his nation, and Salazar having died a year or two before the Communists all but took over Portugal.

People are scratching their heads over such sentences as, "For too many years we have been willing to adopt the flawed principles and tactics of our adversaries, sometimes abandoning our values for theirs. We fought fire with fire, never thinking that fire is better fought with water." Now what on earth does that long rhetorical gargle mean? Even as Commencement Day prose it will not wash down. If we wish to fight fire with water, then let the President dissolve the Pentagon and replace it with a bed of posies. Every time we have used water on the Soviet Union in the post-war years we have germinated a fresh Communist colony.

The "principles and tactics of our adversaries" are indeed flawed, but these are men of blood and guts and ambition who by the exercise of their flawed principles and tactics have managed effective control over half the world, and effective intimidation of the other half. If they are encouraged to treat the West as an alliance of flower children, they will do exactly that.

President Carter's formulations, in his foreign policy speeches, are so maladroit that one can draw reassurance only from the knowledge that he cannot possibly mean what he says.

Consider his well-known position on human rights. "First," he said at Notre Dame, setting forth his credenda, "our policy should reflect our people's basic commitment to promote the cause of human rights." Having a few paragraphs earlier denounced the dictators with whom America has in the past formed morally careless alliances, he announces, a few paragraphs after staking out his policy on the question of human rights, that "we will cooperate more closely with the newly influential countries in Latin America, Africa and Asia. We need their friendship and cooperation in a common effort." Still earlier, he had said, "Because we know democracy works, we can reject the arguments of those rulers who deny human rights to their people."

Attempt, now, to take these discrete observations and splice them together. For one thing, democracy does not always work. It certainly did not work in Argentina. Which are the "newly influential countries" in Asia with whom we must combine in our joint endeavors for human rights and democracy? Vietnam? Cambodia? In his speech at the United Nations, President Carter said, "In Southeast Asia and in the Pacific we will strengthen our association with our traditional friends." Our traditional friends in Southeast Asia are mostly dead.

Or does he mean Taiwan? But at Notre Dame he said, "It is important that we make progress toward normalizing relations with the People's Republic of China. We wish to cooperate closely with the creative Chinese people on the problems that confront all mankind." But the problems that confront the Chinese people, as represented by their leaders, are the Gang of Four, Beethoven and Confucius.

As to Southern Africa, we need "a peaceful resolution of the crisis. The time has come for the principle of majority rule to be the basis for political order, recognizing that in a democratic system the rights of the minority must also be protected. To be peaceful, change must come promptly."

If there is to be majority rule in Southern Africa, why not majority rule in Northern Africa? If there is to be protection for minorities in Rhodesia, who is going to enforce it? The same people who are enforcing the rights of minorities in China? Among all those creative Chinese?

Did you know that "colonialism has nearly gone"? President Ford, as some British will remember, liberated Poland in a single television coup d'état. President Carter chooses now to declare that the whole satellite empire of the Soviet Union is not a colony. "Our policy must reflect our belief that the world can hope for more than simple survival and our belief that dignity and freedom are man's fundamental spiritual requirements."

What policy?

There are Americans who do not believe in the sincerity of Jimmy Carter. I am not among them. Mr. Carter's difficulty is his overweening idealistic appetite combined with the humiliation of living in a sinful world. There are those (among these I do place myself) who believe that a hard, consistent campaign for human rights is both good morals and good politics. It is correct that we need to make distinctions. Senator Fulbright attempted this when ten years ago he wrote that the United States Government has no proper quarrel with the domestic policies of any foreign State no matter how obnoxious, for so long as that State does not seek to export those policies. There is a strong case to be made for exerting pressure of sorts on Rhodesia and on South Africa. But it cannot begin to meet the Fulbright test, which is amply met by China, by Vietnam, by Cuba, toward which countries the Carter Administration has been especially propitiative.

Mr. Carter's random search for fresh partners among "the newly influential countries" in Latin America, Africa and Asia makes our traditional allies wonder, with good reason, whether, in the new vision of the American President, they have been suddenly anachronized.

C. S. Lewis spoke about the sin of disproportion. By committing it so egregiously—the hectic concern for human rights in Rhodesia practically defined as the transfer of power from an orderly white community to a disorderly black faction within the black community, contrasted with an increasingly Platonic concern over the systematic repressions in the Soviet empire, and a total absence of criticism of the practices of a great Oriental Power with which he seeks anxiously to normalize relations—the President loses coherence, disconcerts his natural allies, and douses water on those flames of hope he lit in the first days of his administration when his concern for human rights appeared to be even-handed, and he had not yet advertised his general bewilderment.

The CIA

The stigma of having been one

October 30, 1975

The New Yorker, which has always been respected as a stylistic trendsetter in recent years, as everyone knows who is familiar with this entertaining, instructive, and readable weekly, has gone in for high colonic Conscience-Flushing. It is a pity that the lead writers in "The Talk of the Town" section of the magazine tend to make the rather common mistake of identifying their own conscience with that of the Republic. During the Vietnam years, the screech of pain became all but unbearable, and some of us came close to suggesting to the publishers that they bring out two editions of *The New Yorker,* one with, one without the opening pages—charging double for the shorter, unencumbered, unencumbering version. It is not known what exactly happened over there. Perhaps the editors are seeking to do penance for the fit of idolatry in the issue in which they commented on John F. Kennedy's inaugural address—the one in which the new President swore that we would undertake any sacrifice, bear any pain, proceed if necessary alone, to guarantee freedom everywhere in the world—an exalted rhetoric that greatly impressed many people at the time, and took us to war in Vietnam.

With the removal of U.S. forces, one hoped for remission in *The New Yorker,* but it is very slow in coming. Most recently, "The Talk of the Town" rambled on about the CIA hearings, concluding that it is really very hard nowadays to distinguish between conventional bad guys, like the Mafia and the KGB, and ostensible good guys, like the CIA and the FBI. Indeed, the editorial concluded, "the CIA, the SLA, the FBI, and Charles Manson's family were mingling on our television screens, in our thoughts, and, it seemed, in the real world, and it was getting harder by the minute to tell them apart." Here is a fine example of the rhetorical art put to narcissistic excess. It is one thing to say: "I find it harder and harder to tell them apart." Another to say: "*It* is getting harder to tell them apart."

Me, I have no trouble at all telling apart Charles Manson, say, and James Angleton, but no doubt about it, in the real world—which, however, is a world over-affected by the formative thought of Eastern Seaboard liberalism—they are having that trouble. It is really getting to the point where ex-employees of the CIA, who once were something of an aristocracy among public servants—men and women who worked in anonymity, sometimes risking their lives to forward a foreign policy that had bipartisan political backing and was oriented to the idealistic task of stemming by means short of war the Communist tide—found themselves, on revealing their past association in the course of applying for another job, being treated as cretins. It is both a pity that Mr. Eric Biddle Jr. now feels he has to take the matter to court, and a relief that he is doing so, in what amounts to something of a class action on behalf of all former members of the CIA who are being treated shabbily—by the government of the United States.

Mr. Biddle worked for the CIA between 1950 and 1960, and so far as is known he did not assassinate, or lay the grounds for assassination of, any member of the Kennedy family, or any civil rights leader. When in 1965 he decided to go back into government service, he found himself in due course working for a government agency called Action, about which I know little and therefore suspect it shouldn't even exist.

On the discovery by his employers that he had worked for the CIA, the harassments began, and became so acute that, finally, Biddle was driven to suing the Civil Service Commission. The Commission came up with the most extraordinary finding in recent history: the ban against discrimination by government agencies, e.g., by reason of race, sex, age, etc., did not extend to a ban against discrimination by reason of having worked for another and presumably nefarious branch of government. So: *Eric H. Biddle Jr. v. The United States of America* goes now to the United States District Court for the District of Columbia, and it becomes Mr. Biddle's burden, to return to the language of *The New Yorker*, to persuade the court that there is an observable difference between having worked for the U.S. Central Intelligence Agency, and having camped out with Charles Manson and Squeaky and the girls, honing the kitchen knives. Presumably any juror who reads *The New Yorker* will be disqualified for cause.

The scandals

December 16, 1975

CONCERNING THE FBI and CIA scandals, a few observations:

1. The abuses of the FBI are in three categories. The first is most readily understood, and easily forgiven. It is an excess of zeal in the matter of protecting the nation. The redundant bug is just that—redundant. We should, moreover, bear in mind that at the time of these offenses, the Supreme Court had not imposed its restriction on bugging.

The second category is political, and, although understandable, not easily forgiven. LBJ, bugging Barry Goldwater, in order to profit politically from foreknowledge of Goldwater's plans. This was a forthright abuse of office, and although it transpires that FDR also did it, it was an objectionable and tyrannical violation of privacy.

The third was—one gathers—personal. J. Edgar Hoover's interest in Martin Luther King, let us grant, originated with the suspicion that he had a Communist accomplice. This was reasonable grounds for official attention—the infiltration of the civil rights movement by unregistered agents of the Soviet Union would have direly affected that movement. It became political when Dr. King charged that Hoover was sending agents to the South who would not concern themselves with violations of the civil rights laws.

What seems then to have happened is that Hoover blew his top. He had available tapes, transcribed under a clinical rubric, which were apparently embarrassing, or at least Hoover thought them to be. It was then that the incredible series of events began, the final, ludicrous, pathetic, deranged conclusion of which was a letter inviting Dr. King to commit suicide.

We need to remind ourselves that Hoover for decades was the truly exemplary head of the Federal Bureau of Investigation. His high standards of discipline, and his devotion to the corps he developed, made him respectively loved and feared by law-abiding, and law-breaking citizens. The collapse of the later years tells us nothing very new, but reminds us of things we tend to forget. Power tends to corrupt. The exercise of authority into old age often brings arrogance.

Hoover should not have been permitted to stay in office after reaching the statutory retirement age. Many men and women perform brilliantly into their old age. But it is preferable that their labors are private. Certainly they should not dispose of policemen. Mr. Hoover disgraced himself and his agency, and nobody could regard this more bitterly than the man who labored throughout most of a lifetime to enhance the reputation of his agency—Hoover himself.

2. It is impossible to escape talk about CIA plots to assassinate world leaders, which is obsessing the public, here and abroad. Investigation reveals that CIA complicity was in fact highly limited. And in no case did a CIA agent, or the agent of a CIA agent, participate in an execution.

Three names are most prominently mentioned. Diem was in fact assassinated by South Vietnamese acting on their own initiative. Lumumba was killed by Mobutu in a civil-war situation where bullets fly, and people get killed by being in the way. Castro survives. Meanwhile, everyone takes the categorical position that in no circumstances can a government legitimately conspire in a plot to assassinate any chief of state.

Count me out. Police can shoot down snipers. So, under

rigorously analogous circumstances, would a nation made victim of another neighbor's guerrillas be entitled to strike at their leader. I would not have cavilled, as President of Bolivia during the days of Che Guevara, at ordering the assassination of the foreign official engaged in shooting Bolivians and fomenting civil war. Castro, in 1962, was hardly playing games. The braintrusters surrounding President Kennedy believed that we came very close to a nuclear war. As the result of a primary aggression of Khrushchev to be sure; but the proximate enemy was Castro, in whose territory the missiles, aimed at American cities, were lodged.

What we learn, really, is that a free society cannot conspire to assassinate—because the context of an assassination is never rendered accurately after the fact; and, therefore, the assassination will always appear unjustified, and paranoiac. Free societies have to learn that some transactions—a very few, but some—should properly remain confidential. George Kennan, that wise statesman and scholar, said as much recently. He believes that covert action is justified but doesn't believe it can be carried out in a free society. Another dilemma.

The FBI and Martin Luther King

January 3, 1976

THE WHOLE HOOVER business is getting out of hand. One of the reasons for it is the partisanship of the headlining Congressional investigating committees, which make one think back wistfully on the rough justice of those Nixonites engaged in maximizing the incumbency. Now hear this: Carl Rowan, the prominent black journalist and former director of the United States Information Agency, has actually suggested that the evidence mounts that the Federal Bureau of Investigation, under Hoover's leadership, connived in the assassination of Martin Luther King.

I don't think Joe McCarthy ever made an allegation quite

so breathtaking. They ran McCarthy out of town with wet towels. All that has happened to Carl Rowan, so far as I can see, is that he has received a quiet letter from Ladislas Farrago, the writer, biographer of General Patton, who has been spending the last several years preparing an authoritative biography of J. Edgar Hoover. Rowan would probably have preferred the towels.

Farrago wrote to Rowan to say, in effect:

Look, (1) in 1967 there was a genuine national concern over the company (I do not mean sexual) Dr. King was keeping.

(2) During that period there were periodic threats against the life of Dr. King. These came in part from white fanatics, against whom the FBI was generally able to contend—by bugging certain telephones, keeping some people under surveillance, penetrating their organizations, and providing King with special protections. But it became more and more difficult to protect him against the black extremists—such as, for instance, had assassinated Malcolm X—because the hostility to the FBI engendered by King and a few black extremists had made the work of the FBI extremely difficult in tight black circles.

(3) Moreover, Rowan, back in 1967, was one of the black leaders who knew these facts. His idolatry of Dr. King is strictly a posthumous affair. Mr. Farrago reminded Mr. Rowan of an article published in September, 1967, in the *Reader's Digest*. Martin Luther King is saying "utterly irresponsible things," Rowan wrote then. After the speech in which King compared Americans in Vietnam to the concentration-camp masters of Nazi Germany, Rowan said, "Reaction across the nation and around the world was immediate and explosive. Radios Moscow and Peking picked up King's words and fed them to distant capitals. In the White House, a Presidential aide shouted, 'My God, King has given a speech on Vietnam that goes right down the Communist line!' "

Rowan then gave a list of liberal leaders who had chided King on his excesses—Bunche, Brooke, Freedom House, the Washington *Post*.

Rowan went further. "King," he analyzed, "seemed to develop an exaggerated appraisal of how much he and his crisis techniques were responsible for the race-relations progress that had been made." And he warned:

"Negroes had, in fact, begun to grow uneasy about King. He no longer seemed to be the selfless leader of the 1950's." His visits to the "jail looked like publicity stunts."

Why did King move the civil rights issue into foreign policy? "Why did King," in adopting the Communist line, "reject the advice of his old civil rights colleagues? Some say it was a matter of ego. . . . Others revived a more sinister speculation that had been whispered around Capitol Hill and in the nation's newsrooms for more than two years—talk of Communists influencing the actions and words of the young minister. This talk disturbed other civil rights leaders more than anything else."

And—may we not assume?—disturbed the Director of the Federal Bureau of Investigation. Carl Rowan would perhaps have an easier time understanding the whole mess if he went back to read what he was himself writing about it at the time of Hoover's maximum concern.

The new Intelligence Committee

May 25, 1976

WITHOUT GOING into the detail of the proposed new law governing the activities of our intelligence agencies, it is reasonable to say that it is designed to bring under representative scrutiny a) what our intelligence agencies are doing; and b) how much money they are spending.

It is critical to ask whether that scrutiny is to be exercised by a committee of legislators who can be counted upon to prefer the public safety to the satisfaction of their own political vanity, but that gets you into problems. How do you say in constitutional language: We are going to set up an oversight committee which will exclude Michael Harrington of Massachusetts? The dear old Constitution prohibits bills of attainder, so you have to come up with legal ways of describing Michael Harrington, and that is a tough one.

Then, as a practical matter, you need to ask whether that oversight committee will stop, automatically, drastic covert actions of the kind that wins popular favor and professional criticism.

The distinction is best drawn from the work of our novelists. I have drawn attention before to *The Day of the Jackal*. Here the protagonist is a hired killer, and his assignment is to execute Charles de Gaulle. The suspense is very great, and the huge bestseller owes that success to the narrowness of de Gaulle's escape. But do you know how the French intelligence people managed to save his life? Well, to begin with they kidnapped somebody from Rome. Getting him to Marseilles, they tortured him, and got from him a couple of words—a clue. Oh yes, he died from the torture.

Then the chief of police (of police, mind you), without any authority from anybody, undertook to tap the telephones not of Joe Kraft, but of every member of the French cabinet. And lo, one of these telephones yielded a yummy conversation between the minister of something and his mistress, who, when the minister was snoring, got up and telephoned her contact within the resistance group that had hired the assassin.

All it took, in other words, to protect the life of the president of France was one (1) kidnapping, one (1) torture, one (1) death, and eleven (11) tapped telephones of the French cabinet. The reading public loved it, and Senator Frank Church or Teddy Kennedy has never held up the book as a reason to deny aid to France.

John Ehrlichman, former aide to Richard Nixon, has written a novel in which President Kennedy orders, at the last minute, the assassination of a priest traveling with the invading army to the Bay of Pigs. The idea is that Kennedy discovered that the Russians would counter our invasion of Cuba and come back at us with nuclear ferocity. On the other hand, the invasion was already launched, and could not be aborted.

The President hit on the idea of destroying the spiritual

force behind the military mission: the equivalent of slipping Joan of Arc a mickey finn just before she took on the British. It is not projected that the admirers of President Kennedy will cavil at the action he (allegedly) took, under such circumstances.

The new oversight committee is on the one hand desirable—we *do* need protection against capricious use of intelligence capabilities; on the other hand, it is a schematic example of efforts by lawyers and jigsaw makers to pin down with exactitude the rules by which we govern ourselves in a spontaneous world substantially dominated by tyrants. If we go down, they are saying, it will be with punctilio.

How Robert Redford saved us from the CIA

September 28, 1975

Three Days of the Condor has everything, and one thing too many, wherein alas lies its chic. But for the terminal protuberance, we would have an expertly directed, trimly jigsawed, adequately acted spy-suspense story which catches the viewer with the opening scene: What can that mysterious man in the parked car be about, checking off the names, one by one, of the half-dozen people as they saunter into the "American Literary Historical Society" on Manhattan's East Side to begin a day's work? Why, what he is doing is making sure there's a full house, because at lunchtime, he and his accomplices are going into that staid old building to shoot them all down in cold blood, made colder by the special ice pellets used—at least, that is one inference—by specially designed carnage-machines.

What was Robert Redford doing while his colleagues were being mowed down? He was out for lunch. Specifically, out to fetch lunch for his colleagues, it being his turn to go to the delicatessen. But, in order to avoid the rain, he ignores prescribed security regulations and bounds down the staircase and out the back door, which is closer to the deli; and anyway, it is time to establish him as a man of rather independent habits, who makes the boss of this supersecret CIA front perpetually uneasy ("Are you sure you are quite happy working for us, Turner?") with that roaming, restless intelligence. (The director, Sydney Pollack, is unwilling to blemish Redford's beautiful face with any of the scars of The Thinker, but makes the concession of having him, occasionally, wear glasses. He does not wear glasses when he makes love to Faye Dunaway, but then this is not a moment when his restless intelligence is his dominating concern.)

Redford's job at the "American Literary Historical Society" is to apply his encyclopedic knowledge and omnivorous curiosity to the scanning of routine material in search of surreptitious enemy activity. He has recently come on an anomaly: A certain bestseller has been translated only into Dutch and Arabic. So what, you say? So *you* would never qualify to work for the CIA because of *your* restless intelligence. Redford has sent down to Washington, through his superior at the Manhattan front, the datum, on which he frames a hunch which is mercifully unexplicated, and the lunch-hour carnage is the result. Redford had stumbled over an operation of international significance, and it is a lucky, lucky thing that it was his day to go to the deli and that he used the back door, else he'd be stone-cold dead, along with the boss, the beautiful Oriental secretary, and all the others.

On bringing in the hot dogs and finding everybody dead, Redford decides he had better report the event to Washington, but he is good and scared, and so are you in his behalf, I'm telling you. So when he calls Washington, and is told by the bigger boss which alleyway to report to at exactly what hour, Redford says, No sirree, I'm not going to report to any alleyway to meet up with a perfect stranger. How do I know I'm not talking to the chief killer himself? It is therefore arranged that the unknown boss will be accompanied by an old friend of Redford's from another division of CIA. Recognizing his old friend, Redford will say to himself—and would even if he *didn't* have a restless intelligence—"That's my old friend all right, so the guy with him must be O.K."

But what happens is that as soon as the three men get together, the boss suddenly whips out a pistol and in the general shoot-out Redford's friend is killed, the boss is fatally wounded, and Redford knows he's in real trouble. So he kidnaps Faye Dunaway, a perfect stranger of the kind Robert Redford would come upon, and over the next couple of hours the plot proceeds along its anfractuous way, and the viewer has a superb time as assassins come and go, and gets a true sci-fi thrill out of the display of intelligence hardware, of which my favorite is a machine that flashes a map showing the location of the telephone being used by the caller. However, Redford's restless intelligence at some point in his life put him on to everything anybody ever knew about telephones, and he manages to cross the lines of half the telephone trunks in the city and sits comfortably on a ganglion that makes a laughing stock out of the Central Intelligence Agency's telephone-spotting machine.

By now we all know that the Mr. Big who ordered the killings is very high up in government. Our government. Indeed, by the laws of compound interest, if the movie had endured another half an hour, one would have been satisfied only if the President of the United States, or perhaps even Ralph Nader, had proved to be the energumen behind it all.

Thus it goes, right to the smash ending, as unbalancing as Jimmy Durante's nose. The viewers would, at that point, have been left totally satisfied by a traditional double-agent theme—Mr. Big was really working for the Soviet Union; or, if that is not trendy enough for Pollack-Redford, a Chilean colonel. It transpires, however, that Mr. Big is a 100 percent American who had to eliminate all those people at the "American Literary Historical Society" because they might have become privy to a contingent operation by following the lead turned up by Redford's restless intelligence.

Then, in a dramatic sidewalk confrontation, Mr. Junior Big explains to Redford that it is all high patriotism, working against a future national shortage of oil, and invites Redford to come back into the company and accept the requirements of orthodoxy in the modern world. But Redford says, taking off his glasses, No, never! This very day I have told everything to . . . the camera slithers up to a marquee above the two men who are talking and you see the logo of . . . the

New York *Times*. The director failed only to emblazon under it, "Daniel Ellsberg Slept Here." Mr. Junior Big reacts like the witch come into contact with water. He snarls and shrivels away, and says, half-desperately: "Maybe they won't print it!" But Redford has by now seeded the audience with his restless intelligence, and *we* all know that the New York *Times will* print it, and we shall all be free.

The film's production notes state: "Over a year ago, Stanley Schneider, Robert Redford, Sydney Pollack and Dino de Laurentiis decided to create a film that would reflect the climate of America in the aftermath of the Watergate crisis." "The climate of America" is a pretty broad term. They really mean: The climate of America as seen by I. F. Stone, Seymour Hersh, Susan Sontag and Shirley MacLaine. One recalls Will Rogers, returning from the Soviet Union where he had seen a communal bath. "Did you see all of Russia?" he was asked. "No," Rogers said, weighing his answer. "But I saw all of *parts* of Russia!"

Redford-Pollack-de Laurentiis have shown us the climate in all of parts of America. It sure is cold out there.

II.

Politics

Richard Reeves on President Ford*

October 1975

(1) WHO EVER doubted that Richard Reeves is more *interesting* than Gerald Ford? (2) Wherefore it follows, doesn't it, that a book whose developing thesis is, substantially, that Reeves has more in common with Lincoln than Ford does is a work of supererogation? (3) Made worse, moreover, because the book in question too often reads like "Gerald Ford, the Man and the Myth," by Richard Reeves, as told to Victor Lasky.

Mr. Reeves is among the two or three sprightliest political writers in America, and it is difficult for him to fail to be interesting. But his facility here tempts him to do a lot of coasting—the passing along of salacious rumor, at once unsupported and implausible, and the cultivation of the breezy patois of candor that teeters over the line of spontaneity, and here and there falls into a mudpool.

For instance, on the matter of Nixon's selection of Ford: We are told by Reeves, as matter-of-factly as if he were reporting the temperature in Central Park at noon yesterday, that Ford was not Richard Nixon's first choice. "He was his last choice, in more ways than one." Now it turns out that that sentence dangles there purely for rhetorical and dramatic effect. In the passages that follow, Reeves does not prove that Ford was Nixon's "last" choice. And he certainly doesn't prove that he was his last choice "in more ways than one." In fact, a careful writer, which Reeves normally is, would have scratched out the second phrase for the best reason of all: it is meaningless. If A is B's last choice, there can be diverse *reasons*, but not "ways" for his being the last choice.

What we go on to get is anonymous White House staffers who report the surreptitious contempt allegedly felt by Nix-

---

*A Ford, Not a Lincoln. By Richard Reeves. Harcourt Brace Jovanovich.

on for Ford, and a lot of vague talk about how Ford's manifest "dumbness" would cause the Congress to shrink from impeaching Nixon because that would necessarily mean the accession of Ford. What's wrong with all that is that Congress in due course *did* resolve to remove Nixon, and the dumbness of Ford, which is Reeves's principal theme in this volume, emerges less as a national problem than as a major accommodation for Reeves looking for a clothes horse on which to hang his collected animadversions on a new President.

The candor-talk becomes particularly unpleasant as one comes reluctantly to the conclusion that Reeves is enjoying it for unwholesome reasons. Several times he talks about the whiskey on the breath of a Presidential associate (of course, he gives his name). Ron Nessen, the new press aide to Ford, "gloried in his transformation from asker to asked." (Is that another way of saying that Nessen enjoyed his new job? As in: "Reeves gloried in his transformation from news reporter for the New York *Times* to political commentator for *New York* magazine?") The White House staff under Rumsfeld is allegedly down on Kissinger: "(The anti-Kissinger strategy also had an attractive fringe benefit for Rumsfeld—Rummy wanted the Secretary of State's job.)" Perhaps it is the "Rummy" that makes that sentence odious, though even substituting "Rumsfeld" for "Rummy," it is pretty bad, and the parentheses provide the time warp to Walter Winchell. Still another: The Fords did not relish vacationing with the Annenbergs in California. In fact, "They hated it. The Annenberg servants ordered the Fords not to touch *objets d'art*, warned them not to take photographs inside the house, objected to their children's life style (which included one son's live-in girl friend). . . ." Cholly Knickerbocker would have blue-penciled that one.

Mr. Reeves is a man of unsettled views and ungoverned passion, and my guess is that he is here letting his (well-earned) skills—in glibness, color and candor—lead him into caricature. Candor is king nowadays. A quiet, pedantic economist, Alan Greenspan, informs a meeting of labor leaders that, as a class, the stockbrokers were the most intensely damaged by the current recession. But this becomes for candor-craving Reeves an "asinine insensitive accuracy." I find it as refreshing as I would any stray recognition that stock-brokers, and dentists, and even oil executives, worry about things like adolescent children, harassed wives, lost golf balls, and stomach cancer. There is the impacted cynicism about most things American, and about American institutions—including the press . . . Gerald Ford, the *corpus vile* of American democracy, is the "fair end product of the American political system." From—herewith Reeves's impartiality—Presidents Kennedy, Johnson, and Nixon, we had only "years of lying."

Yet for all that world-weariness, there are certain things Reeves will not put up with. One of them is any suggestion that "history" might speak well of the Administration of Richard Nixon. (My own guess is that history will, and shouldn't.) Most of the flame that flickers in this book is activated by the author's huffing and puffing. But on any matter that touches Nixon, and in particular the pardon of Nixon by Ford, the flame shoots up, a cold merciless blue, a towering inferno. When Ford pardoned Nixon, Gallup showed that Ford's public support went down from 71 to 50. "The press was less restrained, dropping Ford from near 100 to near zero. Reporters just turned a full 180 degrees and began to pound Ford and his lousy English muffins." Right.

I like Reeves and admire his ability, but I'll tell you this, brother. I'd rather have Jeb Magruder and John Dean at the other end of the shock generator when they truss me up with electric wires for getting in the way of the boys who are running things in our Republic. At least they never thought that torture is stylish.

Enter Carter

What are they doing to him?

April 8, 1976

I LIKE GOVERNOR CARTER for much the same reasons others like him, and accordingly I pledge not to observe him at the stump. I find it almost impossible to enhance one's appreciation of a man engaged in asking people to vote for him. Take Carter.

He was appearing before a trade union in Milwaukee, and the mood was surly. Why? Because, as governor, Jimmy Carter had defended right-to-work laws. Now understand exactly what this meant. It meant that the governor of Georgia took the position that the people of Georgia should reserve to themselves the right to decide whether a union shop should be compulsory. The idea that Washington should decide this in behalf of the people of Georgia is an affront not only on the 10th Amendment, but on the whole federal system. However, to have backed, however formalistically, 14(b) is on the order of having defaced an icon. It is a sin of the spirit. So, smiling at his interrogator, now we hear Jimmy Carter saying:

"That was when I was governor of Georgia. Now I think that the repeal of 14(b) means a great deal to a great many people. And if Congress sends me up a bill repealing 14(b), I'll sign it." There were cheers. A little half-hearted, because he was a man who once had disbelieved. Now, having confessed his sins, he was readmitted into the society, but he is still regarded with some suspicion. What those voters—and other voters engaged in humiliating other politicians—never quite think through is what they are doing to the man they propose to send to the Presidency.

You see, to believe that the Federal Government should specify a union shop throughout the United States requires the subordination of libertarian and federalist impulses to the interests of a single social unit—the trade union. Nobody who is prepared to subordinate all other interests to any one interest should be elected President. Not even to the interest of peace. Let alone to the interest of labor unions, or business corporations.

A failure to see this is a failure to understand what it is that makes for a good President. But it is precisely this desire to force the candidate to humiliate himself that the sectarian voter is insisting on. Consider what the reception would have been if Carter had said: "I don't believe that Washington should require states to require union shops—I think it's un-American. But if you vote for me, I promise I won't use the veto if Congress passes that legislation. Closed shops aren't, in my opinion, unconstitutional. So if the people, expressing their will through Congress, insist on outlawing the state's authority to pass right-to-work legislation, I won't stand in the way of that legislation's becoming law."

But that will not do. The voters require the equivalent of what in religious circles they call "internal assent." The candidate is required not merely to say that he will sign that particular measure, but that he *believes* in that particular measure.

The same conservative senators who savage Henry Kissinger over détente appear back home before their agricultural constituencies—and deplore any restrictions on the sale of wheat to Russia. The only thing they are not permitted to say is: "I disapprove of selling wheat to Russia, but I cannot risk alienating the votes of the farmers in my home state."

In New York City there isn't nearly as much freedom to criticize any Israeli policy as there is in the Knesset. Certainly not for a politician hoping to achieve office.

A senator from an oil state, even if he passionately believes in wage and price controls, must make the exception in respect of gas. Moreover, he must write a speech explaining the difference. Perhaps he uses the ghostwriter Senators Kennedy and McGovern used when they managed to distinguish between cutting down on military expenditures elsewhere than in South Dakota and Massachusetts.

Poor Jimmy Carter. He is saying, really: "Look how well qualified I am to serve as President. Is there a *better* hypocrite in town?"

Carter invincible?

May 1, 1976

THE POLL TELLS us that if Senator Humphrey had run in Pennsylvania, he would have achieved one-half the vote—well ahead of Carter. Yawn. In the first place we can't know whether that is true. In the process of running in behalf of oneself, inevitably one runs against somebody else. What Humphrey would have achieved if he had hypothetically run can be very different from what he would have achieved if he had actually run. Senator Humphrey in recent days has all but taken a blood oath to the labor unions, tonsured himself, donned coveralls and lunch-box, and said: "Tell me what to do." It is altogether conceivable that if he had run in his present posture, even in a state as heavily unionized as Pennsylvania, he'd have been rejected.

And, anyway, the game can be played on and on. If Humphrey had run, the poll says, he'd have beaten Carter. Well, if Kennedy had run, he probably would have beaten Humphrey—in the polls. In an actual contest, it is by no means established that Carter wouldn't have beaten the lot of them. You see, Carter is the Democrat on the rise. He is relatively unknown, which can hardly be said about Messrs. Humphrey and Kennedy. The growing excitement that attaches to his name may at some point lead him to the point reached by George McGovern: but I begin to doubt it.

An unexpected aspect of the success of Carter is that his mystery reflects nicely the difficulties Democrats have in being concrete. When a typical Democrat promises full employment without inflation—or full and "free" medical care—the public begins, finally, to sense that it is being trafficked with. Jimmy Carter is not only less than concrete, he seems to take the position that it is somehow vulgar to be concrete. When he is forced to take a direct stand on an issue—forced, for instance, in front of labor union tribunals to drink to the repeal of 14(b)—then he appears to be doing so less out of conviction than out of good nature. A matter of indulgence. "If you want to go to the World Series that bad, sonny, why I'll just dig into mah savings and get you a ticket."

Thus, to a black audience, Jimmy Carter announces that he is for school integration. And to a white audience, he says he is against forced busing. In fact, the two positions are not always incompatible. But, in fact, Jimmy Carter hasn't said what is his position in such parts of the United States where the two positions are indeed incompatible. South Boston, for instance. He would prefer to urge his listeners to believe that under his leadership tensions would dissolve: why should anybody be mad at anybody else, when Jimmy Carter isn't mad at anybody, and loves us all equally?

I tell you, brothers and sisters, it is a formidable posture. And it is in my judgment, and in the judgment of men more practiced in cynicism (the sharp-eyed, sharp-tongued Richard Reeves, for example), entirely sincere, even if it is amorphous. I happen myself to believe in the coming of the Lord, but I do not believe that the Lord takes an emphatic moral position on 14(b), even though I believe that if Jimmy Carter wanted to exclude all but theological arguments, I could make a monkey out of him in a debate on 14(b).

What issues, then, is without any afflatus to specificity. It is, rather, a matter of tone. It is an effective tone because anyone with a slightly better than superficial knowledge of Christianity knows that it is a religion of great discipline as well as great compassion. Thou art forgiven, *but sin no more.* A religion whose paradoxes have inspired the most beautiful poetry and music ever written; whose planted axioms have excited the attention of the most rigorous analytical minds. It is most commonly assumed that religion is mere incantation. A nice ritual, suitable for baptisms, weddings, and funerals, and best delivered by Hallmark. Carter says it is an entirely different context. "In 1967, I had a profound religious experience that changed my life. I accepted Christ into my life."

That, really, is a terrifying statement. And I do not doubt that it is the source of the awe and horror some people are feeling as Carter heads for the nomination. When Jonathan Edwards preached to a generation of deists at Yale, the historian records, "infidelity skulked its head." The prospect of a President who would attempt to rule according to the Word is not only anti-cosmopolitan, it is in the nature of heresy against the commandments of the secular state. Could it be that a President Carter would come out against a particular measure on the grounds that he thought it wrong?

That is the nature of the Carter problem. It is likelier that the system will break him, than that he should break the system. It is also quite possible that the general temper of his indulgence would bring him to stress good nature to the breaking-point of discipline. It has been calculated that, while governor, the whole of his administrative indulgences was equal to more than the sum of its parsimonious parts. Promise them simplicity, and a decent austerity, and give them Macy's window. He will be pressed to the wall in the coming months, but my own guess is that he's going to make it.

New boy in town

June 29, 1976

AT ATHENS, GEORGIA, a month or so back, a young man associated with the University of Georgia and formerly on the staff of Governor Carter told a story at the small dinner before the lecture.

. . . It was April 1973, and Governor Jimmy Carter had flown to Washington to tape an exchange on "Firing Line," the weekly television program. "We"—the reference was to the Governor's staff—"were all anxious to see how the Governor made out, so I had a bunch of them over to my house to listen. Well, after you introduced him, and he started talking—we couldn't believe it. His accent was completely changed. If we had heard the voice without the picture, we wouldn't have known it was the boss talking."

It transpired that Jimmy Carter had been practicing—in total privacy; Pygmalion-like. A new accent. The deregionalization of Jimmy Carter. Decided Southern inflections were left, but what had been there before—the deep Southern accent of deep, traditional Georgia—was gone.

"That's his regular voice now," I was told. I asked whether he was still capable of resurrecting the older voice, like Eliza

Doolittle when slipping on a banana peel. The qualified answer was yes, he could still speak like the old Jimmy Carter and, under special circumstances, before certain audiences, would do so. But the current accent is now the working Jimmy Carter. Presumably if he talks in his sleep, he uses his "Firing Line" voice. That is true self-mastery.

When Jimmy Carter came to New York the other day to give a foreign policy speech, one might put it that his objective was to win grudging praise from the New York *Times*, which has always been rather disdainful of Jimmy Carter, suspecting that under that smooth, calm exterior lies a Georgia cracker.

How do you go about appealing to the New York *Times* in a foreign policy speech? Well, it takes a little practice, but nothing you can't master by exercising in your bathroom, say ten minutes a day, sitting down, reading the *Times*'s editorials.

1. You say something on the theme of interdependence—we all live on one planet, that kind of thing.

2. You say something on the theme of our natural allies—our great postwar alliances with Europe and Japan, and the need to revive them.

3. You say something about the international problems of poverty and population control—and the creative role the United States can play in helping people help themselves.

4. You say something about the emerging nations of Africa—encouraging those "trends" within Africa that point the democratic way—and you deplore the racist policies of South Africa.

5. You deplore, in an age of endemic poverty, the amount of money spent on arms throughout the world, but you make moderate references to the need for a U.S. military capable of serving essential American interests.

6. You deplore the continuing aggressiveness of the Soviet Union—but you stress that we live in an age of accommodation, not confrontation, and restress the need for patience and understanding, which however is not to be confused with weakness.

And what will you get from the *Times*?

"It is unreasonable to expect a candidate for high office to

spell out exactly how he might respond to future contingen-
cies. But in his carefully reasoned statements so far—particularly his impromptu responses to questions—the former
Georgia governor has gone a long way toward dulling
charges of unfamiliarity with the foreign policy challenges
that would confront him as President."

Jimmy Carter can do no wrong these days. It requires not
alone the self-mastery (few have it—even the renowned intellectual virtuoso, Henry Kissinger, can no more shake his accent than Lady Macbeth could her stigmata), but an internal
distillery that pumps out just about what the folks want to
hear, and the folks are rewarding Mr. Carter in the polls
munificently. The current polls show Carter as far ahead of
Ford or Reagan as Nixon was over McGovern, or Roosevelt
over Landon, or Johnson over Goldwater. There isn't a really worked-up anti-Carter Democrat of any prominence left,
with the possible exception of Jerry Brown, about whom it is
sadly concluded among more and more people that Brown's
problem isn't that he loves Carter less, but that he loves
Brown more.

These are heavy odds, and no professional at this moment
would bet against Carter in November without asking for
four, five, maybe six to one. It will require someone of great
skill to cut through this business, and with a talent one might
call theatrical.

The Conventions

The Democratic Platform, 1976

July 17, 1976

DEMOCRATIC ORATORY, this time around as at Miami in 1972,
has been of an order so low as to suggest that the poor darlings don't really have very much to say. There are some
splendid speakers among the Democrats. The good Lord

was prodigal in giving many of them thunderous voices, lofty thoughts, and undulating rhythm. But as to content, this is a lean, lean winter. Let us therefore look at their written platform:

The Democratic Platform is as tame as Jimmy Carter's rhetoric and, in its own courtly-cute way, as inscrutable. Somebody once said about a corporation's annual reports that they are to be compared with a lady's bikini in that they reveal enough to maintain interest, while concealing the vital parts.

Consider, for instance, the simple sentences that concern foreign policy. Under the heading "Middle East," the Democrats say, "We shall continue to seek a just and lasting peace in the Middle East. The cornerstone of our policy is a firm commitment to the independence and security of the State of Israel. This special relationship does not prejudice improved relations with other nations in the region."

Ah, but it does. This is not to say that it *shouldn't:* but quite plainly it *does.* The United States has taken the official position, along with other countries represented in the Security Council way back since November of 1967, that Israel should return the conquered territories. Israel declines to do so, giving reasons some of which are by no means unreasonable. Still, there is such a thing as concern for justice to the Palestinian refugees; and there is no doubt that in the absence of a homeland for them and the return of the conquered territories there is both injustice in the area and a great animosity toward the United States. As James Reston and James Michener, both Democrats, have at one point put it, official Israeli intransigence—much criticized within the Knesset—is an obstacle to Mideast settlement, and the encouragement of it should be something less than a cornerstone of our policy.

Or is that intransigence a vital interest of ours? The next plank of the Democrats concerns "Asia." It is very straightforward. "The Vietnam War has taught us the folly of becoming militarily involved where our vital interests were not at stake. Our relations with China should continue to develop on peaceful lines, including early movement toward normalizing diplomatic relations in the context of a peaceful resolution of the future of Taiwan."

The first part of that could have been written by George Washington and inserted into his Farewell Address—in fact it was. The dangling ambiguities are the vital parts. What is a "peaceful" solution to the future of Taiwan? And is Taiwan's independence from Peking a vital interest of the United States? The existing Treaty presupposes this, but as recently as in the last Democratic Platform dominated by Senator McGovern, the proposal was to rescind that Treaty. Precisely what we don't know from this declaration is everything we really want to know about U.S. policy in the Far East.

In the domestic area, the usual gods are serially oblated. A maximum production is made in behalf of full employment. Not long after that, it is suggested that the minimum wage rate should "keep pace with the increase in the cost of living," which is another way of saying that such unemployment as results from the minimum wage law should not be interfered with.

Welfare reform consists of "income maintenance, substantially financed by the Federal Government." "Financed by the Federal Government" is a code word for "It won't cost you anything," and is the essence of Democratic economic witchcraft: the notion of the spontaneously generated dollar out of Washington, D.C. Which, by the way, ought to have full home rule—almost forgot that one. I truly worry sometimes, after D.C. gets full home rule, how the local politicians are going to talk about "federal subsidies" without stretching the credibility of that superstition.

Since we are going to have full employment, and higher minimum wage, and free medicine, we have to say something about inflation, and we do. We are against inflation. Does that mean we are in favor of wage and price controls? Well, no, not immediately anyway. In the language of the platform, "We do not believe that such involvement [in wage and price decisions] requires a comprehensive system of mandatory controls at this time." If one American can be found who disagrees with that statement, you will have to look for him in Haight-Ashbury, Belmont, Massachusetts, or Walden Pond.

Indeed, there is only one plank in the Democratic Platform that suggests any concern whatever for husbandry. It is listed under the heading "The Developing World." "The United States should not provide aid to any government— anywhere in the world—which uses secret police, detention without charges, and torture to enforce its powers." Roughly speaking, that means the Democrats will authorize aid only to Switzerland.

Well, party platforms should be written and not studied. They are interesting primarily as musical productions. This one sounds like the organ in Radio City Music Hall, unlike its predecessor which sounded like the Rolling Stones. As such, it is guardedly welcome.

Carter adieu

July 20, 1976

IN A SENSE, the two acceptance speeches were reassuring. Nothing, it turns out, has really changed—except for the persona of Jimmy Carter. As for this, I do not underrate it, but neither am I overwhelmed by it; nor is the country permanently in his thrall. After all, he did lose six out of the last nine primaries.

Jimmy Carter came to New York to prove that he was a liberal Democrat, and he succeeded. Almost everything that had set him apart was successfully closeted for the duration of the Convention and, one suspects, the duration of the campaign. The terrible fear harbored in worldly breasts that Jimmy Carter might be a . . . Christian . . . was pacified.

I'd have been surprised, by the end of the week, to hear Jimmy Carter sing "God Bless America." That he consented to end his speech with the words "God bless you" means nothing at all, since at this particular Convention, Robert Ingersoll would not have cavilled at using the expression, which has become the Democratic equivalent of the printer's symbol, "30."

Any delegate afraid that Carter would invoke the aid of the Lord in the accents of Abraham Lincoln went home undisturbed. And I doubt that the Lord will be awakened from His slumber to engrave the ideas of Jimmy Carter onto American destiny.

What ideas? Don't look at his acceptance speech for anything venturesome. It is a smooth effort—his speechwriter has been working on it since May 1976 and clearly should have started in May 1975—full of paradoxes. Throughout, it is a hymn to the high moral character and diligence of the American people. If the American people had been consulted, we would not have had the "tragedy of Vietnam and Cambodia." Answer: the American people were consulted, and they validated and revalidated, directly and through their representatives in Congress, the purposes of, if not the military tactics used in, Vietnam.

"Our nation should always derive its character directly from the people," said Carter. "And let this be the strength and image to be presented to the world . . ." But this same American people, of such high character, Jimmy Carter is now going to look after. He will brush our teeth for us every morning. He will tell us how much of the wages we earn we may keep. He will not confide to us what are the causes of inflation.

And—my favorite of all—he will have universal voter registration. The American people, to whom he intends to "return" government, will receive postage-paid postcards registering them to vote, to eliminate the necessity of going once every year or two to the nearest post office. Perhaps for his second term, President Carter will recommend that federal employees visit the homes of every voter and pick up the voter's ballot.

As for Senator Mondale, he was everything his parent organization, the Americans for Democratic Action, might have hoped for. This was the little-noticed bridge-building of the week: the ultimate Valentine, from Jimmy Carter to the single group in America that, up until almost the end, had refused to endorse him with enthusiasm. So he picked one of its most prominent members for the Vice-Presidency.

Senator Mondale spent half his time talking about the need for compassion, and the other half suggesting that we should yank Richard Nixon out of his house in California and put him in jail. For expressing this compassionate sentiment he was cheered by the delegates as loudly as ever the verdicts of the Jacobinical courts were cheered.

The ideological high-spot of the week was on the last day, when ABC reporter Sam Donaldson caught Senator Scoop Jackson and offered condolences at his not having been selected as Vice-President—but perhaps it was because he was "not as liberal as Senator Mondale?"

Jackson bristled and said he *was too*, just look at his record. Answered ABC, speaking for the media Spiro Agnew used to talk about: "I guess that *was* a bum rap, Senator." And it was a bum rap to think that Jimmy Carter was different.

Naming Schweiker: the afterbirth

August 3, 1976

IT IS INTERESTING how useful politicians find it to express themselves on matters of principle. Ronald Reagan advertises his intention to nominate a domestic liberal as his Vice-President, and is denounced for breach of principle. Breach of principle is here defined as the acknowledgment that there are many Republicans and other Americans whose views in certain areas fall to the left of one's own. Whereupon John Connally (a man I greatly admire) suddenly discovers that Gerald Ford would be the "better candidate" and endorses him. Mr. Connally manages to give the impression that he has been in communion with the Lord Almighty lo these many months, attempting to decide which of the two men is the better candidate for President. With a single move, Reagan convinced him—that Ford was the stronger candidate. Cool observers must be permitted to conclude that John Connally reasoned not that Mr. Ford would be the better candidate, but that he would be the candidate named in Kansas City. That is why he came out for Ford. The Thomists call that "sufficient reason."

* * *

Clarke Reed (a man I greatly like) rose up through the ranks of Southern Republicanism as a conservative of the new school, here defined as a conservative who actually reads books and reacts other than viscerally in arriving at his public positions. Reed promised time and again that he would stand by Reagan, whose positions on most public matters are Reed's own. The pressures on Reed, to give him his due, were awful. It isn't easy to arrive at the point of having to tell your secretary not to take any more calls from the President of the United States. Still, the fact is he crumbled. And it is unreasonable to suppose that he did so for reasons other than John Connally's. After all, he was beginning to wobble before anybody ever heard of Schweiker. Which leaves us with the following summary: Clarke Reed, objecting to Reagan's lack of principle in naming a liberal Vice-President, affirmed his own devotion to principle by rejecting the candidate to whom he had pledged his support, in favor of the candidate who selected his liberal Vice-President two years ago. It is hard to say how the cause of principle is being served by those who in its name are denying the Republican Party the chance to field a candidate who can convincingly articulate conservative principles.

The ironies shine through the situation. It cannot, I think, be persuasively contended that, against Mr. Carter, Mr. Ford would do better than Ronald Reagan. Surveying the general chaos, Mr. Carter issued a wonderfully cool statement to the effect that he thought Schweiker was a very good man. In doing so, he inflamed the resentment of Schweiker by disappointed Reaganites; and, in so doing, strengthened the hand of the adversary he hopes to be contending against in the election campaign. Mr. Alton Frye, of the Council on Foreign Relations, writing in the *Wall Street Journal*, is jubilant about the political effect of Mr. Reagan's maneuver. Look what has happened! he says. By saying he would accept a liberal running-mate, Reagan has knocked himself out. But in doing so, he has revalidated the very idea of a liberal running-mate. And this means that President Ford can take as his Vice-President not a conservative like Connally or Reagan, but a truly qualified candidate, like Percy or Mathias. In other words, Reagan has, however inadvertently, performed a valuable public service.

Clearly it is not going according to plan for the Reagan people. Senator Schweiker hasn't come forward with the names of the delegates whose concern for the elevation of Senator Schweiker was to have led them into Reagan's camp. We do not know, as of now, whether they are intimidated, or whether they were always illusory. All we are given, at the moment, is the spectacle of conservatives assuaging their pique at having to live in the real world by ushering in the Presidency of Jimmy Carter. It seems ages ago, and of no apparent concern to them, that Carter announced as his choice for a running-mate, Walter Mondale.

Enter Buckley

August 17, 1976

THE FORD PEOPLE were displeased by Senator Buckley's announcement that he would permit his name to be placed in nomination. So were the Reagan people. And maddest of all was Mr. Richard Rosenbaum, who is the chairman of the New York State Republican Party, and who sometimes mistakes himself as being rather the Party's master than its servant, a habit he picked up from Nelson Rockefeller over the years.

Briefly examined, the fear in the Ford camp is that Senator Buckley will deprive President Ford of nomination on the first ballot. I have the most enduring respect for Senator Buckley, issuing out of extra-biological considerations—but even so I am constrained to comment that if the junior senator from the State of New York, who achieved his own election by nomination not of the Republican Party but of the Conservative Party, and has been in the Senate for only a single term, can manage to wrest the Presidency away from an incumbent who has operated out of the White House for two and a half years, commands the movements of the army, navy, and air force, dines with the Queen of England, and sends bills back to Congress with strongly worded intimations of imperial displeasure—if Senator Buckley's humble suggestion that he might permit his own name to be placed in nomination threatens the security of the President, then that security is disastrously insecure.

What Mr. Ford's agents are saying in effect—using the Aesopian language of the politician—is that they cannot run the risk of losing a handful of delegates; that they fear that if they do not achieve the nomination in the first ballot, they will not achieve it at all.

Well, let us concede that is indeed their fear; and that the fear is objectively rather than neurotically based. If that is the case, one understands why Ford's legions are so upset over Senator Buckley's modest proffering of himself in order to break the deadlock. But who else should be upset? If the scaffolding under President Ford is that creaky, do we really want to be upset by a man who volunteers to pull the drapes aside permitting us to see the straw on which Ford rests?

As for Governor Reagan, one suspects that his lieutenants' concern is, really, rather thoughtless. It could only be based on the delusion that the Reagan nomination would be won on the first ballot save for the intervention of Senator Buckley. That is not likely to happen, unless President Ford between now and Wednesday runs off with Eddie Fisher. So that if enough votes from the uncommitted and the indecisive were to result in a first ballot that went neither to Ford nor to Reagan, the contest would move into the second ballots: and there, the contribution of Senator Buckley would transpire.

What would happen after the first ballot is a contest substantially freed from the synthetic impositions of first-ballot laws and folkways. These of course differ from state to state. But taking only New Hampshire and California, one sees the nature of the anti-democratic beast. In New Hampshire, President Ford barely defeated Governor Reagan—but he walked off with 100 percent of the delegates. In California, Reagan comfortably defeated Ford—but Reagan walks off with 100 percent of the delegates. How it would come out in a liberated second-ballot vote no one can precisely foretell. For one thing, some states provide that a delegate may switch his vote only after receiving permission to do so from the primary winner. Other states do not, as I suggest, insist on this requirement; and then there are the states that insist on it but do nothing about it when delegates do break away.

It seems another age when one had to wait until the second ballot or beyond to decide what was the true sense of the Convention, but it is not an age from which we should automatically shrink. In the old days, Conventions allowed for an evolution of feeling. It has been, for instance, a long time since the primary of New Hampshire, and there should be an allowance, in the event of a Convention as close as this one, for recrystallized positions. Enter Buckley, who is welcome at my house.

The sights and the smells

August 21, 1976

Kansas City.—WHAT KIND of a show is it? A few observations: After a couple of days, one got the impression that to be a member of the Mississippi delegation is a profession. It is one that requires political skills, high physical stamina, and a theological flair. "What did granddaddy do, Mommy?" "He was a member of the Mississippi delegation" would be an appropriate response.

I would be surprised if at the Council of Trent the delegation from the Manichean states caucused more frequently, or tortured themselves with moral questions more refined, than some of the ladies and gentlemen from Mississippi, one of whom overwhelmed the infidels of NBC by saying yes, she was uncommitted, and she was waiting instructions from above as to whom finally to vote for, but she promised that NBC would be the first to know. And when the afflatus was finally upon her, she signaled to the microphone, and we had as uninterrupted a communication from above to below as we have had in memory.

Indeed, the lady turned out to be a prophet: her instructions had been to vote for Ford. Grant took Vicksburg, but the revenge was absolute: Mississippi took the whole of the Republic a century or so later.

Somehow, the Mississippi people managed it all rather ingratiatingly. One didn't mind the attention one gave them, though perhaps this is because, as they say, when there are no alternatives, there are no problems.

The level of oratory has not been uniformly high. Howard Baker was very good, though he knoweth not the virtue of brevity. Speaking to that huge auditorium requires that the speaker do a good bit of what Mencken once called "plain hollering." The only way you can get a political Convention actually to stop and listen to what you are saying is either to intimate in advance that you are going to do something very dramatic (say, defy the Mississippi delegation); that, or summon the eloquence of a very great speaker. This does not mean that you need to say anything—Barbara Jordan subdued Madison Square Garden as totally as Bob Dylan ever did, and said even less.

Once you have the audience listening to you, your narrative must roll, and you must at all costs avoid telegraphing the huge expanses of wisdom you have left to deliver. Do not, after thirty minutes, say such a thing as: "We come now to the field of foreign policy . . ." Those who view these speeches over television should tilt their heads to one side if they mean to listen because inevitably the television director will distract you—by flashing his camera on a ninety-seven-year-old lady with a Carmen Miranda Reagan hat, swigging from a bottle of hooch.

We must be grateful that Brutus delivered his oration away from the television cameras, or else at the moment the crowd was finally stirred to action, the cameraman would be showing an urchin scribbling on the wall, "Kilroy *hic erat.*"

John Connally made the mistake of over-advertising his oration. There is a danger that attaches to a press announcement along the lines of, "At 8:35 P.M., on all networks, the honorable John Connally will deliver the Gettysburg Address." He is a very eloquent man, but makes the mistake of screwing up his face in a contortion of lapidary concern for the Republic at moments that suit less the requirements of the text, than the rhythms of the paragraph. He must not look equally gloomy in anticipation of a nuclear war, and a rise of one penny in the price of a gallon of gasoline.

Nelson Rockefeller's enemies will no doubt conclude that his speech—which was really quite quite awful—was intended to subvert the ambitions of the Republican Party, now that he will not have an official role within it. I don't really believe that, disinclined as I am to the conspiracy view of history, but I have to confess I can't think of a plausible reason for someone to say about his own unsuccessful pursuit of the Presidency that "somehow I could never get to the church on time." Or to refer to Ford as a "football player without a helmet who led the team." When he got around to deploring the "Nader-day saints," I came as near as I ever have to understanding the John Birch Society.

Having knocked the television people, I should compliment them for some extraordinary achievements, notable among them the scene with Walter Cronkite talking to Barry Goldwater and Nelson Rockefeller, with flashbacks to the dear-sir-you-cur exchanges between them during 1964. Now Rockefeller is saying (ruefully) that he was more liberal than Governor Carey while in New York, and Goldwater is saying (unconvincingly) that his foreign policy was less expert than Rockefeller's. It's like the Sunshine Boys, only with a happy ending.

The GOP triumphant

May 20, 1976

WE HAVE begun to hear from the reactionary wing of the Republican Party about the awful danger of nominating Ronald Reagan. A chief spokesman of this wing of the Party, which is dissatisfied with any form of Republicanism that attempts genuine social movement, is Jacob Javits, senior senator from New York. He is very well practiced in the line he takes. I myself heard him use it in the early spring of 1964. He told his class at a dinner party that a) Senator Goldwater would never be nominated by the Republican Party, and b) if, *per impossibile*, that were to happen, why that would be the end of the Republican Party. A few days ago he said almost exactly the same thing, substituting only Reagan for Goldwater.

It amuses me, though not Senator Javits—who is in any case not easily amused—that the doomsday talk about the dangers of Reagan is almost always accompanied by citations of melancholy statistical ratings of the Republican Party. A typical formulation is as follows: "What are we to say about a party whose popularity among registered voters is down to 18 percent, now considering the nomination of Ronald Reagan!" Now the popularity of the Republican Party has been diminishing since 1952, almost without interruption. Moreover, since 1954, the Democrats have organized both the House of Representatives and the Senate. In 1958, which was the height of the Periclean Age of Eisenhower, the Democrats won their most stunning congressional victory save only that of 1964, the year of Goldwater.

In other words, during an entire generation the Republicans who call themselves liberal have been in charge of affairs. Eisenhower was the progressive alternative to Robert A. Taft. Nixon lost to Kennedy. Goldwater lost to Johnson. Then Nixon beat Humphrey—and ushered in policies which were acclaimed by the New York *Times* in 1971 as having "revolutionized" the Republican Party. Overcome with admiration, the *Times* listed Nixon's achievements—a diplomatic breakthrough with China, the beginnings of détente with the Soviet Union, easing out of the Vietnam War, a huge increase in social expenditures at home, a deficit budget putting human costs above property costs, a progressive tax reform bill, sponsorship of a form of guaranteed annual wage, wage and price controls . . . and although Nixon won hugely in 1972, it is once again perhaps more accurate to say that McGovern lost hugely.

Who cares, really, about the Republican Party? Its soul is the property of the Ripon Society, and a few of the older members of the Council on Foreign Relations. If Reagan ran

on an independent ticket for President, he would get a higher percentage of the vote than the Republican Party would
get if it were led by any other American, with the possible exception of John Connally. The reason the Republican Party
has become nothing much more than an administrative convenience for a few politicians is that it is lacking in any capacity to galvanize. If one were to subtract Simon, Burns, and
Greenspan from the White House, the Republican Administration would collapse under the force of contradiction.
Here are the keepers of the fiscal integrity, spending $40 bil-
lion more than they collect. Our foreign policy on the one
hand boasts of the achievements of detente—but is afraid to
use the word. We conclude an agreement with the Soviet
Union, and are afraid to sign it publicly.

The men who have been in charge of the Republican Party
during the last generation are those under whose leadership
the Party has triumphed by losing two-thirds of its troops.
The pity of it is that it didn't lose two-thirds plus one. On the
other hand, it managed to get rid of John Lindsay. Only
Lindsay's mentor is still with us.

Closing night

August 24, 1976

Kansas City.—DOLE HAD BEEN nominated, and suddenly
nothing was happening. All the attention was being given to
Ronald Reagan, who sat in his box with his wife, and one or
two advisers, and emissaries from Gerald Ford. It soon was
apparent what they were talking about. Should Reagan go
right now—to the platform, to say something pleasant and
ecumenical?

Reagan was clearly arguing against it: for one thing, he
had the sportsman's instinct. The winner's circle belongs to
the winner, not to the loser. But there was a paradox. If he
permitted himself to enter the winner's circle, even if only
for the purpose of complimenting the winner, the crowd

would give him such a welcome as to establish what almost everybody there knew—that Reagan was the dominating presence of the 1976 campaign, even though Gerald Ford was the formal victor. The fight between the two men had been, really, stylistic.

Ford appealed, finally, to that conservative streak in the nation that simply rejects the notion that you throw away an incumbent. Critics of Ford from the left quite correctly point out that on issue after issue, as raised by Reagan, Ford retreated. The most conspicuous symbol of Reagan's ascendancy was the presence in the hall of Henry Kissinger, a magnetic field of supercharged potency who would steal the act from Saint Peter. Yet he sat alone with his wife, his name not once mentioned: because he is associated with that policy of détente condemned by Reagan, and in effect by the Republican Platform.

The delegates sensed that the Republican Party is moribund, and comes to life only when, like Antaeus, it touches the ground of reality. That ground is that the government, the vessel of secular humanism, is too much with us; and that getting and spending in political programs, we lay waste our powers.

So, adamantly, Reagan stayed put, and, facing the awful possibility that the Convention would run right over the edge of prime time, the stage masters put on first Mr. Dole, a bright man and sharp polemicist who simply didn't have the time to come up with anything very bright or unusual in the few hectic hours between his designation and his speech; and then—Cary Grant, who said all those nice things about the girls, making up for the Party's declining to endorse the Equal Rights Amendment. Then there was a vague sort of movie showing pictures of Gerald Ford excelling in college football. And then Ford himself.

You have to hand it to him. It was in itself an electrifying performance. And it was in the circumstances something very nearly miraculous: as if Joe Palooka had appeared in the Roman senate and outshone Cicero. There was determination, fluency, a sense of the spirit of the message.

It was hard to believe that this was the same man who delivered the speech early in 1975 beseeching aid to Vietnam from the Congress, a speech in which, if memory serves, he driveled off finally wondering about the imminent extinction of weeping willow trees.

This was tough stuff, and I do not doubt that it was perhaps the first moment during the Convention when Jimmy Carter felt a little ache in the pit of his stomach wondering just exactly whether he could indeed count on suavely overpowering the man who had jestingly been referred to during the Convention (using the language of Pound on Williams) as "the most bloody inarticulate animal that ever gargled."

Ford had come alive. Whether he will sustain it, one cannot know. One cannot doubt that the strength of his oratory issued from the words he spoke, which were an appeal to a reversed direction in a great American drift to serfdom. Those who talk about the entropy of American Republicanism are something other than mere ideological purists. They are saying, in effect, that the accommodationist programs of a generation of Republicans nursed by Willkie and Dewey can't stand up against the drift of the socialists, even when served, as by Carter, like cream of wheat.

Some time in the future, the Presidential candidate of the Republican Party will have to arrive as though to the Finland Station, grim with historical purpose. The challenge, for which providence provides few precedents, lies in his coming to town not for the purpose of taking power, but of redistributing it to the people. That challenger will arrive preaching the furtive excitements of a republic of law, and he will address a Convention which declines to relegate its Jeffersons and Madisons and Hamiltons to the rear of the hall, yielding the floor to Cary Grant. Until then, it's Gerald Ford, and, thanks to the spirit of Ronald Reagan, he is off to a very good start.

The Campaign

Presidents and cherry trees

September 30, 1976

THE OTHER DAY Mr. Hodding Carter III, publisher of the *Delta Democrat Times*, who is a *summa cum laude* graduate of Princeton University and also very bright, gave it as his reason for devoting his full-time energies to the election of Jimmy Carter that the country was "tired of being lied to" by its Presidents. Now those who believe in the further socialization of American life should go ahead and vote for Jimmy Carter. But someone, even if ungarlanded by a *summa cum laude*, should apply some cold compresses to the fevered brows of those burning idealists who believe that Executive Sin was invented by Nixon-Ford.

Asked about the lies of Mr. Ford, Hodding Carter gave two examples. When asked during his confirmation hearings as Vice-President whether he would run for President, he said, no, he had no intent of doing so. And then when he was asked somewhere along the line whether he would pardon Richard Nixon, he said he didn't think that was appropriate. Well, said Mr. (Hodding) Carter triumphantly—we all know what happened then. Presumably when at Princeton the boys were told that Churchill once said, "Give us the tools and we'll do the job," Hodding and his classmates were introduced to moral squalor.

In his stump speech, Jimmy Carter reverts ceaselessly to the line that he will never lie to the American people. He appears to have convinced some of his disciples that this is literally true. If one were absolutely certain that it was, that would be sufficient reason for voting against Mr. Carter. Because the American people—every people—needs to be "lied" to every now and then, in the sense that Ford "lied" when he said at first he would not grant a pardon, then changed his mind. Knute Rockne lied to his team as all coaches must; even as FDR lied when he said we had nothing to fear but fear itself, when in fact what we had to fear was things like hunger, unemployment, mortgage collectors, Nazis, Communists, and FDR. Professor Hayek has said that the canard that one cannot turn the clock back is the equivalent of saying that one cannot learn from experience. Experience should be an important teacher, and no one knows this better than Jimmy Carter. His experience as a governor of Georgia who sought popularity with his constituency led him to advocate right-to-work laws. His experience as a Presidential candidate led him to oppose right-to-work laws. Is he for that reason a liar? Or, as Carter said of Lyndon Johnson, "a liar and a cheat"?

When the political moralists really want to frighten us these days they dangle the figure of Richard Nixon before our memory. I have resolved from this day on to resist this. My quarrels with Mr. Nixon are not those of the majority— he gave us price controls, and an ambivalent policy in Indochina, and détente with the Soviet Union, and the apotheosis of Mao Tse-tung—that's what I mostly hold against him. Yet these are the measures that brought a détente, however temporary, in his relations with American liberals. The Nixon *they* refer to is exclusively the Nixon of Watergate, the man who conspired to cover up. Well, he did it, he was caught, and he was ousted: so that's that. Chicken thieves should not sit in the Oval Office.

But to suggest that Nixon stands alone in covering up illegalities is to advertise a kind of national parochialism inappropriate to a *summa cum laude* from Princeton, or, for that matter, from San Quentin U. Franklin Delano Roosevelt, during 1940 and 1941, got up in the morning, brushed his teeth, and began a day's lying until, weary, he fell off to sleep at night. The best-seller *A Man Called Intrepid* is substantially an account of the dissimulations and illegal and unconstitutional activity of Franklin Delano Roosevelt, by an ardent admirer who chronicles the critical aid extended by Roosevelt to the Allies before Pearl Harbor. Though I regret the duplicity, I am glad FDR did it. And I doubt that the Carters, either Jimmy or Hodding, will denounce his memory for it. After all, Roosevelt—though he was always talking to Robert Sherwood and other intimates about the possibility of his impeachment in the event he was caught out—won: he got the United States into war. As they say, history is the polemic of the victor.

Are we saying that there is a place for lying in office? That is an awkward formulation. What we are saying is that Presidents *will* "*lie.*" They will change their minds. They will dissimulate. They will smile when there is odium in their hearts, and scowl when they feel serene. They will denounce lying while lying, and preach about chastity when they are sinning with their eyes. On this front there is no relief in sight.

Earl Butz's joke

October 9, 1976

OUTSIDE THE UNITED STATES, when the Earl Butz story broke, the talk among seasoned Americans tended to nonchalance. In Caracas, they do not publish such pith as you can find in *Rolling Stone*, or *The Village Voice*. Under the circumstances, when the Associated Press sent out the actual text of Mr. Butz's remarks, and they spread about by word of mouth, there came the distinctive sense of shock that follows when a community has already made up its mind about something, and learns that it was wrong.

At first, it was supposed that Earl Butz had said something routinely invidious about American blacks. After all, it was only a fortnight earlier that the Vice-President of the United States and the Speaker of the House of Representatives had disported on the subject of what would have happened to Edward Brooke if his ancestors had stayed in Liberia. The microphones were accidentally live, and an entire press section heard the slurs.

They were to be distinguished from those of Earl Butz by their relative mildness; and perhaps by the all-important fact that one of the slurrers is a Republican and the other a Democrat; so that there was no partisan leverage in the episode for one political party to exploit. If Earl Butz had been exchanging views with, say, Teddy Kennedy, who had echoed them, his moral guilt would have been unmitigated but his political career might have survived. Jimmy Carter would not demand the resignation of Senator Kennedy if Teddy came out against Anne Frank.

Most people are aware that, in respect of ethnic jokes, there is something of a generation gap. Not long ago a prominent American liberal in New York told a friend that, throughout his youth, he heard at the dinner table of his distinguished father in Boston racial stories which, nowadays, the New Yorker would leave the room if repeated in his presence.

There is still something of the lure of audacity in the racial story, and it is fair at this heated moment to observe that there is no documented correlation between racial hostility and an inclination to racial jokes or racial slurs. When, four elections back, Jerry terHorst learned about Henry Cabot Lodge's promise that if Nixon was elected, he would name a black to his Cabinet, he was riding on Kennedy's press plane, and scratched out the verse, "Gone are the days when the Cabinet was Jim Crow./Now Treasury has a boss named Old Black Joe./Lodge did it all, that blueblood so-and-so,/He heard a crowd in Harlem calling,/Old Black Joe."

That is the kind of thing it was assumed Earl Butz was guilty of. What he said was breathcatchingly coarse. It betrayed a kind of personal insensitivity that induces sheer wonder. The statement had what one might call KKK wit: but the coarseness overwhelms. It would not have been the charitable thing to say, but Gerald Ford could plausibly have said that he could not feel comfortable in the presence of someone who spoke those phrases.

So much for poor Earl Butz. Now one wonders: what purpose did the ideological tabloid press serve in reprinting the slurs? *The Village Voice*, whose article on the wedding of Tricia Nixon could have been written by Earl Butz, is in the contemptible business of simultaneously moralizing, and sensationalizing. A simple letter to the White House calling attention to Earl Butz's language might well have been justified. But to publish words so offensive to an entire race of people renowned for their gentility is to poison the well.

No doubt John Dean has maximized his incumbency as a free-lance journalist. He and those who publicized his story have done so not so much at the expense of Earl Butz's political career—Butz was expendable—but at the expense of stimulating a dreadful resentment by one-tenth of the American people.

The Polish joke

October 14, 1976

YOU CAN HARDLY blame Carter for opportunizing on President Ford's startling liberation of Poland during their debate on foreign policy, but the roles of the Democratic and the Republican candidates have become almost impossibly confused by the gaffe. After all, it is the Republicans who have traditionally done the most (however insufficient) to keep alive the hope of the liberation of Eastern Europe. The Democrats tend to be associated with a foreign policy of permanent acquiescence in the colonization by the Communists of any part of the world, with the single exception of Israel. A political party that, through Senator Frank Church and his committee, threatened congressional mutiny when the Executive tried to help Portugal and Italy stave off the Communists is not going to lie down for anything in Eastern Europe that tends to threaten their policy of appeasement at any cost. But as a purely political matter, Ford is now on the defensive.

What Mr. Ford said is, frankly, inexplicable—notwithstanding the explanations he and his aides have attempted. It is as if Ford had said, during a general discussion of the great rivers of the world and the problems of flood control: "Fortunately, the Mississippi River doesn't flow through the Unit-

ed States." Everybody looks up and someone finally says—
"You do mean the *Amazon* doesn't flow through the United
States, don't you, Mr. President?"

And he answers, "No, I mean the Mississippi:
M-i-s-s-i-s-s-i-p-p-i."

There is simply no accounting for this. The notion that
what Mr. Ford intended to say was not that Poland was
autonomous and independent but that the United States
does not recognize the satellization of Poland by the Soviet
Union as a permanent arrangement, is simply not validated
by what Mr. Ford in fact said in answer to Mr. Frankel's chiv-
alrous question designed to straighten Mr. Ford out. President Ford said, "Each of those countries [Yugoslavia, Rumania, Poland] *is* independent, autonomous; it has its own
territorial integrity, and the United States does not concede
that those countries *are* under the domination of the Soviet
Union."

Now an explanation for this statement (the last contender
for the Presidency to make such a statement about Eastern
Europe was Henry Wallace, some of whose speeches were
written for him by Communist agents, the others being incoherent) is beyond the grasp of normal men of tidy deductive
habits. The pernicious aspect of the slip is the damage it did
to the whole post-Kansas City image of Ford as an impres-
sively competent Chief Executive.

Mr. Carter is trying to give out the notion that the White
House staff that has so successfully programmed President
Ford forgot to tell him that, in 1945, we lost Poland. Unhappily, Mr. Ford made it easy for him. Those who desire the
truth must settle for a kind of trans-literal confidence. Mr.
Ford is not a specialist in verbal precision or rhetorical inflection, and is certainly not at home with the subjunctive mood.
One is required to conclude that he meant to convey something else—he is, after all, a bright man. But he faces
difficulties now, yet again, of a very broad character, which
afflictions he was successfully pulling away from before he
committed the ultimate Polish joke.

Buckley on Buckley

October 21, 1976

IT IS BEING SAID broadly that the Senate race in New York shapes up as a classic confrontation between traditional conservative and traditional liberal lines, and it's true. The contest, moreover, has been described as the second most important of this fall after the Presidential contest, and that is so. Except for my biological involvement, I'd have written more frequently about it, precisely because of its symbolic importance. Under the circumstance, I shall write only this one time. These observations I have to make or else die of uremic poisoning.

Daniel Patrick Moynihan has one of the liveliest minds in the nation. He is always rethinking those propositions the ideologues cultivate about the time their skin clears, and never again bother to test against experience. That is how Patrick Moynihan became an exciting teacher and writer. The concessions he has made, in his race for the Senate, are dismaying. Take his current speeches, homogenize them, and bless us if he does not sound like Eleanor Roosevelt. That's an awful way to go, and the Senate really isn't worth it.

Here, drastically truncated, is what Moynihan and Senator James Buckley are saying:

Moynihan. Buckley is a reactionary, frightened by FDR as a child.

Buckley. It isn't reactionary to take stock of what is happening to this country under the dispensation of the doctrine that the Federal Government should handle all our problems.

Moynihan. I believe that the Federal Government should work for us, not against us.

Buckley. So do I. And a government works much better for the people in many situations by staying out of their way rather than interfering actively in their lives. There is a role for government, but the statist's presumption in favor of government ends us up busing children to alien schools, telling old people how many days they can spend with their children, and instructing half the population that they can look forward to spending half their time working for the government.

Moynihan. As a senator from New York, I would labor to bring every last penny of federal money into New York.

Buckley. As a senator from New York, I have labored to get every last penny to New York which is New York's due. As a United States Senator I could not in good conscience rob other states—assuming that were possible—for the benefit of such New York lobbyists as the welfare lobby. United States senators are not sent off to Washington with letters of marque and reprisal for use against the other forty-nine states in the union.

Actually, all of it is really there, in these words. James Buckley is an ideologist only in the sense that Thomas Jefferson was ("The country can only do something for the people in proportion as it can do something to the people"). He is suspicious of government only as John Adams cautioned us to be ("The state will turn every contingency into an excuse for enhancing power in itself"). He is a liberal not in the recent mechanical tradition of Moynihan but in the more venerable tradition of Woodrow Wilson ("The history of liberalism is the history of man's efforts to restrain government").

It was the independent-mindedness of James Buckley that brought him to call for the resignation of President Nixon when it had become clear that his continuation in office damaged the country. For this, Senator Buckley suffered every bit as much as Mr. Moynihan for using the phrase "benign neglect." Senator Buckley is rated, even by those who disapprove of some of his policies, as an outstanding member of the Senate. Jack Anderson rates him among the top ten senators.

The voters of New York have the opportunity on election day to accomplish two highly desirable things. Vote to maintain an independent conservative of demonstrated ability, intelligence, and integrity in the Senate. And vote to return Patrick Moynihan to Harvard, where, liberated from the constraints of ideological politics, he will be free once again to shed his grace on all of us.

Citizen Brown?

October 23, 1976

A NUMBER OF AMERICANS seeking election or re-election have contrived, however inadvertently, to politicize our military, and that is a pity. Harry Truman fired Douglas MacArthur on the charge that he was attempting to be a policy-maker rather than a general, and the liberal community cheered this decision. Now they want the chairman of the joint chiefs of staff to make policy decisions.

What General George S. Brown was asked, in the disputed interview, was for his opinion *"from a purely military point of view"*—those are the Israeli questioner's words—about the net bearing, as of last spring, of our commitment to Israel. General Brown said, "Well, I think it's just got to be considered a burden."

Rabbi Alexander Schindler, the chairman of the Conference of Presidents of Major Jewish Organizations, issued a statement that his organization was "deeply disturbed" by the remarks of General Brown. Carter, as usual, proposed firing Brown—he would fire Amy if somebody took exception to her lemonade. Mondale raised the ante and said Brown should never have been hired in the first place—because people like the general "shouldn't be sewage commissioners." Even the sainted junior senator from New York climbed aboard the bandwagon and suggested that General Brown be fired.

Why? Are these gentlemen saying that a general should not be permitted to answer a question posed "from a purely military point of view"? No inference other than this is plausible. Or are they saying that General Brown should be fired because by making that particular statement, he proved himself to be an incompetent soldier? Are we to suppose that Rabbi Schindler's knowledge of military matters entitles him to draw such conclusions about General Brown's military incompetence? I doubt it.

I am certain that the rabbi, like the others, was eliding a military judgment into a political judgment. And that is ex-

actly what ought not to be done in a Republic that prides itself on the division of authority between the military and the
civil orders.

Obviously Israel is a burden—from a purely military point
of view. What has this got to do with whether we should defend it? Or even with the question of whether it might not
become a military blessing in the days ahead? To say that
something is a burden is not even to begin to suggest that it is
not a burden for which we are grateful. The greatest burden
in the Constitution of the United States is the Bill of Rights.
We would hardly elect to be without it for that simple reason.
Children—God knows—are a burden on their parents "from
a purely economic point of view."

From a purely military point of view, our commitment to
Berlin is a tremendous burden. It would be burdensome to
defend, and possibly could only be defended by the threat of
massive nuclear retaliation. South Korea is a considerable
military burden, requiring 50,000 American troops in residence. Israel is hugely expensive to defend, and indeed the
rapid rearming of Israel after the Yom Kippur war severely
drained our military inventory. Yet our commitment to Israel continues. The Arab oil boycott did not budge the convictions of the United States public—its finest hour, that one:
declining to adjust our foreign policy for reasons of economic opportunism.

General Brown was of course presented to the general
press for a statement about his own feelings about United
States policy, and he said the following: "United States policy
toward Israel over the years has been clear: we are fully committed to the security and survival of the state of Israel. I believe in that policy wholeheartedly."

Now that last statement made everybody feel good. Well,
not quite everybody. *I* resent its having been asked. The
chairman of the joint chiefs of staff should say: "I decline to
give my feeling about whether I endorse a public policy.
That is entirely unprofessional. I am chairman of the joint
chiefs of staff to implement public policies set by the com-
mander-in-chief and validated by the people's representatives in Congress. For me to identify myself with a popular
public policy would be easy, but it would be as wrong as it

would have been wrong, let us say, for General Westmoreland to have identified himself as in favor of the Vietnam War."

It is basic failures to understand these distinctions that drive countries into the hands of the military.

Al Smith night

October 26, 1976

JIMMY CARTER did not wish to attend the annual dinner at the Waldorf-Astoria in tribute to the memory of Al Smith but agreed, finally, to do so only after being persuaded by his advisers that here was probably the single invitation the disdain of which could hurt him deeply. I live in fear and trembling that Jimmy Carter will be elected President in virtue of the word having got out that when John Kenneth Galbraith wrote volunteering to serve as a speechwriter, he got back from Carter a form letter advising him to apply to the nearest Carter-for-President office. That grand gesture of indifference to the most ubiquitous liberal ideologue in the United States may very well go down as the equivalent of John F. Kennedy's famous telephone call to the imprisoned Reverend Martin Luther King. "Anybody who rejects Ken by form letter is my candidate" is the impulse that has lifted Carter's lead from two to six points, never mind the official explanation that it resulted from Mr. Ford's Polish joke. But Jimmy Carter's nerve failed him when it came to turning down the Al Smith Dinner.

He was even a little frightened to go, and some of the guests were a little frightened to have him come. Carter and some of his friends feared the possibility that there might be some scattered *boos* by the predominantly (by no means exclusively) Catholic audience. Carter's position on abortion is more variously conjugated than French irregular verbs. One adviser counseled him to make references to James Farley, a conspicuous presence at the Al Smith Dinners until his recent death.

Carter did as he was told, and more—a lot more. He spoke for twenty minutes, twice as long as the speech earlier in the evening by President Ford, and devoted a great amount of that time comparing Al Smith to, well, himself. (Both had been governor of a state, both were criticized for their religion, both were mocked for their accents, both ran against a nice guy whose running-mate was a senator from Kansas, both their opponents said prosperity was just around the corner . . .) And so it went. Reminding one of the Devil's Dictionary, which defines *admiration* as one's polite recognition of other people's similarity to oneself. The 2,000 people present to cherish the memory of Al Smith were invited to deduce that Al Smith was reincarnated in—Jimmy Carter.

But for all this, Carter spoke well. His speech was graceful, well delivered, and felicitously phrased. The nervousness dissipated as he moved along, and he received a warm, if less than ardent, reception.

Mr. Ford also spoke well. His notes look something like an orchestral score, so carefully have his assistants indicated where he is to make an emphasis, where to raise, where to lower his voice. His improvement as an orator during the past few months is remarkable. And he maintained in his speeches enough references to his responsibilities to remind those whose attention wandered that he was, after all, the President of the United States. He was, as he put it, "running the country and the campaign at the same time."

He made a reference possibly oblique enough not to disturb the pro-abortion vote, but palpable enough to please the anti-abortionists, when he spoke of the "dignity of human life," a phrase which in the abstract would alienate only B. F. Skinner. The tough-minded, experienced dais of judges, generals, politicians, and superstars was clearly impressed. If you are going to deliver a bad speech, that is a bad audience to deliver it in front of.

The occasion is impressive. Although the audience is indeed pre-eminently Catholic, the money raised is distributed with iron impartiality among Christian and Jewish enterprises. It is something of a handshake proffered annually by Catholics to Jews, and the dinner chairman, Charles Silver, irradiates the general good feeling. The patron is of course the Cardinal of New York, Terence Cooke, whose charm lies in his diffidence, and in his obstinate political neutrality.

No one is invited to that dinner in order to be ambushed. (In 1968, the guests were President Johnson, and presidential contenders Nixon and Humphrey.) The atmosphere is genuinely convivial, and one finds oneself, surveying all those faces, sensing all those little and great magnetic fields, responding to an electric humor liberated by a transcendent piety, serene, as one is seldom permitted to be these days, at the remarkable concinnity of America.

III.

The Long Reach of Watergate

John Ehrlichman's Testament*

THERE ARE three well-executed passages in this book, which advertises itself as a novel on the inflexible understanding that the reader will not take it as being anything of the sort. It is the ultimate dirty trick of the Nixon era; and, by ironic masterstroke, Nixon is its victim.

The striking passages are one in which President Nixon (he is, of course, given another name in the book, as are Kennedy, Johnson, Hoover, Haldeman, Kissinger and Helms, the narrator) is deftly described aboard Air Force One sitting in a specially constructed hydraulically mounted chair which he causes to rise and lower and swivel and tilt as he lectures to Helms, giving Queeg-like theatrical force to his character as bully, paranoid, misanthrope, cretin. A second scene describes a tantrum by Henry Kissinger. It is splendid, part steel, part helium, as if P. G. Wodehouse had improvised on a description by Speer of an explosion by Hitler. The third is the final scene, when Helms confronts Nixon at Camp David with documentary evidence of Nixon's perfidy, and details his terms for silence while Nixon numbly perseveres with a running travelogue on the features of Camp David.

About the balance of the book, the inventive plot notwithstanding, one can only say that it is so bad it might have been ghosted by John Dean, whose memorandum about maximizing the incumbency stays with us as a relic of the prose style of Nixon's most authentic bureaucrat. "Few Roman emperors confidently gathered to themselves more perquisites than

*The Company. By John Ehrlichman. Simon & Schuster. New York, 1976.

117

did Chairman Esker Scott Anderson" makes one wonder if the author's publishers bothered to gather to themselves the perquisite of an editor. "Jack," the narrator, pauses to wonder about the legendary Harvard professor Henry Kissinger, "How does he survive in that faculty jungle at Harvard?" Well, as a starter I should think by never speaking such a sentence as that one.

The clichés come upon you with the inevitability of nightfall. "I want someone over there who will be spending most of his time looking out for me, Bill, and by Christ I think you're the man to do it." Christ did not mislead the President who placed his faith in Bill. "Seriously, dearest, are you all right?" is the most galvanizing expression of human concern in the entire book. On the other hand, the surrounding flatness of the prose is transformed into a shipwrecked sailor's beach after one experiences the author's occasional high dives into belletrism. "Most Washington cocktail hours," the author notes, "eventually achieve a noise level that forecloses meaningful communication. The crescendo increases with the passage of minutes along a predictable curve which is the algebraic function of the room size and temperature, the number of people, their occupations and gender." It isn't only Washington parties that can drive people to drink.

Now as to the plot. As already suggested, I decline on principle to act as accomplice in the author's bullyragging game of "disguising" the characters he is portraying by such cute artifices as having Kennedy killed in an airplane accident rather than in a car by an assassin; having Johnson quit the Presidency because of leukemia rather than Tet; staging the Bay of Pigs in the Dominican Republic instead of Cuba; and rooting Richard Nixon in Illinois rather than California. As a matter of fact, so frightened is the author that you might fail to match characters, he first describes Charles ("Chuck") Colson in terms his dead grandmother could not mistake, then pauses to say that the President, who didn't usually go in for nicknames, nevertheless referred to his hatchet man as "Tuck." Howard Hunt (who never met Nixon) is brought into the Oval Office by "Tuck," and Nixon is reminded that both Hunt and Colson went to Yale (they both went to Brown).

So. Lifting the veil—as protective of blackheads as a tennis net—here is what happens. Kennedy orders the invasion at the Bay of Pigs. An investigation is subsequently ordered. The investigator discovers that Kennedy, just before the operation, brought in Assistant CIA Director Helms and ordered him to have assassinated the priest who is the spiritual amulet of the expedition. Helms does as he is told, never pausing to reason why, and the demoralized invaders crumble. One copy of the report is made and Vice-President Johnson reads it just before Kennedy is killed and, along with him in Air Force One, the investigator. So Johnson makes Helms head of the CIA, knowing that with the hold LBJ now has over him, Helms will make available all the resources of the "Company" to LBJ for political ends.

When leukemia hits, LBJ steps out and Horrible Nixon succeeds him. In due course Nixon asks to see the "back reports" of the CIA, clearly intending to blacken the Kennedy name. Helms stalls. At the same time Nixon, increasingly resentful of criticism and of Vietnam protesters, begins tapping telephones. CIA sources trip over these taps, and discover that they are proliferating. With the aid of a computer, Helms discerns who are the next likeliest tappees, and when Howard Hunt and Company move in on a famous columnist, they are silently photographed in the act by the CIA's hidden cameras. With the evidence, Helms goes to Camp David to face down the megalomaniac despot—and makes a deal. It includes, for himself—an ambassadorship! No, not to Iran—the author is a novelist. He is writing fiction. I shall not reveal, lest I give away the plot, the country to which Helms is sent as ambassador.

First a minor, then a major observation. The author's intention is to portray Nixon as the ugliest man since Caligula. I do not know whether that is because the author feels this way about a man he once served so lovingly, or because he feels that the Watergate fever is such that if you are writing a book for the purpose of commercial success, you may as well play the odds and indeed raise them. Anyway, alongside Ehrlichman's Nixon, Woodward and Bernstein's is George Romney.

But here the author greatly confuses the student of his

passion play. Helms fears the release of the report on the Bay of Pigs because the disclosed assassination "would be used to destroy the memory of a great, dead President." But the same author leaves no doubt that the late great President ordered Helms to effect the priest's assassination—Nixon, even in *this* book, orders *nobody* to assassinate *anybody*. And as for destroying the Presidency and the integrity of the FBI and the CIA, by the author's own accounting, the full resources of these agencies were routinely used by LBJ and routinely by Hoover for illegal, indeed for indefensible purposes. LBJ, telling Helms what fresh illegal act he must commit, says, "If you think this is politics, just wait until that son of a bitch [Nixon] gets in here. You'll be eating his political shit for breakfast, lunch, and dinner." That has the advantage of sounding like LBJ, but is highly distracting to the ethical crochet. A moment's thought on this aspect of the novel (which is all it is worth) requires the conclusion that the author simply ever bothered to sort out the moral confusions and contradictions. Perhaps they bored him. With good reason.

And neither he nor, so far as one can tell, the critical community has given much thought to the popular new mode for saying anything slanderous one desires to say about anybody at all. Not quite new—there were recognizable characters in great works of art, from Aristophanes to Bosch to Pope. But one supposes that these were committed side-by-side countervailing sanctions that are now either outlawed or etiolated. Exile, imprisonment, the duel, criminal libel, anathema. Truman Capote is lavishing his powers these days saying anything he wishes to say about anybody he wishes to write about. I took the liberty of asking the distinguished editor of *Time* magazine the other day whether his journal could survive a week's competition with *Newsweek* if it were to permit the word *dastardly* to be used to describe what Capote is doing. Perhaps for the same reason you cannot use that word these days (it hurts the user, not the tortfeasor), the offense against which it is appropriately used is all the graver. What defense would Mrs. Woodward have had—assuming she had not committed suicide—against Capote? What defense have the dozen who have not yet committed suicide, against his leering malevolence? To suggest suing is to demonstrate ignorance of the revolution in the libel law, and of the psychological axiom that a victim will often prefer silence, over against prosecution for rape.

What amazes is that the complaint against Nixon began on the grounds of *his* interference in the privacy of other people. Here is a novel that accuses Kennedy of effecting an assassination (clearly, an invasion of privacy); LBJ of the usual and not a few unusual offenses; Henry Kissinger of striking acts of moral weakness not to say depravity; and Richard Nixon of a mind and character grotesque beyond recognition. My argument isn't, at this point, that Nixon is probably someone other than the character in this book. It is that everyone—critic or admirer of Nixon, Hoover, Helms, LBJ, Kennedy—has an interest in resisting such coprophilia as Capote and Ehrlichman are given to.

Last month the court upheld a five-year sentence against Ehrlichman for authorizing the burglary of the files of Daniel Ellsberg's psychiatrist. It is a matter of formal concern whether the sentence is exaggerated under the circumstances. It is a matter of passionate concern that there is no punishment, social let alone legal, as far as one can tell, for such a malevolent, piratical, cynical invasion against historical integrity as Ehrlichman has achieved in this book all by himself. Well, not quite. He had the help of a team grown recently rich by deploring, in another mode, the causes that led to Nixon's Final Days, the story of how Nixon was rightly led to the slaughterhouse for trying to find out the real dirt about his political opponents; when all he had to do was invent it.

Approaching the Anniversary

July 5, 1975

SCENE: The dining room of a former ambassador, and close friend of the former President. He is there, with Mrs. Nixon. Their first night out since the beginning of their exile in San

Clemente. There are twenty or so guests, carefully selected: what the polemical press would call "loyalists." The dinner has been served, and the toasts begin.

The host speaks about his personal debt to his guest of honor, who gave him the privilege of serving the Republic as an ambassador. The guest of honor rises to respond. It is probably the first toast he has given since the year before, when he regularly toasted chiefs of state at the gala dinners in the White House. He is given to non-perfunctory toasts: they seldom lasted less than five minutes, and sometimes went on ten or twelve minutes.

This time around he spoke without any sense of pressure to move the crowd on over to the East Room of the White House for the formal entertainment. So he took his time, and expressed his thanks for the continuing loyalty of his friends, and said such other things as one might have expected to hear from him on the occasion. But he had to end eventually, and he did so by raising his glass and saying to the attentive company: "Tonight I would like to make a toast I was not able to make for five and one-half years. I would like to toast the President of the United States."

It was a moment of great poignancy—but, inevitably, the little creepy-crawly Nixon inflection breaks through, and there is a shaft of intellectual illumination. Though the toast has the air of grace, it sinks, finally, deep onto the ocean floor of gracelessness as one reflects that—it was not, really, a toast to Gerald Ford. It was a toast to Richard Nixon. It was not so much intended to remind the company that another man sits in the Oval Office in the White House, as to remind it that for five and one-half years, the man now raising his glass sat in that august place. It is as if, at St. Helena, Napoleon had risen to toast the king by saying: "May he bring France to the same glories achieved by his predecessor."

For all the effort to institutionalize the problems of Richard Nixon and analyze the causes of his downfall, in the end the key to the mystery lies in Mr. Nixon's character.

The trouble with bad taste, a dramatist once wrote, is that it can lead to murder. In Nixon's case it led to his unmaking, and to derivative institutional consequences everyone is trying to understand—most lucidly, and most readably in recent weeks, Theodore White, whose volume *Breach of Faith* is, as one would expect, engrossing. But it raises at least as many questions as it answers.

There is an explanation for this making the cynical rounds. It is raised by the columnist Nicholas Von Hoffman, who eats lightly sugared icons for breakfast. The trouble with White's analysis of Nixon's downfall, says Hoffman, is that White has to come to terms with what he has written before about Nixon. Indeed, White confesses in his most recent book that way back, like every other American liberal, he began by loathing Nixon, but that somewhere along the line he developed an admiration for him. In full retreat from this admiration, he writes now the book about the Fall of Richard Nixon. But he is unwilling to say what Hoffman would like him to say: that Nixon was always thoroughly evil.

"There are no saints and no villains in history," Hoffman quotes White as saying on a television program, and comments, "Blurting something like that out transcends the embarrassment of looking like a jackass because one once wrote complimentary sentences about Nixon."

White is of course much more nearly correct than Hoffman, who is a caricaturist, and writes columns only because he doesn't draw cartoons. White is a thoughtful man, who has perceived the weaknesses of Nixon, and brought brilliantly into focus—as far as he goes—the bearing of those weaknesses on Nixon's decline and fall. But he fails, in the end, because Theodore White—so kind and good-natured, so ineluctably enticed, even now, by the lures of pot-bellied ideology—fails to nail the principal nexus between Nixon's personal shortcomings, which White traces in as fine detail as Dürer, and the failings of Nixon as a statesman of international harmony: because, as the architect of détente, Nixon continues to be the hero of Teddy White. No man who "opened the door" to China, and who "stopped the arms race," can be all bad.

And yet the same man whose resources failed him at that small dinner party found them wanting in the great state dinners at Peking and Moscow. Nixon's lack of ethical discrimination brought him down: and is even now damaging the prospects of the free world.

Nixon as the Last Picture Show

April 1, 1976

I DON'T KNOW when perspective is going to set in, but until it does, read me, pray, out of that fraternity of self-adulators who surround Woodward and Bernstein as the exemplars of a new journalism fired by ethical concern. I haven't seen the movie, but it is an ironic master-stroke that it should star Robert Redford. The last time out on the boards, Redford was a CIA agent who was finally revolted by his profession. Now he is born again, unburdened of doubts: I Was a Spy for Woodward & Bernstein, and Found Out All about Pat Nixon's Sex Life.

Attempt, for a moment, to recapture perspective. A gang of over-zealous Republican pols decide they should find out what is going on in Democratic headquarters, and to that end organize a team to burglarize those offices and bring out information that might be politically useful. The end result of that attempted invasion of the professional privacy of Lawrence O'Brien was a dozen people in jail, and the resignation of a President of the United States, for the first time in history.

The reputation, meanwhile, of the only prominent surviving Cabinet member of that Administration has been under constant attack because he had a hand—how direct, we do not know—in expediting a dozen telephone taps that sought to isolate the sources of leaks of national security information. It is ceaselessly pointed out by the critics that one or two of the people whose telephones were tapped were in no visible way connected with national security matters, giving rise to the possibility that a Republican Administration had a prurient interest in the private affairs of these men. Notwithstanding these events, about which the contention continues, one fact does stand out. It is that not a single personal detail about the lives of the tappees has ever seen public print. Mr. Morton Halperin is engaged in an extensive civil lawsuit against Henry Kissinger, the abstract merits of which are here extraneous. It remains a fact that the public knows not a single thing about Morton Halperin's sex life, his religious habits, his alcoholic intake, or even whether, at night, he is given to fantasizing conversations with Thomas Jefferson.

It is with this background that one judges the activities of the bunch of people identified with the investigation that brought down a President—featuring *their* invasions of privacy. The difference between Richard Nixon and Mrs. Graham is that he was an unsuccessful snoop with a finite curiosity about human weaknesses; while she, as employer and now as purveyor, is a sponsor of successful snoops whose curiosity is entirely unlimited.

Perhaps their imagination is as unlimited as their prurience. We cannot know how much of the current garbage about Richard Nixon has been fabricated. It hardly matters. It matters very much that Nixon has to skulk out the rest of his life in San Clemente, while those who receive the Pulitzer Prizes and the Woman of the Century Awards take out advertising space telling you how, by merely buying their product, you can learn everything about the private lives of Richard and Patricia Nixon.

It is alleged that, on that final evening, after he had reported to the American people that on the very next day, at noon, he would resign the Presidency of the United States, Richard Nixon called Henry Kissinger to the White House. Kissinger—it is said—saw a broken man. It is not clear what else he might have been expected to see. And that Richard Nixon turned to Kissinger and expressed himself as an imperfect Christian, even as Kissinger was an imperfect Jew, and suggested that they go down on their knees, and pray for help.

One gathers that this is the act from which one is encouraged to deduce that Nixon was *really* bonkers. Praying! On your *knees*! I mean, it's not what the British call PLU (People Like Us). The profiteers of this last go-around against Nixon had better get down on their knees and pray that the Lord is infinitely merciful, because if He is anything less than that, they are in trouble.

Nixon on Nixon

Frost: 1, 2, 3

May 1977

CONCERNING NIXON'S performance the other night, a few observations:

1. Complaints that he spoke "the same old excuses" were not entirely well grounded; and, to the extent they were, were invalid. There was never any reason to suppose that Mr. Nixon's vision of Watergate would change substantially between August 1974 and May 1977. But in fact he made one or two novel points. Principal of these was that he was not a "good butcher." By which he meant that if he had amputated diseased members of the Executive corpus in time, the cancer would have been arrested. This happens to be exactly correct. If he had dismissed John Mitchell (say) at the end of June 1972 on the grounds that his office was the animating force behind the break-in, the Watergate scandal would have ended there and then.

2. The strangest reaction to the Nixon broadcast is the incessant emphasis on the money he is making out of it. There is talk that he will net a million dollars by the time he is through. Let us consider that. He will, by the time he is through, have appeared for a stretch of six hours of television time. The preliminary ratings by the Nielsen Corporation show that the Nixon interview attracted approximately one-half the television viewers in the nation.

At $250,000 per hour and one half, addressing half the nation's television viewers, Richard Nixon is being cheated. Sonny and Cher and Bob Hope would have been remunerated at a higher rate if they achieved those ratings. Any Rolling Stone would have looked at the profit money and fired his agent. Muhammad Ali would have wondered whether there were a couple of zeros missing from the check. Nor is this all. Sonny and Cher can do whatever it is they do next week *ad infinitum, ad nauseam.* Bob Hope has been at it two generations. The Rolling Stones threaten to outlast Ed Sullivan. Muhammad Ali will have to await the development of a new weapons system to stop him.

Richard Nixon will never again speak as he spoke to Frost the other night about the single most lurid, most fascinating political scandal in American history. Is it implicitly charged that he should have done it for nothing? He was not only deposed from office, losing salary and most perquisites. He was disbarred. He is sued by every ideological ambulance chaser in the country. People who stumble into a pothole on the DMZ in 1990 will end up suing Richard Nixon. Is it really a valid cause of resentment that he should be paid money which could never begin to pay the cost of his endless fight to present his case to history?

3. The program, in the opinion of this viewer, was highly revealing. It showed Richard Nixon to be different from his predecessors in one special respect. As an abuser of Executive power he doesn't begin to match FDR, just as an example. As a molester of other people's rights, LBJ and JFK are clearly his superiors. As a man loyal to his cronies, he cannot compare with Harry Truman.

Here is what he distinctively proved to be: stupid. He was incapable of reasoning simply from a position taken, over to the consequences of taking it. He could not see that by flogging the hounds of justice and urging them hotly to sniff out wrongdoing, he was setting these hounds upon himself.

He was stupid to fail to understand that the great movement in government was away from Executive supremacy, in the direction of legislative supremacy, and that therefore the tapes were bound to be given over to the prosecutors by the Supreme Court.

He was stupid to believe that the prestige of the Presidency could survive the exposure of years of barracks talk in the Oval Office.

And, he proved the other night, he was not resourceful enough, even after these months of introspection and pain, to devise a comprehensive formula for giving his case to the people. It is his crowning failure that Nixon isn't really as bad as he makes himself out to be.

* * *

Really, the Nixon-Frost production is high television. It absolutely demonstrates the indispensability of the medium. The program was to a considerable extent a *visual* experience. Reading the transcript is not enough. Nixon is, as Garry Wills wrote almost ten years ago, probably the most interesting man to have entered public life. Mind, Ivan the Terrible was interesting also. But it continues to come out and out, extruded by David Frost with a sense of an infinity of supply. You get the feeling that like Niagara Falls, the cataract could continue indefinitely, a profusion of history, half-history, cunning, self-service, histrionics, poignancy, jabberwocky, and, God save us, even a trace of wit.

How many hours did Frost spend on Nixon and Mao Tse-tung? But imagine coming away from Nixon on Mao with practically the whole of the conversation devoted to "the incomparable humor" of Mao Tse-tung. That is on the order of Héloïse recalling on television about Abélard only that he ate Grape Nuts for breakfast. And truly the infatuation between Nixon and Mao is a fascinating thing. There was the film clip, Nixon and Pat, visiting Mao in the winter of 1976, plucked out from the isolation of San Clemente, like Cinderella, for one day in the Chinese limelight. Nixon grasping Mao with both hands.

Mao was treating Nixon with such affection as is shown to him in America only by Robert Abplanalp and Bebe Rebozo. So we are told that Mao's "sense of humor" is absolutely "devilish." And as evidence of the wisdom of Mao, we are given this from the Chairman's collected thoughts: "Nothing is hard if one dares to scale the heights." Edgar Guest would have been embarrassed by that. In China, it will fuel a whole Cultural Revolution.

. . . Nothing much about Taiwan. Why didn't Frost push him on the subject? All Nixon would say was that the Chinese gave no "express" assurances that they would deal peaceably with Taiwan. But we *knew* that. What we needed to know was what Nixon told Mao we would do about it if the Chinese moved against Taiwan. All we got from Nixon was that it was his opinion "the Chinese don't want to be involved" because of "internal problems." But people representing the Carter

Administration are going around saying that Nixon agreed to "normalize" after the 1972 elections, and that this meant withdrawing from Taiwan. Kissinger is saying that's not true. Why wasn't Nixon asked? Or if he was, why was that section of the tape cut? Will the balance of what was filmed be shown anywhere? At the Smithsonian? If so, please advise.

The human rights business. Nixon said that if he had gone about making "a big grandstand play" about the right of the Jews to emigrate to Israel, he would have accomplished nothing. This was the principal sally of the evening against President Carter. Frost might have observed that, by all accounts, repression in the Soviet Union has increased during the past few years, which, as it happened, are the years of détente. The high point of liberalism in the Soviet Union was reached in 1956, which, as it happened, was the high point of the cold war. There is no necessary correlation, in either direction. Frost should have dragged this out of Nixon, and let us hear directly from his lips whether he disapproves Carter's statement that the Russians ought to live up to their Helsinki obligations.

. . . First-rate stuff, the characterizations of the Russian leaders. Amoral, too, and in a sense that is as it should be. But Nixon charged into the meaning of détente, and by the time he was through defining it, it was left without any meaning at all. He said détente is an "interrelationship," that it is "knowing each other," that it is settling "before the flashpoint." Well, what's new about that? Eisenhower had an "interrelationship," had "conversations," didn't get us into war, but there was never any question in the public mind about his feelings about the Communists. Nixon said about Brezhnev *et al.*, "They want a Communist world." But he said nothing at all about how they propose to achieve the Communist world, nothing about the relative strength of the Soviet Union vis-à-vis American strength on the day he left office, compared to the day he took office.

Then there was the charming blooper. Nixon's own Polish liberation joke. "I'm an old Navy man," he said, to validate his authority for describing the "bow" of a boat as its rear end. No wonder he has trouble defining détente.

* * *

The final hour and one half with Richard Nixon was disappointing primarily in its failure to get from him his estimate of the bearing of Watergate on the loss of Indochina. It is very perplexing that David Frost did not bear down on the point. Here was Richard Nixon, claiming all kinds of immunity for himself in virtue of the exigencies of war, but failing to probe his own contribution to the failure of a national undertaking.

Nixon's summary is as follows: The Democrats began a war which they declined to consummate. A Republican Administration was voted into power. Rather than help that Administration complete the task bequeathed to it, critical members of the Democratic family did everything they could do to undermine what should have been a national rather than a factional effort. The symbol of the opponents was Daniel Ellsberg. (I pause to remark that I thought Mr. Nixon's referring to him as a "punk" was refreshing as mountain water, and I hope Judge Byrne out in Los Angeles can be discouraged from ruling Mr. Nixon's statement out of order.)

Nixon's new approach consisted in intensifying pressures on the field, and diplomatically on the Russians. His principal obstacle during those years was precisely the conviction in North Vietnam that Nixon's efforts would fail because of the strength of the domestic opposition. But when Nixon was re-elected by the landslide of 1972 and ordered the December bombings, finally the North Vietnamese caved in: "We've decided that President Nixon is not going to be affected by the protests," he tells us Le Duc Tho advised Henry Kissinger in January 1973 when they got down to working out an agreement.

But what then happened? In no time at all, the North Vietnamese conquered South Vietnam. Nixon is the king who had lost a war. But about this he said virtually nothing at all. We are all supposed to know the official story: The Gulf of Tonkin Resolution was repealed, the President was stripped of authority to carry out aggressive missions in defense of the terms of the Treaty, Congress turned niggardly in supplying South Vietnam with arms, no one seemed to care that the North was indifferent to the obligations of the Treaty.

The political reality was—Watergate. Richard Nixon, returned triumphantly to the White House, was a slave to Watergate. Whereas under normal circumstances he might have exercised his responsibilities as President and demanded of Congress a consistency of performance, he was, instead, beginning his dreary retreat from victory. Having asked the nation to underwrite the awful sacrifices of Vietnam, he was himself unwilling to risk the humiliation of revealing the complicity of his staff in the Watergate venture.

By the end of 1973, Richard Nixon was far-gone in solipsism. Vietnam had lost its strategic reality. In saying that perhaps he was "the last casualty in Vietnam" he showed an awesome callousness. The last casualty of Vietnam is Vietnam.

As Richard Reeves said the other day, it is probably inevitable that no matter how often one takes the pledge not to write again on the desolate and sad subject of Richard Nixon, it is bound to happen: again, and again. Next year his book will be out. And an endless succession of books. Nixon is the central figure in American postwar politics, who ran five times on a national ticket, and grew progressively in insecurity.

Charles Colson records the utter listlessness of Nixon's behavior on the night he was triumphantly re-elected in 1972. And Frost elicits from him the bitter humiliation Nixon felt on not having been invited back to the White House—notwithstanding that he had been Vice-President of the United States—for eight years, under Kennedy and Johnson. (He did not reflect that Eisenhower banned Truman from the White House for eight years.)

One shrinks from the use of a psychological vocabulary, particularly at the expense of Mr. Nixon, but in the end it is irresistible. He had, and has, a death wish. The huge efforts to stay alive politically had, in the end, only a mechanical meaning.

Arthur Schlesinger, Jr. at Camelot

May 1, 1977

THE BOYS WHO GAVE us the Freedom of Information Act have showered us with unexpected blessings. For instance, we begin to get a real feel for how the knights of the round table addressed King John, back in Camelot. Truly King John was a fine and graceful man, who inspired copious draughts of homage from his knights. Here, for instance, is a secret memorandum from Sir Arthur Schlesinger, addressed to the king, on the subject of how to handle p/r during and after their impending engagement against Cuba in 1961. It shows that the courtly style of communication has not changed substantially since the days when Sir Lancelot addressed King Arthur.

"In the days since January 20," wrote Sir Arthur to his sire, "your Administration has changed the face of American foreign policy. The soberness of style, the absence of cold-war clichés, the lack of self-righteousness and sermonizing, the impressive combination of reasonableness and firmness, the generosity to new ideas, the dedication to social progress, the tough-minded idealism of purpose ["Fill Sir Arthur's glass," I can hear the gentle King saying to the steward]—all these factors have transformed the 'image' of the United States before the world."

Since this memorandum was written on April 10, ten weeks after taking power, you would think the new court would have got over the awful monster Eisenhower who preceded them. But Sir Arthur would make sure, even though there were pressing matters to discuss—the Bay of Pigs was only one week away—that King John should know how happy was the contrast. "People around the world have forgotten the muddling and moralizing conservatism of the Eisenhower period with surprising speed." Indeed. And with surprising speed the world was soon to forget what it was like, under Ike, not to be fighting wars.

Eventually Sir Arthur got down to business. The Bay of

Pigs was planned, and Sir Arthur feared it might boomerang. *Very* important to prepare the p/r. "If Castro [wins the engagement and] flies a group of captured Cubans to New York to testify that they were organized and trained by CIA, we will have to be prepared to show that the alleged CIA personnel were errant idealists or soldiers-of-fortune working on their own." In later years, a successor courtier would call that stonewalling. And the very same errant idealists, a decade later, pried their way into Watergate.

Sir Arthur suggested the need for diversionary action on some other theater. "Could not something be done against the Dominican Republic in the next few days?—some new call for action against the Trujillo tyranny?" Why not? Wish we had thought of that.

King John was not *himself* to be caught out lying. "When lies must be told," Sir Arthur wrote, "they should be told by subordinate officials." That's chivalry, if ever we saw it! In fact, maybe King John should arrange to be out at Chevy Chase playing golf when the invasion actually began? "There seems to be merit in [the] suggestion that someone other than the President make the final decision and do so in his absence—someone whose head can later be placed on the block if things go terribly wrong." King John, feeling his throat tenderly, must have been especially grateful for the solicitude and loyalty and fraternity of his humble servant, Sir Arthur.

In my next dispatch, I shall reproduce a "press conference" as recommended by Arthur Schlesinger to John F. Kennedy in the event the Bay of Pigs went sour. On no account miss it. If Nixon had had Sir Arthur at his side, giving such top-quality advice, Nixon would still be President. Sir Arthur would have figured out a way to repeal the two-term amendment, so that the world might continue to enjoy the soberness of style, the absence of clichés, the lack of self-righteousness and sermonizing, the impressive combination of reasonableness and firmness, the generosity to new ideas, the dedication to social progress, the tough-minded idealism of purpose. Gee. Where was Arthur when King Richard needed him so badly?

* * *

Schlesinger, days before the invasion, is troubled that Kennedy's direct sponsorship of the Bay of Pigs may be discovered by the Woodwards and Bernsteins of 1961. Early in the memorandum he discusses the merits of having someone else actually trigger the invasion, "—someone whose head can later be placed on the block if things go terribly wrong." Some Gordon Liddy, or Howard Hunt, or even John Ehrlichman, or John Mitchell. Then Mr. Schlesinger writes out the kind of press conference President Kennedy might expect, supplying the most appropriate answers to the most embarrassing questions for his boss:

"Q. Mr. President, can you tell us about the reported invasion of Cuba this morning?

"A. We are doing our best to get the exact facts. So far as I can tell at present, a number of opponents of the Castro regime have landed on Cuba. I understand that the Revolutionary Council is trying to make contact with these people."

(How're we doing? Could Nixon have improved on that one? No sir, this is Grade A, Harvard B.A., Harvard Ph.D. Quality Lying. There is more:)

"Q. Sir, according to the newspapers the rebel forces were trained in American camps and supplied by American agencies.

"A. There have been many thousands of Cuban refugees in Florida in these last months. I have no doubt that many of them have been determined to do what they can at the earliest possible moment to restore freedom to their homeland. . . . I suppose that, just as the Castro forces got money and arms from sources in the United States, these rebels may well have too. But, so far as I can tell, this is a purely Cuban operation. I doubt whether Cuba's patriots in exile would have to be stimulated and organized by the United States in order to persuade them to liberate their nation from a Communist dictator."

(Can you imagine what the Watergate Committee, or John Doar's Impeachment Committee, would have done with that one?)

"Q. Mr. President, is the CIA involved in this affair?

"A. As I said a moment ago, I imagine that elements in the United States helped these opponents of Castro, as they helped Castro himself in 1958. I can assure you that the United States government has no intention of using force to overthrow the Castro regime or contributing force to that purpose unless compelled to do so in the interest of self-defense."

That is what one might call Smoking Pistol. But hark! Arthur Schlesinger was worried about it because he added in brackets, "[hardly satisfactory: it is imperative that a better formula be worked out before your next press conference]." It would of course have been better still if, before the next press conference, a better invasion had been worked out.

"Q. Mr. President, would you say that, so far as Cuba is concerned, the U.S. has been faithful to its Treaty pledges against intervention in other countries? Would you say that it has resolutely enforced the laws forbidding the use of U.S. territory to prepare revolutionary action against another state?"

Guess what answer Arthur Schlesinger supplied to that question in his memo to the boss? I quote it exactly as it appears in the secret document:

"A. ? ? ? ?"

Even Mr. Schlesinger had exhausted his reserves of artifice. He had coached the President on how to lie about everything involving the U.S. sponsorship of the Bay of Pigs invasion. But he got stuck on that one point, how to answer that one tricky question. Would that exchange have served as a candidate for an eighteen-minute dubbed-out tape?

Well, we all know what happened. Kennedy launched the Bay of Pigs, and it became obvious that they had been trained and directed by the U.S. government. He then went to the people—and told them the truth; and survived. If he had gone to the people and given such a speech as Schlesinger recommended in his memo, he'd have been as guilty as Nixon. But such memos as in the public mind are identified with the kind of people attracted to Nixon, we see now were quite routinely written by the kind of people attracted to— JFK. My, how history repeats itself, especially at the hands of historians.

IV.

People, Characters

The Long War Against McCarthyism

Lillian Hellman: Who is the ugliest of them all?

January 1977

WHEN *Scoundrel Time* (Little, Brown, $7.95) was first published, in the spring of 1976, only the cooing of reviewers was heard. Up front, in the most prominent seats, they applauded so resolutely, so methodically, that the sound of the metronome teased the ear. Solzhenitsyn, in the first Gulag book, writes about how, during one of the terrors, Stalin's agents would fan out from Moscow to give speeches to the satellite brass, hastily convened in crowded theaters in the outlying cities to receive the details of Stalin's hectic afflatus. After the speaker was done, the subjects would break into applause, and the clapping would go on and on, because no one dared be the first to sit down, lest he be thought insufficiently servile. Indeed, rather than wait for the speaker finally to beckon the whole assembly back to its seats, on one occasion someone did it—stopped clapping, though only after a boisterous while. That man was spotted, given ten years, and shipped off to a prison camp—where, perhaps, he was given to read from the collected anti-fascist *opera* of Lillian Hellman. . . . It seemed for a while the reviewers would be that way all around the town—the New York *Times,* the Washington *Post, Commonweal, America,* the Chicago *Tribune.* Then . . . then, in *The New York Review of Books,* Murray Kempton interrupted his own paean to Miss Hellman to make a comment or two which, however gentle, quite ruptured the trance. It was as if, in Paris during the occupation, an anonymous arranger had, by fugitive notation, insinuated the motif of the *"Marseillaise"* into a great Speer-like orches-

139

tration of *"Über Alles."* Others, after that, came rushing in. It would never be quite the same again for Miss Lillian.

Even so, one has to hand it to her. Though the book is slender, the design is grandly staged, in self-esteem as in presumption. To begin with, here is someone described in the introduction to her own book as the greatest woman playwright in American history. Now this is probably true. But a) Isn't that on the order of celebrating the tallest building in Wichita, Kansas? and b) Doesn't an introduction to oneself in such terms, in one's own book, by one's own chosen introducer, interfere with the desired perception of oneself as a hardworking artist ignorant, indeed disdainful, of the outside world of power-plays and flackery? and c) Aren't the auspices the most alien for making sexual distinctions? I mean, Garry Wills, the Last Kid, talking about the Greatest Woman Playwright as one would talk about the downhill champion on the one-legged ski team?

And here is a writer (Wills) introducing an autobiographical book by a woman who is publicizing now her complaint against an America that, as she might put it, victimized her because of her alleged championship of the regime of Josef Stalin. And what, then, does Wills go and do in his introduction? Quote from the author's pre-McCarthy works, to demonstrate the impartiality of her opposition to tyranny? Not at all. He goes on (and on and on—Mr. Wills consumes thirty-four pages with his introduction, one-fifth of the book), blithely—offhandedly—describing the era of Miss Hellman's travail as the era in U.S.-Soviet relations during which horrible old us, led by Harry Truman, promulgated a cold war against reasonable old them, the startled, innocent Communists, led by Josef Stalin. In *Commentary,* Nathan Glazer quoted from Wills's introduction: *"A newly aggressive Truman had launched the Cold War in the spring of 1947, with his plan to 'rescue' Greece and Turkey. . . . We had still a world to save, with just those plans—from NATO to the Korean War . . ."* And commented: "One reads such passages—and many others— in astonishment. Garry Wills [evidently] believes that Greece and Turkey did not need to be rescued, that one of America's 'plans' was the Korean War. It seems that he prefers the political condition of, say, Bulgaria and North Korea to that of Greece and Turkey." *That* introduction, which might have been written in the Lenin Institute, introducing *that* book, under the circumstances of Miss Hellman's apologia, was a venture either in dumb innocence (inconsistent with Hellman's persona), or in matchless cheek, on the order of Mohandas Gandhi writing the autobiography of a pacifist and asking General Patton to introduce it.

But the difficulties had only just begun for her. Is Ms. Hellman a nice guy? In a way, it shouldn't matter. A sentence from her book, much quoted, asks, *"Since when do you have to agree with people to defend them from injustice?"* By the same token, we shouldn't require that someone be endearing as a prerequisite to indignation at unfair treatment of her. But Ms. Hellman, author of *The Little Foxes*, is quickly spotted as being no less guileful than one of her characters. It's another case of Germaine Greer, filibustering against male chauvinism, while stripteasing her sexual biography across the magazine rack. Ms. Hellman, affecting only a disinterested concern for justice, twangs the heartstrings—with, however, more sleight of hand than craft. She had to sell her country house! She had to fire her cook and gardener! She had to give up a million-dollar contract! She had to take a part-time job in a department store! Her lover had to go to jail! If, unlike the earlier reviewers, you finish the book believing that you have read anything less than an episode in the life of Thomas More, you are either callous—or else her art has failed her.

She takes awful risks, entirely unnecessary. For instance, she exhibits hit-and-run contempt for Lionel and Diana Trilling—for the sin of believing in the sincerity of Whittaker Chambers. Nice people would have handled that differently. James Wechsler of the New York *Post* is denounced for being a *"friendly witness"* before the House Committee on Un-American Activities (he never appeared before HUAC: it was the McCarthy Committee, and Wechsler was hostile). Theodore White is dismissed contemptuously as a *"jolly quarter-historian"*—because he once wrote a book saying that Nixon was a complicated man (Lillian Hellman finds nothing complicated in evil incarnate). Elia Kazan, struggling to appease his conscience, in revolt now against his earlier complicity with the Communist movement, took a full page in the New York *Times* to run his palinode—characterized by Miss Hellman as *"pious shit."*

All in all, her performance is about as ingratiating as a post-Watergate speech by Richard Nixon, and so we quite understand it when Murray Kempton is driven to saying, in concluding his review, that, really, he would not want Lilliam Hellman "overmuch as a comrade." Thus, the scaffolding of the book is pretty shaky. It is, after all, implicitly entitled, *"The Heroism of Lillian Hellman during the Darkest Days of the Republic,* by Lillian Hellman." It would have been a little seemlier if her book had gone out as *"Scoundrel Time,* by Lillian Hellman; as told to Garry Wills." Or—why not just *"Scoundrel Time: How Lillian Hellman Held Her Finger in the Dike and Saved American Freedom and Self-Respect,* by Garry Wills"? He would not have needed to increase the size of his contribution by all that much. In any event—an artistic point, and with apologies to Burke—this martyr, to be loved, should be lovelier.

Then there is the problem of factual accuracy, best captured in the author's unguarded reference to Whittaker Chambers and the pumpkin papers.

Here is what Miss Hellman wrote:

"Facts are facts—and one of them is that a pumpkin, in which Chambers claimed to have hidden the damaging evidence against Hiss, deteriorates."

Now here is a sentence that might have been written by Eleanor Roosevelt. It sounds strange coming from the greatest woman playwright in American history, and is incredible when proffered in support of the proposition that facts are facts.

Yes, it is a fact that pumpkins deteriorate.

But they do not deteriorate appreciably overnight, which is how long the Hiss films reposed in the pumpkin.

As for *"in which Chambers claimed to have hidden . . ."* nobody questions that Chambers hid the films there, not even Alger Hiss. Not even Stalin. Nor could she have intended to write, *"in which Chambers hid the* allegedly *damaging evidence."* Because it wasn't *allegedly* damaging, it was just plain damaging, which indeed is why all the fuss. The films went a long way to establish Chambers's credibility, and therefore the guilt of Hiss. What she presumably *meant* to write was,*"in which Chambers hid the damaging but, it now turns out, meaningless evidence."* Earlier in the book she had constructed an explanatory footnote from which the sentence in question coasted, to wit:*"In 1975 the secret pumpkin papers were found to contain nothing secret, nothing confidential. They were, in fact, non-classified, which is Washington's way of saying anybody who says please can have them."*

Facts are indeed facts. But Miss Hellman's rendition of the facts caught the attention of one of her fans, Congressman Edward Koch of Manhattan. He read her book, and wrote the author a letter of fawning praise reciting his own sustained effort to kill the House Committee on Un-American Activities. But Edward Koch has a streak of Yankee inquisitiveness, even as it is advertised about Miss Hellman that she is curious. John Hersey has written about her—his dear friend—"Miss Hellman's powers of invention are fed by her remarkable memory and her ravenous curiosity. Her father once said she lived 'within a question mark.' She defines culture as 'applied curiosity.' She is always on what she calls 'the find-out kick.'" Well, not quite always. Not on those occasions when she begins a paragraph with the phrase, "Facts are facts." (Like the *Daily World*'s ritual introduction of a lie: "As is well known . . .")

Congressman Koch wrote to the Library of Congress to ask about Miss Hellman's description of the pumpkin papers, and simultaneously wrote to Miss Hellman asking for an elucidation. The lady who lives within a question mark didn't reply. But the lady at the Library of Congress did. As follows: "The footnote statement is inaccurate. On July 31, 1975, Alger Hiss was permitted to see the 'pumpkin papers,' which consist of five rolls of microfilm. One roll, as Mr. Kelly reports, was 'completely light-fogged.' Two other rolls were pages from apparently unclassified Navy technical manuals. The other two rolls, however, contained Government documents 'relating to U.S.-German relations before World War II and cables from U.S. observers in China.' Documents in these two rolls were marked highly confidential. Of the five rolls of microfilm, only these latter two had been used as evidence against Hiss in the trial which led to his conviction for perjury in 1950."

Miss Hellman's reputation as a literary precisionist (she is said to write and rewrite her plays four, six, ten, twelve times) leads one to expect a cognate precision in those of her books and articles that bid for the moral attention of the Republic; so that one is inclined to take literally such a statement by her as, *"Certainly nobody in their [sic] right mind could have believed that the China experts, charged and fired by the State Department, did any more than recognize that Chiang Kai-shek was losing."*

But whom is she referring to? Who is it who was *"charged and fired"* by the State Department for such an offense? The controversial John Carter Vincent was three times *cleared* by the State Department's Loyalty Security Board, and when the Civil Service Loyalty Review Board found against him, Dulles *overruled* that Board, though accepting Vincent's resignation. McCarthy's target, John Paton Davies, was *cleared* by the State Department. John Stewart Service was, granted, finally dropped by the State Department, but only because the Civil Service Loyalty Review Board ruled against him, not the State Department's board, which repeatedly cleared him. And Service was otherwise engaged than merely as a diplomatic technician predicting the ascendancy of Mao. His emotions in the matter were hardly concealed. He had provided his superiors, from the field in China, such information as that "Politically, any orientation which the Chinese Communists may once have had toward the Soviet Union seems to be a thing of the past . . . they are carrying out democratic policies which they expect the United States to approve and sympathetically support." And Service's case was further complicated when he was arrested for passing along classified documents to the editor of *Amerasia*, a Communist-front publication. But of course the principal architect of our China policy, singled out by the Senate Internal Security Subcommittee, hadn't even been a member of the State Department, exercising his influence on policy through the Institute for Pacific Relations. The blurb printed on Owen Lattimore's book *Solution in Asia* went further than merely to predict the downfall of the Kuomintang. "He showed," the book's editors compressed the author's story, "that all the Asiatic people are more interested in actual democratic practices such as the ones they can see in action across the Russian border, than they are in the fine theories of Anglo-Saxon democracies which come coupled with ruthless imperialism. He inclines to support American newspapermen who report that the only real democracy in China is found in Communist areas."

We have learned about democracy in the Communist world. What have we learned about Miss Hellman's credibility?

Nor is she entirely candid in describing the nature or extent of her own involvement with the Soviet Union. She vouchsafes, in a subordinate clause that could be interpreted as contritional, only this much: "*Many* [American intellectuals] *found in the sins of Stalin Communism—and there were plenty of sins and plenty that for a long time I mistakenly denied—the excuse to join those who should have been their hereditary enemies.*" (Interesting, that one. Is she talking about American Jewish socialist anti-Communists? Who else?) Later she says, "*I thought that in the end Russia, having achieved a state socialism, would stop its infringements on personal liberty. I was wrong.*" Isn't there something there on the order of, "I thought that, on buying the contract of Mickey Mantle, the Yankees would go on to win the World Series. I was wrong . . ."? But the ritualistic apology was not enough to satisfy. Soon after Mr. Kempton broke the spell, one began to notice the misgivings of others. William Phillips in *Partisan Review*, Melvin Lasky in *Encounter*, Nathan Glazer in *Commentary*, most notably Hilton Kramer in the New York *Times* (ardently defended by Arthur Schlesinger, Jr. in the letters section), and even Irving Howe, in *Dissent*.

Forsooth, Lillian Hellman's involvement in the Communist movement was not comprehensively divulged in her offhand remarks about her concern for justice and peace, and her stated disinclination for politics. Miss Hellman went to Russia for the first time in 1937, where her ravenous curiosity caused her to learn enough about the Soviet system to return to the United States confidently to defend Stalin's purges and denounce John Dewey and his commission for finding Stalin guilty of staging the show trials during the great purge. She devoted much of her professional career during that period dramatizing the evil of brown fascism. *Watch on the Rhine*, staged in 1941, is devoted to the proposition that *"the death of fascism is more desirable than the lives and well-being of the people who hate it."* When, a quarter-century later, in 1969, she criticized, in a letter to the New York *Times*, the novelist Kuznetsov for fleeing Russia and seeking asylum in England, having first secured an exit visa by "cooperating" with the Soviet Union by giving an obviously fabricated and useless deposition against fellow dissidents, Kuznetsov replied that Miss Hellman's attack on him, "like that of a few others," was "prompted by some surviving illusions about Russia." "The Soviet Union," he explained to Miss Hellman, "is a fascist country. What is more, its fascism is much more dangerous than Hitler's. It is a country which is living in Orwellian times. . . . Tens of millions of bloody victims, a culture destroyed, fascist antisemitism, the genocide of small nations, the transformation of the individual into a hypocritical cipher, Hungary, Czechoslovakia. In literature—nothing but murder, suicides, persecution, trials, lunatic asylums, an unbroken series of tragedies from Gumilev to Solzhenitsyn. Is that really not enough?" There is no recorded reaction from Miss Hellman.

During the war, she traveled to the Soviet Union and was received there as a celebrity. She returned the hospitality in first-rate mint: an article in *Collier's* magazine about the heroism of the Russian people and the Russian soldiers. In that article there is a passage of triumphant irony. She has been implored by her guide to ask more questions. She records her reply: *"I said, 'The first week I was in the Soviet Union I found out that if I did not ask questions, I always got answers. . . . Tell your people to tell me what they want to. I will learn more that way.'"* (Life within a question mark.) And, indeed, she learned everything Stalin and his agents wanted her to learn, and came back to America to share her knowledge, and to despise those of her fellow Americans who insisted on asking questions.

In 1948 and 1949 she was, for a non-politician, very active. She backed Henry Wallace's bid for the Presidency on the

Progressive Party ticket, and was visibly amused on being asked privately by poor old Mortimer Snerd if it were true that there were Communists in positions of power in his party. *"It was such a surprising question that I laughed and said most certainly it was true."* She then put in a call, convening the top Communists in the Progressive Party, and said to them at that meeting, Look, why don't you go paddle your own canoe in your own party? There cannot have been such dumb amazement in Christendom since Lady Astor asked Stalin when would he stop killing people.

A few months later, Lillian Hellman played a big role in the famous Waldorf Conference—the Cultural and Scientific Conference for World Peace. In her book, her running guard Mr. Wills treats most fiercely those who attended the meeting for the purpose of "disrupting" it—such redbaiters as Mary McCarthy and Dwight Macdonald, and officials of the Americans for Democratic Action who, at a press conference, raised with the wretched Russian superpawn, Dmitri Shostakovich, head of the Soviet delegation, questions about the fate of his cultural and scientific colleagues back home, Russian writers, intellectuals, and musicians who had disappeared from sight after the most recent choler of Josef Stalin. Miss Hellman does not allude to any of this. Her quarrel with American intellectuals is over their failure to devote the whole of their time to criticizing J. Parnell Thomas. Presumably, criticism of Stalin could wait until Miss Hellman was personally satisfied that, now that he had established state socialism, he had in fact failed to introduce human freedom.

Indeed, her attitude is ferocious toward those who, looking back on their complicity with Communism, wondered more inventively than she how to make amends. By writing books? (Koestler.) Cooperating with congressional committees? (Kazan.) Doing both? (Chambers.) Miss Hellman, who wrote about how the cause of anti-fascism was bigger than anything, seemed to have lost interest in tyranny, preoccupied now with her material well-being, and that of Dashiell Hammett, her relationship with whom is jovially described by one reviewer—"She was then and had long been a friend of Dashiell Hammett—more than a friend: a wife, off and on, but for the paperwork." In that spirit one could say that thus had been Lillian Hellman's relations with the Communist movement—a marriage, but for the paperwork. If one feels that paperwork, the formal exchange of vows, is essential to a sacramentally complete union, then perhaps Lillian Hellman was not married to the Communist movement any more than she was married to Dashiell Hammett. But the investigating committees, like Miss Hellman's reviewers, were interested in de facto relations.

So off she went to Washington, for her great moment before the congressional committee. There has not been such a prologue since the *Queen Mary* weighed anchor in Manhattan in order to move to Brooklyn. Her device was simple. She wrote to the committee to say she would not answer questions about anybody's activities other than her own, and unless the committee agreed not to ask such questions, she would take the Fifth Amendment. Implicit in her position was her sacred right to be the sole judge of whether her acquaintances in the Communist world were engaged in innocent activity. The committee of course declined to permit her to define the committee's mandate, so she took the Fifth, and wants us to celebrate her wit and courage every twenty-five years. The committee treated her with civility, did not ask Congress to hold her in contempt, and is hardly responsible for the decline in her commercial fortunes. She, not the committee, dictated the script that got her into trouble with Hollywood.

Yet the lady is obsessed with the fancy that she and her common-law husband were specific victims of the terror. "Dash" floats in and out of the book disembodiedly, but always we are reminded that he actually spent time in jail—for refusing to divulge the names of the financial patrons of the Civil Rights Congress, a Communist front (Dashiell Hammett was not a dupe, at least not in the conventional sense: he was a Communist). Miss Hellman makes a great deal of his victimization. Murray Kempton, who would not send Caligula to prison, at this point has had enough. He writes, "We do not diminish the final admiration we feel owed to Dashiell Hammett when we wonder what he might have said to Miss Hellman on the night he came home from the meeting of the board of the Civil Rights Congress which voted to refuse its support to the cause of James Kutcher, a paraplegic veteran who had been discharged as a government clerk because he belonged to the Trotskyite Socialist Workers Party. But then Hammett was a Communist and it was an article of the Party faith that Leon Trotsky, having worked for the Emperor of Japan since 1904, had then improved his social standing by taking employment with the Nazis in 1934. Thus any member of the Socialist Workers Party could be considered by extension to be no more than an agent of Hitler's ghost. Given that interpretation of history, Paul Robeson spoke from principle when a proposal to assist the Trotskyite Kutcher was raised at a public meeting of the Civil Rights Congress. Robeson drove it from the floor with a declaration to the effect that you don't ask Jews to help a Nazi or Negroes to help the KKK." The voice of Paul Robeson lives on, speaking from the same principle: "Oct. 7, 1976. Lillian Hellman, author and dramatist, will receive the third annual Paul Robeson Award tomorrow at 12:30. The award is presented by the Paul Robeson Citation Committee of Actors' Equity for 'concern for and service to fellow humans.'"

The self-pity reaches paranoia. Edmund Wilson once wrote an entire book the thesis of which silts up as suggesting that we went to war in Vietnam for the sole purpose of increasing his income tax. Miss Hellman is vaguer on the subject of motivation, but denies her reader any explanation for bringing the matter up at all, leaving us to suppose that Somebody in Washington singled her and Dash out for Special Treatment. Thus Hammett goes to jail for contempt of Congress (for six months). *"That was a tough spring, 1952. There were not alone the arrangements for my appearance before the Committee, there were other kinds of trouble. Hammett owed the Internal Revenue a great deal of back taxes: two days after he went to jail they attached all income from books, radio, or television, from anything. He was, therefore, to have no income for the remaining ten years of his life. . . . That made me sad."* And again, *"Never in the ten years since the Internal Revenue cut off his income—two days after he went to jail—did he ever buy a suit or even a tie."* As for herself, *"Money was beginning to go and go fast. I had gone from earning a hundred and forty thousand a year (before the movie blacklist) to fifty and then twenty and then ten, almost all of which was taken from me* [note, "taken from me"] *by the Internal Revenue Department, which had come forward with its claim on the sale of a play that the previous Administration had seemingly agreed to."*

La Précisionniste rides again. a) It is, of course, the Internal Revenue *Service*, not Department; b) if she means to say that her companion Dashiell Hammett should have been excused from paying the same taxes other people pay on equivalent income (perhaps because, as a Communist, he was entitled to preferential treatment?), then let her *say* that; c) the IRS doesn't "agree" to the sale of a play, but might have agreed to accept a taxation base: in any event, the tax levied by IRS was on profit; to say nothing of the fact that d) Lillian Hellman is not Vivien Kellems' sister. The latter was the authentic American Poujadiste, and when *she* complained about taxes, she spoke from the bowels of principle. When Lillian Hellman complains about high taxes, she is complaining about the monster she suckled.

What does one go on to say about a book so disorderly, so tasteless, guileful, self-enraptured? The disposition to adore her, feel sorry for her, glow in the vicarious thrill of her courage and decency (her favorite word, "decency": she is apolitical now, she says, desiring only "decency") runs into hurdle after hurdle in the obstacle course of this little book. Consider. It is 1952, and she is living in her townhouse in New York, and the buzzer rings. *"An over-respectable-looking black man . . . stood in the elevator, his hat politely removed. He asked me if I was Lillian Hellman. I agreed to that and asked who he was. He handed me an envelope and said he was there to serve a subpoena from the House Un-American Activities Committee. I opened the envelope and read the subpoena. I said, 'Smart to choose a black man for this job. You like it?' and slammed the door."*

Ah, the decent of this earth. The same lady who in her book tells us that she will not style her life to political fashion, now refers to her visitor, back in 1952, as "black," when of course that word was unused in 1952. Miss Hellman was brought up in New Orleans where, paradoxical though it may seem, the same class of people who institutionalized Jim

Crow never (I speak of the decent members of that class) humiliated individual members of the Negro race. It is difficult to imagine suggesting to a Negro bureaucrat who has merely performed a job assigned to him that he is collusively engaged in anti-Negro activity; impossible to understand a civilized woman slamming the door in the face of someone—a messenger—executing a clerical duty. Truly, the lady's emotions are ungoverned, and perhaps ungovernable. She seems to like to advertise this. *"I have a temper and it is triggered at odd times by odd matters and is then out of my control."* And, elsewhere, talking about her "black" nanny, she reveals that she was given *"anger—an uncomfortable, dangerous, and often useful gift."* To be used against black messengers bearing instructions from Washington, but on no account against white messengers bearing instructions from Moscow.

The author, though she attempts to project a moral for our time out of her own travail, does this less avidly than most of her critics, who seized greedily on this mincing tale of self-pity as the matrix of a passion play. It doesn't work. The heart of her failure beats in a single sentence. *". . . whatever our mistakes, I do not believe we did our country any harm."*

"Dear Lillian Hellman," the socialist Irving Howe writes, "you could not be more mistaken! Those who supported Stalinism and its political enterprises, either here or abroad, helped befoul the cultural atmosphere, helped bring totalitarian methods into trade unions, helped perpetuate one of the great lies of the century, helped destroy whatever possibilities there might have been for a resurgence of serious radicalism in America. Isn't that harm enough?"

What were we supposed to defend, William Phillips of *Partisan Review*, himself an ex-Communist, asks. "Some *were* Communists, and what one was asked to defend was their right to lie about it."

The message of Lillian Hellman, says Hilton Kramer of the New York *Times*, is rendered in *"soigné* prose," causing one to wonder if one ought to be less sensitive than Khrushchev in denouncing the work of his predecessor. But it was Providence that provided the epilogue, the ironic masterstroke. Lillian Hellman, best-selling author of the diatribe against the Hollywood moguls who discriminated against her after she was identified as a Communist apologist. When Miss Hellman finally brought herself to criticize the Soviet Union, she singled out for special scorn Soviet censorship. *"The semi-literate bureaucrats, who suppress and alter manuscripts, who dictate who can and cannot be published, perform a disgusting business."* And lo! the publishers of Miss Hellman's book, Little, Brown, instruct Diana Trilling to alter an essay on Miss Hellman in her manuscript. Mrs. Trilling declines, and Little, Brown breaks the contract—does its best, in effect, to suppress her book. "Miss Hellman is one of our leading successful authors," said Arthur Thornhill, president of Little, Brown. "She's not one of the big so-called money makers, but she's up there where we enjoy the revenue." The principled Miss Hellman, who condemns Hollywood for its base concern for profit, has not severed her relations with Little, Brown, never mind that they sought to suppress and alter a manuscript—in deference to *her!* But, don't you see, the vertebral column of her thought finally emerges. *She* can do no wrong. *"There is nothing in my life of which I am ashamed,"* she wrote to the chairman of the House Committee on Un-American Activities, setting herself, by that sentence, in a class apart from her fellow mortals. Well, it took a long time for her to learn about Communism. She is elderly, but there is time yet, time to recognize that she should be ashamed of this awful book.

Tail Gunner Joe

February 24, 1977

IN THE LATE Fifties, Richard Rovere published a book on the late Senator Joe McCarthy which was greeted as deliriously as Lillian Hellman's recent book, *Scoundrel Time*, the implicit thesis of which is that anybody who thought ill of Josef Stalin before she did, which was some time after he died, was, well, a scoundrel. Rovere's book was called "a brilliant essay in contemporary history" by Professor Arthur Schlesinger, Jr., "one of the most distinguished political documents of the year" by Eric Goldman, and, by Walter Lippmann himself, "the definitive job . . . I can't imagine what else there is to say about him."

In that book, published seventeen years before the networks thought to come up with a dramatization of the Joe McCarthy story, the resourceful Mr. Rovere found Senator McCarthy "a cheap politician" "a guttersnipe" "a seditionist" "a crook" "a foul-mouthed bum" "a mucker" "a liar" "a ranter" "a screamer" "a faker" "an ogre" and "a rattlesnake." Reviewing that book in England, Mr. Evelyn Waugh judged it favorably, but confessed to some misgivings about certain uncompleted bits of narrative. What actually had happened to McCarthy's victims? "There is a curious raggedness . . . in the accounts of the various inquiries which seem to have ended without findings and of the various men who appear and disappear in the story without acquittal or prosecution. What happened to everyone? I wish Mr. Rovere would re-write the book for us ignorant islanders giving us the simple story. We can make the comments."

I wrote to Mr. Waugh at the time and told him that if he was concerned to know such facts, I would send them to him, but I warned that they would distract from the unleavened judgment of McCarthyism in which the Western world basked; and which now, with the television spectacular "Tail Gunner Joe," has been revived. He wrote and asked for the material, and I sent him the book written by Mr. Brent Bozell and me in 1954 called *McCarthy and His Enemies.*

In due course he acknowledged it: "McCarthy is certainly regarded by most Englishmen as a regrettable figure and your *McCarthy and His Enemies,* being written before his later extravagances, will not go far to clear his reputation. I have no doubt that we were sent a lot of prejudiced information six years ago. [I.e., at the height of the McCarthy era.] Your book makes plain that there was a need for investigation ten years ago. It does not, I am afraid, supply the information that will convince me that McCarthy was a suitable man to undertake it. Rovere makes a number of precise charges against his personal honor. Until these are rebutted, those who are sympathetic with his cause must deplore his championship of it."

This, of course, is the crucial point now that anti-McCarthyism has become, once again, the rage. The thrust of the television spectacular was that McCarthy was a mountebank. And indeed by the rules of logic Mr. Waugh could be correct. It could transpire that the anti-McCarthy legend based on his role and the government's in the matter of internal security is altogether false—and still it could stand that McCarthy died of drink, cheated on his taxes, lied in his election campaigns, malingered in the marines—that he was, in Mr. Rovere's elegant word, a Rattlesnake.

But of course, these distinctions are not being observed. There is no significant discussion of Owen Lattimore in "Tail Gunner Joe," none of the successful lengths to which the Communist propaganda machine had gone in convincing such as Lillian Hellman that Stalin who presided over the show trials was a hero, and John Dewey who accused him of staging the trials, a scoundrel. During the Fifties, the Soviet Union consolidated its hold on Eastern Europe, the Chinese Communists theirs on the mainland, our atomic secrets were stolen and exploited, a small group of American Stalinists mounted a major political movement under the titular leadership of Henry Wallace; and now, looking back on the Fifties, NBC devotes itself to the character of Joe McCarthy. It is more than a great cop-out. It is a grand feint. And the most pathetic victims of it are those who write so exultantly about "Tail Gunner Joe."

Mr. John Leonard of the New York *Times*, reviewing the television spectacular, writes that during the McCarthy years "we seemed willing to believe that there were more Communists—in the army, in the clergy, in the State Department, in the glove compartments of our cars—than there were Americans. Books were burned and teachers were fired and writers went to jail and intellectuals cultivated their own gardens . . ."

Now those readers so unfortunate as not to be familiar with the work of Mr. Leonard should know at least this about him, that Tom Wolfe aside, he is the funniest writer in America, the hottest epigrammatist in the language, with a sense of irony the equal of Murray Kempton's, a prose rich as Rimsky-Korsakov—but he suffers from a sad failure quite to connect with reality, notwithstanding a precocious flirtation with conservatism in his early twenties. Hyperbole is one of his wonderful strengths. "One can't disagree that We the People made McCarthy," he writes, "any more than one can disagree with the proposition that death is sad or that sex is less so. But are such pious observations very helpful? On television, there is no shortage of natural gas."

Ah, our tortured poets! But those who believe that Mr. Leonard's delirium is a particular disease have forgotten the history of the era, where the excesses were far less McCarthy's, than his critics'. In those days there actually convened in plenipotentiary sessions six professors at Haverford who dubbed themselves "The Unterrified," and plotted how to rescue America from McCarthy. And there was of course the rabbi who preached that the student panty-raids were the result of the internalization of student exuberance caused by the Terror. There were those wonderful attempts at open-mindedness, of which my favorite remains the Dalton School's response to a girl who complained that McCarthy's side had not once been given. In the spirit of free inquiry, the dean thereupon scheduled a debate on the topic, "Resolved, That McCarthy's Un-American Activities are Justified."

Lord Bertrand Russell actually said that McCarthy had made it unsafe for Americans to read Thomas Jefferson. Mr. Robert Hutchins actually said that so cowed were we all by McCarthy that it took courage to contribute support to Harvard University (where Mr. Leonard was incompletely educated—could it have been the shortage of funds caused by McCarthy?).

McCarthy, up through the Tydings investigation which gave him the notoriety off which "Tail Gunner Joe" coasts, named—and only when required to do so by the Tydings Committee—a total of forty-four persons, whom with a single exception (Owen Lattimore) he designated as loyalty risks.

The writers who went to jail are the Hollywood Ten, for committing exactly the same offense for which Judge Sirica sentenced Gordon Liddy to twenty years in jail, getting for himself in return the Man of the Year award from *Time* Magazine: contempt of a duly constituted government board of inquiry. The loudest protester, Mr. Dalton Trumbo, subsequently revealed *sua sponte* that, what do you know, he had indeed been a member of the Communist Party during the period under investigation.

If anyone undertook today to write a screenplay about the fraternity of teachers, intellectuals, and writers who smeared as fascists or warmongers anyone in America who criticized Josef Stalin, railed against the Hitler-Stalin Pact, defended the innocent at the purge trials, denounced the repatriation of 16 million East Europeans to their death in Soviet camps—that play would likely not be produced. And if by chance it were, it would either be *ho-hummed* to death, or rigorously denounced, probably as McCarthyite. It is more fun to laugh with Woody Allen at those Americans who resented the greatest diplomatic reversal in human history than to wonder, darkly, about the extent to which we were responsible for the Gulag Archipelago.

Let those who amuse themselves by asking that McCarthy be judged by the deficiencies in his character get on with it— this is after all the season for judging Thomas Jefferson on the basis of the mulattoes he sired. But in the process, we are coming very close to judging the decade of the Fifties as one in which the great moral divide was between the McCarthyites and the apologists for the Soviet Union. The substantial anti-McCarthyite, anti-Stalinist liberals received such disdainful treatment as was awarded them in the Lillian Hellman book—which is historically, morally, and intellectually destroyed by Professor Sidney Hook in the current issue of London's *Encounter* magazine. There were some foolish things done and said by McCarthy and some of his supporters during the Fifties. But they cannot hold a candle up against the continuing excesses of McCarthy's critics.

I remember Paul Hughes

March 5, 1977

I HAD RESOLVED to give up for Lent any mention of Paul
Hughes now that we have been catapulted back into a general discussion of the McCarthy years. But this proves impossible now that I have seen a statement by Mr. Alfred Friendly,
retired managing editor of the Washington *Post*, indignantly
denying any wrongdoing in his association with Paul
Hughes. The Hughes story is probably the single most embarrassing thing that happened in the Fifties to the liberal
Establishment. The success of their subsequent cover-up is
the kind of thing Nixon dreams about in his prison at San
Clemente. Mr. Friendly, in his reminiscences about the
McCarthy years, notes that the "best book" ever written
about McCarthy is Richard Rovere's (*Senator Joe McCarthy*,
1959). When *National Review* exposed the Hughes case in
1956, the editors teased the court historians for failing to
write about it. Mr. Rovere replied huffily, "I agree . . . that
the Hughes case is full of import. I know that I shall deal
with the Hughes case in [my forthcoming book]." But Paul
Hughes was not mentioned in the book.

Paul Hughes was a young confidence man. He represented himself, in 1953, to Joseph L. Rauh, Jr., the civil rights
lawyer; to Clayton Fritchey, then editor of the official journal
of the Democratic Party; and to Alfred Friendly, representing the Washington *Post*, as a disaffected member of Senator
Joe McCarthy's Senate staff, willing to feed Rauh, Friendly, *et
al.* confidential information about McCarthy. Rauh's opposition to secret informers vanished overnight, and there was
cranked up surely the strangest transmission belt in modern
history, establishing a credulousness among top American
liberals that would make John Birchers blush.

He gave them "evidence" of a secret alliance between Eisenhower and McCarthy; of tantalizing rivalries between the
staffs of the Internal Security Committee and the McCarthy
Committee; of imminent plans to enter into forbidden communication with Igor Gouzenko, the Soviet defector in Cana-

da; of marital problems developing between Senator and Mrs. McCarthy; of a clandestine White House conference at which a smear campaign against the Democratic Party was programmed; of McCarthy's informers in the White House, in the Louisville *Courier-Journal,* in the New York *Post* (the cooking editor); excruciating teasers about informants whose identity had not been disclosed; and (my very favorite) news that Senator McCarthy had amassed an arsenal of pistols, Lügers, and submachine guns in the basement of the Senate Office Building. All this wrapped up in a chaotic package of notes, official memoranda, interoffice communications, secret transcripts, some illiterate, some eloquent, always steaming with drama and emitting a sex appeal irresistible to the professional anti-McCarthyites.

Now this association continued with, and a sum of almost $11,000 was paid over to, a man who had written what nowadays might be called a premature Huston Plan. The memo dated December 1953, from Paul Hughes to Clayton Fritchey, prepared for Joseph Rauh, said: "Phone taps can be utilized [against McCarthy] . . . Don't discount the tremendous values in just bargaining power of recorded phone discussions . . . A program of this type, although not nice, can result in harm to no one except [McCarthy] . . . As mentioned earlier, being nice, too ethical, or squeamish, will accomplish less than nothing . . . I don't see the necessity for us to send a boy to do a man's work."

Eventually, after *nine months* of association, on the eve of publishing the definitive exposé of McCarthy, researchers for the Washington *Post* went to work and discovered that the whole thing was a phony. There was a trial: at which the jury refused to take the word of Hughes's employers, freeing him and disgracing them. But you won't read about it in the history books, let alone see it dramatized in "Tail Gunner Joe."(You can, however, get the whole story in "The Case of the Secret Informer, *or,* The Terrible Disappointment of Joseph L. Rauh," *NR*, Feb. 8, 1956.) I say it again, the story of McCarthy cannot be told without telling the infinitely more complex story of his enemies.

Commemorating Paul Robeson

February 14, 1976

THE DEATH of Paul Robeson was widely noticed, and his accomplishments, as an athlete, young lawyer, singer and actor, widely remarked. Then there was, to be sure, that other business. Here is how *Time* magazine handled it. ". . . Always he felt hemmed in by the constraints upon blacks . . . In the mid-1940's and 1950's, he was an outspoken champion of civil rights. He moved for a time to the Soviet Union where he thought that blacks had more freedom and where he sent his only son to school. Condemned at home in the McCarthy era as an admirer of the Soviet Union and a friend of Communism, Robeson went into a clouded decline from which he never emerged. Stricken by a circulatory ailment in 1963, he spent his last years in seclusion . . ."

Now the editors of *Time*, who are high practitioners of literary precision, know that the clause, "Condemned at home in the McCarthy era as an admirer of the Soviet Union and a friend of Communism," is intended to denote a fuller understanding than the mere words convey. The statement is intended to be read, "[Falsely] condemned at home in the [hysterical] McCarthy era as an admirer of the Soviet Union and a friend of Communism [which of course he wasn't]"—and it makes one muse ruefully that Senator McCarthy never attempted in his lifetime as much historical revisionism as some of his detractors commit in his name.

Now take Robeson. In 1947, he earned $104,000, singing and acting in America. In 1948, the great decline began. All of America stopped listening. "But for the $30,000 he got for a 1949 concert tour in England, he really might have starved to death," Carl Rowan wrote in the late 1950's, interviewing Robeson.

Now, what happened in 1948? Did Joe McCarthy eat Mrs. Roosevelt? Did he call Shirley Temple a Communist? Did he demand that anyone who defended civil rights for Negroes should be banned from the recital halls of the nation?

No, as a matter of fact. In 1948 Senator McCarthy was totally unknown, a junior senator from Wisconsin who was poking around the edges of one or two controversies, none of them related to Communism. But here is what *did* happen in 1948. The Soviet Union staged a coup in mid-day, collapsing the freedom of Czechoslovakia, for which freedom the British, in 1938 and 1939, promised to fight if necessary by war.

In 1948 the fury of Stalin's purges was becoming known in the West, as defectors wrote about life under his terror. In 1948, crucial atom bomb secrets were delivered to Russia by Soviet agents. In America, the Communist Party mounted a Presidential candidate, dubbed by Mrs. Luce as "Stalin's Mortimer Snerd." By the time the vote came, Henry Wallace was so discredited for his obvious manipulation by Moscow that he got the vote of a mere handful of people.

Senator McCarthy began his notoriety in Wheeling, West Virginia, in 1950. By that time, Robeson was already a pariah in America.

Because of his outspoken championship of civil rights?

Robeson never cared for civil rights in general. He was prophetically right in denouncing Jim Crow. He said he desired civil rights for American Negroes. But it cannot even be assumed that there was a genuine purity in his attachment to black rights, for all his talk about his identification with black people everywhere in the world. Because when such African states as he praised—Ghana, in particular—systematically denied civil rights to their black citizens, there was no protest from Robeson.

Robeson was, quite simply, a Communist fellow-traveler, whose service to the Soviet Union began in the mid-Thirties, who took his son there to school in the late Thirties, who accepted a Peace Prize from Stalin in 1952, who denied in 1946 that he was a Communist but a year later invoked the Fifth Amendment when asked the question again; who was denied a passport when Dean Acheson was Secretary of State— Acheson being the premier anti-McCarthyite in government; who, even when the State Department authorized him to visit Canada, was denied entrance into Canada.

In 1963, a Reuters dispatch from London reported ru-

mors "that the singer would give up Communism." These were denied by Robeson.
Contributions to *Time*'s morgue will be gratefully received.

Honoring Linus Pauling

September 30, 1975

THE BOSTON *Globe* is positively shimmering with pleasure over the award given by President Ford to Professor Linus Pauling. The writers call their editorial "Tardy Honor," and they speak in it of the belated recognition by the President of Dr. Pauling's "contribution to society" which goes "further than his accomplishments in either chemistry or politics."
   Why was the honor belated?
   Because Dr. Pauling "was considered a dangerous radical—a Communist sympathizer, even—by such authorities as Senator Joseph McCarthy, Herbert A. Philbrick, Louis Budenz and William Buckley."
   My dear friends on the Boston *Globe* have never before referred to me so matter-of-factly as an "authority," and I really do appreciate it. But candor requires that I share the honor, however belatedly, with others.
   In 1961, the Senate's Internal Security Subcommittee issued an extensive report on the activities of Linus Pauling. The report concluded: "Dr. Pauling has figured as the No. 1 scientific name in virtually every major activity of the Communist peace offensive in this country. He has participated in many international organizations and international conferences sponsored by the Communist peace offensive. In his statements and his attitudes, Dr. Pauling has displayed a consistent pro-Soviet bias."
   That report was accepted unanimously by: Senators James Eastland, Estes Kefauver, Olin Johnson, John McClellan, Sam Ervin, John Carroll, Thomas Dodd, Philip Hart, Edward Long, William Blakely, Alexander Wiley, Everett

Dirksen, Roman Hruska, Kenneth Keating, Norris Cotton. The editors of the *Herald Tribune* also should share in the honor. In an editorial in the 1960's they said "The Linus Paulings of the world have . . . made themselves not only nuisances, but dangerous nuisances." *Life* magazine's editors also deserve credit. When the Nobel Committee gave Pauling its peace prize, the editors denounced the choice as "A Weird Insult from Norway."

In New York alone, the *Wall Street Journal, The World Telegram and Sun,* the *Daily Mirror,* and the *Daily News* remarked similarly on the activities of Linus Pauling. And it wasn't just Americans who were authorities on Linus Pauling's activities. The Australian Consolidated Press during that period said about him that though no one doubted his scientific ability, in fact "he is the very model of the fellow-traveler of the type who willingly adds respectability to Communist frauds. He signs Communist petitions, he speaks from Communist platforms, he has his speeches published by Communist presses. He has, however, never been heard to say one word of criticism . . . of Soviet terrorism or of the lack of freedom for Soviet scientists."

The Court of Appeals in New York upheld a jury verdict for the New York *Daily News,* sued by Linus Pauling for calling him a Communist sympathizer. Judge Friendly, in his opinion, said in effect that surveying the evidence a jury could reasonably conclude that Dr. Pauling was that: a Communist sympathizer.

We authorities on the subject were influenced by Pauling's organizational affiliations, of course, but also by other things. By his telegram to President Kennedy denouncing Kennedy's Cuban missile crisis ultimatum as "horrifying," "recklessly militaristic," "warlike." We noticed it when he said about President Truman, for deciding to proceed with nuclear testing as necessary, that Truman was "irrational, ignorant or unscrupulous, or any combination of each." And we noticed the telegram he sent to President Kennedy on March 3, 1962, denouncing him for resuming nuclear testing after the Soviets resumed theirs: "Are you to go down in history as one of the most immoral men of all times and one of the greatest enemies of the human race?" And Pauling's support of M. S. Arnoni's publication which compared President Kennedy adversely to Hitler, and described Kennedy as a "bully who knows himself to be a bully."

The Boston *Globe*, which gave its readers the impression that President Ford was righting great historical wrongs against Dr. Pauling, did not bother to give the citation on the Medal of Science, so this authority on Linus Pauling called down to the White House and got it. It reads, in its entirety: "To Linus C. Pauling, for the extraordinary scope and power of his imagination, which has led to basic contributions in such diverse fields as structural chemistry and the nature of chemical bonding, molecular biology, immunology, and the nature of genetic diseases." If President Ford gives William Schockley one of those Science Medals, will the *Globe* write that this vindicates his genetic theses?

A Tory's Tribute to Hubert Horatio Humphrey

December 1977

WHAT IS HAPPENING to Hubert Humphrey is unparalleled in my memory. The apocalyptic word was used by the doctors after his latest operation—he suffered from a "terminal" illness. In what seemed no time at all, he reappeared on the public scene. Scooped up from the clinic by Air Force One, he was to find the entire nation celebrating him like Lindbergh come home. A huge new federal building was named after him. The House of Representatives invited him over from the Senate to give a speech—unprecedented in congressional annals—and he came, occupying the podium used by Presidents of the United States when addressing joint sessions of Congress. He was visibly withered by his experience at the clinics, but otherwise he was unchanged. The same horizon-to-horizon smile, the twinkle in the eyes, the unabashed reference to his longtime ambition to occupy the podium *ex officio*. He was cheered as lustily as anyone in memory, cheered by everyone, on both sides of the aisle, notwithstanding that he has political enemies on both sides—a few on the Democratic side, everyone on the Republican side. It did not matter. There was the familiarity of the figure. His renowned good nature. The tear-drawing physical heroism. The indomitable cheerfulness.

Moreover, the tribute was for a man as partisan as ever sat in the Senate. But it didn't—doesn't—matter. It is worth asking why. To do so requires examining the ideological and intellectual opposition to Senator Humphrey, his works and his ways, if we are to plumb the deepest of the mysteries: How is it that *we* feel this way about him?

We write, all of us, on the assumption that Hubert Humphrey is going down. It is, of course, possible; indeed, in the larger context, probable. All of us who visit the doctor after a certain age do so to frustrate, but only temporarily, a degenerative ineluctability. It is so even for Hubert Horatio Humphrey. The only political promise he neglected to make to his constituencies—and he speaks nowadays to the grandchildren of those he addressed back when he was running for mayor of Minneapolis—was that a vote for the Democratic Party would bring eternal youth.

But having said that, a proper skepticism is in order respecting Hubert Humphrey. He may frustrate the laws of probability, yet again; and surely there is nobody in the world better practiced than he at defying the laws of logic—that being, of course, his profession; and, I assume, not an inconsiderable reason for his appeal. To exercise the politics of joy, it is required to release one's constituency from the depressing restraints of reality and reason.

Dear Lord, you must understand when—many years hence we all devoutly hope—your servant Hubert appears before you that he is *different* from most of your creatures. Deal kindly with him, on the Day of Judgment, and above all, do not instruct the registrar to read back to you any of Hubert's political speeches. We are dimly aware, down here, of the divine tension between the demands of mercy and justice. But so help me, God, if you listen to one of his speeches, the demands of justice are going to get the better of you. And although I am a Tory, born and bred, with absolutely no ambitions to transcend that estate, I do not wish, for Hubert Humphrey, exemplary justice. I will try to explain.

The last coast-to-coast speech by Senator Humphrey was delivered at Madison Square Garden, on July 13, 1976, to the Democratic National Convention gathered together to nominate Jimmy Carter as candidate for President of the United States. The night before had been opening night, with several speeches, the first by keynoter John Glenn. Concerning that speech, the less said the better. One might call it (indeed, on the occasion, one did) "Senator Glenn without Houston Control." Democratic choreographers, clearly worried about the prospective ratings after reading the text of Senator Glenn's speech, scheduled their oratorical Big Bertha, Barbara Jordan. She was airborne by her native eloquence, which is lucky—because for all that the lady stirred the Convention, in fact she had nothing to say, never mind that, when she was done, everyone cooed that here had been a "great oration" (almost everyone's evaluation, including Barry Goldwater's).

I would be surprised if anybody, an hour later, could have written a fifty-word précis of what Mrs. Jordan said with such rapture. But she used with abandon one of the Senator's favorite rhetorical devices, namely paralepsis, with which Hubert Humphrey, the sometime graduate student in political science, is no doubt formally familiar. "I could easily spend this time praising the accomplishments of this party and attacking the record of the Republicans. I do not choose to do that," said Mrs. Jordan, proceeding to do exactly, and lengthily, that. The television cameras focused on Senator Humphrey, seated in his box, beaming. His beam was required over a very long evening, but it did not begin to tax his reserves—Hubert Humphrey could have beamed, start to finish, through the Hundred Years War.

George Wallace had a speech to make, in which he denounced the "monstrous bureaucracy" in Washington that had recently forbidden a father-son dinner at one of HEW's pads, on the grounds that such exclusivity violated the rights of women. Hubert Humphrey was pensive during that one—his jaw resting in his right palm, the striated fingers of wisdom partially covering mouth and cheek. On and on. Jerry Wurf spoke about the need to enfranchise civil servants, and Humphrey nodded his head in solemn assent. Edmund Muskie spoke about the need to "say yes to fair labor standards" as if everywhere in America man was in chains. Barbara Jordan's central point—not entirely unfamiliar to students of political oratory—was that the great American people are possessed of great common sense. This they demonstrated that evening. The Nielsen raters the following day disclosed matter-of-factly that the great Democratic spectacle, covered by all three networks, reached fewer Americans in the New York area than the film *Casablanca*, shown for the tenth time on an independent channel, and filmed in 1942, about the time that Hubert Humphrey, who would be featured on the following night, was deciding to give up academic studies in order to enter politics.

Tuesday evening, as I say, was Hubert Humphrey's. It was generally assumed by the crowd that he would do his very best, which, under the aspect of the heavens, is of course his very worst. From time to time acrid political commentators are inclined to say, after a bad experience, that this, "*surely*," ranked as the "worst speech" in "political history." No one, of course, can pretend to the requisite experience to say such a thing with authority. About Hubert Humphrey's speech on July 13 one could only say that it was so triumphantly awful that he reached the darker partisan heart of his audience, who gave him a standing ovation.

"Do you know how I became mayor of Minneapolis?"— Hubert Humphrey twinkled the technique a generation ago to a former fellow graduate student at a cocktail party. "He spoke *delightedly* on the subject," my professor-friend recalls, without any trace of irritation, let alone condescension. He quoted Humphrey. "Well, I spoke *every* Saturday, and *every* Sunday, at the parks in Minneapolis—there are lots of parks in Minneapolis, you know. And, after the crowd would gather, I would pick up the microphone, and I'd begin to talk. Then—suddenly—I'd stop. And I'd say: 'Wait a minute. Wait a *minute*, I want to see the kids here up front. They're the future of the nation, folks, let's face it, *your* kids. Now come on up here. Don't be shy! That's it . . . right up front, sit down and make yourselves comfortable. Right. Now, as I was saying . . . But I have to say *something else* first. You know, I've been around. I know the great state of Minnesota the way few folks know the state of Minnesota. But I know other states of the Union too, and let me tell you something, ladies and gentlemen: these kids here have got to be the *most* beautiful, the most *wonderful*-looking, the *healthiest* kids I have ever seen . . . *anywhere!'*

"The parents," Humphrey exclaimed to his friend, "would look up at me . . . *adoringly!* Then you know what?"—he put his arm over the professor's back—"*Later* in the *same* afternoon, speaking to *another* audience, at *another* park, at *another* end of the city, I would say . . . *exactly the same thing!*" The miracle of the multiplication of the loaves!

I doubt that anyone in the days ahead will devote much attention to a textual analysis of Hubert Humphrey's speeches. It would be an unfriendly thing to do, and infinitely unprofitable. And, of course, it would miss the point about Humphrey, the point being that he is a great human figure (like Eleanor Roosevelt), never mind that if any civil constitution should ever be written as a congeries of deductions from Humphrey's Laws, the citizenry would all be smiling at each other in a federal zoo that disdained to distinguish between a mole and a giraffe.

At Madison Square Garden—as I say, his most recent coast-to-coast political oration—he began with that brazen defiance of reason that levitates an audience by vacuuming off all sense of reality. What Senator Humphrey said, at the Democratic Convention after the one that nominated for President a Democrat who proceeded to lose every state in the Union save Massachusetts—what he said, referring to the forthcoming election, was: "And once again, [after Carter's victory] the American people will have a friend in the White House, and majority government will have been restored." The sweep of such presumptuousness is its indispensable yeast. It is like the meeting of a Communist International at which the keynote speaker begins by saying, "As everyone knows, the United States is the last surviving imperialist power on earth." It has always been indispensable to Humphrey-the-orator that distinctions, qualifiers, taxonomic niceties, must *never* stand in the way of the Main Purpose. Hubert Humphrey has *never* been publicly distracted by mere events. The San Francisco fire would not have interrupted a tribute by Humphrey to California fire laws. He is out of this world.

But insufficiently so, as we see, with ineffable grief, the workings of the mortal coils, transfiguring his physical image.

No, nothing publicly disturbed Hubert Humphrey's famous equilibrium, in sickness or in health. Even his famous walk-out in the 1948 Convention seems rhythmic, in retrospect. And then twenty years later, late on the Saturday night before the tumultuous Convention in Chicago that finally nominated him for President, Humphrey appeared on the "Irv Kupcinet Show." The show had been taped. In the course of elaborating to Kupcinet the great triumphs of President Johnson's foreign policy in Europe—never mind for a moment the problem of Vietnam—Vice-President Humphrey said happily that, just for example, the East European nations were by now "relatively autonomous." Unhappily, between the time Humphrey spoke those words and the time, one week later, that they were broadcast, the Soviet Union sent tanks into Prague to dispose, for good and all, of any autonomous blooms of the Czechoslovakian spring.

When Mr. Humphrey became Vice-President, he had campaigned on the Atlantic City Democratic platform. "We pledge unflagging devotion to our commitments to freedom from Berlin to South Vietnam." A few days after the Kupcinet show, in the debris of Chicago, Hubert Humphrey managed, with consummate skill, to address successfully the Convention, one-half of which had wanted to nominate Eugene McCarthy, on the Vietnam War. The shadow on his right was President Lyndon Johnson, whose inflexibility on the subject of Vietnam had been validated by a parliamentary majority of the Convention after bitter debate. Without Johnson's support, Candidate Humphrey would never make it to the White House. The shadow on his left was Eugene McCarthy. Without propitiating him and his followers, Humphrey would never make it to the White House.

The performance was superb. Candidate Humphrey got his biggest cheers by insisting he would devote himself to ending the war in Vietnam. What he actually said about his devotion to peace in Vietnam wasn't anything different from what Candidate Nixon—or, for that matter, Superhawk Barry Goldwater—would have said. But Humphrey said it with inflections so wonderfully, so endearingly acquiescent to the shadow on his left, that he succeeded in appearing to draw over his stout shoulders the lonely cloak of righteousness, thus giving the impression that he spoke for the desolate minority, against the obdurate majority. When, listening to his oration, one began to ask oneself, might he be annoying, irritating, that unforgiving shadow on his right?—somehow he would manage a compensating inflection, something on the order of "winning is not worth a compact with extremism," being careful not to identify extremism (let Gene McCarthy think he was talking about Mayor Daley, and let LBJ think he was talking about Gene McCarthy).

But Hubert Humphrey, privately, is no more immune to the irritations of the season than his body is to the impartial appetites of the runaway, roustabout human cell. It was about a year later that ex-President Lyndon Johnson, in one of those exclusive interviews with CBS, said to Walter Cronkite that in Johnson's opinion Humphrey had lost the Presidency by "backing down" on Vietnam in his speech in October at Salt Lake City. A colleague of Humphrey, who had been with him that evening listening together to LBJ, later quoted Hubert's private reaction. It was colorful, definitely not for Kupcinet's show, most definitely not right for a speech to a Democratic National Convention. Turning off the switch, Humphrey said heatedly to his friend, "I really wish I *was* President. Because if I *was*, I'd dispatch the Israeli Army to Cairo to pick up Cleopatra's Needle, take it to Johnson City, and stuff it up the biggest ass-hole in Texas." One always suspected that Hubert's red corpuscles were exercised other than by the universal need for more jobs, better housing, better health care, and equal treatment under the law.

Hubert's animadversions have almost always been general, rather than private. To speak about Republican scoundrels was always easier on his good nature than to speak about individual Republican scoundrels. Fighting for his political future against George McGovern in the California primary in

June 1972, Humphrey began their public debate with an apology. Earlier in the week, he explained, he had said that people who believe in confiscatory taxation are foolish. On reflection, he feared that some people would think that he had said his colleague George McGovern was a "fool." Such people would be wrong, and if he had given them that impression, he wanted here and now to "apologize." Political exchanges are not models of syllogistic form. Granted that in a classroom, Professor Humphrey would have been obliged to put it this way: (1) People who believe in confiscatory taxation are fools. (2) George McGovern believes in confiscatory taxation. Therefore, (3) George McGovern is a fool.

But Hubert Humphrey's career has been spent in ignoring the mute reproaches of logic. In September 1968, Candidate Humphrey intoned before a convention of the B'nai B'rith that Nixon had chosen to join forces with "the most reactionary elements in American society," by which he meant George Wallace, whose third-party candidacy was impinging on Humphrey's Democratic support. One year earlier, Vice-President Humphrey had been photographed arm-in-arm with Governor Lester Maddox in Atlanta, Georgia. On that occasion he had said, "The Democratic Party is like a big house and has lots of room for all of us. I am happy to be in the presence of a good Democrat."

And so on, year after year, sponsoring a bill to outlaw the Communist Party in 1954, expressing himself as devoted, to the end, to South Vietnamese freedom in 1968, preparatory to saying in 1972 that he was in favor of cutting off the South Vietnamese "flat" because they were "in my judgment" "capable of their own defense." When the need would come to dodge on an issue, as in the California primary on the question of busing, he would say deprecatingly that busing "is only *one* of the many tools to effect integration," which was to say something as illuminating as that paper is only one of the constituents of pornography.

Ah, but that final speech at Madison Square Garden, when Hubert Humphrey, having lost the primaries to Jimmy Carter, must have reasoned—his physical health aside—that he had had his last crack at the Presidency. But he would rouse the Convention, after the torpor of Monday night. First, as we have seen, he denied the democratic credentials of the incumbent Administration, which required merely that his audience ignore an electoral victory of 521 to 17. Then he would find just-the-right-word for the Republicans in power, taking care to make no mention that the legislature, which passed all the bills, and spent all the money, and caused all the inflation, was solidly Democratic. He found a new word, or at least one I had not heard him use before. They were . . . "Tories."

"These modern Tories repudiate the magnificent legacy of Andrew Jackson and Woodrow Wilson; of Franklin Roosevelt and Harry Truman; of John Kennedy and Lyndon Johnson.

"There was no room for the Tories in Philadelphia in 1776. And I say there is no room for them in New York in 1976 or in Washington, D.C. in 1977!"

I know, I know. You know. *He* knows. The Tories in Philadelphia, *mutatis mutandis*, were the people who wrote the Constitution. But what does that matter, when the clamor of the crowd rings in the ear, when you know they will shout We Love Hubert! and the band will play, and everyone will rush to congratulate him. "That was a great speech!" the television viewer heard Bob Strauss, National Democratic Chairman, say. Perhaps Strauss had been singularly moved by Herbert Humphrey's passage, "After eight years of phases, freezes, and failure, of start-ups and slow-downs, of high prices and fewer jobs, we are still being asked 'just a little more time and patience.' Go slow, not now, no, no, veto—this is the Republican theme. This is their policy. Well, we've had enough of this defeatism!"

Ah, that causes the analytical blood to tingle with excitement!

Or was it the peroration?

"America looks to new leaders who can make our country both dynamic and just, who have a sense of compassion, but also dedication to individual initiative—leaders who can inspire and are inspired by our history, but who sense that our greatness is in the future.

"America's best days—America's great days—have only just begun!"

They speak about those marvelous new machines that one day will identify each one of us as surely as if they possessed our fingerprints, by scanning a stretch of prose. Hubert's will be unmistakable. Such prose as sets up dynamism and justice as dissonant, let alone antithetical; as suggests that compassion and initiative are disjunctive human impulses . . .

But how futile is the exercise, when we are engaged, in fact, in trying to console ourselves against the inconsolable reality, which is that this preposterous man, this man of majestic intellectual imprecision, this demagogue of transcendent gall, may not be with us forever. What is it about him that causes this sadness to well up, even in those Tories he has sought so diligently to exile?

I confess I do not have the answer. There are emotions—and quite properly so, is a Tory insight—that defy the taxonomic enterprise. Why do we care for him so? Why does his Las Vegas smile in fact light up the room? Why do we sit down and do our knitting, and let our eyeglasses slide down our nose, permit ourselves to smile—when Hubert is on TV, saying all those silly things? Why, when you talk to him, is there that inexplicable rise in human temperature, that makes *you* want to smile, like a blithering Democratic idiot making time at Madison Square Garden? Could it be that all that talk about civil rights and health care and old people and employment and slums and decent housing and nursery care and good education has, imperceptibly, but no less surely, sensitized the public conscience? So that we . . . *feel* more strongly than we used to do before Hubert called us to sit in the front row, and told us we were positively the prettiest children in town—and feel more keenly that concern for each other which, although it was enjoined by Jesus without cosmetics, lights, bands, or Potomac fever, never occupies us as devoutly as it should—is *that* what we love him for?

My experiences with him have been few, but one of them presses the memory. The forward compartment of the Pan Am 747 was very nearly empty. I think there were only eight or ten of us, but when the movie went on there was palpable excitement, because it was to be *The French Connection*, and we unhappy few hadn't seen it. What came on the screen was a frozen oscilloscope of sorts. After several attempts to fix it, the chief stewardess pronounced her apologies—something was wrong with the machine. There is within me, notwithstanding a lifetime's effort to suppress it, an impulse to intrusive do-gooding which from time to time simply takes me over, so that before my wife could succeed in manacling me to the seat, there I was, advising the chief stewardess that if she would get a screwdriver, I would be glad to draw the curtain on the insides of the machine and see if I could not put things right. I did not tell her that a screwdriver in my hand is less useful than a computer in the hands of an aborigine. My unexplicated rule of thumb is that screwdrivers have numinous powers when applied to the tangled webs of technology.

But after I unscrewed the underside panel of the machine and shone the flashlight up on the workings of the projector, acutely conscious of my expectant audience, my heart sank. I stared, as I'd have done at rows of Chinese calligraphy, when the voice under me spoke. "Come on, Bill. Get out of the way. You reactionaries wouldn't know how to fix a broken wheel." I took the flashlight out of my mouth, slithered back down the large intestine of the machine, and handed the light, and the screwdriver, to Hubert Humphrey, until two years earlier Vice-President of the United States. Taking the flashlight, he slid up into the darkness with total confidence, and began to bark orders to me. Screwdriver. Pliers. Something long and thin—"like a giant needle." At my disposal now was the 747's vast tool box, and I strove to please.

In the course of an hour he asked for everything except a Scotch and soda, with which, in my position as apprentice, rump on the staircase, head inside the projection bulkhead, I consoled myself. Hubert chattered on endlessly, reading aloud the arcane instructions that surrounded the tortuous passage the 16-millimeter film declined to follow. Finally the stewardess told me that dinner was being served, and I bellowed the information up to the spelunker, who was chatting away about how, finally, he was confident he had located the difficulty. Eventually I announced that I was capitulating, but that the entire inventory of tools was now within his reach. "You go ahead and eat, Bill. I'll have this licked in a minute."

It was two hours later that, defeated, he climbed wearily down, and exuberantly attacked his cold dinner. But meanwhile I was distracted. The captain of the airship had sent down word: Would I care to witness an instrument landing? He was a fan, and was waiving the no-spectator rule. Excitedly, as the sun came down over London, I strapped myself into the little extra chair in the cockpit, to witness the great technological feat. We were on the final descent when the dialogue was interrupted by a knock. The engineer opened the door slightly, and there was—Hubert Humphrey. "I wonder," he said beaming, "would it be all right if I also peeked?" My wife had given out the word of my whereabouts, and Hubert Humphrey was not about to go through life admitting that he had never witnessed an instrument landing even though a Tory had done so. The situation, in the tight little cockpit, was socially embarrassing because there was no extra seat, and the effort to proffer my own was acrobatically impossible. "No no no no no. I'll just squat down right here." Which he did, and, together, we witnessed that workaday miracle, a 747 making a perfect touchdown under the guidance of electronic hands. My companion, they say, is headed for another touchdown, under the guidance of other hands, but they will look after him, I feel certain, and smile at his inability to fix the machine on the 747, merely one more in a long series of terrestrial failures, but God knows he tried.

Senator Buckley vs. New York?

September 27, 1975

NEW YORK'S CONGRESSIONAL delegation is scandalized by one of its number, Senator James L. Buckley, who has outraged precedent by behaving honorably, which is, roughly speaking, the opposite of behaving politically. The congressional

delegation wants Washington, D.C., which is shorthand for
Duluth, Abilene, Fort Lauderdale, Bridgeport, Atlanta, and
Boise, to guarantee the maturing bonds of the City of New
York. Guaranteeing the bonds means making up the deficit,
because the revenues being generated by the City of New
York are insufficient to pay the obligations undertaken by
the City of New York. Senator Buckley, in a word, is being
vilified for declining to encourage other Americans to subsi-
dize New York City's extravagance and mismanagement. A
few observations:

1. There is in my opinion no reason at all to believe that
the people of New York City are as outraged as their politicians. The people of New York City are overtaxed as it is,
and there are no complaints heard more frequently among
them than against the extravagances of their own officials.
These have been countenanced in part because of the usual
inertia of the voters, in part because somehow the money has
materialized for all those extra services and all that welfare
and all that tuition-free guaranteed admission to city colleges. If the bonds go into default, it will mean very simply
that economies will have to be effected. The people of New
York are bound to benefit in due course from any move that
relieves them of the insidious burden of profligate spending.

2. A senator demeans the office if he considers it his primary function to wage a form of guerrilla warfare against
other states in the union, the purpose of which is to take as
much of the money that belongs to people who live out of
state as he can, in order to spend it at home. A senator especially demeans the office if he considers it his duty to invade
states poorer than his own, for the benefit of his own state.

3. A United States senator, as distinguished from a lobbyist
for New York City, has some responsibility to meditate the
consequences of his vote. Any guarantee by Washington,
D.C., of the obligations of New York City instantly encourages other cities—and quite rightly so—to demand similar
guarantees. And we revert to the old phenomenon of what I
have called a sky black with criss-crossing dollars. The people
who win those wars are the people with political muscle. That
they should also think of themselves—as most New York
congressmen have got into the habit of doing—as the world's

most conspicuous humanitarians, is accepted by people with stronger stomachs than my own, and lesser minds.

4. Representative Edward Koch, who prides himself on his own independence, now says of his colleagues in Congress, "We should be acting as a delegation and speaking with one voice." I find no sanction in American history, in the Constitution, in the Bill of Rights, or in the work of Edmund Burke, Thomas Jefferson, John Stuart Mill, or Oliver Wendell Holmes to endorse this generality of Mr. Koch. Translated, his statement says: "When we guys in New York get together to steal from other Americans, we ought to do it unanimously, since that way as individuals we are less exposed." Mr. Koch makes a demagogic but dangerous crack about Senator Buckley's previous residence in the neighboring state of Connecticut. Demagogic, because he never made such a reference to the previous residence of Senator Robert Kennedy. Dangerous because Connecticut pays out $1.54 for every $1.00 it receives from the Federal Government in welfare, whereas New York, which is wealthier than Connecticut, pays out only 98 cents for every $1.00 it receives.

5. From all of which we must conclude that Senator Buckley is living up to the promises he made to the people who elected him: to guard the federal system, to preserve the independence of the states, to speak the truth as he sees it. I am grateful to Mr. Koch for not proposing that such sentiments should be declared unconstitutional, though if they were, it would certainly relieve us at least of the burden of most congressional salaries.

Eric Sevareid's Disillusionment

October 21, 1975

THE OTHER NIGHT, listening to Eric Sevareid's commentary on the news, I found myself being instructed on "the true catechism" of the right wing.

Here is what I heard him say: "Mr. Ford is daily reciting the true catechism of the right wing, i.e., disorder is worse than injustice; waste in social programs is worse than waste in the military; government regulations that bother business are awful, government regulations that aid and abet business are all right; quick production has priority over saving the environment; inflation is worse than unemployment; street crime must be suppressed; white-collar crime will cure itself, or something; the free market place is sacred but so is the power of great corporations to freeze it by administered prices."

For some reason, my mind traveled to an essay I had read a few years ago by Anthony Burgess, published when he was teaching literature at City College in New York. Professor Burgess passed along a student's analysis of Macbeth—so to speak, a student reciting the true catechism of Macbeth. It went:

"Lady Mackbet says she had a kid not in so many words but she says she remembers what it was like when a kid sucked her tit so I reckon she was a mother some time and the kid must have died but we dont hear no more about it which is really careless of Shakesper because the real reason why Mcbeth and his wife are kind of restless and ambitious is because they did not have a baby that lived and perhaps this is all they really want and S. says notin about it."

As between the two, I find the analysis of Macbeth infinitely more revealing. The difference, of course, is that Professor Burgess's student isn't invited on the CBS network to teach 50 million people the true meaning of Macbeth.

Consider the first of Sevareid's phony disjunctions. Conservatives, he says, believe that "disorder is worse than injustice." That is like saying that women are better than streetcars. What is the relation between disorder and justice? It is a narrow relation: you cannot have justice and disorder—that is to say, they are incompatible. To say that, is not to *prefer* order to justice, any more than to say that women ride on streetcars is to say that women are to be preferred to streetcars.

Conservatives, he says, "believe that waste in social programs is worse than waste in the military." What does that mean? What Sevareid is trying to say is that conservatives are more indulgent about waste in the military than about waste in social programs.

That's true: conservatives feel that if we finish off the century with one more aircraft carrier than we really needed, we will have erred on the side of safety. But conservatives feel that if we keep on multiplying social programs at the going rate, we will kill off the American ethos. That may be arguable, but it is not compressible in the Sevareidian manner. Waste is waste. The problem is defining waste. Conservatives are impartially opposed to waste, even to the kind of wasted time generated by listening to Mr. Sevareid maul orderly thought.

He tells us that conservatives believe "government regulations that bother business are awful but government regulations that aid business are all right." He is all wrong. I don't know a single American conservative opposed to anti-monopoly laws. Unfortunately, I know a lot of American liberals opposed to anti-monopoly laws for labor unions. I know an American conservative who fought AFTRA, and I know an American liberal who weeps about AFTRA but doesn't fight it. And so on.

One is reminded of a recent essay by Professor Lewis Feuer. "Who has ever heard the analysts of one network take issue with those of another? In politics it is taken for granted that the background of every politician will be scrutinized. The reality is that one class in American society, the newsmen, like the medieval church, still enjoys an immunity despite the fact that it is, of all the political elites, the most continuous. Legislators, presidents and cabinet secretaries come and go, but Eric Sevareid is always there, emitting exordia, pronouncements, and sermonettes." [See also page 373, Notes & Asides.]

The Vindication of Sacco and Vanzetti

August 9, 1977

AT THE RATE we are going, the only man left who will be universally acknowledged to have been guilty of anything is Adolf Hitler. Massachusetts is particularly consumed by the passion to exonerate. A while ago the legislature solemnly convened for the purpose of exonerating all those witches hanged in Salem, leaving open the question of whether witchcraft motivated *that* decision. Then somebody appeared with a book insisting that, in point of fact, Fall River's Lizzie Borden had *not* given her father forty whacks with an axe. Then the Massachusetts Bar Association gave Alger Hiss back his license to practice law, and perhaps in due course the legislature will vote to buy him another typewriter and camera, restoring to him the full paraphernalia of his old profession.

And now Governor Michael Dukakis has declared August 23, the 50th anniversary of the execution of Sacco and Vanzetti, will be devoted to their memory, incidentally declaring unfair the trial that sentenced them to death.

Really, Governor Dukakis, who is a very nice man, should do a little reading before contributing to a myth already lapidary in American history. The myth of the unfair trial of Sacco and Vanzetti, and of their innocence of the murders at Dedham. While he was at it, Governor Dukakis might as well have pronounced that the dead bodyguard and paymaster were suicides. Anyone wanting to read the best account of the Sacco-Vanzetti case available should get *Tragedy in Dedham*, by Francis Russell, the historian and journalist. The book was published in 1971, but Mr. Russell's interest in the case continues, and he has most recently published in *National Review* a 50th anniversary summary of the controversy which removes the final straw on which the defenders of Sacco and Vanzetti's innocence leaned.

This is the so-called FBI Secret File.

Two FBI agents volunteered to the Sacco-Vanzetti defense

committee, five years after the trial, that the Bureau had colluded with the prosecution against S & V on the theory that getting the two anarchists out of the FBI's hair via a murder rap was not a bad solution to the Sacco-Vanzetti problem. Passion plays have been written on the theme of the secret FBI files.

J. Edgar Hoover thoroughly investigated the complaint at the time and pronounced it inaccurate. But Hoover would never turn over the files, that being his policy throughout his lifetime. But the Freedom of Information Act of 1975 overrode this policy, and the 701 pages in the Bureau's files have been thoroughly examined by Francis Russell. It turns out that:

1. Far from Sacco and Vanzetti being long-time sources of irritation to the Bureau, the Bureau knew absolutely nothing about them until after their arrest on the murder charge.

2. There was no collusion between the Bureau and the prosecution—until after the conviction, at which point the Bureau sought permission to place an informer in the same prison with Sacco seeking possible leads to the identity of the Wall Street bombing case.

3. The two FBI agents who gave the false information to the defense committee were themselves investigated. One of them (Letherman) had been appointed to the Bureau by an old crony, the head of the Bureau (Hoover became Director in 1924) who was himself a political pal of Harding's Attorney General, Harry Daugherty. The agent was an elderly alcoholic who had once been a drug addict. He had been removed in 1924 because of "neglect of duty, failure to maintain discipline and to properly supervise the work of his division." The other agent (Weyand) began his career as an informer for the Bureau. In 1919 he was made a special agent notwithstanding that he had defrauded his creditors in a bankruptcy proceeding. While an agent, he moonlighted as a bootlegger (remember: this was the pre-Hoover Bureau). He and Letherman used to hold drinking bouts in Letherman's office.

When Hoover was made boss, he retired all politically appointed agents—including Weyand and Letherman. "Trading on the resentments of these disgraced and disgruntled men," Russell writes, "Thompson [the defense attorney] persuaded them to make the affidavit that he himself shaped and formed." Right up until the month of the execution, the files reveal report after report, initiated by Hoover, probing the least possibility that Sacco and Vanzetti were FBI targets. Not a scintilla of evidence was unearthed.

"So," the piece concludes, "after half a century, the secret of the Department of Justice files on the Sacco-Vanzetti case is shown to be that there was no secret."

Chou En-lai, RIP

January 17, 1976

I AM THIS day making provisions in my will to retain the services of NBC's Jack Reynolds as my eulogist. By the time he is through extolling me, they should be able to find not one Mexican bishop but a half dozen to propose my canonization . . . It was *something* to see and hear, last Monday night at 7.

Chou En-lai. His emaciated body lying in state in Peking. The mourners filing by, weeping. All the old soldiers; the comrades-in-arms; their wives; even the wife of Mao Tse-tung. How they wept.

They'd have wept thusly—the old Nuremberg crowd—if it had been a state funeral for Adolf Hitler. Hitler was an absolutely first-rate killer, and I would not wish to disparage his talent, or allude lightly to his appetite. But Chou En-lai was in a class apart. As principal executor for Mao Tse-tung, he presided over policies that, in the first ten years of Maoist rule, resulted in the death not of six million of his own citizens—Hitler's achievement—but three, and possibly five times that many people.

An equal number died, under the reign of Chou En-lai, in the forced labor camps. The estimates range from a total of 30 million people to 60 million people. They were not around to weep at the bier of Chou En-lai; and it is not recorded that NBC's Jack Reynolds ever remarked their departure from this earth, not in a hospital in Peking, but from a bullet in the head, or from starvation, or torture.

The estimates quoted are given by Franz Michael and George Taylor in the book *The East in the Modern World*, by George Beckmann in *The Modernization of China and Japan*, and the collations drawn by the United States Department of State. The Soviet Union made its own official estimate of the high cost of Chinese Communism, giving the figure of "25+ million"—the Soviets are very skilled at estimates of this kind.

Chou was to Mao much more than, say, Ribbentrop was to Hitler (we hanged Ribbentrop, by the way). He was a critical catalyst of Maoism, incidentally in charge of a foreign policy that caused 34,000 American deaths in Korea. Mr. Reynolds was absolutely right in calling him China's "indispensable man."

See them all coming around the bier. "Finally, Chiang Ch'ing, the wife of Chairman Mao, one of the leading forces of the cultural revolution." Mr. Reynolds makes this sound like "one of the leading forces in the European Renaissance." "Although Chou came from a well-to-do background, he had the common touch, and the people responded," even as they did to Hermann Goering, to whom his pet dogs also responded. "They called him China's busiest man, and they respected him for it. Now they came to pay their last respects, wearing the traditional Chinese white patch of mourning." The white patch is one of the few surviving Chinese traditions.

"Chou En-lai," NBC concluded, "was unique. Largely through his efforts, China now has a stable leadership"—the trick is to liquidate all potential rivals—"an improving economy"—85 percent of Chinese are required to work on the land to feed the 100 percent, less those liquidated by the annual purges—"an outward-looking foreign policy"—that, according to Chairman Mao a couple of weeks ago, foresees a world war, and encourages wars of national liberation in places like Switzerland—"and a goal that may be within reach, to make China a major world power by the end of this century"—far less than Hitler accomplished; he brought his country from utter defeat to perhaps the leading world power in ten years. "A fitting tribute to one who has been called China's man for all seasons"—Chou shares such honors with Molotov and Ribbentrop.

At my funeral services, after Mr. Reynolds has recorded my accomplishments, I shall import the bishop of Cuernavaca for the final blessing. His Excellency said, in tribute to the man who killed every practicing Christian he could find in China—sealing the churches and torturing the priests— that Chou should be canonized. The bishop expressed his "regret" at "having lost the chance of knowing one of the greatest men of China."

I share that regret. If the bishop had traveled to China in the high days of Chou En-lai, there'd have been one less bishop, to be sure: But surely providence, returning us then one martyr, would never have given us a better bargain.

Venezuela's CAP

October 19, 1976

Caracas—THE PRESIDENT of Venezuela is not unlike Hubert Humphrey—enthusiastic, loquacious, warm, with an appetite for life and office unrivaled by the conspicuous leaders of this hemisphere. He is, moreover—again like Humphrey—a superb salesman. There is to begin with his conviction that he has taken the proper measure of most problems, which measure he will communicate to you if, like Jimmy Durante, he has to break the piano in two to do it. And apart from that, he communicates with a jaunty lucidity that incorporates the best of the well-ordered academic mind, while rejecting any dreary traces of pedantry. CAP, as they call Carlos Andrés Pérez, was born to talk to people; to lead. As head of the Acción Democratica, he is president for two and a half years more. Then, under the laws of Venezuela, he must step aside for ten years before running for office again. In ten years he'll be younger than Senator Humphrey is now, and I take the opportunity at this moment in Senator Humphrey's convalescence to predict that twelve and one-half years from now, Humphrey will attend the second inaugural of President CAP.

The achievements of Mr. Pérez are, all things considered, quite phenomenal. It isn't every day that the leader of a foreign country nationalizes something on the order of $150 billion worth of oil, paying $1 billion to the people who discovered that oil and capitalized its development—and leaves them if not exactly smiling, at least not mutinous. President Pérez's formula for arriving at a compensatory price was marvelous. He reimbursed the oil companies for the cost of their drilling rigs and refineries, taking the position that the oil itself was at no time the property of the oil investors. It reminds one of the enchanting story by Alexander Woollcott about the French cadet who won the regimental pool and spent a night with Paris's most attractive, well, *poule*. The next morning she asked how he had come on the 5,000 francs necessary to buy her services for the night, and he confessed that his 1,000 fellow cadets had organized a lottery, each man contributing five francs, the winner to spend the night with the renowned mademoiselle. Overcome with sentiment, she wept and wept and, recovering herself, walked to her purse, pulled out a bill, and effusively returned to the cadet his five-franc investment.

How would Venezuela continue to attract foreign investors having dealt thus raffishly with the oil (and the steel) people? CAP smiled, and talked about the splendid opportunities in Venezuela for foreign capital, about the convertibility of currency, the repatriation rights of profits, about the rapid institutionalization in Venezuela of a democratic order which is the best guarantee against such convulsive turns as are common in Latin America and discourage foreign capital.

It seems, at first, strange that Venezuela should need foreign capital. Venezuela is blessed—as few nations outside the Persian Gulf are blessed—with a huge annual endowment, amounting to something on the order of one thousand dollars a Venezuelan a year. But CAP and his planners want everything, as soon as possible. He will tell you that he thinks it altogether possible that oil as fuel will be anachronized by the end of the century, even if oil as a petrochemical will be valuable into the far reaches of history. Under the circumstances, burn the oil, spend the money now, develop a strong capital base, eliminate poverty, raise educational standards.

In doing this he has difficulties, of course. Most societies are slow to rise from lethargy. The Japanese renaissance after 1870 was something of a miracle, like so much that is Japanese. For one thing, Venezuelans do not like to stay out on the farms, preferring the city, never mind the squalor of their lives. For another, the habits of generations of what one would emphatically call a pre-Watergate morality make the journey of a federal dollar dispatched by Caracas to relieve a poor family notoriously hazardous, arriving, typically, only in highly emaciated form. For still another, there is the specter of that political instability which for a while made a mockery of the vaulting rhetoric of the great liberator, Simón Bolívar. One hundred fifty-five governments in one hundred twenty-five years. Mere episodes of self-rule. But beginning fifteen years ago, it appeared that the democratic roots had begun to sink. As so often is the case, Venezuelan democrats overdid it, extending the franchise even to the illiterate. But the hard, revolutionary left has only 6 percent of the vote, and—CAP smiles—that isn't enough. Although he is prominent as a leader of the Third World, the President has in his office, beside the great canvas of Bolívar, only two busts. One of them is of Abraham Lincoln, the other of Winston Churchill. He ought to have, besides, the scalp of John D. Rockefeller. But he is too good-natured to flaunt his triumphs.

Ferdinand Marcos: The Bloody Beginning

November 22, 1977

Manila—To UNDERSTAND Marcos, or—rather—to *try* to understand him, requires a little concentration on what happened to the Philippines, and to him, during the Second World War. Fortunately, the attention does not wander because, in its gruesome way, the story is fascinating. Perhaps the basic datum is that during the occupation of the Philippines by the Japanese, ferocity was rampant. The Japs killed 1 million people, 1/17th of the population in those days. Comparable figures for the United States would be the slaughtering of 12 million people over a period of four years. The reason the Japanese acted so brutally is that in the Philippines—unique among the occupied countries—there was an organized resistance. A young lawyer, recently graduated first in his class, Ferdinand Edralin Marcos, figured prominently in that resistance.

Endeavoring to help the Americans besieged at Corregidor, Marcos was caught by the Japanese, wounded, and dragged along on the famous Bataan Death March. He survived the march, and for his pains was turned over to a Japanese torturer, whom we shall call Mr. Shintu. Instructed to get from Marcos his knowledge of the resistance, Mr. Shintu experimented with a number of devices including filling Marcos's belly with water and jumping on it; though settling, mostly, for simple, savage beatings with a club. Marcos agreed finally to lead a Japanese detachment to the resistance center but contrived instead to lead it into the arms of an ambush which wiped out the Japanese and liberated Marcos. "It was at the hands of the torturers," he said years ago to a reporter, "that I learned to hate."

For six months after his escape, Marcos stalked Mr. Shintu, and when finally the day came and he had him at the other end of his rifle, Marcos called out to him. Shintu turned his head, muttered the name of the young man he had tortured, and died. Marcos had been living on the strength of that purposive hatred, and collapsed with fatigue and fever that took him out of action for six months, leaving him time to win, in the two and one-half years left of the war, only two Silver Stars, five Purple Hearts, one Distinguished Service Medal, and one recommendation for a Congressional Medal of Honor.

In one action, he sought to liberate his father. The Japanese, seeking the whereabouts of Marcos (now renowned in the resistance) and of his younger brother, publicly announced they would kill the elder Marcos unless he led them to his sons. Organizing a rescue operation, Marcos learned that the Japanese planned to kill his father if attacked. Marcos sent word to his younger brother, coming in from the other end of the valley, to hold his fire. But it was too late: impulsively, the attack had been launched. When the smoke had cleared, they learned that their father had been hanged.

Did his capacity to hate survive the war? I asked, and President Marcos said, No. Because when the war was over, the Filipinos suddenly found themselves fighting an internal enemy, the Huk Communist insurgents. Marcos was astonished to find that his own countrymen were capable of cruelties no different from those committed by the Japanese. And then, in 1966, as President of the Philippines, he was given a state dinner by the Emperor of Japan in Tokyo, after which a most extraordinary ceremony took place. Led into a private room, Marcos found several dozen aging little men. They had been the officers in charge of the Philippines, the men against whom Marcos had fought and bled. What did they say? "They apologized to me. And their spokesman said that, in other times, the apology would have been objectified by handing over to the President of the Philippines a freshly severed finger contributed by one of the generals as a token of expiation."

So: Is President Marcos, with that background, himself now the head of a torture establishment? I put it to him, and he denies it with passion and contempt. But there are no grounds for denying that there has been widespread torture since Marcos declared martial law in 1972. And, as always, the same question arises—recently asked about the Greek

Colonels, and then about General Pinochet, and General Videla—Is the barbarity simply the way human beings act toward one another in straitened circumstances: or is there sanction from the top? My own guess would be that a man of Ferdinand Marcos's background—and the man I talked to extensively—would reject the pleasures of sadism. But my judgment is personal.

The Rogues and Heroes of John Greenway*

June 1977

GRANDMA, WHO IS the maddest man in the *whole* world? He is, indisputably, John Greenway, professor of anthropology, University of Colorado, who in his 21st book vouchsafes us autobiographical snippets that suggest his early inclination to high dudgeon. All his work is peppery, whether he is writing *ad libitum* about folk music, or giving us learned anthropological studies of Australian primitives (see his extraordinary *Down Among the Wild Men*). But this work, devoted to crotchets and enthusiasms, is exhaustively self-revealing. Occasionally he lets pass a sigh over the spiked bodice he locked himself into at birth—"Other memories, discontinuous and incoherent, persist with equal indelibility though I have tried to erase them, since they have imprinted in me behavior and attitudes that have done me no good whatever"—but then without drawing breath he is back on the track, recalling his first day in school with long pants. "And my darling little schoolmates howled with laughter at me, too, the bastards. From that moment I have never without good reason liked anybody at first sight." His strengths (which are legion) appear greatly to dismay him, for instance the grandfather who learned Hebrew from a Torah he

*The American Tradition: A Gallery of Rogues. By John Greenway. Mason/Charter. New York, 1976.

found floating near the dikes in Holland: "From [him] I might have inherited my strange tolerance of Jews." One gathers it was an unhappy youth. "There was another good thing that happened to me in high school, but I have forgotten what it was."

And so, this infuriating, engrossing, hilarious book, in five parts. The first is devoted to blasting all Indian-lovers. (Dee Brown's *Bury My Heart at Wounded Knee* "sold well because more than any other [Indian-loving book] it has tears and flapdoodle and squit abounding."

Then to "Halls of Ivy," a fitful, discursive ("Any reminder of Dear Old Rutgers always drives me into profane digression") indictment of education in America ("During the five years I slaved as editor of the *Journal of American Folklore* I could have destroyed nearly the whole of the discipline's hierarchy by printing their manuscripts exactly as they were submitted to me").

On to women's lib, in splendid blend of erudition and feminism. (About Elizabeth Gould Davis, "She hates testicles, thus limiting the men she can admire to Democratic candidates for President. The worst of her world, ironically, is factual: women are dominant among her beloved, red-haired, blue-eyed Celts. That is why most Oirishmen [sic] are on the gargle.")

Then "The Fuzz," a highly illuminating account of his five years moonlighting from the academy as a policeman. His flair for the speech of America is quite wonderful:

"I want my gun back."

"What gun?"

"The gun you PO-leece tooken from me."

"We didn't take no gun."

"Fuck you didn't. You tooken my gun."

"That wasn't no gun, boy, that was evidence. We gets to keep evidence."

And, finally, a sentimental, moving and self-revealing essay on George Patton, Jr. "I enjoy a bloody good cry as much as the next fellow, and again like Patton my eyes are near my bladder, and Christ help the person who thinks it impugns my masculinity. But when something evokes in me such strong emotion for no clear reason, I like to know why. I have an abiding respect for my mind's functioning, but I do not want it knowing more than I do."

The book is irritating, because with so few exceptions it is relentless in its iconoclasm. But it is a very American book, and so free of academic cant one wants to go out and ring bells, and bring on more rogues. There is a deftness to his touch quite magical. For instance, he traces the comforts of womanhood to Andreas Capellanus's *De arte honeste amandi*. "Without the artificial homage Courtly Love gave to women, we would probably still be regarding them as the aborigines of Australia do . . . But because of . . . Andreas, American boys begin their submission to the ladies by carrying their books home from school, continue through much of their inferior lives carrying their groceries from the supermarket, walking on the splattery side of the pavement, letting them in automobiles and elevators first, and giving them the final honor of preceding them to the grave so that they can lollygag on the inheritance in lovelier parts of the world than Gary, Indiana."

Mr. Greenway, to quote the jacket copy, has had professional experience as a master carpenter, builder, professor of English, combat instructor, archaeologist, folk singer and musician, composer, chess expert, photographer, ethnographic filmmaker, and track athlete. He should turn now to fiction.

David Niven Recreates Hollywood*

September 1975

THIS IS A BOOK about Hollywood and incidentally a masterful self-portrait. Inasmuch as what David Niven recalls is mostly what he saw, smelled, and tasted, you wonder, after putting it down, how he managed to bring it off without making it

*Bring On the Empty Horses. By David Niven. G.P. Putnam's Sons. New York, 1975.

sound like a book starring David Niven produced by David Niven directed by David Niven from an original screenplay by David Niven. This does not happen because of a talent for self-effacement which is one of the many things Niven did not learn in Hollywood, the others being a resolute amiability and thoughtfulness. That talent serves him now as a pillar supporting what must easily be the best book ever written about Hollywood. A volume, moreover, that is not likely to be challenged on its own terms because there is no other survivor of the scene from 1935–1960 a) who knew everybody Niven knew and b) who can write the way Niven can write. He is a fine actor and comedian. He is an even better writer.

How does he manage to keep the focus away from himself? Watch. "One Fourth of July he [Douglas Fairbanks] and Sylvia chartered a motor cruiser and invited a small group, including Norma Shearer and Irving Thalberg, to sail with them to Catalina. The idea was to anchor on arrival alongside Cecil B. DeMille's sleek white three-masted schooner. Our captain had an ominous name—Jack Puke . . ." *Our* captain! Is there a neater way to all but inflect oneself right out of an episode?

Yet in ghosting himself out he limns, unconsciously, a portrait that superbly complements the hilarious autobiography of his youth, *The Moon's a Balloon.* One comes to know David Niven as one might one's brother; so to speak, by feel. Hear him again, writing—this time—about Cary Grant. "Through the years to come he made generous efforts to straighten out my private life by warning me of the quirks and peculiarities of various ladies, by giving me complicated advice on how to play a part in a film I was making with him, by telling me which stocks to buy when I could not afford a phone call to a broker, and by promising that he could cure my liking for Scotch by hypnotizing me." We have learned something about Cary Grant, and at least as much about David Niven.

* * *

A book for grown-ups about Hollywood and the lives of Hollywood stars? But the skepticism ends with the first chapter. There is a narrative tension from the beginning, and an ear for piquancy, an eye for the amusing and absurd and the poignant. The compulsion of the entertainer, in Niven's case a blend of exuberance, skill, and good manners (it is after all rude to be dull, if one knows how not to be), keeps the book moving like an Olsen and Johnson production. Even so, he will now and then defer to meticulous but illuminating detail. "He [Edmund Lowe] . . . drove me around the cozily named 'Back Lot'—a 200-acre spread upon which stood the permanent sets, including New York streets, New England, French, and Spanish villages, medieval castles, a railroad station complete with rolling stock, lakes with wave-making machines and rustic bridges, a university campus, an airliner, a section of jungle and another of pine forest, a Mississippi steamboat, a three-masted schooner, native canoes, a submarine, a stretch of desert with ruined fort and, in case anything was missing, several acres of carefully dismantled, docketed and stored streets, villages, cathedrals, mud huts, dance halls, skating rinks, ball parks, theaters, vineyards, slums, Southern plantations, and Oriental palaces."

Thus the paraphernalia of Hollywood. There is much more about the beast. A two-part chapter—he calls it "Our Little Girl," withholding from the reader, for once, the identity of the principal—describes the physical and psychic torture of stardom by giving two days in the life of one star, hour by hour, compressing a decade's exhilaration and decomposition as imaginatively and evocatively as Robert Nathan describing the evolution of a young girl in his *Portrait of Jennie*. David Niven has no illusions about the Hollywood that died in the late Fifties, even if he has not quite yet compounded an antidote to paganism. "[It] was hardly a nursery for intellectuals, it was a hotbed of false values, it harbored an unattractive percentage of small-time crooks and con artists, and the chances of being successful there were minimal, but it was fascinating, and IF YOU WERE LUCKY, it was fun." In a curious sense, David Niven continues to be starstruck, but the reader finds himself—caring. Not because the reader is involved in mankind, but because he actually finds himself involved in Errol Flynn! That makes David Niven something of a sorcerer.

Douglas Fairbanks furtively revealed to him his fear of growing old. George Sanders confided in 1937 that at age sixty-five he would commit suicide, which he did. Errol Flynn suggested the uses of just a touch of cocaine on the tip of the penis. Greta Garbo swam naked in his pool. (Their enduring friendship Niven is required modestly to concede, even as he describes her pathological fear of friendship, recalling Robert Montgomery's acid remark on being snubbed only weeks after co-starring with her, that "making a film with Garbo does not constitute an introduction.") Ronald Colman, noblesse oblige, speeded to his side in his launch and narrowly rescued him from a shark. Clark Gable began by giving him his catch to clean when Niven, broke, worked as a sportsfisherman's assistant—and was soon agitating to get him a screen test. Fred Astaire, a clumsy social dancer, ripped off a wild routine in his living room. Tyrone Power dressed as Santa Claus for his children. Miriam Hopkins acknowledged a Christmas gift of two handkerchiefs by giving him a Studebaker. Charlie Chaplin described in a throwaway paragraph how to contrive to make truly comic a fat lady approaching a banana peel. Charles MacArthur, resentful over the second-class status given by the big producers to writers, took revenge by elaborating to L. B. Mayer the fictitious talents of a London garage mechanic who happened to be entirely illiterate, and landing a thousand-dollar-a-week contract for him. Scott Fitzgerald was numb with gratitude when Niven matter-of-factly offered him the use of his refrigerator for the Coca-Colas Fitzgerald briefly besotted himself with while trying to exorcise demon rum . . .

The book teems with that kind of thing but the incidents are not carelessly catalogued, like a book of jokes by Bennett Cerf. Some of the portraits—of Clemence Dane, for instance, and Errol Flynn—approach art, and easily surpass entertainment. The sentiment, which abounds, stops (usually) short of sentimentality. The descriptions are agile, terse or profuse as the situation demands. And all this the work of an *undertaker*. Because although David Niven is still acting, and hit movies are still being made, the phenomenon of Hollywood has passed, and David Niven has no desire to resurrect it, though in fact he has done so.

James Jackson Kilpatrick Celebrates Scrabble, Va.

December 22, 1977

SOME WRITERS take awful chances, and in doing so many of them fall on their . . . (I have just committed what the verbal technicians call *aposiopesis*). If I or Arthur Schlesinger, Jr. were to attempt to write a book about life in the country, about dogs and flowers and winter and summer, we would both be led ungently to a cell block in which no paper, pen, pencil or typewriter was permitted. While such a confinement would in the one case spare the United States a terrible ongoing affliction, it would, in the other case, deprive the Republic of its principal moral and political gyroscope. All the more reason to wonder, with awe and gratitude, at the accomplishment of James Jackson Kilpatrick.

Everyone knows Kilpatrick as a political commentator. There is no one else who can do such profiles as he has done of Presidential candidates, or political Conventions. That he is the most widely syndicated political columnist is the highest tribute that can be paid to the editors of American editorial pages. He never fails to instruct and to delight. He can be angry without being sour, critical without being catechistic, lyrical and never sing-song. He can see through the least dictum of a Supreme Court Justice and conjugate its strategic mischief before the rest of us have even noticed it. One would assume such a man would be satisfied to have achieved his proconsular rank in American political letters, but no, he has to go and write a book about country life.

Buy it. Letters of gratitude to me for calling attention to it cannot be acknowledged. It is called *The Foxes' Union,* and is published by EPM Publications Inc. of McLean, Virginia. It costs $9.95, and is guaranteed to give you a fix of serenity and pleasure unequaled by any other book of the season.

Kilpatrick was born in Oklahoma, but traveled to Virginia as quickly as he could. It is unimaginable that he was ever other than a Virginian. There he rose to prominence as editor of the Richmond *News Leader,* which he quit after twenty years of hard and distinguished labor to become a syndicated columnist, television commentator, and lecturer. He and his wife Marie, an artist, happened on a stretch of land in Rappahanock County, eighty miles from Washington, and went the way of Mr. Blandings, building his dream house. Happily, he did not permit his new life to remain an entirely private affair.

Many things have happened to him since writing from Scrabble, Virginia, and they happen also to the reader of his book. For instance: in Virginia, people don't really know how to cope with those episodic snowfalls which are routine business in, say, Minneapolis. When the first one came, Kilpatrick and his wife fought it instinctively.

"Then a second thought struck home: accept it. The thought has recurred many times since. In the sum total of man's brief span upon the earth, what would be missed? Truly missed? So the choirboys would not rehearse, nor the Kiwanians convene that day, and the schoolboys of Culpeper would miss the parsing of their sentences. For the time being, there would be no further work upon the new stone wall; but the wall could wait. Somewhere a local court had closed; but justice would be done tomorrow, or the day after, or next week."

These stretches of privacy, in the isolated hills of Virginia up against the Blue Ridge Mountains, have cultivated in the author a consciousness of his natural surroundings that stimulates deep artistic resources. He notes the coming of the spring and the profusion of flowers. Among them "the trillium, loveliest of them all, [which] kneels as modestly as a spring bride, all in white, beside the altar of an old oak stump. If you're not familiar with the trillium, imagine the flower that would come from a flute if a flute could make a flower. That is the trillium, a work of God from a theme by Mozart."

The Foxes' Union is an experience in sensitization. Hark, the spring! It "tiptoes in. It pauses, overcome by shyness, like a grandchild at the door, peeping in, ducking out of sight, giggling in the hallway. 'Heather!' I want to cry, 'I know you're out there. Come in!' And April slips into our arms. The maples do not come forth in green; they are flowering red, soft as slippers, in tassels like a jester's scepter. The flowering almond is pink, absurdly pink, little-girl pink, as pink as peppermint and cream. The apples display their milliner's scraps of ivory silk, rose-tinged. All the sleeping things wake up—primrose, baby iris, candytuft, blue phlox, the Scotch heather that had seemed dead beyond resurrection. The earth warms—you can smell it, feel it, crumble April in your hands." But you can smell and feel this engrossing and enchanting book, and be grateful alike to nature and to its poets.

V.

Reforms

Social Security: The Inside Story

November 8, 1977

INASMUCH AS ECONOMICS seeks to be scientific, it is a continuing wonder that so many people who trade in it should be so
willing to obfuscate. The debate over social security is a case
in point.

Consider the simplest matter. It is argued—endlessly—
what should be the percentage of the payroll tax charged to
the employer, what percentage to the employee. Now, rudimentary economic analysis informs us that if an employer is
prepared to pay, let us say, $20,000 a year to a dispatcher, he
is willing to pay $20,000 a year, that being the budgeted val-
ue of that man's work to that company in contemporary circumstances.

If the government informs the employer that he will need
to pay $2,000 in tax to the social security fund for every em-
ployee earning $20,000, the employer is going to sit down
and make the following calculations: a) If I pay $2,000 in
payroll tax to the government, I shall be earning a $2,000 de-
duction. b) Since my company pays taxes to the Federal Government at approximately the 50 percent rate, we'll be out
net $1,000. c) Since this job is budgeted at $20,000, not
$21,000, I shall advertise to get the services of the dispatcher
to whom I shall offer $19,000, instead of $20,000.

If we assume some kind of meritocratic logic here, the man
who is willing to work for $19,000 is a little less able, or less
experienced, than the man who requires $20,000, so that his
performance will be marginally less efficient. The cost of that
relative inefficiency to the company is difficult to track, but
assume it to be there. Bear in mind that the dispatcher is pay-

199

ing (under the proposed law) one-half the tax his employer is paying. He is really going to work for $18,000, but is costing the company $21,000.

This is what the economists refer to as the "wedge." The bigger the wedge, a) the greater the tendency to unemployment (employers can't come up with the takehome pay the employees want or require); and b) the greater the relative inefficiency of the firm.

The reigning superstition in Congress is that social security funds are in some important way discretely handled from general revenue funds. To be sure, we all go through the motions. But what does it mean? General tax revenues are reduced to the extent corporations deduct their share of the social security payroll tax. Already then, there is the direct subsidy of the system.

The net burden on the company results either in paying less to the employee, in which case the employee earns less; in which case the employee pays less money in tax to the Federal Government; in which case the Federal Government is once again subsidizing social security from the other end. Or, if the worker cannot be hired for less than the $20,000 in question, the company raises the price of its product in order to make up the difference between the budgeted salary and the increased salary. When prices rise, sales diminish. When sales diminish, taxes at all levels diminish. The backwaters all find their way to the federal treasury.

So what is the point in the hocus-pocus? The point is the same our legislators seek to make in so many other circumstances: to obscure reality, because reality in turn obscures the economic facts of life. Briefly stated these are given in the reductionist triumph of Milton Friedman: "There is no such thing as a free lunch."

It is not surprising, then, that Professor Friedman has consistently advocated the abolition of that part of social security that sells itself to the unwary on the occult superstition that we are all engaged in prim exercises in self-insurance, no different from Mutual of Omaha. What we are engaged in is massive acts of income transfers, from younger people to older people. The contributions of the older people, when they were younger, are disguised savings for their own ultimate benefit. In fact they are, increasingly, mere payments to older people. Let it be described as what it is.

Inflation: Senator Kennedy's Funny Money

June 5, 1976

SENATOR KENNEDY has written most provocatively to a number of newspapers challenging an analysis in *On the Right* of his report to the Joint Economic Committee. His reply is given in several seductive paragraphs, and ends with a paternal suggestion. "The next time Mr. Buckley feels the urge to shoot from the hip on economic issues and tax reform, I hope he'll lie down until it passes, or at least check with a responsible economist."

Now Senator Kennedy had written that the notion of the "mushrooming Federal Government" was a "myth." He handles my demonstration to the contrary by holding it up as an example of "how to distort a set of figures." "The big jump in the ratio of federal spending to GNP came between 1951 and 1952, during the Korean War, when it climbed from 13 percent to 20 percent. In 1953 the ratio moved up a notch to 21 percent. Then it settled back, and for the next twenty years it hovered around 20 percent. So much for Mr. Buckley's progression."

Now look. The following figures, taken from the official documents, are *undisputed*. In 1951, federal spending was 14 percent of GNP. In 1956 it was 17 percent. In 1966 it was 19 percent. In 1975 it was 23 percent.

Senator Kennedy says: Ah, but the Korean War was in progress in 1952, causing *that* rapid rise. And in 1975 there was the depression, causing *that* rapid rise. In the intermediate twenty-odd years, "it hovered around 20 percent."

Is Mr. Kennedy asking us to regard as abnormal (14 percent in 1951) a year in which there is a Democratic President—and a war? Or—at the other end—is he asking us to consider as abnormal (23 percent in 1975) a situation in which there is a Democratic Congress—and a depression? These would appear to be the planted axioms of his analysis. Because the historical fact is that a) we have risen from 13 percent to 23 percent, and that b) the *apparent* stability of the intervening years was directly the result of a decrease in the percentage of the GNP spent on defense. Between 1952 and 1972—the critical twenty years—defense spending dropped from 14.3 to 7.2 percent of GNP, while federal domestic spending soared from 3.9 to 12 percent. Federal non-defense spending has been increasing at an accelerating rate—8.9 percent a year from 1960 to 1965; 12 percent from 1965 to 1970; 14.7 percent from 1970 to 1973; and 21.9 percent from 1973 through the third quarter of 1975.

Here is another factor on which Senator Kennedy does not touch. Between 1951 and 1972, in constant dollars, the average American increased his earnings by about 95 percent. But the population increase was only about 38 percent. Accordingly, one notes that the Federal Government, though *apparently* taking the same bite out of the citizen's taxes, was actually increasing its take at about three times the rate of population growth. If, given constant dollars and a constant tax rate, you earn $2,000 a year and the government taxes you 20 percent, and twenty years later you earn $4,000 and the government taxes you 20 percent, what is the relevant figure from your point of view? That the government is still taxing you 20 percent? Or that whereas it *used to* take $400 from you, it now takes $800?

Moreover, none of this takes into account spending by non-federal governments (total spending at all levels hovered around 33 percent of national income from 1956 to 1965, but has since risen steadily to about 40 percent). Those casual one-percentage-point rises in the tax rate, which Senator Kennedy treats like a couple of raisins more or less in the grocery box, represent about $16 billion each.

As for checking my figures with a responsible economist, well, I did so. And if Senator Kennedy thinks him incompetent, why did he vote to confirm him as Secretary of the Treasury? Though, as a matter of fact, the figures are not all that inscrutable, and I'd have had little trouble ferreting them out myself, having earned a degree, however long ago, in economics, passing all my examinations in the subject, without any aid from the public, or even the private, sector.

Resignation: The Neglected Alternative

May 15, 1975

A BOOK HAS been published—*Resignation in Protest*—consisting largely of published statements by American officials about Vietnam. The thesis of the editors, Edward Weisband and Thomas M. Franck, is that in America we have an unlively tradition. It is the tradition of resignation. It is practiced very frequently in Great Britain. When a member of the Cabinet, or even a junior official, is out of sympathy with a policy of his government, he publicly resigns. In America, resignation is taken to be something of an act of petulance, a failure of team spirit: as if the tackle on the football team, disagreeing with the quarterback's proposal, walked off in a huff.

There is something to be said for the American way, whatever the manifest disadvantages. It draws from the idea of the civil servant—who is there to implement policies adopted by the chief of government. In England a very sharp line is drawn between civil servants, who will poison the water supply if told to do so, and the ministries. These, though entirely dominated by the Cabinet, which is dominated by the Prime Minister, are expected to be guided by their political consciences. That being the case, you would not expect, in England, an under-secretary of state to conspire along with Anthony Eden to invade Egypt. If he did, he would be purged, the enterprise having turned sour, along with his boss.

In the United States, the Vietnam war was the great crucible. Nelson Rockefeller lately made a mockery of the notion of the dutiful silence by suggesting that he was bound to keep his opposition silent, in order to increase the flow of federal cash into New York. And there are dozens of names associated with Vietnam about whom the question is asked by the liberal community: Why did they do it? Why didn't they quit?

With the exception of the entirely honorable Rostow Brothers, Dean Rusk, and a few others, the rest—or most of them—have practiced the art of dissociation with great skill. One day you slip away from the government. Maybe indeed you wanted to leave government. Maybe, on the other hand, you weren't getting anywhere, and felt it was time to go. A couple of months later, you sign a gentle manifesto of protest, perhaps arguing against (say) the incursion into Cambodia. Remember, up until now you have said nothing publicly against our participation in Vietnam. Another few months go by and you are suddenly a speaker at an anti-Vietnam rally. You make some sort of effort to distinguish between the kind of policy *now* being pursued, and the kind pursued when *you* were involved in the government. You lean very heavily on the key dissociational word: *incommensurable*. Our effort in Vietnam is *incommensurable* with the ends we seek to achieve.

A few more like that, and you have accomplished an Arthur Schlesinger. You read Arthur Schlesinger of the last few years, and you simply never suspect that there was an Arthur Schlesinger, Jr. who vigorously defended the Vietnam War. You think maybe that was his old man.

I have received complaints over a recent statement asking why George Ball, who recently wrote that our cease-fire arrangements were transparent frauds, didn't say they were transparent frauds at the time. I asked, in the same column, why George Ball, who is so greatly opposed to our Vietnam venture in retrospect, did nothing to dissociate himself from the government that presided over that venture until it was replaced by the electorate? After all, George Ball was Undersecretary of State, and then our principal ambassador to the United Nations, where no question was raised more often than the question of Vietnam. And he did not quit that position until mid-summer in 1968. In order to criticize Lyndon Johnson's conduct of the Vietnam War? No, in order to participate actively in the campaign against Richard Nixon and Spiro Agnew.

The authors of the book about Vietnam suggest that either we should expect more frequent resignations, or proceed on the assumption that cabinet officers are merely civil servants. Their suggestion is not without ingenuity. Let all cabinet officials, they recommend, be selected from the House of Representatives, in the British manner. When they resign they have a political haven, whence they can elaborate their ideas. If George Ball had resigned and gone back to the House of Representatives, he could have been the beginning of a little magnetic field of resentment against Vietnam policy: and expressed himself more forcefully.

The trouble is, you cannot under the Constitution work for more than one branch of the government at one time. But here is a reform that we shouldn't have too much trouble getting through Congress.

The Libel Laws: Desolation

July 1. 1975

LIBEL SUITS INITIATED by public figures are intended to make a public point. In most instances the public figure has not been damaged in the sense that his income has diminished as the direct result of the circulation of the libel. That is why in some of the most conspicuous libel suits of the past season (in some of which I have figured), the plaintiffs have generally stipulated that compensatory damages were not sought. Instead plaintiffs have asked the court to award damages that speak to the intrinsically defamatory nature of the libel; and to punish the tortfeasor for proceeding to write something he had every reason to believe was both wrong and defamatory.

As most people know, in 1964 in *New York Times* v. *Sullivan* the Supreme Court ruled that public officials could not recover unless they could prove "actual malice" on the part of the defendant. Since that ruling, a number of others wandering in disparate directions have been laid down, sometimes appearing to make it almost impossible to libel a public figure; and at other times, urging over toward a metaphysical affirmation that even public figures can appeal to the courts for the protection of their good name. One such case recently arose in New York, and it illuminates the residual injustice in the federal libel law as it has crystallized.

Along comes this jerk feller, the former president of a Protestant college, who is gulled by an organization ostensibly concerned to isolate extremists on the left and on the right, but which is actually concerned to harass the kooky-right. The former college president is back teaching the history of religion, and taking himself most seriously as guardian of the polemical manners of his fellow Americans. He writes me a letter suggesting that unless I reform my ways, he will disapprove of me. I reply that I had never heard of him until a couple of months earlier, was unaware that his approval was a collector's item, ask him to explain any inaccuracy in anything I have written for which I would promptly apologize, and invite him otherwise please to go away.

A year or so passes by and the gentleman publishes a book under the august imprint of a major New York publishing house, alleging that I am to the American conservative movement what Von Ribbentrop was to the Nazis; that I make my living by lying about other people and by insinuating the fascist line into my work. As editor of a journal of opinion which espouses positions that were once thought fit to live only in the fever swamps of the crazy right, I have felt in behalf of my colleagues a collegiate responsibility to resist that kind of thing; so I sued—the publisher, and the author.

From the beginning, I asked for a) an apology; and b) reimbursement of the lawyer's fees, which at that twinkling point in time were only a few hundred dollars. The publishers were too principled to meet the demand, and five years later, after seven days of trial, we settled out of court. . . .

Leaving the college professor who, pleading impoverishment, appeared *pro se,* and for a few horrible moments until the judge told him for gawdssakes to cut it out, the professor actually referred to himself in the third person. The judge, by the way, proved to be one of those exemplary jurists— thorough, fair, courteous. But if a political cell ever stirred in his blood, it was leeched out some time before he reached kindergarten. Intending no criticism, it required the judge as much time to learn to distinguish between permissible and impermissible modalities of political discussions, as it would take me to learn about toxic and innocent varieties of mushrooms. The result was entirely satisfactory—I mean, the judge meditated deeply on the matter, and reached, in an 84-page document, an unassailable conclusion, namely that the wretched professor, while decrying political irresponsibility, had engaged in it: and the judge whacked him $7,500.

Now that may seem a lot of money, but even the judge, who until recently was a successful Wall Street lawyer, knows that is is peanuts alongside the expense of paying lawyers to bring litigation. But—said the judge—7,500 bucks is a lot of scratch for a professor. Which is true. But why isn't there a law like England's—or like Connecticut's?—that says flatly: either a defendant apologizes immediately on being sued, or, if he is proved guilty of libel, he is required to pay the legal costs of the action that brought him to heel.

What can be fairer than that? As it now stands even if you win a token judgment, you lose, net. And, worse, abstract justice is then only for those who can sustain the loss. That is a lousy arrangement, and those who really do worry about free speech should worry about the chilling effect of the practical unavailability of the libel mechanism for men and women who dare to enter public life.

Gun Control: It Won't Work

January 22, 1977

ONCE EVERY GREAT while one comes across a stretch of prose which, ever so calmly and resolutely, picks one up off the ground, and orients one over toward where the sun is really shining. This happened to me on reading in the Fall issue of *The Public Interest* (10 East 53rd Street, New York, N.Y. 10022) an article by Mr. B. Bruce-Briggs, a literate economist. Up until then I was moving toward what might be called creeping acquiescence in the matter of gun-control legislation. Mr. B-B has changed all that in his serene, exhaustive, scholarly inquiry into what he calls "The Great American Gun War."

To let you in on his conclusion, even though it is to deprive you of the exhilarating analytical narrative: he finds that, really, there is practically no correlation between gun control and crime control. One by one he goes down the popular superstitions on the subject, like John Wayne beginning at one end of the town dominated by the outlaws and, on reaching the other end, every one of them is quite unmistakably dead. It is a pity, of course, because it would have been fun to end violent crime by simply scooping up 40 million handguns. But we shall have to come up with a more complicated way of dealing with the problem.

The first thing to bear in mind is that regional, racial, and cultural factors "completely swamp the effects of gun-control laws." It is frequently pointed out that in England, in Switzerland, and in Japan, violent crimes involving firearms are virtually unknown—because there are strict gun-control laws in those countries. Who has not heard that cliché, or been unmoved by it!

But pause. Why do they say "England" rather than "Great Britain"? Because to do so would require us to take stock of the violence by firearms in Ulster, and that would shake up the figures. In Switzerland, there are 600,000 loaded rifles kept in individual homes—pursuant to the tradition of the well-ordered militia. But the Swiss simply do not have a penchant for shooting each other. In Japan, where there is very strict gun control, there are very few gun-inflicted violent crimes. But—among Japanese-Americans, the figures show even less such crime, notwithstanding the profusion of guns.

Although it is correct that most Americans who have guns use them for sport, a great number of them—35 percent—acknowledge that they keep guns for the purpose of self-defense. Now it is true that a gun-in-the-house can cause death: an outraged wife might use it against her husband in passion, or a robber, spotting the gun, might fire to abort being fired at. But intra-family crime is virtually impossible to regulate. If you took away Lizzie Borden's axe, she'd have found something else. As for the robbers, how many of them might leave you alone, if they suspected that a loaded gun might greet them upon entering? (If Larry O'Brien had been armed, Nixon would still be President.) In the South, which is heavily armed, the burglary rate is lower than elsewhere. Moreover, how do you weigh the social value of the serenity achieved by those who have guns at home?

And as a practical matter, no one argues that the professional criminal class will be either deprived of the means of getting a handgun, or even greatly discouraged from using a handgun for such operations as require it: because a criminal will tend to weigh the marginal utility of a gun on the job, not the stretched-out sentence for carrying one.

Professor Arthur Schlesinger has amused himself, and us, with the notion that American gun owners are masking their sexual impotence. Mr. Bruce-Briggs loves that one. "When queried about the source of this suspicion, Schlesinger responded that he thought it was a cliché. Such statements never cite sources because there are no sources. Every mention of the phallic-narcissist theory assumes it is well known, but there is no study or even credible psychoanalytical theory making the point. The germ of the idea derives from the tenth lecture in Sigmund Freud's *General Introduction to Psychoanalysis*, where he maintains that guns can symbolize the penis in dreams—as can sticks, umbrellas, trees, knives, sabers, water faucets, pencils, nail files, hammers, snakes, reptiles, fishes, hats and coats, hands, feet, balloons, aeroplanes, and zeppelins."

But it is true that the great majority of the American people favor gun control. And there is a flare-up of plebiscitary enthusiasm among American liberals, who are less influenced by majoritarianism that favors, e.g., cracking down on obscenity, abortion, and marijuana. Or that favors a return to capital punishment. Concerning this last, there is a nexus. But you must read this splendid analysis by Mr. Bruce-Briggs to find out what it is.

Federal Subsidies: Civil War

July 14, 1977

IN HIS ENDLESSLY heuristic speech of June 27, Senator Moynihan included the following passage:

"The United States Army today is trained almost exclusively to fight a war in Nicaragua, which is to say from training camps in the balmier regions of the Old South. I honor the Marines who, when tons of snow fell in upstate New York last winter, were discovered to have a few companies at Fort Drum on winter training exercises. Similarly, I honor the great Southern congressional chairmen who served their region and this nation so well in sustaining the Armed Forces in an earlier period of isolationist clamor. But the time has come to introduce our soldiery to the thought that in many parts of the world it frequently freezes and sometimes snows."

The levity in tone sustains the passage, which went, perhaps understandably, unnoticed in the coverage of Mr. Moynihan's speech. But coupled with a preceding passage—in which Senator Moynihan, without saying so in exactly as many words, nevertheless unmistakably asked for protection for New York's garment workers—it gives us an insight into what, really, is going on. A war between the states.

"In the period from fiscal year 1968 to fiscal year 1976 California veterans have received $3.17 billion in GI bill payments, while New York veterans have received only $1.12 billion. One might ask whether in this respect this is a direct, if unintended, policy of the Federal Government to make veterans feel that New York is not a good place to settle down."

It doesn't, as it happens, take very long to penetrate the insinuation. For one thing, only 63 percent as many New Yorkers went into the Vietnam War as Californians. For another, more out-of-staters go to California for college training than to New York.

But what is important is that Senator Moynihan should be using arguments of this character, everything from asking for protective tariffs for New York workers, to suggesting that we move our infantry divisions up from warm climates to cold climates: all of it to achieve a higher return on the tax dollar. All of it, one might add, at the expense of other states.

But other states are bound to catch on. Granted, it is a wonder they have not already done so. In 1973, in a small book (favorably reviewed by then-Ambassador Moynihan in the New York *Times*), I pointed out that there were nineteen states in the union whose average per capita income was less than the national average, so that any attempt at economic redistribution had as its implicit purpose helping nineteen specified states at the expense of thirty-one wealthier states. What happened, of course, is that the ideologues discovered it was easier to vote social welfare programs through Washington than through state capitals. Accordingly, states like New York (first in wealth) and California (ninth in wealth) began running money from their citizens, through Washington, back to themselves. But logic quickly advises us that this will only work for so long as the elected representatives of other states are fast asleep in Washington, unaware of real economic movements. "For years," said Mr. Moynihan, "New York has unhesitatingly supported national programs which involve taking out of our private sector one dollar in order to return eleven cents to our public sector. It is not good economics."

But now Senator Moynihan wants Washington to support New York's subways, and to nationalize Central Park. Sure. He is asking back from Washington (he would explain) some of the money New York has been sending to Washington. But the way to avoid these round-trip dollars, and cut down on the furious extravagance of government, is to end the hallucination: to cut Washington out of the picture. Which is why I say yet again that the evidence continues to mount in favor of generic reform: Congress should appropriate funds for social welfare only for the benefit of those states whose per capita income is below the national average.

Federal Wage Increase Reform: *Mea Culpa*

September 29, 1977

I WISH TO ATONE for what I now conceive as a misjudgment, namely my public support of that provision in the federal wage increase package last January which forbids members of Congress from earning more than $8,000 per year from extra-curricular activity. Oh, the rationale sang sweetly to the ear. And, indeed, there was a philanthropic intention: salaries at the highest levels of government were just too low, and it was becoming increasingly difficult to attract non-ascetic types who had obligations to their families to give them the kind of education and shelter which are not available in Washington at forty-four grand before taxes. The practice, as we all know, had been for the most energetic congressmen and senators to eke out their living by doing other things.

Under the new law, they will be limited to earning 15 percent beyond their current salaries (they were raised to $57,500) through extra-legislative activities. I think this wrong both in terms of what it does to congressmen, and what it denies congressmen the right to do for others.

The subject came up during a recent lecture trip when I learned from my hosts that it had become increasingly difficult to engage the services of interesting congressmen or senators to speak. The reason was obvious: after earning $8,000, a congressman may earn no more. He faces the alternative of going to Northwestern State College of Louisiana to give a speech on his current preoccupations—or staying home. It is the planted axiom of the ethics committee's bill that, staying at home, the congressman will devote the time he would otherwise spend talking to students and citizens at Natchitoches rereading the Federalist Papers, or studying up more carefully for tomorrow's committee meeting.

This does not, of course, follow. All that is absolutely known about the effects of the interdiction is that a) the students will not get a chance to hear and question Senator Smith; b) Senator Smith will not get a chance to hear the questions of the students; c) Senator Smith will be deprived of $1,000 of income (assume that the fee is $2,000); and d) the taxpayers will be deprived of $1,000 of income.

(That last point, by the way, is ironically relevant in respect of high-earning congressmen or public servants on the order of Patrick Moynihan, John Kenneth Galbraith, or all those congressmen who used to practice law: in many cases, by their extra-curricular activities they returned to the governments sums of money in excess of that paid them for their work in government. In a way, the Republic was getting their services for nothing.)

In opposing the ethics committee bill, Senator James Buckley argued last December that it was objectionable on several grounds. For one thing it constituted a pre-emption of a property right. It is by no means obvious that anyone can contract for *all* of someone's services—there is an unhealthy feel to such a Faustian contract. For another, Senator Buckley felt that the measure failed lazily to confront the relevant distinctions. It is one thing to frown on the senator who sits on the Maritime Committee and is offered a large fee to give a speech to the Seafarers' Union. It is another to serve on the Maritime Committee and appear as a lecturer at a series sponsored by Northwestern State College.

Senator Buckley's successor, Daniel Patrick Moynihan, opened the floodgates on his tumultuous emotions when his colleague Senator Adlai Stevenson proposed that excess campaign funds should not be permitted to be used for office expenses. The Stevenson proposal was defeated, but not before Senator Moynihan had railed against the senate for desiring to make a "pauper" out of him, having already, earlier in the year, stripped him of an earning capacity as a lecturer that had fetched him $150,000 during his last year as a free agent. A poetic penalty, perhaps, for depriving the nation of the services of his distinguished predecessor.

In the last analysis, there is no substitute for giving public servants the right to make their own decisions—and then spotlighting these decisions so that their ethical adequacy can be evaluated by their constituents. One fears, looking back on it, that unpleasant motives figured in the devising of the bill. Rich congressmen are indifferent to the problems of poorer congressmen. And congressmen whose oratorical gifts are never bid for by Northwestern State College are adept at writing regulations governing the activities of those of their colleagues who are.

The Law: Malpractice

October 27, 1977

ADDRESSING RECENTLY a spirited gathering of law students, I got the reassuring impression that a professional self-concern pricks at their conscience, and there is hope that if they are not soon narcotized by the general preoccupation with getting and spending, this will be a generation that effects reforms so greatly overdue.

Ten years ago, the phenomenon of the self-conscious lawyer was also familiar. But he appeased himself, or tended to, by associating himself gladly with any antiestablishmentarian cause. Those were the lawyers who, driven by a full-blooded antinomianism, egged on their clients to protest this or that mos or folkway. These lawyers are still with us, demanding consumer unions, presuming conflicts of interest, seeing racial and social injustice in the loaf of bread baked by the sweat of an honest baker's brow. Paraphrasing Henry Mencken on the Puritans, a public service lawyer is the man who is afraid that somebody, somewhere, is making a profit.

Although that preoccupation with the law is not the distinguishing feature of this season's discontent, the young men and women about to become lawyers seem to feel that their profession is substantially discredited, and as a matter of fact that is correct. They point to the public attitude poll that recently listed lawyers as having fallen sharply from the plateau they once shared with bricklayers and grape-pickers and other honest men who make an honest living. The explanation they prefer for their fall in the general esteem is that it all has something to do with Watergate. Nixon was a lawyer, Mitchell was a lawyer. So was Ehrlichman, Dean, Liddy, on down the line. Could this be why?

Then there is the very high cost of legal service, about which they feel guilty, though to be sure ambivalent. But they read the figures, and wince just a little bit. A Cabinet officer's income for the practice of law the year before was a half million dollars. They wonder out loud: Can that man have been practicing law, or exercising influence? They read about the bills of the lawyer who defended the Watergate crowd. Two, three, four hundred thousand dollars.

These are surrealistic figures, and they prove very simply one thing, namely that the structure of the law is unsound. Horowitz may be worth $10,000 a day or—if you insist— Mick Jagger. But lawyers who routinely charge $2,000 for a day's work are taking advantage of a system whose protracted rhythms were once enumerated by Hamlet as a cause for suicide. Why don't lawyers effect reforms within their own profession, they wonder?

And correctly so. A young, brilliantly trained, philanthropically-inclined attorney once confessed to me that if he were up on a murder rap, he could not afford to retain a lawyer to take such advantages of the law as he recognized were available to him. Justice beyond the reach of the average individual is injustice. The fatuous solution is to come up with a grand system of federal subsidies. For lawyers. The sensible way to do it is to simplify the law, recodify procedure, make waste unprofitable. Hold those playful lawyers in Washington who amuse themselves by circulating catch-all subpoenas to every tenth name in the telephone book responsible for harassment where harassment is proved.

The deeper problem, as I view it, is that the lawyers, in an age of relativism, nibble away at the root of the epistemology itself. Suddenly nothing is really knowable. The Supreme Court of the United States discovers every year or so something in the Constitution not only that hasn't been discovered before, but something which the formulators of that particular article or amendment to the Constitution specifically rejected. But it becomes law. This is called casuistry, and casuistry is one of the diseases of a decadent order in which people refuse to rely on basic cognitive skills, and have no faith in sequential argument. It is lawyers who can take a plain recitation of facts, turn it upside down, shake it, marinate it with doubts, and trundle it upstairs to a higher court for reconsideration.

"It has become a ridiculously difficult thing to do," one older judge recently said, "to prove plain matters of guilt or innocence." It is lawyers who have come up with an understanding of the Constitution of the United States that makes it apparently impossible to stop wholesale crime. Lawyers, that is to say, whose primary purpose it is to guard the civil order, but who are responsible for much of the chaos within it.

That is the reason so many law students are uneasy about the profession they will soon be practicing; soon, we pray, be reforming.

A National I.D.?: Yes

November 1, 1977

I AM ASSOCIATED, in one of my lives, with what the professionals call a "little magazine." It is a journal of conservative thought and opinion, a small chapel filled with jeweled objects on which the season's lights refract through stained glass windows wonderfully, variously, inexhaustibly, illuminating the truths we live and die for. The tablet-keepers of that magazine received an afflatus recently, causing us to come out in favor of a national identity card, and we woke the next day to find ourselves surrounded by the faithful, hurling objects at us, charging that we had profaned the very foundation of our church. It is un-American to have an I.D.

That is, in my judgment, a venture in ideological mystification. What *is* un-American is the invasion of privacy. The documentation of individual Americans is not *in itself* a violation of privacy. What is done with that documentation is what matters.

Before we had a federal Social Security Act, we did not need federal social security numbers. It would be chaotic to attempt to do without social security numbers now; and, so far as one can judge, Americans nowadays accept not only social security, but social security numbers; and there has been no abuse. Before the age of passports, there were no passport numbers; but there is no rational resentment of passports nowadays, if it is conceded that the identification of the individual is important.

Which brings us to the critical question. Much having been written on the problem of immigration, the subject of an identity card arises. It appears that there is available a technology for the manufacture of an identity card that is virtually proof against forgery. By definition, anything produced by craft can be reproduced by craft: but although it is unsafe to say that the contemplated identity card will be absolute proof of the identity of its holder, experts assure us it would take the resources of a superpower to duplicate it.

What have we got, if we have an identity card? A means not of damming the tide of immigrants coming in (primarily) over the Mexican border; but a means of greatly reducing their number. The population problem in Mexico is as severe as anywhere in the world. I was a student in Mexico when the population of the country was 22 million. In 1975 the woman was born (I quote a Mexican authority) who will become the mother of the 100-millionth living Mexican. The barometric difference between the economy of the American Sunbelt and of the north country of Mexico is of the kind that causes tidal waves. If there are already 7 or more million illegals in the U.S. today, then they are already inundating us: but the floods lie ahead.

An identity card is not the solution, it is merely one device to aid in the regulation of one problem. The presumptive philosophical objections to it ought to be analyzed. If we believe that a country has the right to regulate citizenship by a rhythm suitable to its own priorities, then it follows that a country has the right to seek the means of distinguishing between those people within its frontiers who are citizens, and those who are not. An identity card is, of course, the kind of thing one associates with totalitarian regimes like Russia's and China's, and despotic regimes like South Africa's, which use it for the purpose of doing things no state should ever be permitted to do. But that is a contamination not of the card, but of its uses. This distinction—as we move cautiously into the question of what to do about the illegals—we ought to keep clearly in our mind. If we do so, it should cause the angry armies beleaguering our little magazine to pack up, and go home.

Three Martini Lunch?

December 10, 1977

ONE HAS TO CONCLUDE that Jimmy Carter's crusade is, really, against martinis, not against the revenue lost to the government by their deductibility in certain circumstances. The martini, let's face it, has become a code word. References to the "three martini lunch" are designed not so much to evoke anger at the prospect of a dollar a martini lost in revenue to the government. They are designed to point to a lifestyle against which all the complicated glands in Jimmy Carter's body boil in protest.

I'm not a betting man, and neither is Jimmy, but I'd bet you on this, that if JC were given a lie-detector test, I know what his answer would be to the question: "Mr. President, if you could outlaw the drinking of martinis at lunch, or merely outlaw their tax deductibility, which would you do?"

Now the reason the "three martini lunch" is evocative in a sense that, say, a "three Scotch lunch" or even a "three whiskey" lunch is not, is that the martini is thought to be the quintessentially alcoholic drink. And, really, it is. And the drier you insist the martini be, the closer you come to the essence of alcohol: straight gin. Indeed, there are those who go all the way, ordering straight gin on the rocks. Though, come to think of it, they will not really have gone all the way until they order straight gin without any rocks. Which is what the Dutch do, by the way.

But martinis have a special appeal for certain people. Bernard de Voto, who wrote a book about spirits, dubbed it one of the two genuinely creative American contributions to the repertoire of strong drink (the other: bourbon and water). I know an elderly man who has said that immediately on entering St. Peter's Gates, he intends to seek out the man who invented the dry martini. He tells you why in devout tones: "I just want to say to him 'Thanks.'" But the consensus is that a dry martini even at night is a straightforward invitation for instant relief from the vicissitudes of a long day. And that a martini at lunch is a quick invitation first to exhilaration but then—very quickly—to torpor.

Now Mr. Carter clearly faces emotional difficulties here. He cannot, for instance, outlaw the deductibility of a martini at lunch—without also outlawing the deductibility of, say, champagne. Would he attempt to outlaw the deductibility only of alcoholic beverages? There are restaurants in New York at which for food alone at lunch you can run up a bill of fifty dollars. Is it proposed that the food be deductible but not the booze? That would appeal to the prohibitionist vote, but not very much to the libertarian vote. Will they try to put a limit to the price you can deduct for any lunch? But how would such a price attempt to mete out impartial justice for those who live in New York, say, and those who live in Cedar Rapids?

Ah!—our bureaucrats have come up with an approach. Why not exclude from deductibility the price of the host's lunch, acknowledging as a legitimate business expense only the cost of his guest's? But this is one of those solutions bred in the hygienic laboratories of the bureaucracy, unrelated to experience. If the idea is to take the potential customer to a fancy restaurant to help induce a commercially compliant mood, how can the boss expect his employee to pay for his own fancy lunch? Or should he, having reserved a table at "21," arrive with his lunch box, and order pheasant for the guest? My guess is there would result a certain social uneasiness not conducive to commerce.

It is, of course, one more example of the age-old truth of

the proposition that tax laws are never successful when they try to effect justice. The answer is: Of course, martinis should not be deductible, nor should lunches nor should Tabs. But what would there be to deduct from? Nothing: because, of course, there should be no tax on business.

For the Inflationists: Mug Shots

December 11, 1975

MR. KINGMAN BREWSTER, the president of Yale University, found himself safely in England the other day, out of range of the Kids' Dew line which, round the clock, catches orthodox blips from educational officials and launches deadly missiles against the offenders. Accordingly Mr. Brewster talked to the English Speaking Union in London about problems which, up until now, have been identified in the public mind as problems only the troglodytes worry about. Such problems as overspending, the shortage of capital, the heavy cost of bureaucracy, and, above all, the irresponsibility of Congress.

It is sobering to contemplate that not one of the politicians—or professors—President Brewster is normally linked with could have guessed, reading this speech, who delivered it.

Mr. Brewster said that "[the] inflationary bias of representative government seems to me the greatest threat to the survival of a democratic political economy." That statement is worthy of having been written by, well, myself.

"We need," said the president of the university that teaches its students for the most part to scoff at the dangers of inflation and to support such massive increases in state welfarism as were most recently championed by George McGovern, "some higher law to restrain the natural temptation to use the spending power for political self-perpetua-

tion. If we do not solve this problem, representative government will drive us up to altitudes of inflation which, like
anoxia above 14,000 feet, will not be able to sustain productive economic life."

Then came the clincher. "Until we can devise ways by
which the inflationary consequence of a Congressman's vote
is traced to him with the same particularity which attaches to
a yea or nay on a revenue bill, we will not cure the disease of
public spending motivated by the desire to achieve re-election."

Mr. Brewster's warning is timely. The President last fall
asked for a reduction in taxes but only if tied to a reduction
in spending. The Executive and the Congress are now engaged in an elaborate and complicated exchange, the purpose of which is to blame the other party. Because of such
advantages as Mr. Brewster speaks of, Congress is likely to
escape the blame, and turn an angry public against, not itself,
but the President.

Professor Ernest van den Haag of New York has advanced
a novel notion which, if explored, might provide such countervailing pressures as Mr. Brewster calls for. The President
should "refuse" to borrow the money needed to pay for deficit federal programs. As things generally go, Congress passes
a tax bill which will bring in Revenue X. Then it passes a
spending bill which authorizes Expenditure Y. Y is almost always larger than X. The President has the authority to borrow, through the Federal Reserve system, the differential.

What if he would refuse?

Congress would have to permit the Executive to trim expenditures. Or else it would have to order the President to
borrow, bringing on more inflation. In doing so, it would become far more exposed than it is now. Individual inflationists
might then be traceable with that requisite "particularity"
proposed by Kingman Brewster.

No doubt there are other means. Since we are to have
highly elaborated election laws, perhaps, picking up the
theme of consumer protection, we should require all candidates to list after their names the percentage over revenue
for which they voted appropriations, so that, for instance,
one would routinely refer to "Mrs. Bella Abzug

(D.-N.Y.-50)": meaning that she had voted to spend half again as much money as she voted to tax.

Meanwhile, the sunburst of Mr. Brewster lights the skies, and we pray that having discovered the light, he will one day soon discover the truth.

Energy: Keeping the Issues in Sight

October 6, 1977

IN THE TUMULT and the shouting of the past ten days one has the sense of having lost all idea of economic integration. Highly intelligent people are going about confused over what is going on in the complicated quarrels in Washington having to do with energy. Quite understandably. Concerning all of which, a few comments:

1. The fundamental problem is untouched by all the wrangling over Mr. Carter's energy bill. That problem is the oligopolistic leverage of OPEC over world oil. Since the crack of doom sounded from Saudi Arabia after the Yom Kippur War in 1973, no policy has been arrived at to cope with the quadrupled price of oil coming from the OPEC nations. At a political level, there is an accommodationist fatalism that is absolutely startling. It is as though God had announced, in November of 1973, that He was going to change the seasons around a bit. One professor from Johns Hopkins proposed we should consider military action against Saudi Arabia if absolutely necessary. He was put in Coventry. The Dutch were finally forgiven by the Arabs for siding so conspicuously with Israel during the engagement, and were magnanimously permitted to buy oil at $12 per barrel. The British were secretly enjoying the whole operation because they knew that very soon they would themselves be fellow profiteers of the great oil gouge. The United States meanwhile did nothing, and calmly permitted its imports of foreign oil to rise from one-third of national consumption to one-half.

Everyone in Washington is nowadays arguing whether gas prices should be deregulated. Nobody appears to be concerned about the effect the oligopoly is having on the United States dollar, which is retreating all over the world. And quite rightly, inasmuch as we are predicting for this year a balance-of-trade deficit approximately four times as large as the largest in our history. We are arguing about windfall profits for a few oil and gas producers from Texas, Oklahoma, and Louisiana, while apparently resigned forever to permitting a couple of sheiks to decide, according to their pleasure, the cost of oil, and therefore the value of the dollar.

2. As long as we continue to force American producers to sell oil at a lesser price than we pay for foreign oil, we are in effect subsidizing the purchase of foreign oil. By selling our oil at an artificially low price, we simultaneously increase demand and diminish supply. If oil taken from the ground is sold at less than the price of replacing that oil through fresh discoveries, a subsidy acts to encourage the expenditure of energy-dollars—and to increase general consumption, resulting in a greater importation of oil.

3. The Senate reasons correctly that if oil is taxed at the wellhead (for the purpose of reimbursing certain purchasers some of the cost of oil), there will be no increased incentive to discover fresh oil. President Carter threatens (through Mr. Schlesinger) retaliation, proposing to invoke the authority granted to President Ford to impose a tax on imported oil and then figure out some way to get that money back to the consumers through general tax relief. The whole thing is a mess, subsidizing economic archaeologists who seek to trace the movements of dollars through tariff barriers, entitlement redistributions, wellhead subsidies: a mare's nest of bureaucratic interference. Reminding us that:

4. Economic problems are best solved by the marketplace doing its impartial duty. Political problems are the preserve of the state. It is the job of the American government to upset international conspiracies against the American consumer. The government has done nothing to cope with its responsibilities, but has done its best to prevent the economy from coping with *its* responsibilities. Add to the picture the opposition of the government to breeder reactors for the ex-

ploitation of plutonium power and you have the full picture of government ineptitude and the neutralization of the entrepreneurial function.

The Duty to Vote: Passing the Torch

August 7, 1977

SEVERAL YEARS AGO, addressing students at the University of Texas in Austin, I sat and listened attentively to the young professor who was introducing me. He had clearly done his homework—more homework, it proved, than I myself had done on my ancestry. "Mr. Buckley's grandfather," the professor told the crowd, "was a Texan. Indeed he was the sheriff of Duval County. John Buckley was a law-and-order sheriff and an adamant Democrat. Indeed, although he died in 1904, such was his attachment to the Democrats that he voted for Lyndon Johnson in 1948."

Rumors to the general effect that LBJ stole the election in 1948 were of course rife at the time, and indeed there had been legal action. But LBJ overcame, and in due course he was President of the United States, after which the people stopped sniggering for a little while about "Landslide Lyndon" who had won the big election in virtue of an eighty-seven-vote plurality. When they resumed sniggering it was not to protest the impurity of Texan democracy, but rather the impurity of South Vietnamese democracy.

It reminds one of the delegation of American scholars dispatched by LBJ to Saigon to report on the election of 1967. They all came back and testified to the general hygiene of the event. But one scholar, from Massachusetts, left a little residue of Yankee wryness by saying he had found the election in South Vietnam "every bit as scrupulous as elections in Massachusetts." There was an eloquent silence in Greater Boston when these words were uttered.

Mr. Luis Salas, the aging Mexican-American county judge, announced that he wished to live on good terms with his conscience. He then gave the details of the dramatic meeting at which George Parr, the undisputed boss of that part of South Texas, called in Salas and quoted Lyndon Johnson as saying, "If I can get 200 more votes, I've got it won." Parr went on to say in Spanish to Salas, "We need to win this election. I want you to add those 200 votes."

Salas obligingly did so. What was especially remarkable about the crucial 200 names was that they were handed in in alphabetical order. We have been trained to believe that if you lock up a bunch of monkeys with a bunch of typewriters for long enough, they will eventually type out a perfect edition of *Hamlet*. The notion that 200 individualistic Texans would present themselves in alphabetical order at the polls—including one who had been dead for forty-four years—tends to strain most imaginations: but then Texas excels in most matters, and although the election was contested, it was eventually certified.

Lady Bird Johnson no doubt intended to be reassuring in her comment on the matter. She was in fact anything but reassuring. She said through a spokesman that she "knows no more about the details of the 1948 election other than that charges were made at the time, carried through several courts and finally to a justice at the Supreme Court." What she succeeded in saying is that not only is Texan democracy corrupt, American democracy is corrupt right through several courts and finally to a Justice of the Supreme Court.

Perhaps the incident can be got into the next edition of Victor Lasky's book, *It Didn't Start with Watergate*. On the other hand, I'd like to offer a slightly different view of the matter. Frankly, I rather like the idea of Buckleys voting at every election, never mind the formality of their death.

"Tradition," Chesterton wrote, "may be defined as an extension of the franchise. Tradition means giving votes to the most obscure of all classes, our ancestors. It is the democracy of the dead. Tradition refuses to submit to the small and arrogant oligarchy of those who merely happen to be walking about. All democrats object to men being disqualified by the accident of death."

I am very proud of my grandfather's sense of civic obligation. Clearly it runs in the family.

VI.

Abroad

The Panama Canal: An Opening Statement, Debate with Ronald Reagan

January 1978

MR. CHAIRMAN; ladies and gentlemen: If Lloyds of London had been asked to give odds that I would be disagreeing with Ronald Reagan on a matter of public policy, I doubt they could have flogged a quotation out of their swingingest betting-man. Because, judging from Governor Reagan's impeccable record, the statisticians would have reasoned that it was inconceivable that he should make a mistake. But of course it happens to everyone. I fully expect that, some day, *I'll* be wrong about something. Ronald Reagan told me over the telephone last Sunday that he would treat me very kindly tonight, as he would any friend of his suffering temporarily from a minor aberration. He does not, in other words, plan to send the Marines after me. Perhaps he is saving them to dispatch to Panama.

I find myself, Mr. Chairman, in your company, and in the present company, disarmingly comfortable. I have sat in Saigon with Ellsworth Bunker and heard him confide to me that in his opinion we should militarily cut off the Ho Chi Minh Trail. I have sat in Hawaii with Admiral McCain when, as commanding officer of CINCPAC, he fretted privately over our failure vigorously to work our will on the Vietnamese. Admiral Bud Zumwalt, on "Firing Line," deplored *three years ago* the progressive deterioration in American military strength. Patrick Buchanan is probably the author of every truculent anti-Communist statement uttered by Richard Nixon—the old Nixon—over a period of ten years. Roger Fontaine is that anomaly in the academic world, a scholar wholeheartedly devoted to the anti-Communist enterprise. George

229

Will is probably the most consistent journalistic critic of the SALT treaties, insisting that they play into the hands of the Soviet Union. And my colleague James Burnham is, after all, author of *The Struggle for the World,* and has been the leading anti-Communist strategic prophet in the United States, whose books and articles have illuminated the international understanding of the global threat of the Communist world beyond those of any other scholar . . . And yet here we are, disagreed on a matter of public policy impinging on our common concerns.

We should, I think, make this dispute as easy on ourselves as possible. We are here to ask the question: Should the treaty submitted by the President to the Senate be signed? If I were in the Senate of the United States I *would* sign that treaty. So would Will. So would Burnham. So would Zumwalt. So would Bunker.

Now this does not commit us to saying anything more about that treaty—or, more properly, those treaties, because as you know there are two of them, one governing the role of the United States in Panama until the year 2000, one governing the role of the United States after that time—than that we would vote *for* them, rather than against them. To vote for them is not to endorse the foreign policy of President Carter. To vote for them is not to renounce the foreign policy of Theodore Roosevelt. To vote for them is not to say that we are frightened by any threat directed at us by Omar Torrijos. To vote for them is not to say that we are in the least influenced by the desires of the Security Council of the United Nations, which is dedicated to the decolonization of any part of the world not under Communist control.

I think I speak for my associates when I concede that the means by which we achieved our present position in Panama were a part of what one might call pre-Watergate international morality. But then, if we look about us at the activity during that period of our sister states, we do not—those of us who do not suffer from the sin of scrupulosity—think ourselves historically unique. Indeed—here I should perhaps excuse my colleagues from any identification with my own views on the subject—*I* happen to believe that there is a great deal to be said historically for the achievements of colonialism. Even so rigorous a critic of Western practices as Professor John Kenneth Galbraith manages to change the subject when you ask him whether he believes it was a good thing that Great Britain entered India in the nineteenth century. If anybody wanted to raise the banner of colonialism at this moment in Cambodia or in Uganda, I would salute him and start sounding like a bagpipe. So that what I am saying is that I for one am singularly unmoved by lachrymose appeals to pull out of Panama on the grounds that our presence there is "the last vestige of colonialism." My instinctive response to assertions put to me in those accents is: Maybe we should have a little *more* colonialism, not less of it.

Nor does our belief that it is wise to sign these treaties suggest that we harbor any illusions about the character of the head of government of Panama, or the stability of his regime; or that we find that the thirty-two governments that have ruled over Panama since it became an independent state are tending toward creeping stability because the current government has lasted almost ten years. And, finally, we are not unaware of the friendship struck up by General Torrijos with Fidel Castro, the premier barbarian of this hemisphere. What we are maintaining is that the United States, by signing these treaties, is better off militarily, is better off economically, and is better off spiritually.

Why militarily? The question needs to be examined in two parts. If there is a full-scale atomic war, the Panama Canal will revert to a land-mass, and the first survivor who makes his way across the Isthmus will relive a historical experience, "like stout Cortez when with eagle eyes he stared at the Pacific—and all his men looked at each other with a wild surmise—silent, upon a peak in Darien."

In a situation of hostility short of the exchange of missiles, we would desire mobility through the Canal. That mobility is more easily effected if we have the cooperation of the local population. As matters now stand, 75 percent of the work force in the Canal is Panamanian. It is frequently asserted that the natural economic interest of Panama is sufficient to keep the Panama Canal open and operating. Those who come too readily to that kind of economic reductionism fail to take into account great passions that stir not only in the breasts of members of the Third World, but also in our own. The same man who built the Panama Canal once spoke, in the spirit of Robert Harper, of millions for defense, but not one cent for tribute. Theodore Roosevelt would not have been surprised by the closing of the Suez Canal in 1967 even though the loss of revenues to Egypt was roughly comparable to such a loss to Panama. The Panama Canal is responsible for 12 percent of the gross national product of the Republic of Panama. Subtract 12 percent and you have 88 percent left over—in addition to your pride. I hope that Governor Reagan will not tell us tonight that Panamanian pride is not involved in the matter of the treaties. He may tell us that Panamanian pride must in this case be subordinated to the national interest: and if he convinces me that the national interest requires subordination of Panamanian pride, I shall side with him. But he must not tell us that pride does not count. He must not tell us that the Panamanians should not be expected to share those passions which moved Egyptians a decade ago to make huge sacrifices, closing their canal. And he ought not to suggest that American pride is one thing, Panamanian pride quite something else.

I take it, then, that the cooperation of the 2 million people in whose territory the Canal lies, whose personnel already do three-quarters of the work required to keep the Canal open, is, to put the matter unobtrusively—desirable. At the same time, I deem it essential, along with Admiral McCain, that the United States should continue to exercise responsibility for maintaining access to the Canal, and I note therefore with satisfaction that the first treaty reaffirms the absolute right of the United States to defend access to the Canal and to continue to garrison our troops in Panama until the year 2000; and I note with satisfaction that the second treaty reaffirms the right of the United States to defend the Canal and to guarantee access to it even after the Canal itself shall have become the physical property of the Republic of Panama. It is appropriate to reflect at this moment on the words of William Howard Taft, reiterated by Theodore Roosevelt in another context. Taft said: We do not want to own anything in Panama. What we want is a canal that goes through Panama.

I should add, before leaving the military point, that if we cannot secure access to the Canal after the year 2000 from bases outside Panama—i.e., if our power is so reduced that we cannot control the waters at either end of the little Isthmus of Panama—it is altogether unlikely that the situation would change in virtue of our having the right to bivouac a few thousand Marines within the territory of Panama.

Why would we be better off economically? Because under the first treaty, the revenues from the use of the Canal flow to the United States. The royalty retained by Panama is, at 30 cents per ton, approximately 25 percent of the tolls, plus a share in the profits not to exceed $10 million. Ancillary economic commitments do not spring directly from the treaty, by which I mean our extra-treaty commitment to help Panama achieve credits from the Export-Import Bank, from AID and OPIC; and our commitment to give it, over the term of the treaty, $50 million of military equipment for the purpose of relieving us of expenses we currently shoulder. Those who have made a huge production over the financial price of these treaties—which figure approaches $60 million a year, the whole of it derived from Canal revenues—are perhaps most easily sedated by comparisons that come readily to mind. One billion, 290 million dollars to Spain during the last twenty years—I know, I know: we are paying Spain for the privilege of protecting Spain, such are the burdens of great nations. Or there is Turkey. For the privilege of protecting Turkey from the Soviet Union, we have spent 2 billion, 878 million dollars, and are now committed to spending an extra 1 billion over the next four years. Dear Turkey. Lovely people.

And unlike the Canal, Turkey provides us with no offsetting revenues. Perhaps we should send Mr. Bunker to Ankara to argue that we should receive a royalty on every pound of heroin sent out from Turkey for sale in the streets of the United States. And there is Greece—1 billion, 800 million, with 700 million committed over the next four years— plus reversion to Greece of U.S. military installations. Or the Philippines, which is asking for a cool billion. I do hope and pray that Mr. Reagan, whose propensity to frugality with the public purse is one of his most endearing characteristics, will not devote an extravagant amount of our time tonight to telling us how ignominious it is, under the circumstances, to cede 40 or 50 million dollars a year—out of revenues—to the Republic of Panama.

I said we would be better off spiritually. Perhaps—I fear it is so—this is the most provocative point I have made, particularly in this company. That is so, Mr. Chairman, because we are most of us agreed that the people who have been responsible for United States foreign policy during the postwar years—Republicans and Democrats—have tended to suffer from grievous misconceptions concerning what it is that makes a country popular, or prestigious. The conventional wisdom is that we earn the respect of the world by prostrating ourselves before the nearest Cherokee Indian, and promising to elect Marlon Brando as President. The factual situation suggests that the world works very differently. General Torrijos has criticized the United States far more than he has criticized Fidel Castro. American liberals accept solemnly plebiscites conducted in Panama when they see validated something they want validated, while scorning plebiscites conducted in Chile when they see validated something they don't want validated. I happen to believe that the surest road to international prestige is to pay absolutely no heed whatever to foreign opinion. However, in order to do this successfully, it helps—though it is not required—that you be a gentleman. Nikita Khrushchev had no problems whatever in getting himself admired by Nehru, the great ethical heartthrob of the century: not even when Khrushchev took to expressing his crotchets by sending Russian tanks to run over Hungarian students who wanted a little liberty. In the corridors of the United Nations, the representatives of the anticolonialist world don't rise and walk out in indignation when the Soviet overlords walk into the room, or the Chinese: they don't pass resolutions calling for freedom of Tibet or of Lithuania, let alone Poland—which, we were advised last week by our pleasantly befuddled President, shares American principles and ideals.

No, we do not believe, those of us who favor this treaty, that it is to be favored because it will cause the president of Libya to smile upon us as he lubricates his megaphones with expropriated American oil, happily joining a consortium of extortionists whose respect for the United States—interestingly enough—diminishes as we agree to pay the price they exact from us as a reward for our defective diplomacy.

No, it is another kind of satisfaction we seek—I mean the approval given by reflective men and women to nations that disdain a false pride. Nothing should stand in the way of our resolution to maintain United States sovereignty and freedom. And nothing should distract us from the irrelevance of prideful exercises, suitable rather to the peacock than to the lion, to assert our national masculinity. We have great tests ahead of us: Are we going to disarm unilaterally? Is our word to our allies a reliable covenant? Do we really believe in human rights? Do we really believe in sovereignty? even in sovereignty for little countries, whose natural resources, where and when necessary, we are entitled to use, but not to abuse? The kind of satisfaction a nation truly consistent in the practice of its ideals seeks for itself is the kind of satisfaction, at this moment in history, we can have—by ratifying treaties that, at once, enhance our security, and our self-esteem.

On Hating America from Abroad

January 22, 1976

DR. ROBERT MCAFEE BROWN is Professor of Gloom at Stanford University where, in the Department of Religious Studies, he weeps over American sinfulness. This is all very well, but recently Dr. Brown went abroad to do this, and clearly spoiled the meeting of the World Council of Churches at Nairobi which, like almost every other meeting of that Council, is called for the purpose of indulging one of the principal pleasures of this world: criticizing the United States. He gave a pre-emptive talk about American guilt, so full of mortification, so copious with grief over our sins, that when the time came for the Third World speakers to berate America, they looked as though they had been summoned from the rear of the bus. Everything was anticlimax.

The Third World now has yet another reason for being anti-American: American spokesmen fan out across the globe, frustrating anti-Americans by beating them to the punch.

What specifically did Dr. Brown say? Well, the usual things, one gathers: about warring against the peasantry in Vietnam, and all those other sins of the postwar period during which we spent almost 200 billion dollars trying to help people and keep them more or less free. Dr. Brown summarized his case. "I am ashamed of [America] particularly for what it has done, and continues to do, to so many of your countries." He said that many in the Third World are starving because "American business exploits them economically."

In the current issue of *Commentary* magazine, Professor Peter Bauer of the London School of Economics, who has written extensively on many matters relating to the developing countries, African in particular, makes a number of points which, in turn, would spoil Dr. Brown's fun, assuming he could read without paralysis to his nervous system.

Professor Bauer concedes that the popular notion that rich America is ruining things for the poor nations of the Third World is "axiomatic." In fact, he advises us, this is not only untrue, but more nearly the opposite of the truth. Our acceptance of these axioms has, however, "paralyzed Western diplomacy, both toward the Soviet bloc and toward the Third World, where the West has abased itself before groups of countries which have negligible resources and no power."

Item. When the West descended on the Third World countries, the polarization did not then begin. "The West was [already] far ahead of the present Third World when it established contact with these regions in recent centuries." But surely it is fair to conclude that the underdeveloped nature of much of the Third World is the result of Western depredations? . . . Well, as a matter of fact, no, it is not fair to conclude any such thing. "Some of the materially most backward countries in the world never were colonies (Afghanistan, Tibet, Nepal, Liberia)."

Are trade relations stunting the development of domestic economies in the underdeveloped world? Not at all. "It is paradoxical to suggest that external economic relations are damaging to development."

But doesn't such trade take more and more from the poor nations for the benefit of the rich nations? No. The opposite.

What about the enormous amount of consumption by, for instance, Americans? Well, it's true that we overindulge ourselves—witness Dr. Brown's appointment to Stanford. But the relevant economic index is quite different. "Per capita production in America exceeds production in India by more than the difference in consumption, allowing it not only to pay for this consumption, but also to finance domestic and foreign investment as well as foreign aid."

But Westerners have been responsible for racial and religious discrimination? Yes, but "colonial governments . . . have usually protected the minorities and not persecuted them; and [anyway] discrimination long antedates colonialism."

And a conclusion: So far from the West having caused the poverty of the Third World, contact with the West has been the principal agent of material progress there. Indeed, the very *idea* of material progress is Western.

These are sad tidings for such as Dr. Brown. All his life he has, apparently, shielded himself from them.

The United Nations

Experiencing Carter

March 22, 1977

THANK GOODNESS there was one red corpuscle at the tail end of President Carter's speech to the United Nations, because

up until then it was the worst treacle yet served up by Jimmy
Carter, and is best ignored, which it will be. Toward the end
he made a concrete suggestion—that we move the Human
Rights Commission from Geneva, to New York, where it
would probably accomplish nothing. But it is a good idea, because if you're going to ignore human rights, which is the
principal activity of the United Nations, you should ignore
them in plain view, and that means in New York, not Geneva.

The late Professor Willmoore Kendall of Yale University
gave it as his cynical opinion twenty-five years ago that American Presidents should be elected for life terms—on the
grounds that every President feels free to lose *one* continent
or subcontinent to the Communist world, and the incumbent
having already used up his ration, it would be better to hang
onto him. By the same token, every President of the United
States appears to feel compelled to give one silly speech to
the United Nations, and we can be grateful that President
Carter, who has four and perhaps eight years more to serve,
will not feel any further obligation to appear before the UN
to pronounce such inanities as he pronounced there on
Thursday.

On top of the banalities, there was the strange awkward-
ness of the prose. Listening to the speech, one suspected that
perhaps the speech writers from whom Mr. Carter wrested
the limousines are retaliating by a kind of syntactical slow-
down. Listen:

"Poverty, inequality of such monumental scope that it will
take decades of deliberate and determined effort even to improve the situation substantially." The hybrid metaphors, the
vermiform appendices, the redundancy and alliteration, are
bad enough—but on top of that, the sentence does not make
sense. The word "substantially" was clearly intended to be
"slightly."

Listen again. Mr. Carter wants to "maintain peace and to
reduce the arms race." How do you reduce a race? By making it shorter?

Again: "We must seek to restrain inflation and bring ways
of managing our domestic economies for the benefit of the
global economy." Whaaat? How do you go about bringing
ways?

And on and on. But then the thought matched the syntax: "In Southeast Asia and in the Pacific we will strengthen our association with our traditional friends . . ." Our traditional friends in Southeast Asia are mostly dead.

"We recognize our parallel strategic interests in maintaining stability in Asia, and we will act in the spirit of the Shanghai Communiqué."

Do we have an interest in "maintaining stability" in Asia? We have the same interest in maintaining stability in Asia as George III had in maintaining stability in the colonies, with the rather important difference that George Washington and his gang of fifty-six who signed the Declaration of Independence revolted against conditions which, by contrast with those that continue to enslave 800 million Chinese, were mere bureaucratic inconveniences. If Mr. Carter is interested in human rights, as he does not cease to tell us is the case, he can hardly be interested in maintaining a stability of Asian servitude.

"Throughout the world," Mr. Carter went on, "we are ready to normalize our relations and seek reconciliation with the states which are ready to work with us in promoting global progress and global peace." But of course that sentence is pandemonium. We are in fact seeking good relations with the Soviet Union, which however is promoting global disruption and global strife: in Africa, in the Caribbean—in the situation room at the White House, if we continue to dismember our security apparatus at the current rate.

But let us console ourselves that an important speech by a Chief of State to the United Nations has yet to be delivered. So let us forgive our President, confident that just as his listeners probably don't remember today what he said, neither, probably, does Mr. Carter remember today what he said.

Experiencing Andy Young

June 2, 1977

EVERYWHERE THEY ASK: "What do you think of Andrew Young?"

1. He is said to be a most engaging man. So was Harvey, the wonderful, fanciful rabbit whose creator was everybody's best friend. I will go to see *Harvey* as long as James Stewart revives it on Broadway. Andrew Young is, in the judgment of this observer, somewhere between an innocent and a naïf. Only an innocent could explain his apparent indifference to world Communism by saying he never felt threatened by it. I doubt he was ever threatened by smallpox, but you would like to think he would nevertheless react intelligently to a world epidemic. And of course he is naïve if he believes that stabilization is what happens when Soviet-dominated troops enter a territory. This is true only in the sense in which you can say that the Communists stabilized Czechoslovakia in 1948, the Nazis stabilized the Sudetenland in 1938, and the Ku Klux Klan stabilized the South after the Civil War.

2. His negritude, worn on his sleeve, is not merely distracting. It is counterproductive, and racially offensive. The whole purpose of the civil rights movement in America is to bring on equality. It is, to use the Court's phrase, intended to make the country color-blind. Andrew Young sometimes supposes himself to be the representative of the black American community in the United Nations. He isn't. Daniel Patrick Moynihan wasn't a representative of the Irish community when he served in the United Nations. But Andrew Young, who arrived in Africa giving the Black Power salute, identified himself not only with American blacks, but with a relatively small segment of American blacks. About as many American blacks give the Black Power salute as sing in minstrel shows. Moreover, the rhetoric he used in Africa is straight out of the old song books of the Black Panthers. " . . . When you talk about the infant mortality rate, when you talk about the presence of disease, when you talk about the malnutrition that is the result of systematic oppression

and death dealing, then you have to relate the violence of a military situation . . . to the total violence of the situation." That was Young in Africa.

Elsewhere he found Idi Amin and Ian Smith "similar," which is the same as saying that Jan Smuts and Papa Doc Duvalier were similar. Throughout his tour, he was a Catherine wheel of black bombast, suggesting boycotts here, comparing Jimmy Carter to Afrikaners there, announcing that in the United States the racial climate was in some ways more "brutal" than in South Africa until recently. He was, so to speak, SNCC's representative to Africa, which is not what he was appointed to be, or what he is paid to be.

3. It is both reassuring and alarming that, under the circumstances, he has become not a fighting word in America, but something of a pet. A pet bulldog. *National Review,* a fortnight ago, reproduced the first sentence of an editorial in the New York *Times*—"Ambassador Andrew Young announced in Michigan today that he would continue to speak out candidly . . ."—under *National Review*'s own headline: "Terrorist Threat of the Week." In Europe, during January and February, Andy Young got big headlines in the scary sections of the papers, together with accompanying editorials of hushed and apprehensive gravity, all of which asked the same question: Does Andy Young represent the President of the United States?

Eventually, the White House tactfully dissociated itself from Young sufficiently to quiet this particular worry. The press went on to Phase II: Isn't it scandalous, they would now say, that the President has an ambassador who so regularly is an embarrassment to him and says things that clearly the President would not himself say? But a scandal, if it goes on and on, becomes, somehow, less scandalous. And this is especially so in the current situation because

4. Mr. Young is ambassador to an organization that is so morally inert, it is hard to tease a scandal out of it. The United Nations, a writer who served there recently observed (it was I), is the most impacted institutional hypocrisy in the history of the world. Ostensibly dedicated to enlarging human freedom, it is not only silent but sycophantic toward those powers that practice most diligently the repression of human

freedom. To this assessment of the United Nations there is increasing agreement, from Right to Left. Andy Young becomes just plain Harvey in virtue of the increased disposition of Americans simply not to care what our ambassador to the United Nations says about anything.

So What *Is* Wrong with Great Britain?

May 9, 1976

WELL, to begin with, what's *different* these days about Britain? At least one convention is changing. It is uncharacteristic, not to say unthinkable, for Englishmen to wonder just what it is that foreigners may be thinking is wrong with them, and unheard of formally to solicit their opinions on the matter.

That kind of thing has for generations been an American copyright. We have begged non-Americans to tell us what is wrong with us for more than a century. And we consider that they have earned their keep only if they tell us how thoroughly unsatisfactory we are. Oscar Wilde and GBS would have spoken to empty houses in America if they had arrived with the whispered news that America's achievements, rather than her derelictions, were compulsively the subject of any discussion about America.

The trouble with Britain, I suppose, is that too much is expected of her . . . why should any country continue forever to be "Great"? I remember a dazzling moment with Harold Macmillan when a student panelist on a television program asked him whether it might not sadly be concluded of Great Britain that she no longer was generating great leaders.

He turned on the young lady (rather than to her), and in not more than a few sentences huffily-avuncularly reminded her that England was an island of barely three million people when she defeated the Armada and began, over a period of three centuries, to put three-quarters of the globe under her flag.

But always during those years, Macmillan said, there was

talk, talk, talk of the imminent end of British greatness. Indeed, as a young man he remembered being at White's the day Bonar Law died, listening to an elder statesman at the bar bemoan the loss of indispensable and irreplaceable Great Englishmen. "Bonar Law gone . . . Lloyd George . . . Asquith . . . now," he shook his head sadly, "there are only a few of us left."

Macmillan's serenity was electrifying, and you could hear the strains of "Amazing Grace" in the studio. He was testifying, so to speak, as an Old Boy from British History; rocksure that when the williwaws were done, the air, so preternaturally clear in the sceptered isle, would breathe fresh life into this remarkable breed. As it had done—one of the great prodigalities of history—when simultaneously producing men who could defeat the Armada, and poets who could enshrine St. Crispian's Day. That afternoon I'd have followed Macmillan anywhere—except to the sanctuary of his thesis.

What's wrong with Great Britain is its class structure. The conventional criticism of it is that it keeps Britons separated, frustrates mobility and encourages an abjectness of the spirit. I view the problem differently. The class structure in Great Britain is a tropism, the obsession with which draws Britain to internecine war with itself.

Socialism, that hoary vision of a factitious fraternity which gave theoretical respectability to an untutored generation's superstitions (collective ownership will breed collective satisfactions), fired its enthusiasts only in part because they were seduced by its eschatological pretensions. It didn't take very long to establish that socialized industries tend to produce inferior products at high prices by dissatisfied workers.

You can get a smile even at Brighton—maybe even from Barbara Castle, if the sun is shining—by quoting *Krokodil*'s charming little heresy about socialism ("'What happens when the Soviet Union takes over the Sahara Desert?' Answer: Nothing for fifty years. After that, there is a shortage of sand.")

It isn't that the socialists desire, really, to own the steel companies; it is that they desire that the people who owned the steel companies should cease to own them. One part is envy, but a much more important part is resentment, and the fury of the emotion is, I think, magnified at the polls precisely by virtue of that docility which a tradition of good manners enjoins at home and at work.

The character in fiction who, on his day off as fawning valet to "Milord," marches with the most radical pickets demanding an end to wealth and privilege isn't a character from Shaw. He is Colonel Blimp's stepson.

A guide who took my son and me a few years ago around Copenhagen rattled on about the accomplishments of his remarkable little State and, arriving at the peroration, said rather breathlessly: "Here we have a 99 percent tax on the highest brackets of income." He beamed with pleasure, as if no one could now deny that Denmark had achieved the high-water mark of Western civilization. I remarked that Britain was not far behind, and he said patronizingly that yes, Britain with its 85 percent tax was doing pretty well.

But of course Britain is not doing pretty well, and it isn't only the ravages of a tax rate so preposterously high as to encourage economic stupidity. It is the implicit mandate behind such plutophobic tax rates.

A rate of 85 percent against the most productive members of society, quite apart from what it does to discourage savings, investment and the intelligent allocation of resources, a) abrogates any plausible theory of equal rights under the law (we are *not* all Englishmen; we are, in an involuntary way, servants and masters); b) stimulates a sense of bitterness by a victimized class; c) robs Britons of the morale that makes partnership of endeavor an act of spontaneity (the genius of Switzerland); d) encourages outright defiance of parliamentary authority thus undermining political democracy; and e) causes a few sensitive and important Britons to feel that their only defense is to take residence outside Britain.

Anthony Burgess is not moved primarily by materialist emotions. He feels it an indignity to live in a country that does not need his paltry surplus, but *declines* to let him have it.

Something is wrong with any society a significant number of whose luminaries feel that, Procrustes having taken their measurement, they are found guilty of being too tall; and so, walking past the immigration authorities, they tiptoe out of the country, lest they rouse Harold Macmillan from his reverie.

London Notes: 1975, 1976, 1977

1975

London—THE CONCERN HERE, as one would expect, is largely with British affairs, and these remain steadfastly glum, and if the young De Leonite Tony Benn has his way and takes over control of the British Labor Party, he will make Harold Wilson look like Mark Hanna. The Benn in question began life as Viscount Something, son and heir of the Earl of Stansgate. But when the old Earl died, young Anthony Neil Wedgwood Benn became the Earl and, as such, entitled to a seat in the House of Lords, but most emphatically not in the House of Commons, which of course is where the action is.

The Earl thereupon embarked on a Stakhanovite program of self-proletarianization. It isn't certain whether he has absolutely completed it, but already: a) He succeeded, after a tough fight, in abdicating the title, thus permitting him to stay in the House of Commons. b) He adopted every known position, and some heretofore unknown, that would identify him with the Populists and the Socialists. c) He managed to reduce his name not merely to Anthony Wedgwood Benn, but to pure and simple Tony Benn. At this point, I can only think of dropping the second small "n" from "Benn," to make him more us-folkish; and no doubt this will soon occur to him.

Meanwhile, he is leading the fight on many fronts, subtly undermining Harold Wilson, which is all right, except from the wrong direction. Benn wants England out of the Common Market, and is forever coming up with stratagems designed to effect this: indeed, it was he who, way back in 1968, came up with the idea of a referendum. Just after Wilson went off to Jamaica for the Commonwealth Conference, Benn floated an idea to finance his rapacious nationalization and subsequent impoverishment of all British industries by raiding the city pension plan. Wilson *harrumphed* his disapproval all the way from the Caribbean.

But Benn is undeterred, is the hero of the Greening of Great Britain, and is undoubtedly the most feared man by anybody in England who wants, a couple of years from now, to be able to buy a loaf of bread without carting the cost of it to the bakery in a wheelbarrow.

1976

London—MR. DENIS HEALEY, who is Chancellor of the Exchequer in the socialist cabinet of Mr. Wilson, is plagued by the awful seductions of common sense, which are fatal to the fantasies of ideology. As a faithful advocate of socialism, he manages a fine performance when on duty, and you can sit back and relax in professional admiration, much as you might in hearing Lee Bailey make the case for the Boston Strangler. But when Mr. Healey is engaged in formulating policy, he is required to yield to the vector of forces: England is going broke, her inflation is wild, the morale of the merchant class is shot, the taxation schedule is sadistic and unprofitable.

In a recent seizure of exasperation against ideologues on his left who clamored for more taxation of the "rich" Mr. Healey pointed out that if he were to confiscate 100 percent of the income of every Englishman earning more than 12,000 pounds ($24,000) it would not raise money sufficient to pay 1 percent of the national budget.

More and more Mr. Healey sounds like the man who justifies the necessity for setting fire to the house while doing everything he can, discreetly, to put it out. It is a juggler's act, from which the poor British can take only the consolation that nowadays most of the rhetoric is left-oriented while the deeds are conservative-minded. The trades unions have been forced to ask for only moderate pay increases, there is talk of diminished taxation, and there are high hopes that by letting the pound suffer the discipline of the float, the trade deficit will reverse.

By contrast with Healey, the singular emotional event of the week was Lord George-Brown's statement that he had had it with the Labor Party. A proximate cause of Brown's defection was a single broadcast by Solzhenitsyn, said to have been the most stirring forensic experience by a foreigner since Garibaldi mobilized England on the side of Italian *Risorgimento*. George-Brown has always been an interesting man, in part because of the purity of both his virtues and his vices. It was in the tradition of Ernest Bevin, a child of the labor movement whose eyes were trained on socialism as the instrument for the liberation of the individual.

Brown was made Foreign Minister by Harold Wilson on two separate occasions, but lost his post because he could not manage to win even the safest seat. This was in part owing to his unabashed devotion to the grape, which he is frank in considering to be, even ahead of the dog, man's very best friend. Accordingly, after listening to the speech by Solzhenitsyn, after enduring the latest assault on private liberty—the government-backed closed shop bill—and the coincidental death of a beloved father, he called a rather boozy press conference at which, however, he spoke of the ideals that many years ago had brought him to socialism: the quest for liberty.

These ideals, he said, were no longer being served by the Labor Party, from which he said, just before falling on his face, he now chose to dissociate himself. Paradoxically, he has at least earned that financial security the socialists have wanted for everyone. Mr. Wilson stuck him in the House of Lords where, characteristically, instead of choosing to call himself something like Lord George of Wick Hampshire, he renamed himself, simply, Lord George-Brown.

Though, come to think of it, he is not entirely safe. The left wing of the Socialist Party continues in its ravenous search for neglected liberties and traditions to obliterate. Anthony Wedgwood Benn, who will not be happy until he has nationalized the swans in Windsor Park, proposes yet another assault on the House of Lords, and incidentally on the monarchy.

The Young Socialists, in their newest resolution, have come up with a marvelous idea for limiting criticism of themselves and other socialists. Simply a) nationalize the newspapers, and b) instruct printers to remove editorial copy offensive to them. Why didn't we think of that? Perhaps I can persuade the sainted junior senator from New York to sponsor a bill nationalizing book reviewers.

1977

London—WHEN THE BRITISH learned—it was an incidental piece of intelligence, filed as filler copy adorning the main event—that on the day that President Jimmy Carter addressed the joint session of Congress it was the very first time he had stepped foot in Congress, they were unbelieving. Because in Great Britain the House of Commons is the center of political life. To become Chief Executive without having had extensive parliamentary experience is at least inconceivable, probably unnatural, and possibly aberrational. For this reason it is indispensable that an aspirant Prime Minister perform well in the House of Commons. We speak every four years about the requirement that a Presidential contender do well in a public debate. In the House of Commons such debates as we set up as quadrennial spectaculars, they run off once or twice a week. And if you do poorly in these, before long you are out of contention. That is why the showing a couple of weeks ago of Margaret Thatcher, leader of the Conservative opposition, was so important. She took the pants off James Callaghan, the Prime Minister, and Denis Healey, the Chancellor of the Exchequer; and all England was abuzz with the word that the lady is a tough and knowledgeable polemicist.

Nothing is more embarrassing to a British socialist than to quote his utterances over the years. It is a wonder that Tony Benn hasn't proposed a law that all past speeches of socialist politicians be hidden in the British Museum along with the sado-masochist collection.

Mrs. Thatcher quoted the Chancellor of the Exchequer when he said, in September 1974, "If the social contract is maintained"—the social contract is the term used to describe the willingness of the trades unions to limit their demands for annual increases in pay—"we can get inflation down close to 10 percent by the end of next year and into single figures the year after." The social contract was maintained.

Mrs. Thatcher quoted the same man speaking a year later: "There is now every prospect of inflation getting down to a single figure, year on year, by the end of 1976."

Mrs. Thatcher quoted the Prime Minister speaking in 1976: "If you can grin and bear it for twelve months more, then by the end of 1977 the inflation will be where that of our major competitors is now."

Mrs. Thatcher quoted the Chancellor of the Exchequer speaking on July 15, 1977, after the breakdown of the social contract: "The inflation should fall below 12 percent well before this time next year."

Ah, but the lady was not through with Mr. Healey. She quoted a statement made by him in March of 1974, in which he spoke of a £4.2-billion deficit as "intolerable," announcing that the Labor Government would reduce it to £2.7 billion. Three years later it was £9 billion.

In 1974 the Labor Government pronounced the unemployment intolerably high. Since then it has risen by 800,000. The inflation rate is at 15 percent. The pound is down to $1.70. Public spending is at 60 percent of the GNP. The Chancellor of the Exchequer was forced to admit that the revenue that would come in (only once, because after that Englishmen would make other arrangements) if all salaries in excess of $12,000 per year were taxed at 100 percent would take care of the government's expenses for only four and one-half days.

Mr. Peter Jay, our new ambassador from Great Britain, and Mr. Samuel Brittan have written, in the volume *The Future That Doesn't Work: Social Democracy's Failures in Britain* (edited by R. Emmett Tyrrell Jr. and published by Doubleday): "The marketplace for votes and the marketplace for goods operate according to vastly different and frequently incompatible criteria. The political entrepreneur asks what most people want. The economic entrepreneur must ask himself what people want most."

Social democracy, observes Mr. Ferdinand Mount, a learned British journalist, isn't the same as socialism. Social democracy presumes a continuing responsibility for social policy. Socialism presumes a one-time entry into the maw of socialism without opportunity seriously to reconsider. England has "democratic socialism in that its introduction follows the democratic process. Its operation is totally authoritarian, bureaucratic, and unresponsive to public feeling. It is a furtive, squalid masquerade, foisted upon an unwilling, bewildered, and increasingly apathetic electorate. . . . The difference between this state of affairs and the clarity and certainty with which private industry has usually been allowed to operate in Sweden and West Germany can hardly be exaggerated."

The parliamentary pressure being exerted by Mrs. Thatcher must necessarily awaken the dormant intellectuals of socialism. Mr. Mount comments on their performance. "For all the cant about Labor being the intellectuals' party, nobody in the Labor movement has applied any real thought to the central questions of social democracy in the last twenty years. If I were a social democrat, I should blush to be associated with such a bunch of careerist numbskulls."

The political situation is warming up in England, now that summer's there.

A Day in Israel

May 17, 1975

Tel Aviv—LEAVING ISRAEL IS A revealing experience. It is hard to begrudge an air terminal that has suffered what Lod has suffered the right to impose any indignity on transiting passengers. So when the lady asked me what was my profession, I answered good-naturedly, "I am a journalist."

"Show me your journalist card."

"What do you mean my 'journalist card'?" I answered. "In America, we don't have 'journalist cards.'"

Well then, she said, how could I prove I was who I said I was?

When you come to think of it, proving you are who you are, when your interrogator declines to accept your passport or your American Express card as proof, isn't the most obviously easy thing in the world to do. But that was when my inspiration took me. In my briefcase I was carrying a copy of one of my recent books, promised to my host in Athens. I reached for it triumphantly, because on the back of it is a large photograph of seven scruffy looking people of whom I am one, and the central figure is most indisputably Dr. Henry Kissinger, Secretary of State of the United States, whose signature appears on all our passports beseeching foreign officials to permit us pass without let or hindrance. The occasion of the photograph was the swearing in of the United States delegation to the 28th General Assembly of the United Nations.

On seeing the face of Dr. Kissinger, I regret to report, the lady instantly left and came back with a man dressed in khaki, about thirty years old, sinewy, tough.

"How long have you been in Israel?"

"One day," I said.

"What did you do?"

The Lord, I thought, had delivered him into my hands.

"Well, as a matter of fact, I spent an hour in a television studio with Prime Minister Rabin."

With this, the gentleman became forthrightly hostile and suspicious as, one supposes, he'd have done if I had said I was Napoleon.

"Where are you going from here?"—he answered his own question by examining my airplane ticket which showed I would spend two days in Athens, and an evening in London, before going on to Washington.

"Why are you going to London?"

I thought it best not to yield to the temptation of saying, "I can't go on any longer without listening to Big Ben."

"Because you cannot get to the United States if you leave Athens after 2 P.M. , and my business in Athens does not end until 2 P.M., so I am hitching a ride to London where I shall spend the night visiting with my goddaughter's parents in Wiltshire, catching the early flight the next morning to Washington."

"That isn't true. You can get to Washington or New York directly from Athens."

"Look," I said, "what business is it of yours where I go after I leave Israel? What if I wanted to go to Iceland?"

"I am the chief security officer," he said.

We had, really, reached an impasse; and so he decided, grudgingly, not to detain me. Instead, the two of them inspected my baggage with lascivious care, even unto squirting my Right Guard, thus further diminishing the Ozone Barrier.

"They are really uptight over there," a journalist in Athens commented, on hearing the story. He used a word which, mercifully, has very nearly gone out of fashion. But he used it truly, and there is every reason for Israel to be in a high state of jitters.

Yet having remarked this, I found in conversations with Mr. Rabin, and with a newspaper editor, an academician, and an author, that there is a mood of subjective fatalistic optimism in Israel. They figure that the price of bringing Israel down is a price the world, really, isn't prepared to pay. Don't ask me how I found out, and thank God Ninotchka at Lod airport didn't know I was leaving the country with this piece of knowledge, but the Israeli high command secretly calculates it could survive only six weeks of war before finding itself in the logistical jam it was in after six days of the Yom Kippur War. The feeling is that the Arabs simply do not want another war, and that the claims of the Palestinians will not drive the Arabs to another war. It is obvious that the Israelis are genuinely ready for some horsetrading, and through it all, they are sustained by a great spirit, which tells them that if Apocalypse is ahead for them, they must accept the fact—fatalistically. But the feeling is that Israel will survive.

A Light on Darkest Africa

August 12, 1975

THE DECISION, reached at Kampala, by the Organization of African Unity, not slavishly to endorse Arab motions in the

General Assembly of the United Nations at the forthcoming session is significant and heartening. The Arab-African bloc has spoken for several years with a dismaying unity that belied not only the strutting rhetoric of independence with which representatives of these nations traditionally announce themselves, but gainsaid whatever little use the United Nations might serve the freshly independent states. To persuade Uganda—for instance—that its interests are identical with those of Saudi Arabia reminds one very simply of the surviving powers of superstition. For Kenya to vote against an effective anti-terrorist resolution is a venture in self-destruction.

No doubt repeated threats by authoritative American officials to have done with the United Nations if it deprives Israel of its right to speak in the General Assembly brought caution to the big meeting in Kampala. United States support for the United Nations is quite simply critical at every level: financial, diplomatic, and psychological. It is also the one world stage to which the African nabobs can repair to show off their sovereignty in extra-parochial surroundings.

Mr. V. S. Naipaul, an Indian novelist, has given us in a recent issue of *The New York Review of Books* a sensitive look at the state of Zaire, the old Congo of the Belgian Kings. The principal figure in Zaire is of course General Mobutu. He used to be plain old Sergeant Joseph Mobutu, son of a cook, in the local Force Publique. Now he is Mobutu Sese Seko Kuku Ngbendu Wa Za Banga, which means a number of things in the Lingala dialect, none of them unflattering. General Mobutu traveled to New York to give an ardently anti-white speech in the fall of 1973, and managed to make the journey without hardship with the aid of a supporting retinue of eighty-six persons, including his wife's hairdresser.

All this kind of thing, Mr. Naipaul points out, is not resented in the least by the impoverished people of Zaire. As Mobutu succeeds in promoting the vision of himself as not merely *citoyen* (he does not disguise his humble origins) but King, and even . . . divinity . . . the people participate in his elevation. There is very little else for them to participate in. General Mobutu, by Mr. Naipaul's account, presides over one of the supremely tatterdemalion states in the world, cursed by the eternal bush, creaky with the rust of junked

Belgian hardware, stitched together by a nearly impenetrable tapestry of corruption, boiling under the equatorial sun.

Mr. Naipaul describes a visit by a state commissioner to a nationalized coffee plantation whose workers had not been paid for five months. "Everywhere the commissioner went he urged the people, for the sake of their own liberty and well-being, to follow the principles of Mobutuism to the letter; everywhere he urged vigilance." Mr. Naipaul does not try to improve on the brief description in the capital newspaper of the voyage to one outpost, a mere twenty miles from the principal artery of the Congo, the River Zaire. "At the very entrance to the canal thousands of mosquitoes cover you from head to ankles, compelling you to move about all the time . . . After a whole night of insomnia on the Lubengo Canal, or rather the 'calvary' of Lubengo, where we had very often to get out in the water and make a superhuman effort to help the paddlers free the pirogue from mud or wood snags, we got to the end of the canal at nine in the morning (we had entered it at 9:30 the previous evening), and so at last we arrived at Bomongo at 12:30, in a state that would have softened the hardest hearts."

These are the workaday problems of much of Africa, and it is appropriate to feel compassion for those who seek to plumb the heart of darkness, and prescribe for it. The Belgian colonialists made scant progress, and ruled with a cruelty Mobutu, in his excesses, can hardly be accused of doing more than imitating. The United Nations and a fawning audience, the kingly palaces, the servants and presidential parks and parades and marching children, are the sponge filled with vinegar, held out to the tortured thirst of generations of humiliation. Africa has unconvincingly rejected Western ways—the women of Zaire are by law forbidden from imitating Western dress. But their dreams are of Mercedes cars and huge factories, devolving to Africa after the decadence of the West finally launches us all into the bush. But clearly the leaders of these countries wish for the United Nations to survive to see it all happen.

General Franco's Executions

October 4, 1975

IT IS HARD to go for very long these days without thinking of James Burnham's masterpiece *Suicide of the West*. There is a fresh book, elaborating the same thesis, in a way. A novel, by the Frenchman Jean Raspail, which treats of a kind of amphibious invasion of the southern coast of France by a sampan Indian fleet of a million refugees fleeing their over-populated and plague-ridden homeland, and the drama be-comes: Will France resist? It is called *The Camp of the Saints*, and it might just as well have been called *Suicide of the West*.

The chorus of that plot has been singing very stridently in recent days, ever since a military court sentenced to death eleven Spaniards for—murder. General Franco commuted six of the sentences for extenuating circumstances, e.g., two of the girls were pregnant. The others he had taken out and executed by a firing squad. It was bad enough in the United States, where reports of the executions were as lugubrious as if it were Edith Cavell they were shooting. In Europe, you would have thought that Franco was executing five of Our Lord's twelve apostles: for the sin of going about the world preaching faith, hope, and charity.

One does wish that His Holiness Pope Paul would stop in-terfering in these matters. This is the third time now that I can remember. He has the power, unchallenged in the Cath-olic community, to declare that capital punishment is a moral crime. Let him use it, if he feels the afflatus. He would, to be sure, be required to revise those passages in the Old Testa-ment that specify capital punishment for certain kinds of crime. But I do not see why the Pope makes no gesture against Catholic France for guillotining assorted criminals (some ten in the past ten years) who kill people, while pro-testing the execution of Spaniards who kill people.

The only generic distinction one can come up with is that in Spain the murders were "political murders." So? I cannot see that the victims—simple policemen—were in any way affected by the distinction. And I do not see that a state should consider that anyone within its borders who kills someone for a political motive should be treated more gently than someone who kills someone while robbing a bank. The argument, as a matter of fact, is entirely in the other direction. The principal corporate responsibility of the state is to guard itself: *salus publica, suprema lex.* Attempts on civil authority are attempts on civil order. And this statement is a generically safe one to make. One wishes that tyrants were regularly popped off by heroic assassins. But one cannot expect that those who are caught will go unpunished. Why didn't the legions in Europe rise up in protest against the public execution of the assassin of King Faisal? Probably because they were afraid they'd have to pay more for the gas they use up driving to town to make their protests.

President Echeverria of Mexico, who is doing his best these days to sound like Algeria's Bouteflika, proposed expelling Spain from the United Nations. It is safe for somebody like Echeverría to say that kind of thing because he is used to being ignored. When in 1968 some of the students in his own country got a little frisky, he gave the order to his executioners, who did their work not against convicted murderers, but, Kent State style, against waves of students, killing hundreds. Even today, the exact figure is a military secret.

Franco has executed eight people in fourteen years. Almost two years ago, the revolutionists executed the premier. How many policemen and other innocents would have been dead if the law had not been enforced? Let France, which averages one new republic every twenty years as a result of the failure of the preceding one, prescribe for herself. And Germany, which should have executed Hitler and spared the lives of 30 million Europeans and Americans. Great Britain has come a long way since she used to execute schoolboys for stealing anything in excess of the value of one shilling. But the hangman, so dreadfully missed in England, is keeping his rope limber against the day when people there begin in earnest shooting down British policemen. I do not doubt that even now, a convicted terrorist exploding hand grenades in hotel lobbies would be gladly strung up by the British people. Franco would have the grace to remain silent.

Revisiting the Soviet Union

Russia contra naturam

December 27, 1975

Moscow—IN THREE YEARS, the people of Moscow are better dressed, slightly better housed, slightly less harassed, it would appear. There isn't any reason for this that issues out of any recent access of Soviet efficiency or benevolence. The top rulers of the Soviet Union aren't sadists, like their predecessors. But cruelty does not particularly disturb them, if they can think up uses for it, and there are plenty. It is useful for staying in power, maintaining a worldwide force of menacing potential, and suppressing any organized effort to provide the Russian people with an alternative life. What progress the Russian people have made in recent years can be said to have leaked through. If 95 percent of the bureaucracy retired tomorrow, along with their rules and regulations, the Russian people would prosper as never before.

One hears, in the West, about the few conspicuous Soviet dissenters. Most notably, now that Solzhenitsyn has gone, Sakharov; echoes, every now and then, from Amalrik, who gave one interview too many to a CBS correspondent, producing that distribution of justice to which we have become accustomed: the CBS man was booted out of the country, sentenced to life outside the Soviet Union. Amalrik was sent to a labor camp, with special treatments at a neighborhood psychiatric asylum that specializes in blowing the minds of dissenters. But it has been four years now since an American correspondent was tossed out of the country. And although they are monitored as keenly as ever, they do not, any longer, disguise their movements as diligently as they used to. They reason as follows: if the Kremlin is going to permit traffic with the dissidents, as journalists they must go ahead and pursue those contacts. If the dissidents, knowing they will be observed, want to take the risk, why there isn't very much the foreign correspondents can do about it. It is an entirely unpredictable matter when, on what pretext, or in what numbers the dissidents will be rounded up and sent off to torture. Those who collect the benefits of détente like to think that official Russo-American amity serves as something of a life insurance policy for the dissenters. This needs to be said slowly, carefully. Because no one believes that the Soviet mind has been lobotomized and is incapable now of doing spasmodically what yesterday it did routinely. But some American observers continue to believe that the uneasy toleration of dissent is traceable to a new self-consciousness about Soviet barbarism, induced by détente.

For instance—one foreign correspondent pointed out—there was the scene a year ago that shook the artistic world: a bulldozer running through an outdoor exhibit of unlicensed Soviet artists. The repercussions in the art world were damaging to Soviet authorities, who noiselessly permitted a subsequent exhibit, on a smaller scale, to proceed without interference; and indeed it is reported that one or two of the offending artists have been invited into the Artists' Union. This is revolutionary indeed; or, more properly, counter-revolutionary, it never having been previously supposed that the day would come when any Russian artist would be permitted into the Artists' Union.

For the rest, détente has meant little to Soviet citizens. The rise in the standard of dress and consumption is a tribute not to the relaxation of tensions, but to the sophistication of the so-called counter-economy. Although the standard of living in Russia is very low—less than one-half our own—there is a good deal of cash income around, for the very good reason that for years there has been nothing to buy with it. American tourists shopping in Russia can patronize shops out of bounds to native Muscovites. Having come to these oases, you can buy a) caviar and vodka, b) a fur cap, or c) an enameled box. The techniques of the counter-economy are designed to find something to buy with the money you save. A license to buy a car. Blue jeans. A silk scarf. A short-wave radio. A record by the Rolling Stones. The right to live in Moscow (price: marry somebody who already lives there, divorce him/her, pay him/her off). The counter-economy is beginning to thrive in the Soviet Union. It is nature's defense against totalitarian socialism, and the antibodies thrive on corruption, bring a small measure of contentment to the fortunate few among the Soviet people. The Soviet Union would be infinitely better off if corruption were absolutely universal. It would remain, then, only to declare corruption to be legal—and you would approach a free market system.

Sunday in Leningrad

December 30, 1975

Leningrad—Forget Gulag for a moment. In Russia it is also the little things. You are much better off traveling here in groups, because the Soviet state thinks macrocosmically. Twenty, thirty, a hundred people are palpable. One is a nuisance. But the trouble now was a subgroup. Twelve of us wanted to go to church on Sunday. This is not, by the way, a Provocative Act for a foreigner in Russia—he is free to attend church, and leave the country peacefully.

We are at the newest, largest hotel in Leningrad, a city of 4 million people. You would suppose that the lobby is bustling at 8:30 in the morning. It is not. You look outside the door, into the Arctic dark, and there is no taxi line. You go to the desk where the sign tells you they will call you a taxi for thirty kopeks, but there is no one there. You go to one end of the main desk, and the lady hears you out; and then points to another woman, at the other end of the desk—*she* is the one who speaks English. You go through it again. She tells you you must go to Information on B Floor. You go to Information on B Floor. There is nobody there. You return to the main desk. She tells you to talk to the lady on your own floor who keeps the room keys. You complain that she does not speak English. You are told she will understand you. You go back to Floor 5 and explain that you desire f-o-u-r taxis, counting the fingers on your hand as in This Little Piggy Went to Market, to take t-w-e-l-v-e people to church. She nods, and picks up her telephone. But it does not work. She says something in Russian which has got to be earthy. FLASH! She reaches for a key, obviously to an unoccupied guest room, halfway down the hall. In two minutes she is back, and scribbles the number of a cab which will come to the door of the hotel in a matter of minutes. What about the other three cabs? Go down, she says, and advise four members of your party to occupy the cab with number 76-30. Then come back here, and I will tell you the number of the next cab.

You go to the elevators, but four of them are out of order, and three are not enough to handle rush hour traffic, which has now begun. So you run down 4, 3, 2, 1, PAST THE MYSTERY FLOOR—nobody knows what's there; perhaps Howard Hughes has hedged his bets—B, A, bark your orders to four communicants, and bound back up the six flights. She is at her desk. As you reach her, she hears the telephone ring, bounds down the hall, returns with the number of the second cab, and instructs you to rush down and Fire Two. You ask if you might not simply wait downstairs as all the taxis arrive, and she says No! Under no circumstances! How would you know what the number is of the cab that is dispatched for your use? You do not argue in Russia. I expect you would not argue even if you knew how to argue in Russian. The logical gears are non-reciprocating. On the other hand, the management of the largest hotel in the most cosmopolitan center of Russia finds nothing abnormal in organizing something like Houston Control to round up four taxis at nine in the morning on Sunday. On the other hand, you have the feeling that if you had appeared at the main desk and asked for six B-52s, you would not have been required to make any extra exertions.

We got there. There were perhaps two hundred parishioners. The priest was venerable, and he spoke to a congregation that must have been born, every one of them, before the revolution. The priest read extensively in Russian—from the Scriptures, one supposes. You take fugitive delight in calculating that there probably isn't enough religion left in Russia to attract the attention of the new liturgists.

So the old priest spoke the Mass in Latin, in the old rite, and the old women, and a few men, bowed their heads. Behind the altar is a huge florid painting of the romantic school, the cross figuring large with the legend, IN HOC SIGNO VINCES: *by this sign, ye shall conquer.* You sigh under the weight of all that is undone, in Russia, and outside Russia, before the Church can be called triumphant; but then you ponder the fact that it—the little tatterdemalion church—is still there; and ponder even the demisemiquaver of a miracle— that all twelve American tourists got there. And anyway, after a half-century's experience with Communism in Russia, impatience with chiliastic Christianity is childlike. Someday, when the statues of Lenin are as windblown as his thoughts, the major shrine in Leningrad will probably be that little Christian church, that went on and on, Sunday after Sunday, as if nothing had happened.

Restoration in Russia

January 1, 1976

Leningrad—IN HIS BRILLIANT forthcoming book (*The Russians*), Hedrick Smith of the New York *Times* confirms the worst we have suspected, namely that the exhilarating movement of the dissidents in the Soviet Union has been skillfully choked back by the Communist nobility, to ghostly proportions. It is reduced to three superstars, on whom brilliant but episodic lights continue to shine as they sweatily perform their death-defying trapeze acts in a progressively sequestered ring of the huge auditorium, once filled with an elated constituency of artists, intellectuals, poets, and pilgrims; who for the most part are absent now when, with increasing frequency, the act goes on. The crowds are back in their crowded quarters, queueing up for a fresh orange, reading—or not reading—the Soviet press; dolefully appeasing the ugly demands of their ugly society, even though this requires them to join in ritual denunciations of the three great dissenters among them, Solzhenitsyn, Sakharov, and Medvedev.

They take you, in Leningrad, to Peter and Paul Fortress, built in the beginning of the eighteenth century when Peter the Great decided to Westernize Russia through a resplendent new capital. The prison cells at P & P bear the pictures and biographies of the latest occupants before the revolution, the most celebrated of whom are the older brother of Lenin, and the poet Maxim Gorky. The guide will tell you in catch-throated sentences about the horrors of prison life under the czars. He then tells you that the prisoners were seldom incarcerated for more than six months, dying thereupon on the gallows, or of tuberculosis; or, subsequently, of overexposure in Siberia. It is true that Lenin's brother died on the gallows. His infraction was that he contributed his scientific knowledge to the production of a bomb designed to explode the czar. The bomb, however, misfired. "Upon his death," the guide tells you, "we lost a young genius, already at twenty-one recognized as the leading young light of Soviet science." Those who have followed the vicissitudes of Soviet science will understand that its provenance was a misfired bomb.

But that observation apart, it is hard to get worked up about the execution of somebody who tried to blow up his emperor eighty years ago. We will deal with Squeaky with condign severity.* The other prison cells record matter-of-factly the death dates of their former occupants—in the '30's and '40's of this century, for the most part—comfortably escaping execution, TB, and terminal experiences with Siberia.

The craze in Leningrad, so greatly devastated by the German siege of 1941–44, is for *restoration*. The exquisite palaces of the czars and czarinas of the past 200 years are recreated with brilliant eye and numinous hand, and there is nowhere in the world such repristinated splendor of decorative detail,

*[Squeaky Fromme received a life sentence for attempting the assassination of President Ford—W.F.B.]

achieved by a society that will hang a sign: *DO NOT TOUCH!* on a hard marble staircase, which sign it would not hang over the genitalia of political dissenters, dragged into the torture chambers for interrogation; unavailable for inspection by American tourists.

There is something about the past of Russia that modern Soviet Russia cannot let alone. The exception is intriguing. It is the desolate palace of Nicholas and Alexandra, the last czars. They will drive you right by it to Catherine's Palace, only 300 yards down the road. You need to make a major scene to slow the bus down to let you look at the one unreconstructed palace in the great complex around St. Petersburg. When, finally, the guide sulkily consenting, the photographs are taken, she divulges "our resentment" that "so many Americans" should be "interested" in the habitation of the last czar. "For us," she says—I would guess she was born twenty-five years after the czar and his family were murdered—"the Czar Nicholas is not history, he is still evil, he did much to hurt Russia. . . . How would you like it," she asks, "if I went to New York and took a picture of, of—the Bowery?"

Her audience was greatly amused, and one of them suggested she would probably get a prize from the National Endowment on the Humanities, provided the picture were gruesome enough.

Why, one wonders, do they fear so much the memory of that pallid, awkward, maladroit monarch, drawing curtains over his relatively modest palace, while restoring busily every gilded filigree in every antechamber of his ancestors? Is it a psychic fear of illegitimacy? Anastasia-in-the-closet? The felt need to immure the link between the fastidiously restored past, and the gruesome present? Lest Restoration should become more than a craftsman's passion.

An Evening with Fidel Castro

October 12, 1976

Panama City—FOR THOSE antiquarians who cherish an occasional vignette of the kind which in better days would stir the blood of free men, here is one the hero of which is a Panamanian banker.

For reasons irrelevant to the story, this young businessman had a mission to transact with Fidel Castro, and the contacts to arrange for a meeting with him. He made his arrangements to go.

But these arrangements are to be distinguished from those apparently made by the typical visitor to Cuba from the United States, whether congressman or civil servant or journalist. The visitor put all other cares aside and spent an entire fortnight familiarizing himself with the Cuba from which Fidel Castro—it is now being all but universally said—rescued the people. He was sophisticated enough to know that for years the Russian Communists quieted Western apprehensions by reciting the horrors of life under the czars. Recent studies establish that the period of greatest growth in virtually every direction in Russia was during the first fifteen years of this century. But all Communist arguments are orchestrated around the conditions in Russia in 1917, and those in Russia today. It is not even asked what would Russia under the czars have done between 1917 and 1976 in the absence of Lenin and his successors.

Having done his historical homework, the banker visited with Cuban refugees, getting from them in detail figures, descriptions, locations. On arriving in Havana, he knew that Castro would play his seigneurial game of refusing to indicate an hour for the scheduled conference. He took accordingly two precautions. He devoted his time to touring Havana and the countryside demanding that his official guide stop the car at this school, or that grocery store, or at this medical clinic: and into the memory bank the descriptions were stored: How it was now, almost twenty years after Castro's takeover, compared with how it was then.

The second precaution was to train the body. *Mens sana in corpore sano.* Castro, like Stalin—whose legitimate son he is—rejoices in midnight conferences. They suit, to begin with, Castro's personal habits. They are, moreover, psychologically intimidating. Stay up until midnight doing whatever you do in the evening hours, get awakened by a knock on the door at two in the morning with the news that Castro is expecting you *at that moment*, and you are not likely to be at your best. The visitor, anticipating that Castro could not postpone much longer the interview, went to bed at 8 P.M.—and indeed, at two in the morning, in the safe house where he had been told to stay, the knock came to inform him that Castro was in the east wing.

With, incredibly, very nearly all of his Cabinet. He likes that kind of thing. The full court, any hour of the day or of the night; and the conversations began.

In thinking back to when something of the sort happened to another dictator, one can only think of the great moment when Stalin, at a reception in Moscow, was accosted by Lady Astor who asked when was he going to stop killing people. Castro swaggered in with the kind of stuff that overwhelms American senators and Latin American archbishops: and he found he had run into a stone wall. Courteously, but confidently, the young banker confuted virtually every claim made. He corrected Castro's pre-revolutionary statistics. He challenged, giving the evidence of his own eyes, Castro's claims to the quality of modern medicine in Cuba; to the availability of all basic foodstuffs; to the pupil-teacher ratio.

Castro began then to squirm, and to look aside at his Cabinet, as if to say: How did you permit me to get into this mess with this argumentative bourgeois? One could not tell—the banker reported—whether the glance meant that the next morning the Cabinet would be sent to the sugarfields and a new set of sycophants brought in; or whether the deadly glance suggested that Castro's pride was maimed at having been himself deceived, even as the czars were regularly deceived by their courts. In desperation, Fidel Castro pulled out a book—on himself, by Frank Mankiewicz, former aide to Senator Robert Kennedy, campaign manager to George McGovern. A paean to Castro's Cuba. Of course, the banker had already read it: and held it in the contempt it deserves. He handed back the volume to Castro, as if to say: give it to your propaganda minister.

I learned the story the afternoon that the good archbishop of Panama, the Most Reverend Marcos McGrath, praised the achievements of Castro for his people. He did this most sincerely. Why should he be expected to know more than Frank Mankiewicz about conditions in Cuba? And the next morning—sometimes the prodigality of providence is breathtaking—the morning newspaper in Panama reported that Castro had rationed the consumption of coffee in Cuba to one and one-half ounces per person per week.

Terror in Argentina

February 3, 1977

Buenos Aires—MORE PEOPLE have been executed here by terrorists and counterterrorists in the past couple of years than in France during the revolution. The killings here are less ritualistic: there is no guillotine, no roll of drums, but the results are as conclusive. Yesterday, a dear young thing, third-year student in psychology at the university, a businessman's daughter who had ingratiated herself with the local police chief, left a package on his desk which in due course exploded, killing the chief, his assistant, and wounding several others in the area, including an eleven-year-old boy.

She would be a so-called Montonero, not to be confused with the ERP. The latter, a tightly organized, military revolutionary group, were attacking police and military installations in force during the last days of Isabelita Perón. They are mostly dead now. The former, though left-ideologists who think of themselves as vaguely Trotskyist, behave rather like the Narodniki in Russia, early in the century, going about killing people, preferably officials of the Argentine government but, failing a nubile target, anybody will do. The best friend of Argentina's leading sociologist was driving down the road with his seven children. His car was stopped, a stranger leaned into the window, drew a pistol, and killed the father in the sight of his seven children.

The Montoneros were originally the militant fighting division of Peronism. But when after eighteen years Perón was finally permitted back in Argentina and took power, he condemned the terrorists. But he turned the army loose only against the ERP, hoping to domesticate the Montoneros by extra-voltages of his special charisma. In fact they flourished. When Perón died in July 1974, his wife Isabel succeeded to the presidency, and, although she was the formal chief executive, the army and the police began exercising their own initiatives and the general crackdown began. Mrs. Perón, who trained for the presidency of Argentina as a young nightclub dancer, and as a graduate of three years of formal education undertaken at ages five to eight, relied primarily on her "super-minister" López Rega for decisions. López Rega, in turn, relied on the moon, and chicken entrails—he was a devoted astrologer and mystic. The decisions he made in due course brought on a 600 percent inflation rate, and a chaos so general as to cause universal relief when the army finally took over in March of 1976. López Rega not only wrecked the country, he set back the cause of astrology for years to come, and discredited an entire generation of chickens.

And so Argentina began to limp its way back. Back to what? It can't be said, with any sense of historical conviction, that Argentina is heading back toward a democracy that never took convincing root here. If Argentina could get itself a Francisco Franco, the people would probably settle for him gratefully; forty years of peace, minimal terror and repression, though, to be sure, none of the delights of political liberty. As it is, the principal member of the junta, General Videla, is that unusual creature, a truly reluctant President. Technically, he is *primus inter pares*: that is to say, his two partners, the heads of the navy and air force, can jointly overrule him, though he serves as chief executive officer. It is generally believed that nothing would please General Videla more than to become, once again, just plain General Videla. He is criticized, paradoxically, not for taking too much power, but for taking too little. Without power, there's no responsibility. It is unquestionably the case that there is excessive violence in Argentina, even though motivated by the desire to repress violence. It is extremely difficult to fine-tune an anti-terrorist campaign. People who reach for their pistols or their shotguns at the sight of a terrorist or a suspected terrorist are not trained at West Point. In the United States we trained Lt. Calley at Fort Benning, and his approach to terrorism was My Lai. When the police in Los Angeles moved in on the Symbionese Liberation Army, and cremated practically the entire thing, the American public sat watching the firestorm on their television sets and eating popcorn without much thought to due process. It is so in Argentina, though the question is unanswered: If the Montoneros are finally controlled, will the blood lust slake?

Jorge Luis Borges tends to avoid politics. He is, after all, preoccupied. At seventy-seven, arguably the best living writer in the world, he is blind and has been for twenty years; having read *The Divine Comedy* in Italian only eleven times, he is in a hurry to get back to it, though of course it will need now to be read to him. He has written thirty-five books, so he is busy at work on three new ones simultaneously.

When Peron first came to power thirty-two years ago, Borges exerted himself politically to the extent of signing a manifesto against him. In return, Borges's mother and sister were put in prison, and Borges lost his job in the library. He will engage himself politically nowadays only "when the barbarians are at the gate." Then the big question: What is his position on the ruling junta in Argentina? "They are gentlemen." He would go no further.

In a sense he did not need to do so. General Videla, by almost everyone's estimate, is that. Well, will he lead Argentina to democracy? Borges's answer: "Perhaps in a hundred years." But on reflection a few moments later he interrupted

himself. "You had better make that five hundred years."
Now, General Videla has said he wishes to head his country
toward democracy, but he would no sooner venture to put a
date on its realization than Abraham Lincoln would have giv-
en a date for the ending of the Civil War after the Battle of
Bull Run. There is simply too much to do, too many people
suffering from the economic dislocation caused by the terrorists.

Life, to be sure, goes on. During the Second World War,
Oxford and Cambridge still rowed against each other. The
other day, the annual International Ocean Sailing Race, Buenos Aires to Rio, took off: thirty-two boats, one American entry. At the Yacht Club here it was all clutter, bars doing great
business, beautiful women coming in to see their husbands
and sweethearts take off.

Only strangers noticed what Argentines take for granted:
several dozen soldiers with automatic weapons. There was
enough firepower at the Argentina Yacht Club to level a
moderate-sized town. At the local school for the children of
foreign executives, the enrollment is down 75 percent. Foreign companies cannot afford to pay ransoms in excess of
$10 million to keep a man in the field, and cannot afford the
only kind of security that is effective. There are seventy-two
persons guarding the American ambassador and his family:
at a cost of $1 million per year. Among the effects being pro-
tected at the American ambassador's residence is a plaque
commemorating the visit in that building of President Franklin Delano Roosevelt between November 30 and December
2, 1936.

The plaque features a single phrase from a declaration by
the President on that occasion: "Democracy is still the hope
of the world." In Argentina, democracy brought them Perón, twice. Democracy proved not the hope of Argentina,
but the undoing of Argentina.

And now they need to go back and start all over again.
There is total freedom of the press, which abounds with criticism of this or that act or this or that government official.
The policies of Martins de Hoz, the ascetic, scholarly minister of the economy, are hotly debated. But the government

has the right not to censor, but to close down newspapers, and did so last week, ordering *La Opinión* closed for forty-eight hours. The fight against inflation is painful, but progress is being made.

Americans owe them patience and understanding. That is why it is absolutely critical to know whether in fact we are dealing with gentlemen.

South African Impasse

April 12, 1977

THE OTHER EVENING a visitor from South Africa put it this way to the guests at dinner:

"I abominate present arrangements in South Africa. I always have. I am public in that opposition, and have devoted a good deal of my time to endorsing and subsidizing the activities of the energetic opposition. I do think that progress is being made there, and that that progress is insufficient. But here is what confounds me about the criticism from the United States.

"That criticism fails to acknowledge any formula for South Africa that would be satisfying to our critics in America. One thing that will not happen in South Africa—and should not happen—is the subordination of three to four million white people to total black domination. We are not, after all, colonialists. Our claims to South Africa are at least as legitimate, racially and historically, as those of the black Africans. In the last analysis it is irresponsible to tell South Africa what is expected of it if what is really expected of it is euthanasia for the white race. What do our critics desire?"

The question is difficult to answer. The other day, riding about the Transkei, Jacques Soustelle, former intimate of de Gaulle, sociologist and archeologist, sometime governor of Algeria, wrote that the reason the Transkei has been subjected to universal boycott is that Chief Matanzima did not get that territory after killing a lot of white people. It was a matter of negotiation, and indeed South Africa is the godfather of the whole Bantustan idea, rather than the wounded ex-colonialist power petulant after a revolutionary amputation. Indeed it is true: if the Transkei had declared its independence after shooting a bunch of white African soldiers, and won concessions from South Africa exactly identical to those she has freely got, there would be a representative of the Transkei in the United Nations, at the Human Rights Commission in Geneva, and at the International Conference of the Law of the Sea. Instead, it is a non-country.

Western critics of South Africa seem to be saying the same thing. Rhodesia's experience with Mr. Kissinger is in point. The concessions made by Ian Smith went much further than any in prospect by the South African government: and yet in a matter of weeks, these concessions progressed in the public mind from substantial capitulation by Ian Smith, to Ian Smith the Irreconcilable. All it required was the propaganda of the worldwide leftist machine, plus the demagogy of the front line states. South Africa cannot have failed to read the lesson.

The late Saul Alinsky once observed about Liberia that the reason it was sluggish in the conduct of its own affairs is that it was handed its independence by the United States (more than 100 years ago). According to that thesis a country, to act independently, must fight for its independence.

The conduct of other self-governing states in Africa hardly validates Mr. Alinsky's thesis. What is wrong in Liberia is endemically wrong in much of Africa: one-man or one-party rule, corruption, sloth, oppression. But that notion combined with the vaguely theological notion that white Africa must be made to suffer for the sins of the past, even as the white South was made to suffer during Reconstruction, persists. There is a feel, in the rhetoric of much of the criticism of South Africa, that only a Nat Turner solution would suitably avenge history.

Never mind whether a case for this can be made. Such a solution is not one the South African whites are likely to be attracted to. Under the circumstances it becomes clear that the whites there will need to make their own way, effect their own compromises, their own adjustments. What we cannot sincerely offer them is any relief from the incessant criticism with which we now threaten to worsen matters. Pressure is one thing, but those on whom it is visited should be convinced that there is relief short of the act of suicide. America would profit from observing the axiom that it does not pay to cut off the enemy's line of retreat.

The Beauty of Chinese Shadows

November 5, 1977

THERE IS LITTLE in politics that is truly beautiful. A great oration, every now and then—one or two of Churchill's qualify. A vignette that transcends politics—as Solzhenitsyn did in *One Day in the Life of Ivan Denisovich.* A cry from the soul: this has come to us now from a Belgian Sinologist trained in the appreciation of art. He has written a book of such searing beauty about what Mao Tse-tung has done to China it is safe to say that people will be reading *Chinese Shadows* by Simon Leys after Mao Tse-tung is reduced to fetid memory, occupying a common grave site with Hitler, Stalin, and Caligula.

Mr. Leys's lyre is his wit, and his passion. He began his love affair with China, with its people, with its history and art, at nineteen, devoting himself for twenty years entirely to the study of China, its language and its culture, living there, indifferent to politics. But the Cultural Revolution aroused him, and as he surveyed its ruins—contemporary China—he wrote, sadly, this volume. Sadly because he knew that its publication would bar him forever from revisiting "the country I love more than my own." His book is the only bloom of the Cultural Revolution.

He describes the evening banquets presided over by Chou En-lai (I attended six of these in 1972, and any co-survivor will corroborate Mr. Leys's description, while envying his wit). "Each table seats 12. How the places are chosen and where everyone sits is the result of some complex algebra that would have fascinated the Duc de Saint-Simon: it takes into account the rank of each guest as well as the degree of warmth in relations between China and his country.

"These delicate equations are not easy to solve, and one can easily understand that the civil servants in charge of etiquette do not want to repeat such mathematical efforts too often: this means that once you have been given a seat at one table, you will always have the same fellows with you, barring death or transfer, in all subsequent events. After a few such evenings, the conversational topics are exhausted (provided, of course, that a common language made it possible to converse in the first place, which is not always the case). During lulls, there is music: a band from the People's Liberation Army plays at regular intervals, like a well-oiled music box, from its vast repertory of about a dozen tunes."

Alexander Pope could not have done better. But transcending the anger, there is something that approaches dumb grief—as he describes, for instance, the architectural ruination of Peking. And, riding in the train from Peking to Shanghai, he looks out the window at Mao's new China, the latest hobby of the Ideological Smart Set, from Shirley MacLaine to Barbara Tuchman.

"In the harsh Shantung countryside I rediscovered for the first time the graves scattered in the fields, marked by a stele, an old tree, or a copse, that are such a feature of the Chinese landscape. Instead of our death-ghettoes, our corpse quarters, here the whole earth is a vast and welcoming cemetery: the dead nourish the earth that had nourished them, and their tombs, like a protecting presence, witness the work of their offspring from generation to generation. The new regime—both for technical and economic reasons (regrouping the fields, levelling the countless tumuli that prevented continuous plowing) and for political and ideological reasons (the fight against 'superstition,' the desire to break the old clan ties, woven around the tombs of common ancestors, that bridged the class differences between 'poor farmers' and 'rich farmers')—started long ago to expropriate the dead, and has generally succeeded, despite desperate peasant resistance. Shantung was about the only place that I could still find some remnants of this celebration of the mystical union between life and death, between man and earth, which once could be seen all over China."

George Orwell in his book *1984* fascinates Simon Leys. "Re-reading this book, written before the People's Republic was founded, one is aghast at its uncanny prophetic quality. Without ever dreaming of Mao's China, Orwell succeeded in describing it, *down to concrete details of daily life*, with more truth and accuracy than most researchers who have come back from Peking to tell us the 'real truth.'"

Mr. Leys's book, published by the Viking Press, is as engrossing and as beautiful as *1984*. But the heart stops at the awful realization that it is not a work of fiction.

The Chastened Dollar

May 13, 1975

Geneva—THE FRIGHTENING stories you hear about prices in Europe are largely true. It will require a major change in the American mind to revise the fiction that Europe is where you go to have a cheap vacation. A generation's experience with a dollar swaggering down the European marketplace taking a little of this, a bunch of that, filling the basket to overflowing is now as remote as the Paris of Hemingway.

A few concrete examples. I and my six bags and briefcases needed, this afternoon, to get from Geneva to Montreux, which is superhighway all the way, about sixty miles. Price? Three hundred francs. The easiest way to translate Swiss francs into what we used to call Real Money is to multiply by four. It comes to $120—for an hour's car ride. (I write these words on the train.)

Two weeks ago I spent one night at the Dolder Grand in Zurich, a lovely hotel I have known since childhood. I asked for the smallest suite. The bill was $160. A few months ago, driving by night to the mountains and having gagged at the

food proffered on the airplane by BEA, my wife and I found
a country inn, ordered two sandwiches each and a bottle of
the local wine. Twenty dollars.

The Swiss will tell you, quite politely and quite cogently,
that, really, it isn't their fault. Only two and a half years ago
you could take a $10 bill to a bank and get forty-three francs
for it. At that rate the hotels, taxis, and ham sandwiches in
Switzerland have risen only by that almost universal 10 percent a year that everybody seems to get used to. But when
you add to that 10 percent two devaluations of the dollar,
you get a polarization that makes travel in Switzerland—and
France, and Germany—terribly expensive. It is, I think, not
an exaggeration to say that travel within America is substantially cheaper than in Europe. Our gasoline is half as expensive. Our typical motel rooms are half as high. Except for the
fancy spots in the fancy cities, our cuisine is, I would guess,
about three-quarters as high. Inflation, as Lord Keynes reminded us, is a most evil disease not least because its consequences are so subtle, so pernicious, so difficult to track
down. The United States has gravely mismanaged its economic affairs, but it is only lately that we begin to realize that
all that scope we thought we had in virtue of our dizzying per
capita wealth is very largely illusory.

Everyone knows, of course, that the richest per capita state
is one of those places in the Persian Gulf, where there is an
oil pool per goat-herder. And this is true—specifically, of
Kuwait, which has a per capita gross national product of
$11,000. But surely we are next, and well ahead even of the
Europeans?

No. The second richest country (I use per capita income,
of course) is Switzerland, at $7,270. After Switzerland comes
Sweden, with $6,840. Then Denmark ($6,800); and only after that, the United States with $6,595. We are only a little
way ahead of West Germany ($6,215) and France ($5,390).
We are just a hair ahead of Canada, after which come Norway, Australia, Belgium, the Netherlands, Libya, Austria,
and Japan.

The big dip comes at this point with Great Britain at
$3,385. Recently Mr. Denis Healey, the Chancellor of the Ex-
chequer, proudly announced that the government is spend-

ing $2,400 per year on every member of the working population. He doesn't have very far to go before he spends more on Englishmen than Englishmen earn.

But not to stray from the point: the United States is massively rich because it has a huge capital plant geared to produce for 200 million people. That capital plant can accomplish marvels: it can land people on the moon, produce 10 million automobiles, provide a huge percentage of the foodstuffs of the entire world. But it is powerless to defend itself against the depredations of politicians who abuse it: by taxing it into premature senility; by improvident fiscal and monetary policies. And by a kind of disgust-with-it-all, of which the best expression was the formative book of Professor Galbraith, *The Affluent Society*. The United States has done more than any country in the world to lift its own people and—by the export of capital and technology—other people out of material misery. But a few days in Europe, with humiliating trips to the money changer's window, reminds us that an era is over.

Airline Update

February 8, 1977

Rio de Janeiro—IT HAS BEEN a while since I filed one of my occasional reports on air travel, but now I must caution against flying by Viasa, the Venezuelan airline, if you are among those who a) desire to read aboard an airplane; or b) prefer not to eat lunch at three in the afternoon; or c) tend to prefer the company of an amiable crew. It is probably unfair to file a report based on a single experience, but it is equally unfair to fail to pass along the word after two consecutive experiences.

To be sure, waiting at the airport in Rio de Janeiro is especially trying. The other day the temperature there was 110°. The airport is not air-conditioned. There is a single room there that is cooled, but access to it requires that you call twenty-four hours ahead to reserve a seat. This may strike you as unreasonable, since in the United States we are not accustomed to going to airports for the purpose of going to waiting rooms. But it makes a certain amount of sense in Rio where—just to begin with—the habit of mind is bureaucratic. At that same airport, if you want to check a bag in the baggage room, a form must be completed in quadruplicate, including your passport number. But the main reason for waiting at the Rio airport is, presumably, because flights by Viasa don't usually land on time. Why then not wait at home, or in your air-conditioned hotel, knowing that the flight will be late? Because there is no way of ascertaining whether a particular Viasa flight will be late: You see, Viasa does not answer its telephone.

Two and one-half hours late, the flight to Buenos Aires finally took off, and since it had turned dusk, the handful of passengers on board turned on their reading lights. A faint glow issued, rather like wartime London protecting itself against the blitz. Questioned, the stewardess tells you blithely that no one has ever complained before. You respond that, as of this moment, the record is broken, but she does not smile with you. FLASH! Why not go forward to the compartment with the table in the first-class lounge!

You do so, and the light is gratifying. But, in a moment, in storms the Jefe de Cabina. "This lounge is reserved for the crew."

Surely not, you say: it is clearly an amenity for all the first-class passengers?—and nothing less than an oasis for those who have work to do, and need light to do it? Besides, there are approximately 104 empty seats on the plane, wherein, provided they don't want to read, the crew could relax? The steward retorts that the crew has been working for nine hours. You retort that *you* have been sitting two and one-half hours in Rio, and, before that, worked seven hours, and that it is not *your* responsibility that the airplane is late. Whereupon—the ultimate weapon!—the Chief of Cabin, who ought to be featured in Viasa's next series of advertisements, turns off the overhead light by master switch, leaving you in the dark. Ah so. The Jefe de Cabina does not know something; I can type in the dark!—which I am now doing.

* * *

Three months ago, I boarded Viasa in Panama at 2:30 P.M. for a three-hour flight to Caracas. A Teutonic stewardess with brushed-back blonde hair plunked assorted cold matter in front of me at 2:45, and I observed that having lunched at 1:00, I had no appetite at 2:45, but would be grateful for the sustenance at, say, 4:30. She *harrumphed*, as if I had made an improper proposal, that refreshments were being served *now*, and not again! There is of course no point in eating when you are not hungry—unless you are a bear preparing for hibernation: so I passed. But I did observe the lady who, a good two hours before landing at Caracas, everyone having been served, reclined in her chair, there being nothing to do. Save possibly hate passengers. If her thought turned to contempt for patrons of Viasa, I must concede that she was intelligently occupied.

By and large, Venezuelans are the most hospitable people in the world. But there are some who become positively Russian in their attitude toward customers. The Russians, as readers of Mr. Hedrick Smith's wonderful book will recall, actively resent patronage of any facility by which they are employed. My own experience suggests that the Teutonic lady, and the Jefe de Cabina of Viasa, will be happy only when their airplanes are entirely empty of passengers. They may not have long to wait.

VII.

Manners, Morals, Mannerists

Abortion as a Campaign Issue

September 23, 1976

IN THE SPACE of a week, from two august sources, we were all advised to stop asking the Presidential candidates how they feel about abortion. Mr. James Jackson Kilpatrick was one, and there is no one around whose advice, as a general rule, I'd sooner take even blindfolded. The other is the editorial board of the New York *Times*, a huge magnetic field useful primarily for orienting your compass to the wrong direction. The convergence of the two requires one to examine the proposition.

It is this. Abortion (they tell us) is fundamentally a religious issue—most conspicuously, a Catholic issue. It is a violation of the traditional separation of church and state to impose upon members of other religious sects the views of any one religious sect. Moreover, there are simply too many issues around—population, energy, crime, foreign policy, unemployment, taxation, inflation—to warrant the superordination of abortion over all others. Under the circumstances, in addition to its being a violation of the protocols of church-state, it is something approaching fanaticism to go about asking candidates how they feel about abortion, and then deciding, on the basis of their answer to that one question alone, how you are going to vote. To do this is to be maimed by what the frogs call a *fausse idée claire*.

Now this analysis appears to be plausible, but it breaks down under scrutiny.

Let us concede that abortion as a single issue can be taken to ludicrous lengths. During the Thirties and Forties, there was a doctor-professor in New Haven who would join any organization that favored socialized medicine. He asked only that one question, no other: and by that mechanism, he managed to end up belonging to something like forty-five Communist fronts—for the simple reason that among the de-

281

mands of the Communists is the socialization of everything, including medicine. By the same token, the anti-abortionist who asks only what a candidate's position is on abortion could conceivably end by supporting on election day a pacifist, or a Nazi, or, God help us, a prohibitionist.

But allowing for the intelligent avoidance of silly reductionism, what question is more important than whether the fetus is human? A great moral insight is a great moral insight irrespective of its provenance. It is true that the anti-abortion movement is perceived as a substantially Catholic movement, but it is by no means nourished by exclusively Catholic theology. Jews and Protestants in significant numbers are opposed to abortion for religious reasons. Anyway, religion nowhere tells them thou shalt not kill a fetus; religion tells them simply thou shalt not kill a human being. It is scientific evidence, not religious evidence, that leads them to believe, as so many doctors and scientists are coming to believe, that a fetus is in every crucial respect except one a human being, entitled, therefore, to be treated as one would a day-old baby.

A little more than 100 years ago the abolitionists began to move in on the political parties. For them, too, there were great problems confronting our adolescent society. But the greatest of these was the need to answer the question whether a man born black is nevertheless a man. It is difficult to persuade ourselves, one century later, that these men were parochial, or morally misguided. John Brown gave abolition a bad name, as some Americans by unconstructive behavior have given anti-abortion a bad name. But the issue is a genuine issue, and it takes only a little thought to recongnize that it is the pre-eminent moral issue. Because if it is true that the fetus is human—if one hundred years from now Americans will look back in horror at our abortion clinics, even as we look back now in horror at the slave markets in Charleston, S.C.—then to destroy him as insouciantly as, say, we would squirt a blast of insecticide at a mosquito or order another drink, is appalling. Those who believe that the fetus is human, like those who believed the Negro was human, cannot do less than seek to share their insight with others, and to demand that their politicians accept corporate responsibility for the protection of human life.

Auction Time at the ACLU

June 30, 1977

THE ASSOCIATED PRESS brings us an item on a recent fund-raising auction in New Orleans. Let me relieve the suspense—the auction was a success. It brought in about $3,000, which, apparently, is average.

The custom in such matters is for tradesmen to be invited to contribute items which are then auctioned off. But the ACLU deals in a different métier, so that instead of collecting color television sets, round-trips to Israel, two-ounce bottles of Sortilège, and dinners for two at Antoine's, it offered a smorgasbord of professional services from all those people who hover around the ACLU taking advantage of the liberties it secures for us. The most exciting contribution—the most generous, one gathers—was: one free abortion.

That contribution was, presumably, by a practicing abortionist—a doctor. Last week, you will remember, the Supreme Court ruled that it is not required that states pay for abortions out of tax money, and this caused a great hue and cry, with the suggestion that from now on only Doris Duke can get an abortion; everyone else will need to go to the nearest Snidely J. Whiplash in a grimy basement, or—as in the movie *The Other Side of Midnight*—to a clothes-hanger. Well, spirited bidding in New Orleans resulted in a selling price of $30. That must have disappointed the folks at the ACLU. Who knows, it may have embarrassed the doctor. If you make a grand gesture before an appreciative house where, moreover, the tradition calls on the bidders to be extra generous in their donations—which are usually tax-deductible—then you normally get bloated prices. But $30!

* * *

An economist, taking this datum, would authorize one of several inferences. The first and most obvious is that $30 is the true free-market rate for an abortion in New Orleans by a licensed practitioner. If that is so, it teaches us a great deal about the hysteria of those who have said that, with abortion no longer paid for by the government, it will be priced out of the popular market. Just about everybody can afford $30. And since you can't have an abortion more often than once every couple of months, you can keep a special piggy bank for the purpose.

There is, a properly trained economist would insist, the alternative explanation: perhaps in New Orleans there is no demand for abortions. The old problem of selling refrigerators to Eskimos. But common sense suggests otherwise, New Orleans being a city of passionate people, and, although heavily Catholic, by no means exclusively so. No—it has got to be that science has brought down the price of abortions to a very low level.

Speaking of very low levels, another item auctioned by the ACLU was a free divorce. This went for $19. Now, understanding this requires a little more concentration. A licensed doctor administering an abortion is engaged in a pretty routine event. The objective is absolutely straightforward: kill the fetus. But divorces are, to a certain extent, artistic instruments. There are all those little points of bargaining, and evidently the bidders at the ACLU auction feared that the lawyer offering the free divorce was an ambulance-chasing type, not up to looking after the sophisticated demands of such classy people as attend ACLU auctions. As much might explain why free legal services for driving while intoxicated brought only $10. The explanation is not only reasonable, it is charitable. The entire price structure of the legal fraternity would collapse if divorces sold for only $19, and drunken driving defenses for ten bucks.

The leadership of the ACLU has shown considerable originality. Next year it might auction a free defense for rape. If they maneuver the very best lawyer in New Orleans into making that contribution, then the successful bidder might figure he has in effect bought himself one free rape. In the land of noblesse oblige, the same bidder might also buy the free abortion voucher—which he could then stuff down the dress of the girl.

The implications are fascinating. I do wonder, though, whether there aren't some problems here the ACLU hasn't thought through. Suppose the intoxicated driver runs over the guy with the free rape and abortion vouchers, and they are discovered among his assets. Who pays the estate tax? The ACLU? But surely the ACLU would find that unconstitutional. If the ACLU really wanted to jazz up its fund-raising, it should auction off the reconstitutionalization of prayer in the schools. Or would that demean the spirit of their auctions?

The Trials of Christianity

May 29, 1976

Time magazine's biennial essay on the vicissitudes of the Roman Catholic Church is launched with an epigraph attributed to an "elderly woman parishioner of St. Thomas Aquinas Church, Ames, Iowa": "I hope I die soon so that I can die a Catholic." The lady expresses the misgivings of many Catholics, here and abroad, though the statement of her frustration is philosophically perplexing. Rather like the story of the man whose doctor informs him that he has terminal cancer, and asks what he proposes to do. The patient reflects for a moment, and then says he will join the Communist Party. "Better one of them should go than one of us."

The travail of the Catholic Church is of continuing interest to non-Catholics, for reasons analogous to the curiosity Republicans feel about Democratic sentiment, in the historical knowledge that their own platform of a few years hence is being written. As Catholicism is, so to speak, Protestantized, so is Protestantism. If you find Catholics wondering out loud about the doctrine of the Trinity, you will find more Protestants like the famous Unitarian who believes in "at most one God." At the same time, you find a growing hunger for the formal stuff of Christianity. That formal stuff is really quite simply stated in the Apostles' Creed, or whatever they decided to rename it at Vatican II when, on a rainy afternoon, they ran out of more subversive ideas. It is of course the notion of the Incarnation—that's about it; all the rest is derivative, and interpretive.

Much has been written about the Christianity of Jimmy Carter. Everything evil is being imputed to his Christian belief, short only of the allegation that he is a secret Catholic. Ten years ago, they'd have been saying *that* about him. But nowadays to be a secret Catholic is no more arresting politically than to be a non-secret Catholic. People do not seem to care, because Catholicism has lost so much of its distinctive flavor. "The Catholic Church of today," Clare Boothe Luce says, resignedly, "isn't the same Church I joined." That is certainly true, and as its moorings weaken, so, *pari passu*, do the dogmatical moorings weaken of the coordinate Christian religions. Again, with the exception of fundamentalist Christianity, which it is widely assumed is what Jimmy Carter subscribes to.

What are the implications of that faith? For a President of the United States? It is very difficult to say. Consider the most pressing question a President might need to answer: whether to use nuclear force to defend the independence of the United States. How would a Christian answer that one differently from a non-Christian? Well, we all know that there are Christian pacifists. But there are also non-Christian pacifists. Speaking for what was in those days a fairly dutiful flock, Pope Pius XII said that some things were of "such great value"—for instance, the freedom to worship—that they should be defended "at any cost." That was interpreted as a papal blessing on the use of the atomic bomb under certain circumstances. It is not recorded that the Pope's sanction affected in any way American policy on the use of the bomb. When that statement was uttered, we were committed to building a substantial nuclear arsenal with which to defend this country and even some of its allies.

*   *   *

Suppose that the Soviet Union succeeded with a first-strike against our counterforce weaponry, leaving us merely with nuclear submarines which we would petulantly dump on the Soviet Union, killing off a half-hundred million Russians but leaving us then exposed to a retaliatory strike against our population centers. Leaving the Russians with the last laugh, to put the thing into the jargon of black humor. Is there a distinctively Christian response? Or is it unfair to construct the deductions after positing a successful first-strike by the Soviet Union? Would the Soviet Union risk a first-strike if they knew the American President would instantly put his submarines into action? Is it possible for a President a) to convince the Russians that that was exactly what he intended to do, while b) secretly committing himself not to initiate mutual slaughter, if it came right down to it? Is there a shaft of Christian reason that illuminates the problem? Is it explicable in the vocabulary of fundamentalist Christianity, or, for that matter, of Jesuitical casuistry?

What does it mean to be a Christian is easier to answer, and Christ, the authority on the matter, did so repeatedly, usually in the form of a parable. But there are no parables that quite fit the apocalyptic responsibilities of a President. With the important single exception that the life we lead here on earth is not the final experience of the human being. Though on this much everyone would gratefully agree, that it is certainly our last political experience.

His New Prayer

November 17, 1977

THOSE OUTSIDERS (I am not an Anglican) who have been following the agony of that Christian communion oscillate between feelings of sorrow and anger. It is conceivably a part of the Lord's design to torture His institutional representatives on earth, and of course it is generally conceded that the special object of His displeasure in the past decade has been His old favorite, the Roman Catholic Church, which He has treated with stepfatherly neglect. But as if some providential version of equal treatment under the Law were guiding Him, it has been recently the season of torment for the Anglican Church, which indeed is now riven in factions so resolutely opposed to one another that schism itself has set in.

This last was precipitated by the question whether to ordain women priests. There is an Episcopal bishop in New York who is given to extreme formulations in any field whatsoever. About a year ago he was anathematizing businessmen who were driven from New York having looked at their ledgers and decided that, on the whole, they and their flock would be better off in an area in which the tax overhead was less, and also the incidence of murder, rape, and mugging. Bishop Moore would have lectured Moses himself on his lack of civic pride in departing Egypt in search of greener pastures. Well, the Bishop not only came out for ordaining women, for which there is at least a coherent argument, he proceeded to ordain a self-professed lesbian, which struck his flock as less a gesture of compassion, than of defiance. Anyway, when last heard from, entire individual churches were busy renouncing their ties to the central church.

This morning, the Church of England has issued its rewording of the Lord's Prayer. Now, the head of the Church of England, at least titularly, is the Queen of England. She continues to be addressed with all the euphuistic pomposity of Plantagenet prose, but now they are modernizing the form of address appropriate to God. One continues to refer to the Queen as Your Majesty, and as "Ma'am," but for God, "Thee" and "Thou" are—out. The Lord's head has been placed on the Jacobinical block. He is not quite yet addressed as Comrade, or even Big Brother: but He is definitely made to feel at home in the modern world.

It now goes not, "Our Father, Who art in Heaven, hallowed be·Thy name"—but "Our Father in Heaven, hallowed be Your Name." Granted, they have left the capital letter in "Your," which must have been done after grave debate in the relevant councils. But clearly it was felt that "Thy" was simply—too much. Who does He think He is? The Queen of England?

It goes on, "Your will be done on earth as in Heaven."

One wonders what has been gained by that formulation over the traditional formulation, which read, "Thy will be done on earth as it is in Heaven." There is transparent here something on the order of a Parkinsonian imperative: A venerable passage will be reworded by a rewording commission insofar as a commission to reword possesses the authority to do so.

Is it suggested that more people will understand the phrase in the new formulation? In the first place, we are hip-deep in the aleatory mode when we say, "Thy will be done"—since we all know that it is very seldom done; and, indeed, some would go so far as to say that it is most unlikely that it is being done by the Royal Commission on the Vulgarization of the Book of Common Prayer when they take such a sentence as "Thy will be done on earth as it is in Heaven" back from the alchemists who worked for the Lord and for King James, and beat it into the leaden substitute which they have now promulgated.

One wishes that were all, but there is no sin of omission for which we might be grateful. "Lead us not into temptation, but deliver us from evil" has been changed to, "Do not bring us to the time of trial, but deliver us from evil." Why? For the sake of clarity? (That is the usual answer.) I know, because every sense in my body informs me, and every misinclination of my mind, what is temptation, from which we seek deliverance. But *"the time of trial"*? That sounds like the Supreme Court is in session. I grant that is a time of trial. But what are we doing bringing in old metaphors in the name of clarification?

Perhaps it was ordained that the Anglicans, like their brothers the Catholics, should suffer. It is a time for weeping, and a time for rage. Do not go gently into the night. Rage, rage against the dying of the light. That would be the advice of this outsider to my brothers in the Anglican Church. They must rage against those who bring upon Christianity not only indifference, but contempt.

The Quinlan Case

September 20, 1975

THE KAREN ANNE QUINLAN case settled not very much, but brought to prominence the whole question of the right of the individual to command the movements of his doctors under dire circumstances. Dr. Milton Heifetz, a prominent California neurosurgeon, has written a subtle and informative book on the subject called *The Right to Die*. He testified in the Karen Anne Quinlan case on the side of the petitioners, Karen's parents, who begged the doctor to "pull the plug," the earthy term, for which however there is no satisfactory substitute conveying exactly that meaning. The distinction is between letting a patient die of natural causes, and causing him to die.

It is in the opinion of Dr. Heifetz the critical distinction, and it has distinguished ethical lineage. Karen Quinlan's parents are Catholics, and before approaching the doctor to recommend that he turn off the respirator that keeps their vegetated daughter technically alive, they consulted their parish priest. Relying on a papal allocution seventeen years old, that priest told them to go ahead. There was controversy up the line, when a Franciscan priest writing in *Osservatore Romano* called for keeping her alive. But a prominent Italian Jesuit disagreed. And everyone, including the judge, studied the relevant phrases of Pope Pius: quite properly, I should think, since ethics are best defined not by legislators, but by moralists.

The Pope began his address to the anesthesiologists in 1958 by saying that questions of science, such as *when* is someone in fact dead, are best settled by scientists. But "considerations of a general nature allow us to believe that human life continues for as long as its vital functions—distinguished from the simple life of organs—manifest themselves spontaneously or even with the help of artificial processes."

The question concerning which there is discussion is the emphasis that is properly placed on the word "or." It would appear, if read literally, to make the word "spontaneously" entirely meaningless. Either vital organs are working spontaneously, or they are not. If, as in artificial respiration, they are made to work by artificial processes leading to their resuscitation, after which they will resume working spontaneously, then the answer would be clear. Indeed, in *John F. Kennedy Memorial Hospital* vs. *Heston* a court ordered, against the will of her parents, a Jehovah's Witness to receive a transfusion of blood—which resulted in the girl's recovery.

There is crystallizing agreement that in cases of irreversible paralysis, doctors should be permitted to pull the plug if that is the will of the patient. The practical problem is ascertaining the will of someone in a comatose condition. We know what Karen Anne's parents believe she would wish. But we do not, in fact, have her word on the matter. Her attending physician—although one doubts that he would disagree that Karen, if competent, would agree with her parents—is simply not qualified to transcribe the desires of an unconscious human being. And the judge ruled that her parents were not authorized to make so grave a decision in their capacity as surrogates. What is coming up, then, is the question of how to anticipate such circumstances.

The fear of reasonable men is that ordered arguments against protracting technical life, as in the case of Karen Quinlan, will end us up at the mercy of Norman Cousins. My dear friend Mr. Cousins has a genius for blurring distinctions by suffusing all subjects with a kind of corporate pity which a very little misunderstanding could transform into a recommendation of Euthanasia for Appalachians. Thus, in considering the Quinlan case, he writes in *Saturday Review,* "Our failure [to protect our poor] poses at least as great a problem to public morality and sensibility as the debate over disconnecting a comatose young woman from a device that keeps her technically alive . . . In Appalachia every day, men are gasping for air . . . "

I am not in Appalachia, but I gasp for air—at such stuff, which obscures the question. The fact is that Karen Anne Quinlan is not to be confused with a coal miner or a ghetto resident, whatever hardships they suffer. Efforts to say the contrary can succeed only in causing resistance to the subtle distinctions made by such as Dr. Milton Heifetz in his book, *The Right to Die.* Dr. Heifetz is talking about medical problems that are clinically definable. His assumptions are that (1) the law is on your side on the question of whether you desire medical treatment; and therefore (2) with forethought, you can anticipate such quandaries as the Quinlan family faces.

I reproduce, with here and there an interpolation, the form recommended by Dr. Heifetz, completed copies of which should be sent to the next of kin, to the family attorney, and to the family doctor.

A DIRECTIVE TO MY PHYSICIAN

This directive is written while I am of sound mind and fully competent.

I insist [Dr. Heifetz is here pleading with an imaginary court of law] that I have complete right of self-determination. That includes complete right of refusal of any medical or surgical treatment unless a court order affirms that my decision would bring undue or unexpected hardship on my family or society [I do not know why this last clause is there: I cannot imagine its relevance].

Therefore:

If I become incompetent, in consideration of my legal rights to refuse medical or surgical treatment regardless of the consequences to my health and life, I hereby direct and order my physician, or any physician in charge of my care, to cease and refrain from any medical or surgical treatment which would prolong my life if I am in a condition of:

(1)   unconsciousness from which I cannot recover,
(2)   unconsciousness over a period of six months,
(3)   mental incompetency which is irreversible.

However, although mentally incompetent, I must be informed of the situation [he means, "a ritual effort should be made to inform me of my situation"], and if I wish to be treated, I am to be treated in spite of my original request made while competent [fair enough; and this safety clause should satisfy many doubters].

If there is any reasonable doubt of the diagnosis of my illness and prognosis, then consultation with available specialists is suggested but need not be considered mandatory.

This directive to my physician also applies to any hospital or sanitarium in which I may be at the time of my illness and relieves them of any and all responsibility in the action or lack of action of any physician acting according to my demands.

If any action is taken contrary to these expressed demands, I hereby request my next of kin or legal representative to consider—and, if necessary, to take—legal action against the involved.

If any of my next of kin oppose this directive, their opposition is to be considered without legal grounds since I remove any right of my next of kin who oppose me in this directive to speak for me.

I hereby absolve my physician or any physician taking care of me from any legal liability pertaining to the fulfillment of my demands.

Signed [in this case] Wm. F. Buckley, Jr.

September 20, 1975
Witness: The Washington Star Syndicate.

Feminism: Unsex Me Now

April 29, 1976

WHAT DO Mary McCarthy, Joyce Carol Oates, Muriel Spark, and Joan Didion have in common?

Ans. They are first-class writers. If you like, you can say they are "first-class woman writers." But it must be somewhere along the line communicated that by that you mean that they are first-class writers who are women. Otherwise there is a patronizing residue, as in "he is a first-class junior skier." Ironically, one of the reasons these ladies (patronizing? All right, these women) are first-class writers is that they would shun like the plague such exhortations as are being urged on all writers by the National Council of Teachers of English (NCTE), in the name of eliminating sexism.

As a rather agreeable surprise, the latest bulletin from the anti-sexist league is itself fairly literate. We are told: "The man who cannot cry and the woman who cannot command are equally victims of their socialization." The trouble is that by the time they are through with their recommendations, they make everybody cry who cares for the mother tongue.

Unhappily, there is no way in the English of Shakespeare, Milton, Pope, and Faulkner, to get rid of the synecdoche "man," which, as in "mankind," means man and woman. Clifton Fadiman wrote years ago that the English language is wonderfully resourceful, but that "there are some things you *just can't do with it.*" One of them is to replace "man" in some situations. Consider the efforts of the NCTE.

The common man becomes *the average person,* or *ordinary people.* Try it out . . . "The century of the average person." No. Why? If you don't know, I can't tell you. Ditto for "The century of ordinary people." Here, at least, you can point out that ordinary has several meanings and that whereas common does too, the conjunction of *common man* instantly excludes all but the Henry Wallace use of the word common; whereas the conjunction *of ordinary man* does not exclude such a sniffy remark as, say, Lucius Beebe might have made about vulgar people. Clarity is one of the objectives of good writers, which is why Mary McCarthy would never write about "the century of ordinary people."

The bulletin offers you a typical sexist slur: *The average student is worried about his grades.* Suggested substitute: *The average student is worried about grades.* There again, you will note a difficulty. The two sentences do not mean exactly the same thing. In the first, the student is worried about his (or her) grades. In the second, the student is worried about grades as a generic concern. Perhaps he is worried about, say, the role that grades play or do not play in getting into graduate school. Anyway, there is a residual indistinction, and English teachers shouldn't be teaching people how to write imprecisely.

The bulletin notes that English does not have a generic singular common-sex pronoun, the convention being to use the male. This will be proscribed . . . *If the student was satisfied with his performance on the pre-test, he took the post-test.* This becomes, *A student who was satisfied with her or his performance on the pre-test took the post-test.* That is called killing two birds with one stone. You eliminate the generic male singular, and reverse the conventional sequence (her and his). The distortions ring in the ear.

At one point, the NCTE wants us to validate improper usage. Here we are asked to rewrite *Anyone who wants to go to the game should bring his money tomorrow* to *Anyone who wants to go to the game should bring their money tomorrow;* and I say anyone who does that kind of thing at this point should not be hired as a professional writer.

So mobilized are these folk that they do not stop at a war far from the cosmopolitan centers, designed to wipe out little pockets of vernacular resistance. *Gal Friday* has to become assistant. A *libber* must become a *feminist* (here I think they have dealt from the bottom of the deck: what's inherently sexist about libber?). A *man-sized job* becomes a *big* or *enormous* job. Question: How do you describe a job that requires physical exertion beyond the biological powers of wopersons?

It is comforting to know that this effort to correct the language will precisely not succeed because the genuine artists among woman writers are more concerned for their craft than for fashionable sociological skirmishes. Nothing more persuades the general public of women's inferiority (which doctrine is of course preposterous) than efforts at equality achieved by indicting good prose.

Personal

Does anyone know Elton John?

September 6, 1975

Excuse me, but does anybody out there know someone called Elton John? This is very important to me, and maybe you can help. . . .

A little girl called Maria came to live in our household with her mother about ten years ago. In those days she spoke only Spanish, though her deceased father was American. But now, after ten years of schools in New York City she speaks Spanish, however perfectly, with some reluctance. She is entirely American. The other change is that she has grown into picture-book beauty. She is just now fourteen, and one has to go back to *National Velvet,* to the fourteen-year-old Elizabeth Taylor, to find a face as breathtakingly lovely. I don't know how Elizabeth Taylor was at that age, though I suspect the worst; but Maria is entirely unspoiled, the least demanding of God's creatures, so that when, a week ago, my friend and I, drinking iced tea in the sun, engaged her in conversation, she was her characteristic reticent, undemanding self.

Marvin asked her what she wanted for her birthday. She replied that she wanted nothing, nothing at all.

Marvin, who has the tough-Jewish sentimentalist's way with children, accepted the challenge. "Suppose," he said, "you could have anything you wanted in the whole world, what would you choose?"

She giggled self-consciously and said she didn't need anything.

Undeterred, Marvin said: "How about a Lear jet?" She laughed, like Alice in wonderland.

"How about Queen Elizabeth's jewels?" She broke out in a bright smile, flashing her pearl-teeth.

"How about the S.S. *France*—you can get it cheap now, you know?"

Now she began to laugh, joyously.

Marvin told her she had twenty-four hours to decide what she wanted for her birthday, and the next day, driving to church, I asked her gravely if she had come to a decision.

I knew this would take a good deal of wrenching, but after several times repeating that there was nothing in this world she needed or wanted, I got her to say, "Except maybe one thing."

"What?"

"Well, never mind—sir."

It required two more assaults before she blurted it out. "I'd like to meet Elton John."

Now, Elton John is one of my many lacunae, along with institutions like the Dallas Redskins, and 90 percent of the people talked about in the hagiographical pages of *Rolling Stone*. Since at this point Marvin and I had privately resolved to devote ourselves entirely to realizing Maria's dream, knowing her to be sensible enough not to commission a raid on the Tower of London to extract the coronation jewels, I was stunned by my impotence.

Between us, Marvin and I know Jerry Ford, we know somebody who knows the Pope, and Golda Meir. But we don't even know somebody who knows somebody who knows Elton John. Moreover, it required great delicacy at once to participate in her idolatry, and to fix exactly the identity of the man Maria loves. Marvin asked if Elton John was the young blind singer who just got 13 million dollars from a single contract, and Maria said no, but he wears big glasses, so— her delicacy here was very nearly paternalistic—she could understand it if we thought him to be blind. Well, where does Elton John live? Maria didn't know. In America, she thinks. Marvin whispered to me that he has the impression that Elton John is English. I seem to remember a cover story in *Time* magazine on, I think, Elton John, and make a note to look it up—but it is missing from our collection.

We managed to get her ten Elton John records for her birthday. My wife plunged collusively into the picture and came up with an Elton John sweat shirt and an Elton John pin, of sorts. I am surprised there are no Elton John toothbrushes—or perhaps there are? But, when you come down to it, we are not delivering on our great macho-swaggering boast, and we have let Maria down, which is why I reach out and ask you, please, to help. Maybe you are his brother. . . . His mother (born without original sin?). . . . His agent, sweetheart, banker, best friend, lawyer, stockbroker. . . . Could you please arrange it? I would do anything in return. Teddy—Teddy! You are wanting maybe a little interference, right-wise, in 1976? . . . It isn't as if Maria had asked, as a birthday present, to meet Howard Hughes. Or is it? [See also page 379.]

Up from misery: Kenneth and AA

January 27, 1977

A FRIEND OF LONG standing who has never asked me to devote this space to advertising any enthusiasm of his has now,
diffidently, made the exception. He does not want to do anything less than what he can do, through his own efforts and
those of his friends, to pass along the word that, within walking distance of the great majority of Americans, there is help
waiting which can lead them out of the darkness, as indisputably as an eye surgeon, restoring sight, can lead someone
into the sunlight.

Kenneth (we'll call him) is a cocky feller, something of a
sport, tough-talking, an ace in his individualistic profession,
who remembers getting drunk at college in the late '20's on
the night he won an important boxing match, but at no other
time during his college career. Emerging from college into
the professional world, he revved up slowly, hitting in his late
30's his cruising speed: two or three martinis per day. These
he was dearly attached to, but not apparently dominated by:
He would not, gladly, go a day without his martinis, but neither, after the third, did he require a fourth.

Then in the spring of 1972 his gentle, devoted (teetotal-
ing) wife had a mastectomy, the prognosis otimistic; but with
a shade of uncertainty. So, to beef up his morale, he increased the dosage just a little. When, later that year, the
doctor called to tell him the worst, he walked straightaway to
the nearest bar. After she died, he began buying a fifth each
of bourbon and gin on Saturdays, a week's supply to eke out
the several martinis he had been drinking at and after lunch.
Fascinated, he watched himself casually making minor alter-
ations: "Make that quarts" was the modest beginning. Then
the resupplying would come on Friday; then Thursday. In
due course it was a quart a day.

In the morning he would begin; one, then up to five snorts
before leaving for the office—later and later in the morning.
Before reaching the door he would rinse out his mouth. But
always—this fascinated him, as gradually he comprehended
the totality of his servitude—he would, on turning the door
handle, go back: for just one more.

At night he would prepare himself dinner, then lie down for a little nap, wake hours later, go to the kitchen to eat dinner—only to find he had already eaten it. Once he returned to a restaurant three hours after having eaten his dinner: he forgot he had been there. Blackouts, he called the experiences.

On the crucial day it was nothing special. He walked home from the office, full of gin, and vomited in the street (this often happened), struggling to do this with aplomb in the posh backdrop of the East 60's. On reaching his apartment he lurched gratefully for the bottle, sipped from the glass . . . and was clapped by the hand of Providence as unmistakably as any piece of breast was ever struck by a lance.

He heard his own voice say, as if directed by an outside force, "What the hell am I doing to myself?" He poured his martini into the sink, emptied the gin bottle, then emptied the bourbon bottle, then went to the telephone and, never in his life having given a second's conscious thought to the organization, fumbled through the directory and dialed the number for Alcoholics Anonymous.

One must suppose that whoever answered that telephone call was as surprised as a fireman excitedly advised that a house was ablaze. Kenneth would like to . . . inquire—but perhaps AA was too busy tonight, perhaps next week sometime? . . . What? Come today? How about tomorrow? Do you have a meeting every week? You have *800 meetings in New York a week?* . . . Scores every night? . . . Okay. Tomorrow.

Tomorrow would be the first of 250 meetings in ninety days with Alcoholics Anonymous. AA advises at least ninety meetings in the first ninety days. Kenneth had assumed he would be mixing with hoi polloi. Always objective, he advises now that "on a scale of 1-10"—incorporating intelligence, education, success, articulateness—"I would rank around six or seven." He made friends. And he made instant progress during those first weeks, quickly losing the compulsion for the morning drinks. But for the late afternoon martinis he thirsted, and he hungered, and he lusted. He dove into a despair mitigated only by his thrice-daily contacts with AA. His banked-up grief for his wife raged now, and every moment, every long afternoon and evening without her, and without alcohol, were endless bouts with the haunting question: What is the point in living at all?

And then, suddenly, as suddenly as on the day he poured the booze into the sink, twenty-seven weeks later, he had been inveigled into going to a party. Intending to stay one dutiful hour, he stayed five. On returning, he was exhilarated. He had developed anew the capacity to talk with people, other than in the prescribed ritualisms of his profession, or in the boozy idiom of the tippler. He was so excited, so pleased, so elated, he could not sleep until early morning for pleasure at re-experiencing life.

That was two months ago, and every day he rejoiced at his liberation, and prays that others who suffer will find the hand of Alcoholics Anonymous. And—one might presumptuously add—the hand of the Prime Mover, Who was there in that little kitchen on the day the impulse came to him; and Who, surely, is the wellspring of the faith of Alcoholics Anonymous, as of so many other spirits united to help their fellow man.

Mrs. Ford on chastity

August 16, 1975

ONE HATES to respond, or even comment, on the casual effluvia of spouses of important people, but what, really, is the alternative other than to take it lying down, a posture recommended by Mrs. Ford for young unmarried American women? Mrs. Ford's interview (on CBS's "60 Minutes") was in fact an act of aggression. What she did was to use her high office as First Lady, achieved by a concatenation of romantic and felonious coincidences, to rewrite the operative sexual code of Western civilization. It is bad enough to hear the same kind of thing from Margaret Mead, returned from a winter in Samoa and overwhelmed by the spontaneity of it all; or from Dr. Kinsey, whose iron rule was that if 50 percent plus one of the people do it, it is okay. But the role of the

civic leader is to defend standards, even if the barbarians are
at the gate; which they most definitely are. Her husband's
policies of detente with the Soviet Union may, by some, be
excused as a necessary capitulation to overwhelming force.
But Hugh Hefner does not dispose of hydrogen bombs, leaving Mrs. Ford without a practical reason for insouciantly undermining the traditional presumption in favor of chastity,
and fidelity.

What she did *not* say was that if her daughter Susan had an
affair, she would understand, and forgive her. What she said
was that she would not be "surprised"; that, in effect, she
would approve, subject—here was a strange qualification—to
an investigation of the boy-lover who took Susan to his bed.
"I'd want to know pretty much about the young man that she
was planning to have the affair with—whether it was a worthwhile encounter or whether it was going to be one of
those . . . ."

One of those what? What qualifications would Mrs. Ford
look for, in a suitor who aspired to be the lover of her eighteen-year-old daughter? That he be a moderate Republican?
Surely not—that would be politically strait-laced. That he be
a WASP? That too would be atavistic—HEW would not approve of any such discrimination, nor would the 14th
Amendment, or the Supreme Court. That the young man
should be genuinely attached to eighteen-year-old Susan? I
cannot imagine whom that would exclude, Susan being attractive and nubile. That he be rich? Or—at the opposite extreme—poor, and therefore otherwise unindulged? That he
be handsome and attractive? But surely Susan is the exclusive arbiter of those qualities in any courtship? One concludes—happily, in this case—that Mrs. Ford really hasn't
thought the matter through, and one is left ignorant of
whether she is capable of thinking the matter through.

President Ford, who was suddenly cast into the role of
poor John Mitchell a few years ago, authorized a spokesman
to say limply that he had always encouraged his wife to
"speak her mind." Well, clearly the Republican platform of
1976 should commit the President to discouraging his wife
from speaking her mind. It is a rationalist and psychological

superstition that it is always a good thing to speak your mind. It is nothing of the sort. If we all always spoke our minds, the situation would be entirely chaotic.

Civil behavior requires exactly the opposite: that we often *refrain* from speaking our minds—in deference to the sensibilities of others. In the last season there has been a good bit of breast-beating in the intellectual journals by writers who confess that they have always really disliked blacks. Under carefully controlled auspices it is permissible to discuss this kind of thing: but always with the understanding that it is a failing. Of the people who have thus written, I know none who would intentionally affront a black. It makes no difference that they might continue to harbor prejudice against blacks, any more than it makes any difference at all that all of us are sinners and that sexual permissiveness is in vogue. Hypocrisy, La Rochefoucauld said, is the tribute that vice pays to virtue.

Mrs. Ford's evangelistic and dismayingly superficial view of women's rights was not to be curbed that day on CBS. Asked about abortion, she commented that the Supreme Court's decision to legalize abortion was "the best thing in the world . . . a great, great decision." Now as a matter of fact, even lawyers who are enthusiastic in their belief that a woman should have the right to abort her child, agree that it was a very poor decision. But the quality of judicial thought aside, the enthusiasm of Mrs. Ford was a disastrous breach in tone. To apply to a Supreme Court decision affirming the right of a woman to abort, the kind of cheering-section enthusiasm Mrs. Ford gave it, is dismayingly insensitive. As if the head of the World Population Council were to appear and report gleefully that one million Biafran children had starved, thus relieving the population problem in West Africa. A moment's thought should have sufficed to inform Mrs. Ford that the Supreme Court was not endorsing abortion in *Roe* v. *Wade*. It was merely explicating its understanding of rights exercisable under the Constitution. That which is permitted is not *ipso facto* commendable; nor is that which is practiced *ipso facto* desirable.

It is very surprising, and very bad news, that Mrs. Ford

abused her husband's position by speaking out in contravention of ethical values established, according to her husband who not infrequently invokes His assistance, by an authority higher even than the Supreme Court.

Your ethos is slipping

October 2,˙1975

THERE ARE STIRRINGS in Western Europe. From some of them we can take heart. The Danish political parties are finally running into genuine resistance over the lengths to which welfarism has taken them. One estimate puts the cost of social services at 55 percent of the Gross National Product. Continue at that rate for a little longer, and the Danish people won't have money left over to buy porn with; though one supposes that the Social Democrats would come out for Free Porn. Perhaps some time before then, the people will rediscover their taste for freedom, and the great body of socialists who have written all the laws will be led to the gates of the city and given free passes back home.

In West Germany a recent survey suggests that something of profoundly alarming consequence is at work on the ethos. If one had to select the country that has most greatly prospered since the ravages of the Second World War, all indicators would point to West Germany. Here was not only the rubble of an atomized country, but the awful corporate sense of shame at having been dominated by a mad savage who was a popular leader. The Germans worked hard, and sincerely, for their prosperity and their democratic freedoms.

Suddenly things are beginning to go sour. A recent survey shows that among workers under the age of thirty, 39 percent, if given the opportunity, would not work at all. The corresponding figure in 1962 was 22 percent. The indisposition to work, then, has almost doubled in a dozen years. And hearken to this: In the age group between sixteen and twenty, a total of 76 percent would just as soon not have to work.

No doubt there are those who will find nothing in the least unusual about the figures. Work can be very unpleasant, and sloth achieved its standing as one of the capital sins because of the social recognition that what is unpleasant has nevertheless to be done. But the need for it does not make it pleasant. Dishes have to be washed, and fences painted, but it takes a con man like Tom Sawyer to persuade people that it is fun to do it. The substitute for Tom Sawyer in a modern society is an ethos—the work ethos. It was known intuitively for thousands of years that people feel better after exerting themselves. Modern psychologists, as usual certifying the obvious, establish that work is necessary to a sense of mental well-being. Sir Harold Nicolson wrote that "industry is the enemy of melancholy."

So what does it mean when three-quarters of the young people of the most enterprising and industrious nation on earth decide, with some suddenness, that they would just as soon not have to work for a living? Politically, the meaning of their decision is obvious. They are boob-bait for the demagogues of the Left who will whisper to them how they can get it for nothing—how, in the phrase of Albert Jay Nock, they can substitute political for economic means of aggrandizing themselves. What then happens, we all know. Everyone gets poorer, and there are fresh reasons—or are there?—for misery.

The surveys seem to be telling us that the standards of the bourgeois world are not accepted by people who rise up into that world by commanding high salaries in the free market. It is, says Professor Noelle Numann of the Allensback Institute for Opinion Research, the other way around. The London *Times* paraphrases. "The bourgeoisie are adopting not only the blue jeans but also the social values of the workers. For over ten years, she finds, there has been a steady decline in traditionally bourgeois values such as respect for property, hard work, politeness, modesty, thrift, and the belief that one is responsible for one's own fate. There has been a corresponding spread of what she perhaps libelously describes as traditionally lower-class attitudes such as lack of interest in work, avoidance of effort and risk, the desire for immediate gratification, doubts about the fairness of rewards, and fatalism about status."

Here was an interesting test question put to the respondents. A father has to decide which of his two sons to send on an exchange visit to England. He resolves on the one who has been getting the better grades in school. Obvious? "The percentage of people who approved his decision dropped from 62 to 49 between 1962 and 1972. In another question two secretaries of the same age do the same work but one gets paid more because she works better and faster." Right, said 73 percent in 1962—but only 62 percent in 1972.

Patrick Moynihan, who continues to startle the free world as well as the unfree world, made bold to say on television a couple of weeks ago that some countries are not as well off as they ought to be—Argentina, for example. But what do you do when the ethos begins to go? How do you revive it? The trick is to do something about it quickly, because if you let it go too late, a big jackbooted man usually appears, and he carries a lash.

Please don't eat the daisies

October 14, 1975

THEY HAVE MADE a pretty good effort in recent months to adjust to the problem of the anti-smoker, so that now when we board an airplane we are politely asked, "Smoking or nonsmoking, sir?" I have been giving routinely the answer, "I don't smoke, but I don't mind it if others do"—the only answer I could plausibly give, unless my wife and I occupied separate dining rooms.

Of course such an answer is the horrible equivalent of saying at a cocktail party, when asked, "What can I bring you from the bar?"—"Anything. Anything at all." People who say that mean to be accommodating. Actually, they merely confuse and exasperate. I'd rather a guest asked me for a Brandy Alexander than for "anything at all." To be sure, I would have to learn to make a Brandy Alexander.

But there remain uncrystallized civil accommodations, notably the typewriter. Now I am, for reasons unknown and irrelevant, the most instinctively undisruptive of men. I even hesitate to hang on the doorknob outside my hotel room the sign that says DO NOT DISTURB without first attempting to write in, "Please." It horrifies me as much as the English that we decorate our national parks with such barbed-wire phrases as "KEEP OFF THE GRASS." I'd have made a very good Jap. All the above on the understanding, of course, that when the bugles sound, I am ready and dressed to defend Pearl Harbor.

Like other journalists, I am saddled with the problem of The Typewriter. Wherever I go, I must use it. No, I don't mean at restaurants, or at public receptions at the White House, or at funeral processions. But other times: notably, on planes and trains.

The other day, traveling New York to Washington, I elected to go by Amtrak, thinking to have my dinner and begin typing my notes for a television program that would begin at 9:00 in the morning, followed by a second program beginning at 10:15. I chatted with a friend during the brief dinner hour, then went to work. I had no sooner begun to type than I was accosted by a tall middle-aged man with the bearing of an ex-colonel, who approached me and said in tones loud enough to sound over the hundred MPH noise of a train whistling through the night on tracks laid down during the Grant Administration: "I want you to know," he said without any introductory civility, "that I think you are the rudest man I have ever seen. My wife and I paid over $60 to travel on this train and to have a little peace and quiet, and all we get is the sound of your typewriter." He marched away, and all eyes were on me. Did I want to move? the porter asked me. Move where? I replied—the car was full.

I resumed typing but, actually, I found that I was not concentrating on my work. Suddenly every stroke of a key sounded like an acetylene torch triggered under a honeymooner's bed. It is a psychological cliché: the ticking of a clock that is entirely unnoticed can be made—in a movie, say—to sound like the rumbling of a juggernaut merely by having somebody say casually, "When that clock reaches midnight, London will be destroyed."

* * *

Every note I tapped sounded louder than the others. Every pause between strokes sounded like a provocative attempt at cacophony. People around me who had been dozing or reading, utterly unaware of the sound of the typewriter, were suddenly looking at me malevolently. This I'd have understood easily enough if they knew what I was writing. But for all they knew, I was copying out "Twinkle Twinkle Little Star" . . .

I don't like rules, but they can be liberating. If the sign says, "Smoking Permitted Aft of These Seats," then it is only a matter of ascertaining which way is aft before lighting up; and nobody has a legitimate case against you. You guessed it. I think they should get around to signs that say "Typing Permitted Aft of These Seats." Aft of *those* seats could put you with one foot in the baggage compartment, but at least you would have your own turf.

Some will say that, really, we are asked to make too many concessions: that people should try to curb their sensibilities. There is a case for this too. I don't like magenta. Should I have said to the gentleman on the train: "I'll make a deal, pal. I'll stop typing if you will tell your wife to go to the ladies' room and come back dressed in another color—any other color." "Magenta Permitted Aft of These Seats." To be sure, we are left without a solution for the man aboard an airplane who can't stand wings.

Just call me Bill

October 28, 1975

VERY SOON I will be fifty, a datum I do not expect will rouse the statisticians, or revive the fireworks industry. I reflect on it only because of a personal problem of general concern I had not solved twenty years ago, the nature of which keeps . . . changing, as you grow older. It is, of course, the first-name problem.

My inclinations on the matter have always been formal. In part this was a matter of inheritance.

I heard my father, days before his death at seventy-eight, refer to his best friend and associate of forty years as "Montgomery"; who, in deference to the ten-year difference in their ages, referred to him only as "Mr. Buckley."

I grew up mistering people, and discovered, after I was fully grown (if indeed that has really happened), that in continuing to do so, I was bucking a trend of sorts: the obsessive egalitarian familiarity which approaches a raid on one's privacy.

So on reaching thirty, I made a determined effort to resist. Even now, on the television program "Firing Line," I refer even to those guests I know intimately as "Mr. Burnham," or "Governor Reagan," or "Senator Goldwater." (This rule I simply had to break on introducing Senator Buckley, but even then the departure from the habit was stylistically troublesome.) The effort, I thought, was worthwhile—a small gesture against the convention that requires you to refer to Professor Mortimer Applegate as "Mort" five minutes after you have met. Jack Paar would have called Socrates "Soc."

I came on two difficulties. The first was the public situation in which mistering somebody was plainly misunderstood. Or, if understood at all, taken as an act of social condescension. For a couple of years I would refer, on his program, to "Mr. Carson." In due course I discovered that the audience thought I was trying to put on an act: Mr. Carson does not exist in America. Only Johnny does.

The second problem, as you grow older, lies in the creeping suspicion of people a little older than yourself that your use of the surname is intended to accentuate an exiguous difference in age. If you are eighteen and the other man is twenty-eight, you can, for a while, call him Mr. Jones without giving offense. But if you are forty and he is fifty and you call him Mr. Jones, he is likely to think that you are rubbing in the fact of his relative senescence.

The complement of that problem, which I fear more than anything except rattlesnakes and détente, is trying to be One of the Boys. "Just call me Bill," to the roommate of your son at college, is in my judgment an odious effort to efface a chronological interval as palpable as the wrinkles on my face, and the maturity of my judgments. On the other hand, one has to struggle to avoid stuffiness: so I arrived, for a while, at the understanding that I was Mister to everyone under the age of 21, or thereabouts, and only then, cautiously, Bill. It is a sub-problem how to break the habit. Here I made a sub-rule: that I would invite younger people to call me "Bill" exactly one time. If thereafter they persisted in using the surname, well that was up to them: a second, redundant gesture on my part could be interpreted as pleading with them to accept me as a biological equal.

My bias, on the whole, continued in the direction of a tendency to formality, so in the last few years I made a determined effort to overcome it, wherein I came across my most recent humiliation. Mrs. Margaret Thatcher was my guest on "Firing Line." Rather to my surprise, the English being more naturally formal than we are, halfway through the program she suddenly referred to me, once, as "Bill." I declined to break my "Firing Line" rule, and so persisted with "Mrs. Thatcher." However, the next day when we met again at a semi-social function, I braced myself on leaving and said, "Good-bye, Margaret." And a week later, writing her a note congratulating her on her performance, I addressed it: "Dear Margaret."

Today I have from her a most pleasant reply, about this and that. But it is addressed, in her own hand (as is the British habit: only the text is typed): "Dear Mr. Buckley." Shocked, I looked at the transcript—only to discover that, on the program, she was talking about a "Bill" that lay before the House of Commons. The trauma has set me back by years, and I may even find myself addressing "Mr. Carson" next time around. I suppose, though, that at fifty, the problem becomes easier in respect of the twenty-five-year-olds. At seventy it will be easier still. Well before then, I hope to be able to address Margaret, I mean Mrs. Thatcher, as Madam Prime Minister. [See also page 350.]

Reflections on gift-giving

December 23, 1976

GUESS WHAT Shirley Temple is doing right now? As chief of protocol, she has to decide whether William Simon should be permitted to buy from the United States Government some of the gifts he was given while Secretary of the Treasury, or whether that would be opposed to the "spirit" of the law. The gifts Mr. Simon desires to hang on to are those that "mean something special" to him, namely, a Russian shotgun, a cigarette box from Saudi Arabia, two silver-colored necklaces from Israel, a set of matched pistols from Argentina, a wristwatch from Leonid Brezhnev with Brezhnev's name engraved on it, and a porcelain sculpture from Spain. The law says that any gifts from foreign officials worth more than $50 must be turned over to the United States Government. What then happens to them, if you were President of the United States, is that they end up decorating those shrines ex-Presidents and their friends build to preserve their sacred memory; or, if you were a lesser light, they are quietly auctioned off a few years down the line by the General Services Administration.

Mr. Simon is a gun collector, which explains in part why he wants to hang on to the shotgun and to the pistols. The silver necklaces apparently have sentimental value (they alone are valued at less than $50, so there is no problem there). The porcelain sculpture from Spain presumably has nostalgic as well as artistic value. It isn't plain why he wants to hang on to the watch. The only gift I would accept from Brezhnev is an urn containing the ashes of the Brezhnev Doctrine. On the other hand, if every time you look at your watch you see Brezhnev's name, that's not a bad idea either, since it is good to remind ourselves that life is nasty, brutish, and short, thanks substantially to Brezhnev. Furthermore, William Simon being one of the world's exemplary libertarians, there are no grounds for suspecting any alienation of affection. If Mr. Simon goes back to Wall Street, he will no doubt want to be the only guy in the board room who tells the time by looking at Brezhnev's watch.

When I was a little boy, though not so little I shouldn't have known better, a lady at a souvenir shop in Stratford-on-Avon gave me, after my sisters and I had loaded up on Shakespeareana, a miniature *Hamlet*—the whole play, reduced to a book the size of a passport photograph. I was delighted, and fished out of my grubby pocket a shilling, which I, in turn, insisted on giving the lady. With us was an old friend who taught me piano, but has had no other recorded failure during her lifetime, and later she told me I must learn gracefully to accept gifts; that any methodical attempt to requite a gift has the effect of squirting cold water on acts of spontaneous generosity.

One supposes that the law binding William Simon was written on the assumption that foreign officials are not engaged in acts of spontaneous generosity, but rather in formalities, or even cynicism. The exchange of gifts between heads of state is a ritual that began with the beginning of history. The question arises whether it is possible for a foreign leader to make a spontaneous gift. Sadat, for instance, is clearly attached to Henry Kissinger, not to the Secretary of State. Will he wait until Mr. Kissinger is out of office, and then make him a gift? Not To Be Opened Until After Your Resignation?

It is one of the uglier aspects of public service that such spontaneities are forbidden because they are presumptively suspect. The next man who takes you to lunch may turn out to be the Korean ambassador. The late Democratic Senator Paul Douglas once wrote on the subject, laying down the law that $7 was the maximum value for an acceptable gift to an elected official, $7 being, in those days, the price of the most expensive book. A few Democratic Congresses later, you need to pay twice $7 to buy even a socialist primer to give to your local congressman.

I hope Mr. Simon gets to keep his presents, and if he doesn't, I'm going to send him two silver-colored necklaces, and pretend they came from Israel.

Sex scandal in Mormonland

June 19, 1976

I CONFESS I have been consciously hunting out an opportunity to say something friendly about the Mormons for several months, after a half-dozen impressive hours spent mostly with students at the University of Utah, but including also a few minutes with the venerable sages who lead the church.

The opportunity comes on reading that a prominent lawyer in Salt Lake City said quite matter-of-factly that the incumbent Congressman had "committed political suicide." How come? By propositioning *two* (shades of Brigham Young?) ladies of pleasure to spend the evening with him. The two ladies happened to be policewomen wearing recording devices, and now these tapes (how did we *manage* before tape recorders?) have been shipped over to the prosecutor's office, and it is assumed that the Congressman will be had up for "soliciting sex for money," which is what they call patronizing a prostitute in Utah.

The Mormons, like other Christians, believe in forgiving a sinner seventy times seven times. But their experience in forgiving has not caused them to lose the very idea of wrongdoing. In what we choose to call the more cosmopolitan centers of America, everyone rushed forward to say, in the matter of Congressman Wayne Hays, that his "private" life was entirely his own affair, that it mattered only whether he was using the taxpayers' money to appease his lubricity. There has been no noticeable ideological division on this point. That is to say everybody in Congress—even Senator Humphrey—appears to take the position that prostitution should remain in the private sector. It will be several Democratic conventions down the line before the Right to Sex as a state responsibility is discovered.

Now it isn't only the Mormons, of course, who believe in good conduct, even in private. President Ford, in a speech to a convention of Baptists, talked about the need for public morality. "Public officials," he said, "have a special responsibility to set a good example for others to follow—in both private and public conduct." His reference was everywhere taken to be to the sexual misbehavior highlighted during recent days.

What President Ford says to a Baptist Convention is, however, to be taken less seriously than what apparently occurs as a matter of course to members of a religious community that takes quite seriously the basic commandments of the Christian religion, which call for marital fidelity, among other things.

The Mormon idea is that the political leader is also something of a moral leader. That praiseworthy men should be elected to positions of power. In hanging on to this notion they cause to survive a great political tradition that traces to the Hellenic notion of the aristoi—men of singular quality, performing the necessary functions of the leaders. The aristoi were supposed to distinguish themselves not merely by giving great orations, let alone defining social justice. But by exhibiting a kind of temperance, a reverence for quality, a kind of cosmic piety that set them gently apart from the roisterers—and these were as common in Athens as in Washington.

The reason it sounds so strange—this axiomatic belief by the Mormons that their Congressman should, as a gentleman, resign—is that the notion of a "private" life that is entirely "private" has gone, really, to quite extraordinary lengths. It is one thing to say that no one should be permitted to peer into a man's home. Another to say that the public should be unconcerned as to what in fact goes on there.

There are interesting questions raised about the appurtenances and stratagems of the anti-vice girls in Salt Lake City: but these do not affect the appropriateness of the public judgment. We may have had no business knowing what Congressman Jones said or did to Fanny Hill. But if it transpires that what they did together affronts the public ideal, then surely there is a Christian reconciliation: affirm the ideal by dismissing the Congressman. And then forgive the Congressman his transgression—while insisting that that is what it was.

Pity Harry Reems?

December 21, 1976

BOYS WILL be boys, but to judge from the 'proliferation of committees to defend Harry Reems, grown men are determined to be boys. I know, having joined, and indeed helped to found, the ABCDEF Committee, as a schoolboy aged fifteen: to wit, the American Boys Club for the Defense of Errol Flynn, who a generation ago was charged with siring a child via a teen-aged girl. Harry Reems is endeavoring to persuade the community that if his conviction is upheld, lights will go out all over the world. Not quite, the situation being as follows:

Harry Reems, one day in 1972, gave himself over to a movie studio and for the sum of $100 performed sex for the benefit of the lewdest camera in town. The movie went out as *Deep Throat* and became the *Gone with the Wind* of the smut circuit, for reasons nobody quite understands. Somewhere along the line the Federal Government decided to move.

It did so by taking a dozen of the persons principally involved in the venture and charging them with conspiracy to violate the law that prohibits interstate commerce in obscene materials. As we all know, the jurisdiction of the Federal Government is everywhere: so the prosecutor decided on Memphis as the place to try Reems. In the choice of that city, the defense finds dark cynicism. The implication is that only in Rubesville would a jury find *Deep Throat* to be obscene. This is difficult to follow. *Deep Throat* would be found obscene if shown in Sodom and Gomorrah.

The so-called Memphis argument goes on to say that if the conviction of Reems is upheld, the Federal Government would have at its disposal the means of setting obscenity standards for the whole nation by the simple act of finding the chastest corner of the Republic, and prosecuting a film or book there, gaining a conviction and then driving the product out of the projection rooms and bookstores of the more cosmopolitan, raunchier parts of the country. Moreover, they warn us, if the government is allowed to succeed with

Deep Throat, where will the government stop? Will it go back and find *Ulysses* was obscene after all, reversing a generation of progress since Judge Woolsey made his liberating decision?

Then—the defense goes on—there is the *ex post facto* problem. In 1972, when Harry Reems made the movie, the courts were being guided by the Roth standard. That decision, handed down by Justice Brennan in 1957, held that something was obscene if it appealed exclusively to the prurient interest and had no "redeeming social importance" whatever. It wasn't until 1973 that the Supreme Court revised that definition, doing away with the social importance clause and leaving the definition of obscenity to be if the "average person, applying contemporary community standards, would find that the work, taken as a whole, appeals to the prurient interest." That means that in 1976, Reems was tried by 1973 standards for doing something he did in 1972.

Where are we left?

In a way, *Deep Throat* is the perfect target precisely because those who defend it cannot, however resourceful their reserves of sophism, maintain that it is anything less than what Harry Reems was paid $100 to do: make obscenity. All other positions on the film are not worth listening to.

The two questions that survive are: Is the government legitimately concerned with obscenity? If so, then it must be legitimately concerned with *Deep Throat*. The argument that if the government is permitted to move against *Deep Throat*, tomorrow it will move against the Song of Solomon, is the old argument of give him an inch and he'll take a mile. It is not without merit. The government that was given the right to tax income by a Congress that spoke as if 10 percent was higher than the government would ever reach out for, in a generation or so was happily taxing at a 90 percent rate. Still, a self-governing people has primarily itself to consult when setting standards. The history of capital punishment suggests that the government can retreat from the exercise of a drastic sanction, rather than the necessity that it will (adapting the obscenity logic) move in the direction of electrocuting double-parkers.

The second question has to do with the authority of the

community, and with the question whether Memphis can "set standards" for San Francisco and New York. Well, as a libertarian the whole business makes one uneasy. But isn't it a fact that standards are in fact being set by San Francisco and New York for Memphis?

Even little gulls do it

November 29, 1977

IN A RECENT period spent mostly aboard airplanes, my wife, at the end of a long leg of the trip, threw down a book and said, "*That* is the worst *and* the most disgusting book I've ever read." That was a challenge, so I picked it up and, a day or so later, arrived at pretty much the identical conclusion. The book in question is the latest by Harold Robbins, who is an American industry specializing in sex & power books.

The minor difference between the incumbent Robbins and the one I had read a decade ago is that scant attention is given to a plausible plot. The major difference is that a third of the sex scenes are explicitly homosexual.

Robbins is one thing, John Cheever is something quite other. Cheever is a marvelously gifted writer who made his reputation by chronicling the decline of the aristocratic Wapshot family of Massachusetts over the course of two books in which is recorded with splendid imagination the attrition of gentility by creeping poverty, sexual promiscuity, booze, and a social tempo at odds with traditional concepts of life and leisure. The latest Cheever novel, *Falconer*, continues on the general theme of social and personal disintegration, but it ups the ante, so that we have degradation rather than mere disintegration; and a number of the metaphors used, and the descriptive tissue of the book, are—quite suddenly, for Cheever—homosexual. What's going on?

That was on a Saturday I read *Falconer*.

On Sunday I read the account of the tergiversation of Betty Friedan at Houston. It came, appropriately enough from every point of view, with tears in her eyes. You see, Betty Friedan was really the founder of the modern feminist movement in the United States, and a couple of years ago she dug in her heels. No lesbian stuff for her, she said. This greatly outraged the left wing of the feminist movement, which considers lesbianism the highest form of emancipation from male sexism, or however you want to put it.

Betty Friedan had said all along that there was nothing whatever in the women's movement that argued against the cohesiveness of the family unit. But she was beginning to lose her popularity, and last weekend, in Houston, she capitulated. In an emotional statement, she said to her sisters that, really, she had been wrong. Woman must be free to love woman. The ineluctable laws of nature require us to conclude that there is nothing then left of the family to *be* cohesive. Although perhaps Bishop Moore of New York will, while he is at it, go beyond the redefinition of marriage to redefine a family as consisting of two girls. Or, of course, two boys.

It was a rough week, and then on Wednesday, the headline in the New York *Times:* "EXTENSIVE HOMOSEXUALITY/IS FOUND AMONG SEAGULLS/OFF COAST OF CALIFORNIA." One would like to think that the Seagulls/Off New England would not engage in such a thing, but resignation is in the saddle, and one must suppose that It goes on everywhere.

Now it is one thing to shrink from the excesses of Anita Bryant, who, it is rumored, is toying with the idea of making homosexuality illegal. While she is at it, she might go on and make lust illegal. But it is alarming when a Harold Robbins, for reasons purely commercial, and a John Cheever, for reasons poetic, find that homosexuality has wide appeal.

Such homosexuality as went into the popular play, *The Boys in the Band*, was intended to amuse (I say intended, because even some of us who are not Victorians did not find it amusing). But it was not designed to arouse. And clearly the passages in the Robbins book *are* designed to arouse. In that sense, Robbins's experiment is more significant than Cheever's. Because Cheever is a serious man, and it must be presumed that he intends to probe something or other when he goes on about homosexuality in a prison. Robbins has done one of two things. Either he has discovered that the gay readership is now large enough to make it lucrative explicitly to pander to it; or else he is experimenting with the notion that male homosexual sex is erotic for the woman reader. Or— most extraordinary—he is probing the notion that homosexual sex in general is arousing to the heterosexual.

This last thesis one can only suppose Mr. Robbins will find wrong. There is something perversely interesting in perversion. The most normal people in the world will have read one or perhaps two books by de Sade. But for magazine-rack reading, the thought that current novels with their OSS ("obligatory sex scene"—V. Nabokov, 1975) will have to go on to obligatory gay sex scenes, to appease the movement, makes one think, suddenly, lustful thoughts about Anita Bryant.

Do you know Barney's?

July 16, 1977

FEW THINGS better dispose a man to smile upon the world of getting and spending than an imminent vacation. It is, to be sure, a scandalous act of irresponsibility to suspend this column for a period of an entire week: rather as if the Magnetic North Pole were to take off a week to recharge its batteries. What will people do for orientation? It would be appropriate for Congress to adjourn for one week, and for President Carter to put all business in abeyance . . . But before I go, I must reply to Barney's.

I have written on the uncrystallized ethic of product-endorsement. The general attitude on the subject is lackadaisical. People do not dislike Joe DiMaggio for puffing a bank whose policies he probably knows less about than the bank's advertising manager knows about batting averages. Everyone knows that, like professional wrestling, it is phony; and nobody appears to care. Laurence Olivier can move from playing Coriolanus, and disdaining the imperfections of human nature, to shilling for Polaroid: so what? Politicians read the lines someone writes for them, poets laureate can be got to praise a monarch notwithstanding their private opinions of him. Art is for hire.

Still, I have come recently across a category of people known in the trade as "virgins." They are public figures who decline to endorse a commercial product, period. I saw a list of prominent virgins recently, but recall only the name of James Stewart. I believe the definition is over-severe. One should be permitted to endorse a commercial product provided there is no remuneration involved. It is an overly antiseptic world in which one cannot say publicly: I had a marvelous experience on _____ Airlines the other day.

Now stratagems for deflorating virgins are wonderfully varied. For instance, I have here this most engaging letter.

"Dear Mr. Buckley: Would you be interested in appearing in a print ad for Barney's Men's Clothing Store? The ad would say: 'I'd like to commend Barney's for its incredible selection of conservative clothes.'

"I realize your answer will be predicated on a) whether you'd like to commend Barney's for its incredible selection of conservative clothes (there being the possibility you've never been to, heard of, or cared about Barney's or conservative clothes), and b) whether you care to do any endorsements whatsoever. At any rate, if you're interested, please get in touch with me at your earliest possible convenience."

There is a fine gentility in that letter. "[Advise] whether you care to do any endorsements whatsoever" suggests resignedly that there are still some of us who are stubbornly devoted to spinsterhood, but also leaves open the possibility that we are playing the role of the coy mistress—maybe we just wanna be coaxed. Another nice touch: "There being the possibility you've never been to, heard of, or cared about Barney's or conservative clothes." That possibility is, by the rhetorical construction of the sentence, held up as sheer hypothetical contingency: as if to say, "Of course, it's always possible you have never *heard* of Abraham Lincoln . . ." And the closing phrase is a subtle blandishment. As if to say, ". . . and it's always possible you don't *care* about Abraham Lincoln."

The virgin blushes, and, to defend her intellectual rectitude, comes close to sacrificing her chastity.

It is the soft sell, the cool sell: more English than American, but becoming modish over here. Is it a coincidence that
that which is becoming rhetorically modish should declare itself enthusiastic over "conservative" clothes? Would Barney's
launch a national campaign for funky clothes? If so, whom
would they approach to advertise them? The Led Zeppelin?

The only appropriate answer to the author of so beguiling
a letter is: I *do* care about conservative clothes. If I knew Barney's, I'm sure I would love Barney's. But I intend to remain
a virgin until the time comes when no one will any longer
care to seduce me.

The selling of your own books: a bill of rights

July 1976

YEARS AGO, A COG in the man-eating machine having mal-
functioned, I found myself in midsummer in the deserted
deep-South residence of my parents (they summered in New
England) with ten days to wait before my induction into the
United States Infantry. I had come south expecting merely
an overnight stay at the ghostly residence, only to learn that
the date on the induction notice was incorrect. During that
period I spent happy evening hours cultivating the friendship of a middle-aged lawyer of aristocratic attitudes, huge
and cosmopolitan erudition, and gentle manner, a bachelor
crippled in his kindergarten days by polio who managed nevertheless to drive a specially built car and to fly an Ercoupe,
which required no pedal motion, the ailerons having been
synchronized with the wheel. At eighteen it never occurred
to me to wonder why he consented to spend almost every
evening with me at the local chicken and steak joint; now I
know that he sensed the loneliness, and fright, of a boy from
a large family experiencing an unscheduled hiatus before

the ghastly procrusteanization ahead and no doubt felt that the war, inasmuch as it had to be fought by men of sounder limb than his, could at least benefit from whatever kindness he was in a position to pay to a prospective young soldier.

We became very good friends, and much of what he spoke about I remember. But I suppose I remember most vividly what he told me casually in one conversation, because it so much offended my sensibilities, which at that time suffered from not having been coarsened by experience. He spoke about a rendezvous a few weeks before with an attractive young lady from our town, who agreed to drive with him for a weekend at Myrtle Beach, which is the Gold Coast of South Carolina. They arrived, checked in at the hotel, puttered about the beach, had an extensive and vinous dinner, after which she declined to accompany my friend back to his little suite. His greatest strength was his irony, and, concentrating his energy to appear judicious, the effect was arresting. "Bill, that woman is a cheat. She broke an implicit contract."

I tended, under the impulse of congeniality, to agree with him whenever he asseverated about this or that, which was not all that often. But now I said nothing. My reasoning quickly became obvious to him. I was clearly having trouble associating the ethics of contract law with the ethics of seduction. Perhaps the lady had thought all along that the gambol at Myrtle Beach was to be entirely chaste. Perhaps, on discovering otherwise, she maneuvered as best she could without calling the police. Still, if my friend's accounting was correct, one had to take sides: either in favor of sin being committed or a contract being broken. Which was the greater offense?

It occurs to me, after much experience with the same dilemma in another form, that worldly authors of worldly books are, paradoxically, the most regularly cheated class of people on earth. We are always taking them to Myrtle Beach—Barbara Walters, Johnny Carson, Merv Griffin, Dick Cavett, Dinah Shore, Mike Douglas—time after time after time, and when the moment comes, what do they do? They talk about New York municipal bonds. What the profession needs is a code of fair practices, toward a formulation of which these words are dedicated.

*   *   *

Let us begin by laying down a few distinctions. Some authors are willing to appear on television and radio for the fun of it. It is, after all, a form of entertainment and, as such, something of an act of self-discipline. It requires a kind of straitjacketed geniality that is good for people inclined to sourpussery. George C. Scott was recently on the circuit to promote his movie, and one could detect the awful burden the medium imposed on him, straining a nature so clearly inclined to misanthropy, toward that ingratiation required to effect his seductions. Some people—believe me, this is true—find it enjoyable. Some, because they are born evangelists and are happiest instructing others, whether on how to conduct foreign policy or how to make tomato soup. Some, because they find it stimulating. Some, because they find it gratifying to the ego to appear before an audience.

I think, however, that it is safe to say about most authors that we do *not* enjoy working the talk shows. Here, too, there are good and bad reasons. Perhaps because we are a little lazy. Perhaps because we are too fastidious, too used to the luxury of editing our remarks; horrified at the licentious results of extemporaneity. Vladimir Nabokov, who has this problem, solved it pretty much the way General de Gaulle solved it. General de Gaulle hated press conferences, so he all but abolished them. He conducted about two a year. And he pre-stipulated the questions and memorized the answers to them. Nabokov does about two television appearances a decade. And he memorizes every single thing he permits himself to say, wisecracks and all.

Others dislike the talk show because they feel that necessarily it will trivialize any subject under discussion. Still others lack confidence in their capacity for small talk and are afraid of sounding either simple-minded or arrogant.

Even so, most authors will consent to do almost anything to promote their books. Doing *anything* to promote one's book I define as appearing on the David Susskind show. Doing *almost* anything, I define as appearing on the other shows. John Kenneth Galbraith lives by the rule, "I write 'em, you [he is addressing Houghton Mifflin] sell 'em." But even JKG will appear on the "Today" show to promote his books. And when he does, there is an air of no-nonsense. He is not there, at seven-thirty in the morning at Rockefeller Center, to give free advice on public policy. He is there to talk about his new book. It happened once, riding in the car with him to a joint appearance on the "Today" show, that I complained to him about his cupidity, even as a co-beneficiary of it. "Because your agent insisted we get paid so much money for our appearance this morning," I explained, "it was made discreetly clear to me through an intermediary that they are *not* going to mention my new book." His legs stretched out in the car and he tilted his head, looking and sounding more Scottish than Annie Laurie, and with wry delight suggested a formula. "When *you* say whatever nonsense you are bound to say in defense of poverty and ill health and atom bombs, *I'll* say, 'Bill, that reminds me of your new book, *Execution Eve*, which I believe is published by Putnam's and is in any case available at any bookstore.' And then when *I* am defending the poor and the sick and advocating peace in the world, *you* break in and say, 'Well, Ken, you do take those positions very persuasively and eloquently in your book on *Money*—was it Houghton Mifflin?' " We giggled like schoolgirls and of course didn't. We are pros. We were getting paid not to talk about our books. But when you aren't getting paid (and by being paid, I don't mean scale), the other guys should act like pros.

I am among those authors who agree to appear publicly to promote their books; to do almost anything to promote them, as I have put it, though I set a limit of approximately one week and eight appearances. I am not a Stakhanovite book promoter on the order of, say, Jacqueline Susann, one of whose tours consumed three months, or Joe McGinniss, who wrote charmingly on *The Making of a Best-Seller*. Still, like so many authors, I recognize that there is no easy way to make excuses for not making a few public appearances. There are two important reasons for this. The first is that to refuse to put in the dozen hours necessary to appear on the top five or six shows in order to bring to the public's attention a book on which you spent a dozen hundred hours is not quite logical. The second is that it is difficult to prod a publisher to promote a publication at great cost to himself which you decline to promote at very little cost to yourself.

324 A HYMNAL: THE CONTROVERSIAL ARTS

Now, when I say at little cost to the author, once again we
need to pause to consider the snares. One of them is being
made to become, so to speak, a member of the Beverly Hill-
billies. Usually I have contrived to appear and depart, resisting that commingling that can transform an appearance on a
talk show into a prolonged nightmare. During my youth,
promoting my books on the old Dave Garroway "Today"
show, I once found myself thinking of J. Fred Muggs as
probably my closest friend. Nowadays, I gently, but firmly,
insist on in-and-out, even if this means I am placed at the tail
end of the program.

My worst tumble, snarewise, occurred in connection with
the Dinah Shore show. I can only say in self-defense, have
you ever tried to defend yourself against Dinah Shore? I
found it, after her third letter, impossible.

It wasn't only that she wanted me to appear on her show. It
was that . . . she wanted me to play something on the harpsichord on her show. This was several years ago, when her
formula was fairly rigid. She would give the audience the
recipe and there and then cook a particular dish, her guest
acting as straight man, passing her the salt and the onions
and so forth. Bad enough. But there is worse to come. The
guest must perform at his hobby. I must play the harpsichord for her. One of the difficulties with the harpsichord is
that it cannot be made to sound, at the hands of an amateur,
endearing—like Jack Benny's violin. It just sounds like amateur night.

I tried and for two years succeeded in putting her off. But
that third letter—in which she said she had learned I would
be in Los Angeles to appear on the Johnny Carson show—
wasn't that wonderful—because now I could appear that
same afternoon on her show as I had promised one day I
would. . . .

It was Appear or Break with her. There was no Middle
Way.

But then I thought of something that suddenly gave me
great comfort. In my entire life, I had never met anyone who
had ever seen the Dinah Shore show. I say that this thought
crossed my mind with no intention of slighting the most attractive woman in the entire world. But, after all, it is another

. . . set . . . of people who watch daytime television shows; so I felt that I could safely make a fool of myself playing the harpsichord on the Dinah Shore show. I felt as secure from detection as if I had contracted with the CIA for the loan of a safe house wherein to play the harpsichord, the kind of place in which I ought to play the harpsichord. And—who knows—perhaps the mention of my book might effect a sale or two. A week later, I had forgotten it all, save the wonderful persona of Dinah Shore.

Two weeks after that, I landed in a small private airplane with a friend from Mississippi who was taking me to meet, and lunch with, my hero. My hero is Walker Percy, the novelist. We pulled up to the terminal of the little airstrip east of New Orleans and a tall lanky man in Levi's approached the airplane and, as I emerged from it, shot out his hand. "I'm Walker Percy, Mr. Buckley. I feel I know you. Just saw you on the Dinah Shore show." (Providence was looking after me, as it happened. Before lunch, mint julep in hand, I was dictating my column over the telephone to New York. Halfway through, the operator in my office interrupted to say that Dr. Kissinger was on the line, which he was; he told me, apropos of this or that, that the terms had finally been arrived at for the Paris accord on Vietnam. Accordingly, when I returned to the porch I managed to say to Walker Percy, as theatrically as possible, "I bring you peace in our time." Just in case he got the impression that all I do in life is play the harpsichord that way.)

I forget which book it was, but I remember that Miss Shore—excuse me, Dinah—lived quite scrupulously up to her implicit part of the bargain. She mentioned the book several times, asked me a couple of questions about it, and flashed the jacket on the screen. That was her *quid pro quo*. In return for that, she got me playing the harpsichord; *she* could have got me doing anything, though now I know that her show isn't run on closed-circuit TV.

The first thing, then, is to watch out for the snares. And then to make it unmistakably clear to the prospective host (best done through an intermediary) that the purpose of the visit is *to talk about the book*. Thought should be given to what it is about the book that is of general interest. It is obviously easier for Jacqueline Susann than, say, Alfred North Whitehead. Joe McGinniss was somewhere in between, but he had it pretty easy. He had a story to tell (narrative); it took a while to tell it (making it impossible to interrupt him without killing the narrative); and the victim of the story, Richard Nixon, was very much in the public mind (he was President). McGinniss had no problem at all. His book occupied center stage in all his appearances.

As all authors know, the safest assumption in the trade is that the host of a talk show has not read your book. (The notable exceptions in New York are Arlene Francis and Barry Farber, whose industry is both exemplary and astonishing; and, of course, Robert Cromie.) There is no point in taking offense on this score. It is simply impossible to do a program five times a week, of which the author will occupy perhaps only 10 percent of the time, and prepare for him by reading his entire book. What not every author knows is that *some* talk-show hosts haven't even read the one- or two-page digest of the book prepared by the publisher. Mary Ellen Chase, of Smith College, once asked at the bookstore for a new volume by a colleague in the history department, *The Gateway to the Middle Ages*, and was offered in its place, by the salesgirl, *Life Begins at Forty*. That salesgirl was borrowed from the talk shows. It appears to make no difference at all that the major talk shows dispatch a conscientious lieutenant either to visit with you personally or to speak with you over the telephone about areas of interest in your book, the better to brief the host. Generally the host is slimly informed about your book; sometimes he is *entirely* ignorant of it.

Now, collections are especially hard to handle. I have attempted to promote five and cannot remember a single successful network talk-show encounter. A year ago, I published *Execution Eve*, subtitled *And Other Contemporary Ballads*. The difficulty was that there is virtually no subject the book neglects to impinge upon.

"... So let's have a big hand for Mr. William F. Buckley, Jr. ...

"Bill, why did you call your book *Execution Eve*?"

"Well, you know, you've got to call a book *something*. And I got a telegram from my publisher and he said: SEND TITLE FOR YOUR NEW BOOK BY NOON MONDAY. So, I thought maybe that some of the essays in the book are pretty pessimistic, so, you know . . ."

"Pessimistic? Tell me, Bill, are you pessimistic about the future of New York City?—Mr. Buckley here, some of you will remember, ran for mayor of New York back in, in . . . when was that, Bill?"

"1965."

"1965. That's right. Against John Lindsay. And when they asked him what would he do if he won, he said . . . tell 'em what you said, Bill."

"Uh, can I tell a story?"

"Of course. But hang on just a minute for a station break."

"Now, where were we? Oh, yes. New York. Do you believe the Federal Government should help out New York City with more or less aid than it sends to Afghanistan?"

Since I didn't get to tell my story, I must unburden myself of it, even though the lights are off now and the house is empty. It has to do with Rachmaninoff, and the occasion was his seventieth birthday. His friends (it is said) organized a big celebration for him at Carnegie Hall.

Arthur Rubinstein was now at center stage, sitting in front of a concert grand. Rachmaninoff was sitting onstage in the place of honor and did not know what was coming. Silence. Rubinstein's hands descend on the piano and the majestic opening octaves—POM, POM, POM (this story is easier to tell than to write)—are sounded. Rachmaninoff, hearing them, lurches forward, pale: but then, unaccountably, the music goes off in an entirely unfamiliar direction. (Rubinstein premieres a prelude, specially composed by a chic composer in honor of Rachmaninoff.) Rachmaninoff leans back, visibly relieved. The crowd howls with delighted laughter.

It is an inside joke. You see, Rachmaninoff was nineteen when he composed the C-sharp Minor Prelude. He has not succeeded in playing a single recital since then without having to play the goddamn prelude as an encore. It is his *Clair de Lune*. He has become so sick of it, it turns his stomach. When he heard those telltale notes, he actually thought he was going to have to *sit and listen to somebody else play his C-sharp Minor Prelude*—on his seventieth birthday! Some birthday. . . . You see, Johnny, that's how *I* feel when I am introduced as the man who, on being asked what he would do if he won the election, replied, "Demand a recount."

Pretty rococo stuff for a talk show. Anyway, the story wouldn't have been a conduit back to *Execution Eve*. But it will appear in my next collection. [And welcome!—W.F.B.]

So: when you have a collection, or a tricky novel, you need more cooperation from the host than when you are dealing with books easier to talk about. Dan Wakefield complained, in an article in the New York *Times*, that people on talk shows tend to resist *any* discussion of novels, and he gave as an example, coincidentally, my brother Reid, interviewed on the "Today" show on the publication of his novel, *Servants and Their Masters*. He was introduced as the author and within forty-five seconds was being asked to comment on Nixon's trip to China. He did as bidden—we all do—and his novel never saw the light of day again.

This last time around, I thought that, finally, I had the problem licked. I had written a novel. My first, as it happened. But see, this is no *Naked Lunch* or *Giles Goat Boy*. The hero of my novel works for the CIA. In the course of pursuing his quarry in England, in 1951, he s-c-r-e-w-s the queen. No, no, not the incumbent—a fictitious queen. Then he fights a duel, ostensibly a demonstration at an air show—actually, the *real* thing!—and, and, well. . . .

"Mr. Buckley has written a novel, *Saving the Queen* [a book jacket is shown on the screen. Unhappily, it is the jacket of a book I didn't write and have never heard of]. It is a novel about the CIA"—that much the host could have gotten by reading just the jacket.

"Mr. Buckley, you were yourself in the CIA, weren't you?"

"Yes, I was—in 1951 and 1952, for eight months."

"Tell me, do you believe the CIA has the right to assassinate people?"

"Well, I think that is a complicated question. I don't think the CIA has the 'right' to assassinate people, but I can think of things that are worse than a CIA assassination—a world war, for instance. It's hard to answer categorically. In *Saving the Queen* . . ."

"Well, take the case of Patrice Lumumba, did the CIA . . ."

What's going on, I wondered? This was publication day. *Surely* the interviewer will get plenty of mileage—from the *interviewer's* point of view let alone the author's—out of such a question as, "Mr. Buckley, in your novel, the CIA agent has an affair with the Queen of England. Would you say that was in the line of duty?"

So help me, the two interviewers did not even know that that was, so to speak, the climax of the book we were all supposed to be talking about. I had the feeling, after going out of the studio, that if I had revealed in my book that it was I, not Alger Hiss, who gave Whittaker Chambers the Pumpkin Papers, we would still have spent our twelve minutes talking about yesterday's accusations by the Church committee. If you can't find a way to interest a general audience in a book in which the Queen of England does it with a CIA agent, what are you going to do with *Execution Eve?*

That was the first of the eight days allotted to promotion. Another day, the producer having faithfully promised that my book would be the only subject for discussion, I found waiting for me on the set in Philadelphia Jack Anderson. Now I like Jack Anderson, and I don't mind discussing the CIA with him—*another time.* My book occupied exactly thirty seconds of that half-hour. My final experience, on the eighth day, was on a network show. The entire hour would be given to my book. I was brought in to visit briefly with the host in his makeup room. He reached out and shook my hand, then warmed me with the following words. "Just got back from a week's vacation in Nassau. Took your book with me but couldn't get past the first six pages." I was affronted—

but only for a very little while. After the first six minutes on the air with him, it became clear to me that he had never got past the first six pages of any book. You will assume that we devoted the hour to a general discussion of CIA; and you will be correct.

I have just completed a new book, and, a few months from now, I shall face the question all authors face so agonizingly: Shall I do it again? Must I? There is no way to be tougher than the publisher's agents, and my Miss Bronson, have been. They have gotten, from representatives of the big shows, everything short of tattooed promises to keep to the subject of the book. But when you are on the air, though you can attempt, for a little bit, a King Charles's head approach to your book ("What do I think of Jimmy Carter's chances? It's a funny thing about Jimmy Carter. He looks just like the father of the protagonist in my novel—Blackford Oakes, the guy who, you know, has this secret mission in London which ends up him sharing state secrets—and, ho ho ho, other secrets—with the Queen of England"), the trouble with that approach is that it makes you feel exactly as you should feel using it. Vulgar. It is better to be angry with the talk-show host than with yourself.

What is needed is a formula: AUTHOR AND HOST; BOOK AND NON-BOOK—SEPARATE AND EQUAL.

It is based on these propositions:

1. The desire of an author to bring attention to his book is entirely normal. Perhaps the author's interest is only commercial. Even if that is the case, so what? Actually, most authors write books for reasons not exclusively commercial. Agatha Christie, it is somewhere recorded, once said that she would write books even if they were read only by her husband. Most books can be legitimately advertised by their authors as meaning something to them not completely transcribed in their royalty statements. Obviously this is so in respect of books that are forthrightly evangelistic. But it is also so about books that are merely ventures in entertainment. Jimmy Durante, Bing Crosby and Bob Hope performed, in part, because they wanted to perform or felt the need to per-

form. Under the circumstances, the attendant hypocrisy in authors' appearances on talk shows is really unnecessary.

2. If an author is invited to make an appearance on a talk show, it is generally true that the producer has judged the author to be interesting or else newsworthy; and, of course, possibly he is both. In any event, extremely dull authors of even very popular books do not get invited to talk shows, so that the mere appearance of a guest is a presumption that he can hold the interest of an audience. That presumption should be carried forward to the presumption that he can be interesting in discussing his own book.

3. Even though that is the case, it is true that a particular author may be more interesting to the audience curious about other matters than those the author discusses in the book. A novel by Spiro Agnew is a case in point. When he completes his novel, and if he consents to publicize it, it cannot reasonably be expected that, appearing on the "Today" show, questions would be limited to the content of the novel.

4. Under the circumstances, producers and authors should agree that where this is the case there will be a rough division of time. Part of it spent on the book, part of it on other matters.

The question of how to *deal* with a book is, I think, less difficult to answer if a formula is agreed upon rather than day-by-day improvisation. The obvious springboard is the reviews.

"Mr. Buckley, the reviewer from the San Francisco *Chronicle* says that the experiences of your hero are obviously autobiographical."

"Yes, he did say that, Johnny. But then the reviewer for the Kansas City *Star* said that since the hero is irresistibly handsome and charming, at least the reader can take satisfaction from knowing it is not autobiographical."

"Several of the reviews make reference to the extraordinary wit, charm, and good looks of the hero. Did you have any design in mind in making him so?"

"Yes, as a matter of fact. One thing I was doing intentionally, the second, I realized I was doing only when the book was well along. As you know, I have had no experience in fiction. Or, rather, my experience was limited to one session with two editors at Doubleday and one reading of John Braine's book, *Writing a Novel*. One of the editors told me that a novel tends to succeed if, early on, the reader forms an attachment to the protagonist and comes really to care about his future. So I tried to make my hero appealing. Beyond that, I found myself resisting, as I went along, the craze for the anti-hero—so much so that I permitted something of Billy Budd to enter into my portrait."

"Billy Budd? Who is he?"

And so on.

The host of the talk show would, of course, be furnished with provocative excerpts from reviews of the book. (These, limited to one page, he would *have to read*.) This becomes easier as the season advances. The "Today" show tends to want to weigh in on publication date, which would require that the interviewers be satisfied with the *Publishers Weekly* review and Virginia Kirkus—and the two or three reviews that, inevitably, break the publication date. Even so, there is always plenty to talk about, and my guess is that the interviewers would find themselves emancipated by the candor of the format. Consider the difference in the introductions:

A. "Mr. William F. Buckley, Jr., whose recent book, *Saving the Queen*, is just published, is a man with many views on many subjects, almost always controversial. There's a lot to be controversial about these days, so let's hear from Mr. William F. Buckley, Jr."

B. "Mr. William F. Buckley, Jr. is here to talk about his new book, *Saving the Queen*. After we have discussed that book, we'll turn to other matters about which—you can depend on it!—Mr. Buckley is bound to have some controversial things to say."

I should think that the formula would be appealing not only to authors but also to the hosts. And certainly to the audience which, intuiting the real reason for the author's appearance on the program, resents the conventional obliquity of the references to his new book; or—depending on where his sympathies or interests lie—feels cheated by the victimization of the author, who is suddenly being made to talk about

New York municipal bonds; or grateful to the host who conned the author by getting his book out of the way with such dispatch. And the host can't help experiencing relief at the crystallization of an implicit contract which relieves him, in the eyes of the audience, of any alternative other than spending a few minutes on the book. They might even find that the audience likes it that way. At least they should feel better. And if they do not institute such a reform, they should be made to feel worse. Authors of the world, unite! We have nothing to lose but our publicity.

VIII.

Notes & Asides

WHAT FOLLOWS is a few items from the editor's column at *National Review*, which is labeled Notes & Asides. It has developed a distinctive tradition over twenty years. People write to complain about something over which, as often as not, we have no control; to correct the editor; to insult the editor; to bring something to the editor's attention; to take umbrage over something that previously appeared in the space. The editor comments on these letters about half the time, leaving the others pristine. The space is also used as a bulletin board for the purpose of sharing staff communications of general interest. The column is sometimes used for unabashedly pedagogical reasons. For instance, I have nowhere seen a short definition of Keynesianism I like better than the one given here by Edward Meadows. And, finally, the space is used by the editor for extraordinary communications to his colleagues, friends, and others. In the previous selection (*Execution Eve*, 1975) I noted that entries can be loosely classified under the headings: *NR* Staff, Kookdom, Pedagogy, Up Yours, Setting the Record Straight, Very Personal Observations, and *Sui Generis*. The divisions continue to hold up. There is some attempt at grouping in the selection published here, but mostly I just hop about, not entirely unintentionally.—WFB

■Dear Mr. Buckley:

Calling our putting a man on the moon "an aristocratic caper" was a nice use of words and would have been even nicer had you pronounced the adjective from the Greek as it is pronounced by the *best* English speakers.

Sincerely,
Rives Matthews
The Society for the Prevention of Cruelty to English
Paradise Valley, Arizona

* * *

Dear Mr. Matthews: You must mean "as it is pronounced by *some of* the best English speakers"?

Cordially,
WFB

■Dear Bill:

I did not give you the good oil, as the Australians say, in my previous note. I implied that *Homo phoenicopteros* was Latin. Of course the coinage is macaronic—Latin and Greek. Oy!

A note on Joseph A. Rehyansky's ["Letter from the Edge of Détente," February 20, 1976] mention that the U.S. garrison troops along the East German border carry .45 calibre automatic pistols.

The American Army .45 is a ferocious weapon. In the continuing controversy over what handgun to keep in the bedroom against burglars, Democrats, and other shootable creatures, I recommend the .45 Colt automatic. One has to pull the slide back to place a round in the chamber, an effort that prevents one's shooting oneself after a bad dream, as one can do with a revolver. Moreover, pulling back the slide is beyond the strength of most women (*vide* the abortive attempt to shoot President Ford), and so the husband of the house has a good chance his wife will not be able to shoot him. Placing weapons on the top of the wardrobe or locking the trigger is not advisable, since most burglars and Democrats will not wait until the victim gets his gun down, finds the trigger lock key, and gets the thing in operating order. Moreover, in dispatching Democrats, one must be forehanded—if one shoots them, the remaining members of that party will surely call louder for a gun control law—so in their case I recommend using a bow and arrow. That might also turn the current fashion against the feathered Indians.

Best,
John Greenway
Oppressor of Anthropology
University of Colorado
Boulder, Colorado

* * *

Dear Bill:

As a Democrat and a one-time expert with an Army .45, I was delighted with John Greenway's advice ["Notes & Asides," April 2] that this is the ideal weapon to keep in the bedroom to eliminate, *inter alios*, Democrats. (That is, unless one is prepared either to use it as a club or to throw it at the rogue.)

The .45's kick is such that—unless one is prepared to spend several hours a day on the range instead of the tennis court—a normal "Oppressor of Anthropology," aiming at a rascally Democrat, would blow a hole in the ceiling. Most Democrats I know rely on cocker spaniels for defense against Republicans.

Ciao,
John P. Roche
The Fletcher School of Law and Diplomacy
Medford, Massachusetts

Dear Mr. Buckley:

As a mossbacked Republican, as well as the director of a small-arms school, I must point out that, quite contrary to Dr. Roche's remarks on the subject ["Notes & Asides," May 28], the recoil of the U.S. service .45 auto pistol is a completely trivial consideration. I am prepared to teach even a small, thin Democrat to fire the fearsome .45 easily with just the thumb and forefinger of one hand, in one short lesson, providing he or she (or it) undertakes in return to bore from within against the confiscation corps in his own party.

Cordially,
Jeff Cooper
The American Pistol Institute
Paulden, Arizona

Dear Mr. Buckley:

Regarding John Greenway's and John P. Roche's little disagreement over how best to eliminate Democratic voters, I just want to report that we Texas Republicans found a foolproof method for cutting down on the number of Democrats.

We ran Ronald Reagan in the Republican presidential primary. We found this to be far more effective than practicing on our shooting ranges every day, and we even had time for a little tennis.

Cordially,
Tom Tyler III
Houston, Texas

■Mr. Buckley:
You are the mouthpiece of that evil rabble that depends on fraud, perjury, dirty tricks, anything at all that suits their purposes.
I would trust a snake before I would trust you or anybody you support.

A. Ruesthe
(No address)

Dear Mr. Ruesthe: What would you do if I supported the snake? Cordially,

—WFB

■Dear Mr. Buckley:
I am a teacher with credentials in English, political science, history, mathematics, humanities, and Japanese, and yet I barely have the ability to decipher your vulgar prose.
I can't recall ever having seen such an obvious search for and display of archaic vocabulary and overall obfuscation in an apparent attempt to be "the learned one." You stink!
You are a complete joke, a pedant, a phony conservative. You're an upstart. You may be a New Englander and a Yale man, but, in no wise, do you have the class of a Cox, a Richardson, or even a Kennedy.

Yours truly,
John M. Herlihy
Seaside, California

Dear Mr. Herlihy: Sorry. English, political science, history, mathematics, humanities, and Japanese are not *quite* enough. But don't give up, Herlihy. Don't ever give up.

—WFB

■   Elsie Meyer, RIP

AT MIDAFTERNOON on Sunday, April 27, Elsie Meyer, whose husband Frank died of cancer three years ago, called Priscilla Buckley, and engaged her in one of those routine, chirpy, business-pleasure telephone calls by which business tends to be done at *National Review* if at one end of the line you have Priscilla Buckley, and especially if, at the other end of the line, Frank Meyer had been talking, or, now, his wife Elsie. Frank, who was a founding editor of *National Review*, transformed the telephone into his special genie—his blackboard, his couch, his Scotch and soda. His friends were legion, and when he died we were left with the sensation of an indispensable ganglion having suddenly stopped functioning. His habits had been resolute. He rose in the early afternoon, and retired sometime after dawn. In between, he would engage two or three dozen people in conversation over the telephone: deep and trivial, about matters cosmic and personal. He was beloved of young people, whose concerns became his own; and, among established echelons who wrote for the book section in *National Review* that he edited, he was beloved also, and admired for his persistence, good humor, but also for his total seriousness. He and Elsie had been not merely fellow-traveling members of the Communist Party, but most serious functionaries of it, and when they defected, it was in exchange for no escapist alternative: they sought to do no less than improve the universe. It was only their coordinates that had changed. Instead of Marxist orthodoxy, they discovered the glamorous and intoxicating orthodoxy of individual freedom. Hours before he died, Frank Meyer, who had many years earlier discovered Christian orthodoxy, made a commitment to it, and was received into the Catholic faith. Elsie had already begun instructions in Christianity, as had their eldest son John, a chess champion and law student, a lawyer now with the Community Services Administration in Washington.

One hour after Elsie spoke to Priscilla about the routine problems of the forthcoming issue of *National Review*, she took from the farmhouse in Woodstock, New York, sagging under the weight of a generation's accumulation of Frank's books, an old blanket, went out into the desolate backyard, wrapped herself in it, and shot herself with Frank's .22 pistol.

After Frank died, the editors of National Review assigned the job of book review editor to our Washington correspondent, George Will. Elsie presided over the transitional period, and settled down to a widow's rustication, one son about to graduate from law school, her younger son Eugene a freshman at Yale. After a few months she came to us and said that she could not bear the loneliness of life in the remote little house on the mountain at Woodstock, her sons away at school—without Frank. Her sense of loss was easily communicated to those who found their own lives significantly diminished by the absence of Frank's pestiferous, inquisitive, unyielding, refreshing, demanding telephone calls. And so Priscilla suggested that Elsie replace Pat Simonds as copy editor for National Review, Mr. and Mrs. Christopher Simonds having decided to quit NR and take jobs at a country pre-prep school.

Elsie asked only that she be permitted a four-day week, which in the collage of NR timetables is a venture in orthodoxy. If she had asked for a job that would keep her occupied from midnight to six in the morning on odd days, she'd have come to the right place. To be sure, she had working for her the advantage that she was probably the single most popular figure in National Review's professional periphery. Frank was occasionally impossible; and Elsie would, soothingly, discreetly, make it all right. She did everything for him, from feeding the children to teaching them Latin, to taking down Frank's columns in shorthand and transcribing them. She was a graduate of Radcliffe, and, notwithstanding, was proficient in the essential intellectual disciplines. She was a fastidious grammarian, etymologist, and stylist, and had done all of Frank's correspondence, and much of the editing of his book section.

She was also unabashedly homely. Or that, at any rate, was the impression she, with the active connivance of her extraworldly husband, cultivated. Her hair was in perpetual disarray. Her nose was obstinately crooked. Her teeth were a flowering of the free enterprise system. After Frank died, she suddenly permitted herself just the lightest dab of lip-stick, and occasionally her hair was moderately in place. What never changed was a smile that lit up her entire face, an irresistible warmth, a sense, uncontrollable, of the humor of things—she laughed wholesomely about everything without (one thinks of Whittaker Chambers) losing her spiritual orientation. Within forty-eight hours of coming to work she was everybody's friend. A year later, overseeing the editorial copy and calling gently to the attention of transgressors their offenses against the rigors and the purity of the language, her little cubicle had become something of a grotto, a plea-sure to pass by, and to pause at.

When the news of her suicide reached us, there was uni-versal concern over the question: *Why?* She had, of her own volition, acquiesced in stern philosophical principles; in be-coming a Catholic, she had implicitly committed herself against suicide.

While in New York she enjoyed the opera, the ballet, the theater, above all the company of her colleagues, as she eked out a sustenance, by hard work, for herself and her two sons. She was editor of the American African Affairs Association newsletter, on the side; and of the Educational Exchange, a private newsletter available to college faculty and administra-tors seeking to employ scholars of libertarian and conserva-tive inclination. Late on Thursday afternoon she would take the bus back 100 miles to Woodstock, returning to us on Monday. Over the weekend she would work on a mountain of manuscripts and galleys. But every now and then, almost unnoticeably, she would confide, most discreetly, to one of her colleagues that she could not "stand" life "without Frank." It may have been that that loneliness gained the criti-cal ascendancy on that Sunday afternoon when she scribbled out a brief note to her sons and, with her fastidious concern for neatness, elected to go outside to perform the act. Twenty years earlier she was called in the middle of the night to their neighbor and best friend, Eugene O'Neill Jr., the playwright's son—after whom Elsie and Frank named their younger son. He was dead by his own hand, in the cellar of his house, a hideous end, of course; and also messy. In those days, we learn, the Meyers and others who had escaped from the miasma of Communism were to talk late into the night about suicide. It was the fashionable alternative during a period when the dichotomies of Albert Camus were the center of philosophical attention. Frank Meyer resisted the impulse to suicide, and instead did much to instruct a generation of conservatives. His wife was at his side serving him, while he lived, in every capacity, and, after he died, with apparent cheerfulness doing her best to survive him. She failed, finally. But in behalf of her colleagues, I record that in our experience there was never anyone more cheerful, or whose company was more cheering. And, strange as it may sound, no one in our memory who had grown more physically beautiful than Elsie Meyer.

■Memo to: Bill
    From: Priscilla
    Delicious, from an *American Opinion* piece (January) by Alan Stang in which he reports on telephone interviews with conservative columnists and comments: "Needless to say, none of this applies to William F. Buckley. This article deals only with those columnists who, so far as your reporter knows, may safely be assumed to on our side—which naturally excludes members of the Council on Foreign Relations and those who conspire with the Bilderbergers."

Priscilla:
    Don't tell anyone, but the Bilderbergers conspired to make Alan Stang write that. Boy, are they powerful. On the other hand, since they are powerful enough to run the foreign policies of the entire world, why should we be surprised that they should succeed in dictating policy to the John Birch Society? XX Bill

■Memo to: Bill   November 1, 1976
    From: Priscilla
    Bill von Dreele, always the professional, sent two verses. One in case Ford wins, the other in case Carter does.

HERE COMES CARTER

If you're over thirteen thou'
Pushing pencil, truck, or plough,
Be prepared to bleed a bit
When the Carter taxes hit.
In the meantime, try to be
As compassionate as he;
Later, when you lose your shirts,
Try to smile until it hurts.

—W. H. von Dreele

LEVITATION

Some do it for the Gipper;
    Scots do it for the clan.
Some, like the little choo-choo,
    Repeat, "I think I can."
Some rise just like the Phoenix;
    Some, just before the bell.
As for the Ford's assumption,
    The Lord alone can tell.

—W. H. Von Dreele

■INT WILLIAM F BUCKLEY ETAL
CARE US EMBASSY
MOSCOW (RUSSIA)*
WILLIAMOVICH PRISCILLANOVNA IVANOVNA VOTSISSDRAWOWE
MIT MUSCOVICHES? VOTS TO HAPPEN CREDIBILITOVICH NATION-
AL REVIEWOVICH? CHECKOVICH BUGSOVICH ROOMSOVICH YOU
BETCHUM BETTER KOMMEN SIE HOMEOVICH QUICKOVICH
                                        REIDOVICH [BUCKLEY]

*On the 20th Anniversary of *National Review*, I took the staff for a tour of the Soviet
Union (see page 257). The American Ambassador, Mr. Walter J. Stoessel, Jr., had a
reception for us and presented us with a telegram from my brother, Reid.

■Dear Bill:
What does Sobran know about good actors, great generals, fine movies, and geniuses? Get rid of that fool.
Cordially,
H. G. Wright
Waldo, Florida

Dear Mr. Wright: Who then would advise us concerning bad actors, bad generals, bad movies, and fools? Cordially,
WFB

■Dear Mr. Buckley:
I've taken *NR* for the last year. I enjoy it. I'm not a conservative, *per se,* but I am a pragmatist and tend toward Friedman in my economic thought.
Economics is at the root of social and political problems: crime, unemployment, slum housing, etc. Often conservatives identify the problem with a clearer reality than others. But then they drift off in the fog and forget to attack solutions, for the problems identified.
So here's a chance for conservatives. As you know I am a prisoner. I am not a political prisoner. I am not innocent. I am tired of the revolving door of the criminal justice system (five felonies, three imprisonments). You will recall my last scheme—a computer fraud of the IRS of $565,340.31 FROM OUTSIDE THE IRS AND BY MYSELF.
Come September 29 I'll be paroled. I need *meaningful* employment. If I don't find it *and fast,* I'll just put into effect another scheme I've already got a handle on—this time for over $3,000,000. Not much was recovered last time, none will the next. Of course I know I'll likely be caught and . . . well you know the rest. More revolving doors.
But as I said, I'm tired of wasting years in prison. I have a lot of abilities *and* qualifications (of course I'm prohibited from being an accountant again). The last time out I spent thousands on becoming a qualified pilot for charter work, etc.
Soon—like in the summer—I must have concrete plans for my parole. This is for me—not the parole commission—they no longer count employment plans because so many parolees

went to "slot" jobs that were meaningless, devoid of promise, etc.

If some conservative, or whatever, really wants to put his money where his convictions are, then I'd hope he'd consider taking a 33-year-old, highly intelligent and sophisticated ex-felon on as a really productive employee.

An employer truly does get what he pays for—business is business. I don't expect a free ride—but I won't accept a "slot" job. If someone needs a topnotch co-pilot-manager for a corporate flight department, then I hope he'll contact me. Nothing less than 400 hours of flying per year—commercial or corporate. Cargo or passengers. No flight instructing.

It is the businessman and taxpayer that pays when I rip off $500,000 every six months. They also pay when I'm doing time. Prison isn't so bad that the risks aren't worth it. But I would like to change my act.

David Robinson
Reg. No. 18443–148
Federal Correctional Institution
Box 7, Terminal Island
San Pedro, California 90731

Dear Mr. Robinson: I shall consult with Milton Friedman, your mentor, on the matter of a free market solution for your problem.

Yours faithfully,
WFB

■Dear Mr. Buckley:

The esteemed Dr. Rinfret ["Firing Line," August 28] declared that "Keynes said the capitalist system could never reach full equilibrium." Absolutely wrong. Keynes only suggested that equilibrium need not occur at the point of full employment. From a historical perspective, the Neoclassical paradigm, on one hand, assured automatic full employment equilibrium, while on the other, the Marxist dogma assured automatic disequilibrium. Keynes came along and patched up the capitalist system by introducing into it the mechanism for the disequilibrium that was and is so obvious in real life.

The heart of Keynes's schemata is the psychological "law"

of the consumption function, $C = f(Y)$, i.e., people's spending is a function of their income and, specifically, $f(Y) = a + bY$ in simple form, which shows that consumption varies directly with income but less than in proportion, given $b > 1$. Now, given this behavioral assumption, Keynes was merely trying to point out that the "automatic" tendency toward equilibrium is diverted by means of the fact that notional demand (what consumers would like to buy if they had the cash) cannot be transmitted through the economy. (In other words, Say's Law isn't a "law" but an identity true only in equilibrium.) For example, assume incomes are lowered. People buy less. Thus signaled, producers produce less. With less being produced, incomes fall further. A downward spiral. But wait! All those consumers out there would happily buy goods and services if only they had the money. That is, if producers would rehire them and step up production, the economy would take off. But producers have only their effective demand to go by. They have no measure of what consumers might like to buy. All they can judge is what consumers are buying. Hence Say's Law, that demand creates its own supply, doesn't work except at full employment equilibrium. And hence unemployment equilibrium may instead be reached. This is all one needs to know about Keynes (except that he was a gentleman and a pederast).

Sincerely,
Edward Meadows
Columbia, South Carolina

Professor George Stigler
Department of Economics
University of Chicago

Dear George:
    When Bill Buckley told me you were reviewing *The Age of Uncertainty*, I expected the worst and you did not disappoint. It seems to me an example of fair polemics, and I'm not sure that I didn't learn a thing or two, however reluctantly. You worried me about the absence of a reference to competition and I concocted an easy excuse—that I took it so completely

for granted. Then to my joy I found that in the broadcast, at
least, it is safely there.

On one point I would solidly disagree. On balance, I think
it more important to be known as a good writer than as a
good economist. There must be hundreds of our profession—I could name a dozen—with an original, perceptive, or
otherwise interesting view of matters, large or small, who
have been unable to communicate it beyond at least the nar-
rowest circle, often not that.

In a way you are an example of the opposite case. I naturally consider you, on balance, a bad economist, a thought
from which you will doubtless recover. You are an unduly
predictable exponent of the stereotypes. You would have
had no influence whatever save that you are able to write
with clarity, some grace, and occasional humor. And I can
think of no economist from Smith to Milton Friedman who
has earned any reputation in the field without some competence as a writer. I've said on many occasions that Marx and
Ricardo both owed something to the obscurity of their prose
and the ability of their disciples to find therein what they
want to believe. But both had a stunning capacity to make
themselves heard when they wished.

Yours faithfully,
John Kenneth Galbraith
Harvard University
Cambridge, Massachusetts

cc: Mr. William F. Buckley Jr.

Professor John K. Galbraith
Harvard University

Dear Ken:

You are more charitable with me than ordinary good manners dictate, and I thank you for your restraint under provo-
cation.

You will not be surprised that I disagree with you on what
makes an economist important. I believe that you confuse
popularity with importance, and I enclose an article which
argues that an economist is only important when he is mak-

ing scientific contributions. My own merits as an economist will rest, not on the desultory expeditions I make into policy discussion, but on whatever value attaches to my work on the economics of information, regulation, etc.

Sincerely,
George J. Stigler
University of Chicago

cc: Mr. William F. Buckley Jr.

Stigler wins. Discussion closed.

—WFB

■House of Commons
London SW1

Dear Bill,
    Having just read your article in the Washington *Star* of 28th October,* I have made my first New Year Resolution. From 1st January, 1976, Mr. Buckley shall be "Bill."
    I shall assume the appropriate reciprocity.

Yours sincerely,
Margaret Thatcher
*See page 307.

■Dear Bill:
    I remember a column you wrote a while back in which you clucked about unseemly familiarity in modes of personal address. I agree with you. In fact, I'm rather standoffish myself; I've been at Dartmouth for over a month now, and I haven't even met Jeffrey Hart. Oh, I've *seen* him, but I haven't actually met him, and when I do I'll certainly call him Mr. Hart, at least to begin with.
    But I presume to call you Bill. There are several reasons. I did actually meet you once, years and years ago—you were on the lecture circuit at St. Michael's College in Winooski, Vermont (and you spoke very well). Also, I got a nice little note from you several years back, in which you signed yourself "Bill." I had responded to your annual appeal for funds to keep *NR* afloat by saying that I wished I could kick in a

hundred or two but I didn't have any money (I was writing my dissertation at the time and really didn't have any money—still don't). Your reply was a gracious gesture, and it made me feel as though I knew you a little better. In fact, as an almost-charter subscriber to *NR* and a regular viewer of "Firing Line" I feel that over the years I have grown to know the contours of your mind excruciatingly well.

Still, I don't think I would be calling you Bill even now if it weren't for the startling familiarity with which you greet me, through your subalterns, every other week when I rush to the mailbox to pick up my copy of *NR*. What do I see?:

```
M BRWNOOIR 010 7721 – 3 25 –
ROBERT E BROWNE
CLAREMONT ANUS
1 VALIANT WINTER ST
CLAREMONT NH 03743
```

Never mind that this perfectly captures my feelings about Claremont, New Hampshire; do you think you could send future issues in a plain brown wrapper with the address on the inside? Or change it to "Arms"? Or talk to Mr. McFadden? Him I shall continue to address with decorous formality. Thanks, Bill.

Yours appreciatively,
Robert E. "Bob" Browne
English Department
Dartmouth College

Dear Bob: I checked with Jim McFadden. He is awfully busy, and began by muttering something that sounded like "Up Claremont." But he was mollified, the correction will be made, and he says you can call him Jim.

Cordially,
Bill

■Dear Bill:
Kreon, Haemon, Antigone, Ismene, and the boys in the back room are going to miss you! But I'll take note of the

proceedings and send you a report of the outcome. The smart money is on Kreon, because he owns the guards, but there have been upsets from time to time, just enough to keep monarchs off balance. Hedge all bets.

Your original plan was to set something up for the next weekend. Let's fall back to that position and think of a picnic Sunday—we'll call it the Annual Awards Banquet of the Hack Journalists Klub, all three of us (you, Stan, yo mismo), and with hot dogs and français fries and Moet & Chandon how can we go wrong? Falling back position, *en cas de pluie*: the Admiral Benbow Inn, right around the corner from your pad, and suitably martially yclept.

I got a note from Tim Wheeler, telling me he can now type with both hands—an aberration that automatically disqualifies him from membership in our Klub. Rumor has it he has written a book. Probably the same book, but critical judgment must defer to the objective correlative. Tim is among the few who could have written the same book first instead of second. Sorta *déjà phooey.*

I have other thoughts, but I am exhausted in contemplating what I have already done. A thousand *paredones.* (To err is mural.)

See you Sunday? I am disarmed and should be considered harmless unless terrified.

Fondly always,
Bill Rickenbacker
Briarcliff Manor, New York

■Dear Bill:

Now that I'm fully recovered from my latest mild bout with the force of dementia praecox super schizo triple paranoia *praise the void* (Yiddish accent), I am happy to announce the construction of ontological apparatus with transmission capabilities of 7/8ths of an ounce—hmm—new lexicons—Sing Sing nexus listen close—you've heard the expression "Next year in Jerusalem!"?—no doubt—anyway I got it straight from the horse's frothing mouth—it is Time to

Begin the Beguine
Beguile the Begule
Begume the Bitume

or there won't be a Tel Aviv to tell about nor a Jerusalem to journey to nor a planet to plot peace upon, and blood will run nigh over the johnny pumps. America the Reneger— death is a rubber disease! Ha—spoked and spun like a vandal son in de roamin' sky—I is entitled to ire and—free peanut butter. Wot? Duh, peace, Me puzzling, tho promising summer behind these danged walls. Enough to make a saint out of a sinner. Good to hear from you. Be well.

Chuck Culhane
Sing Sing Penitentiary
Ossining, New York

Dear Chuck: Celebrating decriminalization? Cordially,

Bill

■Dear Mr. Buckley:

You got anything in the way of corrective or preventive therapy for guys who get tempted by the romance of radicalism? I feel it coming on like a plague, just like it did in '69, and I really don't think I'm gonna be able to fight it off this time. I've been sitting here listening to the library's collection of Sir Winston's wartime speeches, looking at my pictures of General MacArthur, fondling my toy elephants, doing everything I can think of to keep myself straight, but there's something in the air this spring that keeps bringing back all them tastes of college nonsense, going off to Fort Dix in October to get a taste of tear gas, just going out and raising hell for the sake of raising hell, no principles, no burning issues, just get four or five hundred people out in the streets and dress up funny and make pig noises and be a perfect ass and *love* it. Yeah, except all the people who were doing that kind of garbage five years ago are practicing law in Paramus now. Tough break, huh?

But it was so lovely, particularly in early 1970, the fever pitch was there, you didn't have to make sense to feel vindicated, you could handle any confrontation with the right words, maybe it was all this *ecology* nonsense that fouled it up. It used to be that you'd . . . well, take Woodstock. Everybody left all their empties right there in the mud, right? Hey, let Yasgur clean it up, it's *his* farm. Even if you *could* by some miracle pull off another Woodstock in '75, these kids would spend the next week "policing the area." Yeah, I saw *that* business when it began, we should've nipped it in the bud then. In October 1969, the Moratorium, behind the Public Library, 40,000 people jammed into Bryant Park to see, ohh. . . . Gene McCarthy, Javits, Lindsay was there, Senator Goodell, all this fun and commotion, Hare Krishna guys, Weathermen with VC battle flags, right, then when it was over these characters from Columbia were going around picking up *candy wrappers!!* Hey, if we'd been *really* bright, we would've seen it developing. Within a year you couldn't talk Revolution to those candy-wrapper people, all they wanted to do was save Lake Erie and mumble about ZPG. I figured it was time to up the ante, cure their Realism with stronger medicine, make the fantasies *more* and *more* bizarre, so I started writing this thing about how the CIA had murdered Luther Burbank in 1926 because he was on the track of Petrochemical Hybrids, growing oil in plant form, the oil billionaires from Dallas had put out a contract on him, then some guy told me there *wasn't* any CIA back then, but it didn't matter, by then I was being asked to leave the university anyhow and before long I was off at the factory making ra--dio dials and thinking about becoming a Republican for the summer.

Oh, now I don't remember what I was writing about when I began the letter. A fatal digression. If you get to the point of typing really fast, you get hypnotized by the sound of the keys, you just let yourself go and all the stuff you normally would've concealed or edited comes flowing down your arms and out your fingers into the text of what you're writing. Maybe that's why I couldn't finish college. I'd get halfway into a paper on some frog's digestive system and end up talking about Theodore's sinus problem. No bother. I've decided to be a rock star next. That should keep me busy until autumn. I hope you have a nice summer.

Stanley Matis
Jefferson, Massachusetts

Dear Mr. Matis: Thanks. We both need a rest.   Cordially,
WFB

■To the Editor:

William F. Buckley's high sense of moralism is his Achilles's heel. He falls into the trap of seeing matters, however complex, as right *or* wrong, good *or* bad. He takes the National Council of Teachers of English to task [See page 293] for recommending the use of plural pronouns with indefinite pronouns (everyone, anyone, etc.) when those words refer to groups including members of both sexes. According to the *Oxford English Dictionary*, "the pronoun referring to *everyone* is often plural: the absence of a singular pronoun of common gender rendering this violation of grammatical concord sometimes necessary."

If Mr. Buckley wants to disagree with the *OED*, that's his privilege. But anyone as authoritarian as he is will surely understand if we side with the *OED* . . .

Sincerely,
Robert F. Hogan
Executive Secretary
National Council of Teachers of English
Urbana, Illinois

Dear Mr. Hogan: You aren't siding with the *OED,* you are co-opting it for your *evil* purposes. *"Everyone was happy. They raised their glasses in a toast to the winning team."* Okay. But *your* proposal to extend that license so as to be able to say, *"Everyone requires food. Otherwise, they will starve,"* is *not* okayed by the *OED,* since "he" in this case clearly represents both sexes, as in, "he who laughs last, laughs best." Ho ho ho.

Sincerely,
WFB

■Dear Mr. Buckley:

Your reply to the language instructor who found it "irresistible . . . to overlook your rare slip in syntax" should have been not *"Nolo contendere,"* but rather *"Tu quoque."*

Charles Floto
New Haven, Connecticut

■Dear Mr. Buckley:

Pray tell us readers the difference between "certain inalienable rights," as I read in my copy of The Declaration, and "certain unalienable rights," as printed on page 554 of *National Review*.

Sincerely,
Colonel Fred W. Miller
Scottsdale, Arizona

P.S.: My dictionary says that "inalienable" and "unalienable" are synonymous.

Dear Colonel: "Unalienable" is the word Jefferson used. "Inalienable" is what is nowadays used. "Alienable" is what describes the rights we fought for.

Cordially,
WFB

Dear Mr. Buckley:

In "Notes and Asides" for June 25, 1976, you stated that Jefferson wrote the phrase "certain unalienable rights" into the Declaration of Independence, while "inalienable" is the word nowadays used. An all-time Bicentennial goof, Mr. Buckley. Jefferson used the word "inalienable"; Congress eventually adopted the "unalienable" reading, so *that* is the word we nowadays use—at least, when we're being accurate. (The switch, Carl Becker argued, was made by John Adams who was also on the Committee of Five that Congress charged to draft the document.)

Furthermore, in the last quarter of the eighteenth century, "unalienable" meant "unalterable," whereas "inalienable" had a stronger, more juridical import, relating to undivestable Lockean natural rights. *Pas de quoi*.

Sincerely,
James Viator
Claremont Graduate School
Claremont, California

P.S. In case *NR* should continue perpetrating crimes against historicity, my retainer fee is quite reasonable.

Posh. Academic pish. You don't go around saying Thomas Wolfe didn't write that word from *Look Homeward, Angel*,

Maxwell Perkins did. Jefferson listed himself as author of the Declaration of Independence, which is good enough by us. As for your *fee*, learn first how to use the word historicity correctly. *Abi, Viator, et imitare si poteris.*

Cordially,
WFB

■Dear Kilpo [James J. Kilpatrick]:
A splendid column on Cornell. However, I disagree that a letter cannot be both verbose and redundant. Verbosity need not be redundant. Correct?

But I would write more confidently if it were not that you are Number One, being addressed by your faithful servant,

Number Two

Numero Uno:
I venture no positive pronouncements on this difficult issue. My tentative feeling is that it is quite possible to be redundant without being verbose, but I would think it difficult to be verbose without being redundant.

To say, as so many of our friends in broadcasting so often say, that a meeting will be held "at 10 A.M. in the morning" is to fall headlong into redundancy. But this is not verbosity.

I encounter verbosity (or what strikes me as verbosity) whenever I travel to the Senate press gallery and spend an hour marveling at the butter and marmalade professions on the floor. "Permit me to yield, Mr. President, to my able and distinguished friend, the senior senator from thus-and-so, for whom I entertain the highest regard and the warmest admiration. Indeed, Mr. President, I must say that no member of this deliberative body is held in higher regard, or more justifiably so, than my brilliant and erudite colleague, to whom I deferentially yield such time as he may require." That is verbosity; it is also redundancy.

I am supported in these impressions by the lexicographers of *Webster's.* Under the heading of "redundant," they encourage us to seek amplification under "wordy." At "wordy," we are educated in the subtleties that distinguish *wordy, verbose, prolix, diffuse,* and *redundant.* From these first cousins we are led to a remarkable array of second cousins, great-uncles, step-sisters, and great-aunts once removed: *tedious, garrulous, repetitious, loquacious,* and so forth. From all this I conclude that there are times, alas, when I am both verbose and re- dundant, while you, my mentor, are merely richly detailed.

Deferentially,
James J. Kilpatrick

Dear Kilpo: We ought to put our act on the road. Herewith a trial balloon.

Cordially,
Bill

■Dear Mr. Buckley:

Having long been a sincere admirer of your intellect and versatility, I think I am entitled to be indignant about a silly and easily avoidable error you made in *Saving the Queen.* See p. 25, para. 2:

". . . sent the three professors each a two-volume set of the Diabelli Variations, played by Leonard Shure . . ."

What on earth . . . ?! Beethoven's "33 Variations on a Waltz by Diabelli," i.e., the Diabelli Variations of your refer- ence as it is popularly called, is recorded—whether by your apparent personal friend Shure or by others of higher inter- pretive level—on two sides of a single 33-rpm recording. There cannot possibly be a "two-volume set" such as you cite. Painful; it suggests that you do not know the work, Beethov- en's Op. 120, and nonetheless wish to display familiarity with it. This being so, I am almost inclined to suspect you even in connection with Antigone, which you mention just a few lines further below the spot quoted above.

Unworthy of you, Mr. Buckley.

Best wishes and regards,
Dr. Andor C. Klay
Washington, D.C.

Dear Dr. Klay: Know the Diabelli Variations? I could hum you all 33 of them! Leonard Shure, whose virtuosity com- pares favorably with your knowledge of music, recorded the Variations in a two-volume set issued by Amvox in 1949 (No. 6360 VLP). The Variations occupied three sides, the fourth was given over to the six variations in F Major, Opus #34. So you know now that Blackford Oakes *never* errs. As for Antigone, she hated her brother Polynices, whence the term antagonistic, which will be the tone of any future answer from me to a letter from you unless you have in the interim done something about your sciolism, which I suspect comes in *more* than 33 variations.

Yours cordially,
WFB

Dear Mr. Buckley:

I believe you're mistaken as to the derivation of the word "antagonistic."

"Antagonistic" does not derive from, nor does it share its Greek root with, Antigone. The two words do share the use of the preposition, *anti,* which carries much the same meaning it does in English. But they derive from different basic roots. The progenitor of "antagonistic" is a variation of the verb *agonizomai,* which carries the general sense of "to struggle." Antigone, on the other hand, descends from a noun, *gone* (go-NAY); it means "offspring, relation." In the context of Sophocles' play, the meaning of the word is more specifically "brother."

Hence, Antigone's name verbalizes her struggle "against her brother." The word "antagonistic" conveys only the more general sense of "struggling against." The assonance of the words is coincidental, implying no essential etymologic relationship.

I trouble you with this minutia only because I admire your philologic zeal.

With respect,
Douglas C. Clemensen
Minneapolis, Minnesota

Dear Mr. Buckley:

As I understand it, the two words have in common only the prefix, the root being different, and the "anta" of the one and the "Anti" of the other should have alerted you to this possibility. I would say that Antigone derives from the Greek noun *gonos* (omicron), which means, among other things, "kindred" (Antigone opposed her brother), whereas our word "antagonistic" derives from the noun *agon* (omega), meaning "a contest." This is seen clearly in the two Greek verbs *agonizesthai* and *antagonizesthai* (omega in both cases), meaning "to struggle" and "to struggle against" respectively.

My authority for this is the father of Alice (of Wonderland fame), Professor H. G. Liddell. Who is yours?

Sincerely,
Murl J. Manlove
San Antonio, Texas

Dear Mr. Manlove, et al.: Mine was a put-on, including the bit about the relations between Antigone and her brother. To tell the absolute truth, I was running short of material for N&A, whence the ambush. Thanks for your energetic corrections.

Cordially,
WFB

∎Dear Hugh:

A year or so ago—maybe two years—I wrote Bill several letters about his persistent usage of the dreadful word *solipsism*—and he finally gave in and wrote me he would *stop* using it if I could find him a substitute—and I then wrote you asking if you could provide me with one, but you did not respond. In the meantime, Bill, faithfully, did not use the word again until about two weeks ago, and there it was, causing me sorrow again. I cannot think of a better source than you and pray that you will send me not one, but *several* alternatives, that I may again take up the matter with Bill.

Charles Wallen Jr.
Millbrae, California

Dear Charles:

But Bill's point is precisely that there is *no* substitute for "solipsism." If what pains you about it is simply the fact that you seldom hear it, then the fault is not in the man who grinds it against your ears, but in the millions of part-time and largely inadvertent solipsists who are so convinced the universe emanates from them that they feel no need of a word to designate such a condition. Fish, on the same principle, know nothing of water, and for aqueous terminology you should not apply to a fish. If on the other hand your ears are assaulted by its impacted sibilants (as the ears of Tennyson were aggrieved by the word "scissors"), then I can only fetch you the cold comfort that for a graceless condition the wisdom inherent in the language has afforded us a graceless word. And if, finally, your grievance is that Bill uses it too often, then I can only tax you with inconsistency, since you report that after one to two years of not hearing it from his lips you were wounded anew by a single occurrence—perhaps, I will grant, on the principle of a man who has been sensitized to penicillin. Such a man's comfort should be that others need the remedy that inflames him, and that principle I commend to you.

Hugh Kenner
Santa Barbara, Calif.

■   **VN-RIP**

THE COVER of this magazine* had gone to press when word came in that Vladimir Nabokov was dead. I am sorry—not for the impiety; sorry that VN will not see the cover, or read the verse, which he'd have enjoyed. He'd have seen this issue days ahead of most Americans, because he received *National Review* by airmail, and had done so for several years. And when we would meet, which was every year, for lunch or dinner, he never failed to express pleasure with the magazine. In February, when I last saw him, he came down in the elevator, big, hunched, with his cane, carefully observed by Vera, white-haired, with the ivory skin and delicate features and beautiful face. VN was carrying a book, which he tendered me with some embarrassment—because it was inscribed. In one of his books, a collection of interviews and random fare, given over not insubstantially to the celebration of his favorite crotchets, he had said that one of the things he *never* did was inscribe books.

*["Vladimir Nabokov interviews Madame Butterfly ('Poor Butterfly, come into my net; you are the handsomest and most exotic of lepidoptera yet') . . ."]

Last year, called back unexpectedly to New York, I missed our annual reunion. Since then I had lent him my two most recent books, and about these he now expressed hospitable enthusiasm as we sat down at his table in the corner of the elegant dining room of the most adamantly unchanged hotel in Europe: I cannot imagine, for all its recent architectural modernization, that the Montreux-Palace was any different before the Russian revolution.

He had been very ill, he said, and was saved by the dogged intervention of his son, Dmitri, who at the hospital ordered ministrations the poor doctors had not thought of—isn't that right, Vera? Almost right—Vera is a stickler for precision. But he was writing again, back to the old schedule. What was that schedule? (I knew, but knew he liked to tell it.) Up in the morning about six, read the papers and a few journals, then cook breakfast for Vera in the warren of little rooms where they had lived for seventeen years. After that he would begin writing, and would write all morning long, usually standing, on the cards he had specially cut to a size that suited him (he wrote on both sides, and collated them finally into books). Then a light lunch, then a walk, then a nap, and, in nimbler days, a little butterfly-chasing or tennis, then back to his writing until dinner time. Seven hours of writing, and he would produce 175 words. [What words!] Then dinner, and book-reading, perhaps a game of Scrabble in Russian. A very dull life, he said chortling with pleasure, and then asking questions about America, deploring the infelicitous Russian prose of Solzhenitsyn, assuring me that I was wrong in saying he had attended the inaugural meeting of the Congress for Cultural Freedom—he had never attended *any* organizational meeting of anything—isn't that right, Vera? This time she nods her head and tells him to get on with the business of ordering from the menu. He describes with a fluent synoptic virtuosity the literary scene, the political scene, inflation, bad French, cupiditous publishers, the exciting breakthrough in his son's operatic career, and what am I working on now?

A novel, and you're in it.

What was that?

You and Vera are in it. You have a daughter, and she becomes a Communist agent.

He is more amused by this than Vera, but not all *that* amused. Of course I'll send it to you, I beam. He laughs— much of the time he is laughing. How long will it take you to drive to the airport in Geneva?

My taxi told me it takes *"un petit heure."*

Une petite heure [he is the professor]: that means fifty minutes. We shall have to eat quickly. He reminisces about his declination of my bid to go on "Firing Line." It would have taken me *two weeks* of preparation, he says almost proudly, reminding me of his well-known rule against improvising. Every word he ever spoke before an audience had been written out and memorized, he assured me—isn't that right, Vera? Well no, he would answer questions in class extemporaneously. Well *obviously!* He laughed. He could hardly program his students to ask questions to which he had the answers prepared! I demur: his extemporaneous style is fine, just fine; ah, he says, but before an audience, or before one of those . . . television . . . cameras, he would freeze. He ordered a brandy, and in a few minutes we rose, and he and Vera and I walked ever so slowly to the door. "As long as Western civilization survives," Christopher Lehmann-Haupt wrote in the *Times* last Tuesday, "his reputation is safe. Indeed, he will probably emerge as one of the greatest artists our century has produced," I said goodbye warmly, embracing Vera, taking his hand, knowing that probably I would never see again—never mind the artist—this wonderful human being.

■ "There were a few of us who proposed the use of nuclear weapons (on Khe Sanh). We felt it important to establish that these weapons would not trigger a nuclear war." [From a column by WFB.] *This* is a reason to unleash the hydrogen bomb on innocent men, women, and children? Think what you are saying. The sheer, stinking obscenity of that statement makes me want to retch. If I ever get as sick as *that,* I hope I die before I have a chance to spread the infection.

Very truly yours,
Father M. M. DeWalt, S.J.
315 East 46th Street
New York, New York

Pax vobiscum, padre. (1) The proposal was to use *tactical* nuclear bombs, (2) there were no women and children in Khe Sanh, just U.S. Marines, surrounded by armed, non-innocent North Vietnamese aggressors, on whom (3) we ended up dropping much greater firepower than would have belched out of a few tactical nuclear bombs; making it (4) really unnecessary for you to retch, although such missives as this one are not the best way to persuade your congregation that you are in good health.

Cordially,
WFB

■Dear Sir:
You possess one of the most unacceptable and unpleasant faces of capitalism I have ever seen,

Yours sincerely,
Michael R. Morritt
Pontefract, Yorks.
England

Dear Mr. Morritt: Have you ever seen the face of Ulysses S. Grant?

—WFB

■To my dearest Mr. Buckley:
Where would you be today if you were Puerto Rican?

Cordially,
Colleen Baldwin
Denton, Texas

To my dearest Miss Baldwin: Probably I'd be minister of propaganda in the administration of Governor Carlos Romero Barcelo, my classmate at Yale.

Cordially,
WFB

■Sir:
It is my opinion that you and your brother, putting Israel first, would rather see taxpayers charged billions for the benefit of Israel and your oil interests in the hope of having

the country go to war with the Arabs (and Russians) than see one dime of federal aid go to New York City. You are revolting.

Sincerely,
Eliot H. Sharp
1 Pierrepont Street
Brooklyn, New York

Dear Mr. Sharp: Revolting? Well I should hope so. This is the 200th anniversary of our revolt. How do you plan to spend the Fourth? Cordially,

—WFB

■To the Editor
Playboy Magazine

Dear Sir:

Karl Hess, replying to your interviewer's question in the current issue of *Playboy* ("Although you admire Buckley, you no longer agree with him. From your point of view, where did he go wrong?"), answers: "He went wrong because, in the end, he actually believed he was preserving God's will. I remember a dinner party Bill had at his place in Connecticut soon after the first issue of *National Review* was published [twenty years ago]. This fellow kept staring at him and finally said, 'You know, Bill, you have the profile of a young Caesar.' Well, instead of being embarrassed by that preposterous remark, Bill reveled in it. And in retrospect, I conclude that people who do not blush when they are compared to Caesar end up being Caesar."

I remember the scene very well. You see, at my dinner parties I try to guide the discussion into profitable directions of common interest and substantial purpose. On the agenda that particular evening was the question: Does my profile more closely resemble that of Julius Caesar, Alexander the Great, or Rudolph Valentino? The argument raged for hours, and I attempted to be entirely dispassionate on the subject, believing as I do in untrammeled democratic authority. The guests were pretty well divided when one of them, with singular authority, announced that my profile is indisputably more like that of Caesar, and although I admit to a certain wistfulness at the rejection of Alexander and Valentino (a strong minority case can be made in their favor), I was secretly pleased that Caesar had won out. I thought I had kept my pleasure safely undetected. But I must congratulate Mr. Hess on his acuity. *He* saw through to my true attitude, even as now he has penetrated to the *real* intentions of God, the Founding Fathers, and Mankind.

Cordially,
—WFB

■From the Congressional Record, H9700 *et seq.*

PARLIAMENTARY INQUIRY CONCERNING ALLEGED VIOLATIONS OF THE RULES OF THE HOUSE AND THE RULES OF COMITY

(Mr. Cleveland asked and was given permission to address the House for one minute and to revise and extend his remarks.)

Mr. Cleveland. Mr. Speaker, I have asked for this time for the purpose of addressing the Chair so that I may make an inquiry, which will be in the nature of a parliamentary inquiry, of the Chair, in regard to the following matter:

On last April 17, at page H2884 of the *Record,* I was commenting on the manner in which the Senate was handling aspects of the New Hampshire Senate election, remarks that were critical of the Senate, and the Speaker at that time called me to order, and, quoting from the Speaker's remarks, the Speaker asked me to desist and stated that my remarks were in violation of the rules of the House and the rules of comity.

For this reason, Mr. Speaker, I wish to bring this to the attention of the Chair: I noticed on October 1 that at pages H9424–H9425 of the *Record* the gentleman from New York [Mr. Koch] addressed the House under the one-minute rule and had been extremely critical of the junior Senator from New York [Mr. Buckley].

Mr. Speaker, I would like to inquire if the remarks of the gentleman from New York [Mr. Koch], like those of mine earlier in the year, are in violation of thr rules of the House and the rules of comity.

The Speaker. Does the gentleman from New York [Mr. Koch] desire to be heard?

Mr. Koch. I do, Mr. Speaker.

First, I will not object at this time to the use by the gentleman in the well of the name of a Member of the other House.

Instead, Mr. Speaker, I would like to say this.

Mr. Cleveland. Just a second. I not only used the name of the gentleman from New York [Mr. Koch], but I told him I was going to be here today and for what purpose.

Mr. Koch. No, no. The gentleman from New Hampshire [Mr. Cleveland] misunderstood me. My reference was to the other Chamber. The gentleman referred to a Member of the other Chamber by name, something we may not do.

Mr. Cleveland. No: I thought I just said "the junior Senator."

Mr. Koch. I believe the gentleman from New Hampshire mentioned his name. I thought I heard it distinctly.

In any event, Mr. Speaker, I examined the precedents of the House, and I know the gentleman is familiar with *Jefferson's Manual,* a book that I revere, and, indeed, there are only two others that I have a higher regard for. One is the Bible, and the other is *Cannon's Precedents.*

In *Cannon's Precedents,* Mr. Speaker, there is a statement that it is not in order in debate to criticize Members of the other body, but such rules do not apply to criticisms of statements made by Members of the other body outside the Chamber.

In my remarks to which the gentleman from New Hampshire [Mr. Cleveland] refers, I did discuss the remarks of a Member of the other body, the younger brother of a noted columnist.

Mr. Cleveland. Mr. Speaker, I might say that that is being pretty critical right there.

Mr. Koch. That he is the younger brother of a noted columnist?

In any event, as a result of those remarks, this noted columnist, for whom I have high regard and personal affection—I know him quite well and, thank God, he is not a Member of the other body, so I can even mention his name, Bill Buckley—he took exception to my remarks in his column.

In examining the precedents, I have come to the conclusion that I ought not to have mentioned the exact name of that Member of the other body. Therefore, with the Chair's permission, I would consent to a withdrawal of that unutterable name and have substituted in each and every case where that name was mentioned a reference to the fact that I was referring to the younger brother of a noted columnist.

The Speaker. The Chair is ready to rule.

The Chair has, accordingly, checked the precedents. The precedents of the House indicate that it is not in order for a Member of this body to refer to the actions or remarks of a Member of the other body occurring either within the other body or elsewhere—Speaker Rayburn, May 5, 1941. The motives of the Member making the remarks are not relevant to a determination of whether they are or are not in order, as even complimentary remarks have been held to violate the rule of comity between the two Houses—Volume VIII, 2509.

The rule of comity has clearly been violated and, without objection, the remarks of the gentleman from New York will be stricken from the *Record.*

There was no objection.

Mr. Speaker! Mr. Speaker! Point of order. This is the noted columnist speaking. He wishes to advise the gentleman from New York that the columnist is the younger, not the older brother of the junior Senator from New York, and that that should be well known to the gentleman from New Hampshire who, at Law School, was the roommate of the future junior Senator from New York at a time when the future junior Senator's younger brother was a classmate of the gentleman from New Hampshire's younger brother, indeed the two younger brothers and the future Senator co-owned an airplane. Let's have comity, *and* accuracy, and full disclosure!

—WFB

∎Dear Bill:

I have just uncovered the authentic text (in *Transition #1*) and cannot dally in apprising you that what Gertrude Stein actually wrote was:

"Suppose, to suppose, suppose that a rose is a rose is a rose is a rose."

Note, four roses. And three supposes. And do not omit the two commas. Now, you are ONE UP.

As ever,

Hugh Kenner
Johns Hopkins University
Baltimore, Maryland

■Memo To: All Concerned, which I hope is everyone
From: WFB
Re: My imminent disappearance for thirty days

I plan to sail the schooner *Cyrano,* beginning at 1000 EDT May 30, from Miami, to Bermuda, to San Miguel (the Azores), to Marbella (in Spain). There I shall leave the boat in the hands of a captain and crew who will hire out the vessel, and themselves, to charter parties in the Mediterranean. The boat will be based in Cap Ferrat, just east of Nice. For information, write to Mrs. Flynn at *National Review.*

During that period I shall be virtually incommunicado, although the ship has an excellent radio telephone for outgoing calls which, I pray, will be few in number. I shall serve as captain and navigator, and if I call to say, "Where am I?" I would appreciate a non-derisory reply, even if it offends the stylistic preferences of my colleagues. I shall write three of my newspaper columns before setting sail (careful readers will note in them a certain detachment from highly contemporary affairs); and then I shall take my two weeks annual vacation from the column. The three columns for the last week of June prior to our landfall (ETA June 30) will be filed from the Azores. If you detect a sharp shift in my general political position, you may draw the appropriate conclusions about our reception by the Portuguese.

I have been hoping to make such a trip for a very long time. Now the opportunity coincides with the need to transport the vessel to the Mediterranean, and a contract to write a book (with photographs!) about the journey for Macmillan's. It has been a busy winter and spring with, in addition to the usual things, a novel (Doubleday, February), and another collection (Putnam's, September). In November, *NR* will be twenty, and I'll be fifty. It is unsafe to put off forever things like sailing across the Atlantic. For those of you who have been kind enough to express a concern over my physical safety, a reassuring statistic: for $500, Lloyd's will be giving us a million dollars' insurance. And remember there is always the silver lining. Since our policy is in favor of *National Review*, if the ship goes down, you'll have two entire years without a fund appeal!

Dear Mr. Buckley:

I just finished your column on John Lofton. I lost my temper, of course. You always do that to me. As, indeed, does Mr. Lofton.

But that isn't why I'm writing.

I read the col last week (and probably lost my temper then, too) and noted that you can do celestial navigation. I must say I am terribly impressed. I spent a week on Mixter, a couple of hours on the text issued by the Naval Academy in 1940, and my publisher sent me a snappy little number called *Commonsense Celestial Navigation* by one Hewitt Schlereth. All three of these books I'm sure are wonderful. But I don't understand a word in any of them.

Is there a text called something like *Self-Taught Celestial for Dumb Micks*? If there isn't, I'm going to have to get loran which, like powerboat ownership, is ungentlemanly. If you know of such a book, I would dearly love to hear about it. Your help in this matter won't make a conservative out of me, but it might keep me out of the country more often and on the ocean where my pernicious and kneejerk liberalism will harm none but the fishes.

Today's column, by the way, didn't make me angry because I disagreed with anything in it. It is true that on some matters sometimes journalists of both the Left and the Right get lucky and catch their opposite numbers in jackassy mistakes in public. What angered me about the column was its triviality. That Lofton was right all along is pretty small beer compared to that multi-billion dollar cruiser Dumb-Dumb wants to spend our money on or the fact that this note will probably be read by the CIA, possibly before you read it and almost certainly after.

Anthony Lewis's column today gloats that Sy Hersh was right all along and Mr. Colby is a liar. I don't disagree with Mr. Lewis, as I didn't with you. But I do think that during a time when the government has forgotten that it is ours and not vice versa, there are more important things to do than gloat.

To go from gloat to float, if you do know of a self-taught celestial book, I'd like to hear about it.

Best regards,
William J. Slattery
Box 239
Jamestown, Rhode Island

Dear Mr. Slattery: But gloating is a *great* delight. A real sensual treat, and you are only half a man if you don't ever engage in it. Hence even Our Lord gloated over His tormentors when He remarked to His fellow victim that this day they would be together in heaven. Granted, that is a Higher Gloat than anything one is entitled to at the expense of Shana Alexander. But actually, Slattery, gloating over the silliness of the mighty and the opinionated is a form of levelling iconoclasm, and very much in the spirit of the anti-authoritarianism which animates *National Review,* which you ought to read. Re celestial navigation, it is really very easy, though I have never read a book that made it sound easy. Accordingly, I intend to write one. Where the pedants make a mistake is in trying to tell you *why* it works. Never mind. Do you know how a computer works? Exactly. My book on my transatlantic sail, which will be written next winter, avoids the trap of intellectual curiosity. It will merely tell you how to do it, and gloat over yet another exegetical triumph. Cordially,

WFB

The Editor
The New York *Times*

July 3, 1975

Dear Sir:

Having only just now crawled out of the ocean in Spain, I have begun to catch up on my reading. I note in a recent column by Mr. James Reston the following sentence: "When we arrived [at the Azores] it was reported that a 'foreign vessel' had arrived at the port of Ponta Delgada. We checked this immediately . . . and discovered the 'foreign vessel' was a yacht skippered by Bill Buckley, en route from Long Island Sound to the Mediterranean, with John Kenneth Galbraith, celebrating his retirement from the Harvard faculty, as part of the crew."

Alas, the consequences of congressional parsimony on U.S. Intelligence are already beginning to show. (1) We sailed from Miami, not Long Island; (2) the Galbraith on board was not my friend the 6-foot 11-inch emaciated Menshevik, John Kenneth, but my friend the chunky 5-foot 11-inch Manchesterist, Evan; and anyway, (3) surely it was Harvard, not Professor Galbraith, that had reason to celebrate?

Yours cordially,
WFB

■Dear Mr. Buckley:

I've a friend who is given to adducing examples of one-in-a-million shots in order to buttress his frequently improbable arguments. In the course of a career of contentiousness, he has, to my personal knowledge, cited the case of the first German bomb to fall on Leningrad during WW II—you've heard this one, surely: the bomb, the first of its number, remember, is said to have killed the one and only elephant in that unfortunate city's zoo—at least a dozen times.

In my opinion the case of the Leningrad elephant has long palled, and lately even my friend has shown signs of casting about for a more improbable statistic, especially since I, while shingling an argument of my own, asked him what he thought the probability was that the following comic blunder could appear in a column by WFB ("The Trials of Christianity"): "leaving us merely with nuclear submarines which we would petulantly dump on the Soviet Union, killing off a half-hundred million Russians but leaving us then exposed to a retaliatory strike against our population centers."

Sincerely,
Jan Ophus
Scobey, Montana

Dear Mr. Ophus: If Reagan wins, we would, in the event of a
Soviet strike, dump on the Russians not merely the nuclear
bombs in the submarine, but *the whole submarine!!* So back to
the elephant, Ophus. Cordially,

—WFB

■Mr. Eric Sevareid
CBS-TV
New York, N.Y. 10019

Dear Eric:
   Mr. Paul Sweeney, the associate producer of "Firing Line,"
advised me a week or two ago that your publisher declined,
in your name, an invitation to appear on "Firing Line" on the
grounds—she represented herself as quoting you—that "Mr.
Sevareid is offended by recent writings by Mr. Buckley about
himself and about Teddy White." I called Teddy White, and
he told me that although he has very nearly total recall about
animadversions at his expense, and although I have frequently disagreed with him, he cannot remember when he
found my criticism personally offensive. So much for Teddy.
Now I sit here wondering what I did to you . . . Could it
have been the column in which I disagreed with your definition of "conservatism," as you gave it out to your listeners
some months back? Do you have handy—I'd be pleased to
consult it—a Guide to Permissible Criticism of Eric Sevareid?
If so, I hope it contains a supplement listing the names of
those of your friends any criticism of whom you do not tolerate. Since I criticize practically everybody, yet you name only
Teddy White, am I to gather that only he enjoys your special
protection? Or that he is your only friend? But that really is
preposterous, because even *I* have always thought of myself
as, among other things,

Your friend,
Bill

[See page 176.]

Dear Bill Buckley,
   I am referring back to your letter of September 20 on the

matter of friendship. My friendship is not easily given or easily withdrawn and I have arrived at the age when nothing else is quite so important.

But I'm afraid I take a view different from yours on permissible strains; and your logic confuses me. Because you have informed your many readers that Sevareid is not worth listening to I could not see why you would wish me on your TV hour.

When you began your AFTRA suit I made a published comment in support. What followed were repeated sneers in your column because I chose not to join the suit. You did not inquire as to why, but implied, as I read it, that it was due to cowardice. If there is anything in the world that does not frighten me, it would be that union. I declined to join simply because my time, my health, and my money were already painfully overextended and because lawyers assured me the suit had no chance.

You have, I am told by a source I believe, publicly described Teddy White as a national bore. If he chooses to disregard that, it's his business.

Sincerely,
Eric Sevareid
CBS News

Dear Eric:

Concerning your letter, a few observations:

1. My friendship, by contrast, is easily given, but does not preclude concurrent disagreement.

2. I do not remember telling my readers that you are not worth listening to. And even if I thought you were not, I would not hesitate to put you on "Firing Line"—because people whose views are not worth listening to are often listened to nevertheless. "Firing Line" has the advantage of giving its guests an opportunity to test their views under pressure.

3. I have indeed publicly pondered why you have not joined a lawsuit which you approve of. You never inquired whether it would cost you money to join me in the lawsuit to bring First Amendment protection to news analysts on the airwaves. The answer is No—the National Right to Work Legal Defense Foundation is defraying all expenses. Nor was

any investment of your time required. I do not see how the lawsuit would have impaired your health, unless your nerves are shattered by bad judicial decisions, in which case you are probably a nervous wreck anyway. As for the lawsuit's having no chance, remember we won at the circuit court level, and, despite setbacks, the case proceeds. Do I understand you to be saying that you will not associate yourself with a cause you believe will fail? How can you then associate yourself with so hopeless a cause as Immunity for Eric Sevareid from Criticism?

4. I have not publicly or privately described Teddy White as a national bore, because I do not believe him to be a national bore. Indeed I have acclaimed in print, even while criticizing some portions of them, several of his books. Pray inform your Deep Throat that he is incorrect. Is he, by the way, the same source you regularly rely on when composing your news analyses?

5. "Dear Bill Buckley"! Oooo! Dear Eric, I fear that in that protracted tug-of-war between yourself and a terminal stuffiness, you have, finally, lost. And that is everybody's business.

Cordially,
Wm. F. Buckley Jr.

■Dear Bill:

Somebody asked, specifically, so let me say it directly: some of the best journalism in America is being printed in the *National Review*.

Just wanted you to know.

Sincerely,
Dan Rather
CBS News
New York

Dear Dan: Many thanks.

—Bill

Dear Mr. Buckley:

As a long-time subscriber, more or less generous contributor, and sincere admirer of *NR,* I was terribly disappointed to read in "Notes & Asides" of the April 25 issue the laudatory remarks from Dan Rather. Where do you suppose *NR* went wrong?

Yours truly,
Joseph Voyles
Department of German
UC, Berkeley

Dear Mr. Voyles: *NR never* goes wrong. If Dan Rather likes it, Dan Rather went right!

—WFB

■Dear Mr. Buckley:
Upon the request of my roommate I began reading your article, "Letters to the Editor," in the TWA *Ambassador*, October 1977 edition. Although you are quite an accomplished writer, and the article was rather humorous, I could not force myself to finish reading it, due to the fact that I had a great deal of studying awaiting me. Putting the article aside started my previously mentioned roommate bitching at me. For you see, he is a great admirer of yours. Therefore on behalf of my roommate, I am sending this letter of apology for not having completed your article.

Apologetically yours,
Donald Jones (Tom's roommate)
218 Jamestown Rd.
Williamsburg, Virginia 23185

Dear Mr. Jones: Many thanks. Take your time. It's easy, at Williamsburg, to take one's time. The perspective is right.

Cordially,
WFB

■DearBill:
Cancel fund appeal! Will send details later!

Chilton Williamson
MGM Grand Hotel
Las Vegas, Nevada

■Dear Mr. Buckley:

I was looking around the yard for the Ninth and Tenth Amendments the other day, but couldn't find them. Have you seen any sign of them lately?

Yours truly,
Greg Christainsen
Wellesley, Massachusetts

Dear Mr. Christainsen: The amendments in question disappeared not long after the Civil War. Although there was interest in discovering them, it proved episodic, and there are only a half-dozen living Americans who would recognize them if they met them face to face. In 1950, the Supreme Court (widely suspected of showing only a formalistic interest in them) declined (*FPC* v. *East Ohio Gas Co.,* 338, U.S. 464) to pursue an obvious lead that might have led to the discovery of their whereabouts.

Cordially,
WFB

■Dear Mr. Buckley:

Recently I attended dedication ceremonies for a new sports complex at one of our large universities. Above the main entrance, sculpted in stone, stood the time-worn motto: *"Persona sana in corpore sano."*

Needless to say, the ceremonies ended with a rousing chorus of the "Battle Her of the Republic."

Sincerely yours,
Sean E. Sullivan
New York, New York

■Dear Mr. Buckley:

I recently purchased your book *Inveighing We Will Go,* and—forgive me—it fell apart! Now I am sure your hardcover books do not do this but, being 15 and having access to limited funds, I bought the paperback version.

You can imagine my dismay when, after 15 or so pages, each subsequent page fluttered to the floor. This can get to be a problem, especially when one reads in school. The bell rings and a score of people trample over some of your finest selections.

I was sitting outside reading on a particularly warm day when, after my attention was sufficiently distracted, the page I had been reading flew off into the sunset. I did run after it and managed to grab it following an exhilarating run.

My reason for writing this letter is to inform you of my mishap. Possibly you could get in contact with your publishers, Putnam, and ask them to secure their bindings better. Really, the condition of your books surprisingly reflects on you! One of my more liberal teachers found one of the pages to your book and when I said who wrote it the teacher looked at the decrepit condition of your book and said, "It figures, *his* books *do* fall apart." Our relations have never been the same.

Well, I managed to get through the whole book and thought it marvelous. It encouraged me to buy: *The Unmaking of a Mayor, The Committee and Its Critics, Saving the Queen,* and *Execution Eve.* The last two purchases were a splurge on my part and the first two I bought at a second-hand bookstore. I thought them all great and they substantiated and helped to define my already conservative views. I also subscribe to your magazine.

I was wondering how I can purchase your 25th Anniversary Issue? I read part of it in our library and would myself like a copy.

Is this a "fan letter"? You can say that as I both admire and enjoy both you and your afflatus.

Sincerely,
Bill Pavlovich
West Springfield, Massachusetts

P.S.: I enclose the cover which fell off your book *Inveighing We Will Go* in the hopes that you would autograph it.

Dear Bill: Since we are only twenty-one years old, and you have absorbed the contents of our 25th Anniversary Issue, clearly it is you who's got the afflatus. We'll pass the word along to Putnam, and replace your copy.

Cordially,
WFB

•Dear Mr. Buckley:

In a footnote on pages 73 and 74 of a little paperback entitled *The Rockefeller File* by Gary Allen, I have just read that you are a member of the satanic Council on Foreign Relations.

If this be not true please deny the statement that was made by Mr. Allen. But if it be true please cancel my subscription to *National Review* immediately. I shall destroy the copies I have carefully filed, even rereading them because I trusted you!

Yours truly,
E. M. Scorpio
Johnston, Rhode Island

Dear Mr. Scorpio: That's not enough! (1) Take mustard with lukewarm water, and swallow one pint! (2) Then call an exorcist! (3) Then throw yourself down nearest Memory Hole! Don't just *stand* there! Move!

—WFB

■Dear Mr. Buckley:

I was touched by your column "Does Anyone Know Elton John?" Mr. John seems a nice enough fellow and his music is interesting—not just noisy. I keep hoping Mr. John will consent to see your Maria. She sounds like an enchanting child. I hope you'll let me and/or your readers know if the meeting took place.

Sincerely yours,
Sandra J. Madden
New Canaan, Connecticut

Dear Miss Madden: Thank you, the meeting took place finally, in Denver, Colorado. The headline in the paper was ELTON JOHN FROM LONDON/MEETS MARIA CERVANTES FROM NEW YORK.

[See page 295.]

■Dear Mr. Buckley:

I have read two of your recent books, alas.

Airborne is totally without merit, except for its title which, although clever, is a misnomer, since a substantial part of the trip was under power, with barrels of fuel lashed on deck, no less. The book has no substance, no message, no entertainment, no value. Your publisher should be more discriminating.   ·

Saving the Queen is a good story, but you have abominable taste and insensitivity.

These two books are no recommendation for your *National Review* or any other of your publications.

Sincerely yours,
Louis E. Prickman, MD
Mayo Clinic
Rochester, Minnesota

Dear Doc: Please call me Bill. Can I call you by your nickname?

Cordially,
WFB

Dear Bill:

Saving the Queen was great fun, and an elegant spoof on the James Bond genre of machismo-fantasizing. Blackie is a comic book hero for the sophisticates of the jet set, and New York intellectuals. To get birched on the bottom by a snobbish Britisher, and to settle the score by screwing his Queen, is Royal tits for a commoner's tat, and a male chauvinist piece of imagination without parallel in fiction.

Love,
Clare [Boothe Luce]

■Dear Mr. Buckley:

You are one of the leading conservatives in this country, but you wear your hair like a way out liberal hippy. It is nasty looking, unkempt and subtracts tremendously from your appearance. You would be a fairly good looking man if you would get a haircut. With best wishes,

Sincerely yours,
Fellow Conservative
Box 1588
Greensboro, North Carolina

Dear Fellow Conservative: If I were also good looking, don't you think it would all be just *too* much?

Cordially,
WFB

■Dear Mr. Buckley:

I was a mere nineteen-year-old college sophomore the first time I read *Up from Liberalism.* I fell madly for your sarcastic wit and incredible logic.

Recently, I heard you speak at McFarlain Auditorium on the SMU campus in Dallas. I'm a twenty-four-year-old graduate student now, and your wit and logic are no longer enough. Mr. Buckley, I want your body.

Do you fool around?

M_____ W_____
Tipton, Oklahoma

Dear Miss W_____: Mostly in Notes & Asides.

Love,
WFB

IX.

Crime and Punishment

Crime in America

November 2, 1976

As ONE THINKS back on the campaign, one wonders how was it possible that so much time was spent, and effort given over to, the ventilation of national problems without any mention that one can recall of: crime.

One has the feeling that there is something akin to national despair over the problem of crime. George Wallace, who became famous by asking for law and order, was criminally assaulted, and crippled. When he rose shakily again to renew his bid for the Presidency, his voice faltered: and he lost out to a man who raises his voice at such horrors as the pardon of Richard Nixon, and tax loopholes. Jimmy Carter's only resonant sally against crime in America was at a speech long ago in which he said that rich and powerful men don't go to jail, but poor black boys do. Well, here's a poor black boy who didn't.

Mr. Donald Singleton of the New York *Daily News* gives the story. It is of two young men caught beating and robbing an eighty-two-year-old woman in the Bronx. One of the boys was let out right away. The second, Ronald Timmons, had little difficulty raising the bail. It was set at $500 by the judge, one Jerome Kidder. The District Attorney had asked Judge Kidder to set bail at $25,000, but Judge Kidder, perhaps moved by Jimmy Carter's speech, didn't. An appeal before another judge, Murray Koenig, didn't work either, so off Timmons went.

Now Timmons was convicted in 1972, when he was sixteen years old, of murdering a ninety-two-year-old man. Timmons and his brother broke into the man's apartment, apparently tied his arms and legs and gagged him with a towel and locked him in the bathroom. "When the man managed to remove the gag and yell for help," Mr. Singleton writes, "the boys replaced the gag, breaking the old man's rib in the process. The man died several days later."

385

Timmons is a rare one. Or—perhaps this is the point—not quite so rare. He has a record of sixteen other juvenile arrests, dating back to the age of eight. He has escaped from a state training school to which he was sent for a variety of violent crimes against older people, and from which he evidently emerged impenitent. Is this what Jimmy Carter is talking about?

A few months ago, a former Democratic leader, Mr. Edward Costikyan, who managed Mr. Beame's first campaign for Mayor of New York, went to the rescue of his son who was mugged by a young white man on the east side of New York. The assailant had a record of four or five violent crimes, and apparently makes a game of going in and out of New York courts.

A few weeks ago, in another borough of New York, an elderly couple, one in her seventies, the other in his eighties, were assailed and tortured in their apartment where they had lived for forty years. It was the second time in a short time, and when the assailant left, the couple apparently had a serious philosophical conversation. They decided that life was not really worth living. So they drew out their savings and dispatched them to a favorite charity—something on the order of $23,000. They then explained why they were doing as they were doing, and hanged themselves.

On the same day that Timmons made Judge Kidder jump through his hoop, John Ehrlichman committed himself to jail. Ehrlichman was, so to speak, rich. Certainly he was powerful. He never committed a violent crime. Is this what Jimmy Carter invokes, when he protests the operation of criminal justice in America?

Where are we going when a suicide pact by octogenarians, to avoid living in the Big Apple—a story which if written by Paddy Chayefsky would have been thought something of a Black Mass—fails to arouse sufficient interest to engage the attention of any public figure? Ronald Timmons is free because Judge Kidder—what? Acted as he *had to* under the law? If so, was that law handed to us by a leering providence, to mock the Bill of Rights? But Jimmy Carter and all the judges, high and low, who countenance this, are mocking the very idea of a free society.

Chicago Is Not the Worst

November 25, 1976

ONE WONDERS why he is so obstinately good-natured, but some people—not enough, alas—are simply born that way. His beat, in Chicago, comprehends an area near the University of Chicago distinguished by the highest homicide rate in the United States. He is thirty years old, was married at nineteen, has two children, and you would think his beat was the Garden of Eden. He does, however, tell you that the system is simply not working. In Chicago, as in so many other places, crime is something of a licensed activity.

At the moment, he is involved in a case involving three boys, aged fourteen, fifteen, and sixteen. They have had a merry old time during the past season. Their specialty was breaking silently into a small house, or apartment, immobilizing the mother at gunpoint, bringing down the children and the father, tying them up, and ceremonially raping the mother in their presence. Then they would pick up the portable artifacts—color television sets were specially prized—and, with exemplary filial devotion, give these to their mothers, who, when questioned about the appearance of their homes, which had begun to look like Macy's bargain basement, informed the police that they assumed their sons were profitably engaged, which is certainly true, crime being extremely profitable in Chicago. What, the visitor asked, would the boys receive in the way of prison sentences, now that they were finally apprehended? "Two years, maximum," the policeman said,

How did they get their guns?

Nothing, it appears, could be easier. There is a gun-registration law in Chicago, indeed in Illinois. The effect of it, said the policeman, is to make it more difficult for people who are straight (his word) to arm themselves. Others have no problem at all—guns abound. And get this. There is one outfit, apparently known to just about everyone, which rents you guns. The rental is very simple: 10 percent of the money that gun helps you to rob. Besides, Indiana is only twenty miles away, and there are no effective registration laws there.

But what if you get caught with a gun on your person, without a permit? What happens then, said the policeman, smiling, is—nothing. What do you mean, "nothing"? Well, the policeman takes you before a judge, and the judge says, "Case dismissed." *"That's* what I mean by nothing."

Why are things so bad? Well, the cop says, there is one obvious reason why. The prisons are full, and there isn't any room for extra people. So when anybody who has done anything less than torture his grandmother to death comes before the judge, the judge tends just to shove the case to one side, grant continuance after continuance, and, eventually, the case, if not formally dismissed, sort of dies from attrition.

"Isn't that pretty demoralizing for the police?" "Yes," he said, beaming.

Then there is the problem of getting people to testify. If there are ten witnesses to a felony, you are lucky if you can persuade one, or at most two, to testify. There are reasons: the general solidarity of a culture resigned to living on the other side of the law. Fear of reprisal. But above all, a sense of uselessness. It isn't as though you were a party to collaring a rabid dog, and removing him from the playground, so that your children could ever after be safe. These rabid dogs are simply sent to the pound for a day or two, or a week, perhaps a month, and they are back. And in any case, the density of the dog population does not visibly diminish.

It is as useless as swatting the legendary mosquito on your arm when traveling up the Amazon. Why bother yourself? The judges don't care. The lawyers will make you out a liar. The legislature won't vote the money for the prisons. The politicians don't even bother anymore to run for office calling for law and order. And indeed it is significant that the most prestigious civil rights organization in the country (in the world?) has given more attention during this period to the right of a Utah killer not to get killed even though he wants to be killed, than to a half-million people in Chicago who, every day, are deprived of their life, liberty, and property by a criminal class that enjoys permanent predatory rights to mug, rape, and kill.

"But believe me," the cop said happily, "Chicago isn't the worst. Not by any means."

Death for Gilmore?

November 23, 1976

IN THE MATTER of Gary Mark Gilmore, we note the strange behavior, as so often is the case, of the American Civil Liberties Union, which has entered the case in opposition to Gilmore's plea to the state of Utah to get on with its capital sentence.

The reasoning of the ACLU is roughly as follows: Capital punishment is evil. Therefore, if you cannot persuade a state to repeal its capital-punishment law, and if you cannot persuade the Supreme Court to declare such a law, if passed by a state, unconstitutional: then use whatever devices you can to stand in the way of the execution of such a law. Never mind that the condemned man asks the state to proceed. All that man is doing is saying that he would rather be shot than live a lifetime in prison. His wish should not prevail, for the simple reason that an individual's opting for an end the state ought never to have authorized does not have the effect of baptizing that end. If—let us say—a prisoner offered to permit his hands to be amputated, preferring that punishment over a ten-year sentence for theft, the state ought not to comply with the prisoner's choice. That which is barbaric remains so irrespective of an individual's preferences.

The logic, so far as it goes, is good. Although it is at odds with the overarching commitment of the ACLU to the notion of sovereignty over one's own body. Let us examine one or two variations of the argument:

1. Does an individual have the right to submit to sadistic treatment? To judge from the flotsam that silts up in the magazine racks, there is a considerable appetite for this sort of thing. Let us hypothesize an off-Broadway show, featuring an S/M production in which the heroine is flailed—real whips, real woman, real blood—for the delectation of the depraved. One assumes that the ACLU would defend the right of the producers to get on with it, trotting out the argument that no one has the right to interfere with the means by which others take their pleasure. The opposing argument is that the community has the right first to define, then to suppress, depravity. Moreover, the community legitimately concerns itself over the coarsening effect of depravity.

2. Does the individual's right over his own body extend to suicide? Most states have laws against suicide, notwithstanding that of all unenforceable laws, this is probably the most conspicuously unenforceable. Still, the policeman who at great risk to himself succeeds in aborting a suicide by climbing up to the window of the skyscraper in which the woman hovers, and grabbing her before she jumps, more often than not aborts an impulse permanently. The figures show that the inclination to suicide is more often than not permanently choked off, if only the suicide is prevented. Moreover, the theological argument is profoundly relevant. That which is vouchsafed to the human being by providence, he must not dispossess himself of. It is the right to life. Gilmore has greatly confused matters by attempting suicide. Strangely, there are few voices to be heard saying that the prison authorities were wrong in using a stomach pump to revive Gilmore. No doubt the judiciary in Utah would have taken quiet satisfaction if Gilmore, by successfully ending his own life, had relieved the state of the necessity of coping with the difficult questions he has raised.

3. Assuming that there were no capital punishment, what would be the position of the ACLU toward a prisoner who, having been sentenced to life in jail, presented himself before the authorities and asked for drugs sufficient to end his own life? Here the state would not be executing the prisoner, merely making available to the prisoner the means by which the prisoner could legislate an alternative for himself. Or are

there people around who believe that the state should be permitted to prescribe the exact nature of the punishment? We saw that impulse at work in Nuremberg when Hermann Goering managed to swallow poison on the eve of his scheduled hanging. (The memorable lead on United Press Radio on that occasion was: "Hermann Goering cheated death today by committing suicide.") There was general consternation, stomach pumps working overtime, because it was decided that Goering undergo the ritual execution. The condemned man is not free to mull over the known means of extinguishing human life, and then express his preference.

The arguments are complex, and Gilmore, perhaps inadvertently, has confronted the community with them by his bizarre request. In theatrical terms, after ten years without capital punishment, his request is something of a bridge between total abstinence and systematic resumption of capital punishment. Moreover, he has made it plain for all to see that capital punishment is cruel and unusual insofar as it is eccentrically meted out. The state has the right to take life, when the right to life is forfeited. The torture is the result of indecision.

The Electric Chair and the Mayoral Campaign

September 15, 1977

THE RACE in New York, barring a welcome upset by the candidate of the Conservative Party Mr. Barry Farber, is between Edward Koch and Mario Cuomo, and you will never guess what Mr. Cuomo is spending his time on. Edward Koch's qualified endorsement of capital punishment.

One must assume that this is viewed as a shrewd maneuver by somebody, else presumably it would not happen. As things now stand Representative Edward Koch, whose credentials are impeccably liberal, but who appeals to a great many independents precisely because of the independence of his mind and his inquisitive disposition, has the slight edge. He has the advantages and disadvantages of being Jewish, even as Mr. Cuomo has the advantages and disadvantages of being Italian in an ethnic-oriented community (the melting pot was buried about fifteen years ago by Nathan Glazer and Patrick Moynihan in a slender book appropriately called *Beyond the Melting Pot*). Call it a draw.

Mr. Koch has the advantage of five terms in Congress during which he gradually crystallized as an institutional municipal fixture as solid as Grand Central Station. Cuomo has the advantage of backing from Albany, backing from the Liberal Party, and a certain mysterious freshness that wafts in from the image of the Italian-intellectual-romancer. As so often is the case, the two men facing each other during the run-off don't quite know how to go about disparaging each other, and therefore Mr. Cuomo elected to highlight his opponent's endorsement of the return of capital punishment.

Here exactly is what Representative Koch had said: "Society has the right to show its sense of moral outrage in particularly heinous crimes by providing that the death penalty be an option available to a judge and jury."

To judge from Cuomo's reaction, Koch was sounding the tocsin for the nuclear obliteration of our crime centers. Addressing a congregation of worshipers, mostly black, at a local church, Mr. Cuomo retorted, "*The electric chair cannot produce jobs for the poor.*"

That statement can only be met by a retort of equivalent intellectual profundity. If I had been there, I swear I'd have risen and said, "B-b-but Mr. Cuomo, wouldn't it provide jobs for executioners?"

Cuomo went on: "*The electric chair cannot balance the budget.*"

One possible comment on that would be: "Well, it could *help* balance the budget. Convicted murderers cost the state $30,000 a year to keep alive." Would Cuomo have thought this a niggling economy? One could have answered that piggy-bank savings add up to balanced budgets.

Did Cuomo finally stop there? Not at all. "*The electric chair cannot educate our children.*" No no no no no, I'd have said. *Surely* it would help to educate those of our children who are considering a life of violent crime? Surely if the prospect of a hairbrush, at the margin, can help to educate some children (if Cuomo had demurred here, Koch, citing the Old Testament sanction for the use of the rod, could have denounced Cuomo as anti-Semitic), the prospect of an electric chair might deter an eighteen-year-old from ice-picking an old lady to death?

Was he through *yet?* Oh no/Never Cuomo. *"The electric chair cannot give us a sound economy or save us from bankruptcy or even save my seventy-seven-year-old mother from muggers."* Why stop there? He might have added that the electric chair cannot give us rainbows in the sky, or chocolate malted milk shakes, or skating rinks.

It is interesting that Mr. Cuomo should choose to elevate one part of Mr. Koch's program as the most conspicuous and presumably the most vulnerable. The attitude of the majority of New Yorkers is that something needs to be done about crime beyond that which is now being done about crime, and there is the intuitive feeling about the return of capital punishment that it may have *something* to do with incidence of murder. To deduce that Congressman Koch (or any other American politician) proposes capital punishment as a panacea is to play the old logical trick of *ignoratio elenchi.* The voters will probably see through that. And having seen it, they may be reminded to vote for Koch because, besides everything else, he believes in the use of capital punishment under certain circumstances. The electric chair cannot elect Cuomo mayor.

Thinking about Crime

August 11, 1977

THE CONVENTIONAL wisdom is that one needs to spend one's time in probing the *causes* of our social maladies. A few very bright men (e.g., James Q. Wilson, Ernest van den Haag) have been trying to tell us, particularly in the field of penology, that it would be splendid if we were to discover the causes of crime, or the techniques of rehabilitation, but it is our absorption with these pursuits that distracts us from coping with crime. Weeks after the anarchic outburst in New York City, the talk still tends to dwell on the causes of it. But what should be *done?*

Herewith a few propositions:

1. More people than are now in jail ought to be in jail.

2. The objection that there are not enough jails is an insufficient one. There are two ways of dealing with the problem. The first would be to build more jails. The second would be to release from jail prisoners who have been sent there as punishment for committing non-violent crimes. In federal institutions, only 25 percent of the inmates are there for having murdered, kidnapped, raped, or mugged. In New York State prisons, 30 percent of the inhabitants are not guilty of violent crimes. These people could be punished in different ways, outside jail.

3. There being no way to make parents responsible for the behavior of their children when there are no parents (it is estimated that more than 50 percent of black teenagers in New York City live without one or both of their parents), legal distinctions between children and adults should be abolished where there are no parents; and where there are parents, these distinctions should be abolished after repeated offenses.

4. Judges or parole boards who release, before he is twenty-five years old, a prisoner of whatever age who has been convicted three times of a Class A misdemeanor, or twice of a Class E felony, should be subject to impeachment proceedings.

5. The community should acknowledge responsibility for failure to grant adequate protection to a member of that community. Victims of violent crimes should be compensated; so also should victims of theft, under reasonable regulations.

Now none of this suggests thought should cease to be given to the causes of every kind of misbehavior. If the future holds for us some thaumaturgical medication that will transform the Son of Sam into St. Francis of Assisi, we should by all means do our best to get it past the Federal Drug Administration. But the methodological breakthrough is overdue: we must reason from the particular back toward the general, rather than the other way around. It is nice to see old Spencer Tracy movies with Father Flanagan saying such things as: "There's no such thing as a bad boy." But the broken arm, the ravished girl, the tortured old man, are the concrete realities. It does not preclude any kind of inventive ministrations to bad boys to rule that these should be given inside prison walls. Going after the symptom of the disease (a cognate cliché) is unreasonable only when it is known how to treat the disease. Since we do not know how to treat the disease, lacking—for instance—the authority to require people to procreate children only in wedlock, then we must ask whether dealing with the symptom isn't to be preferred to doing nothing at all.

The answer should be plain. But of course it isn't; and that is why no reform movement has grown out of the awful events of the past weeks, and years.

The Return of Edgar Smith

November 20, 1976

I AM BEHIND the curtain of the auditorium at the University of Alabama in Huntsville, and my host now slips through to the podium. Presently he will introduce me; I am to follow in his footsteps, and begin my speech. Just then a student puffs in, having taken the steps three at a time. Before I go on—he stammers out—I am to telephone Bodino Rodino at the *Bergen Record*, re: Edgar Smith. I stuff the message in my pocket, a bottomless pit by now for messages from people who wish to speak to me about Edgar Smith.

Now it is a television studio, a live show, coast to coast, "Good Morning, America." I am there to discuss a new book

I have written on a subject far removed from the world of getting and spending and killing: sailing boats. The props— enticing pictures, taken at sea—are all in place, and the star of the show opens up: "First, Mr. Buckley, I'd like to ask you about Edgar Smith . . ."

Very well, I surrender.

1. Edgar Smith was tried and convicted in 1957 of murdering a fifteen-year-old girl. In 1964, we began a correspondence. Over the ensuing seven years, he wrote me 2,900 pages of letters (he counted them). I became convinced that he had not been fairly tried, and that he could not have committed the murder in the time and under the circumstances alleged.

Two gifted attorneys, for the most part volunteering their services, persuaded a very bright judge that Edgar Smith had not been fairly tried. Rather than re-try him for first-degree murder, the New Jersey court bargained with him. If he would say that he killed the girl, the prosecution would reduce the charge to second-degree murder. Counting "good" time, his release would be effective one hour after he stood up in open court pleading guilty. One hour later, he emerged from Trenton State Prison into my waiting car and drove to New York City where, before the cameras, he retracted his confession, which he attributed to the requirements of "court theater." He had been in the death house longer than anyone in American history. The judge who let him out was profoundly convinced that Smith had in fact, as a seedy, shiftless twenty-three-year-old, killed the girl. But, said the judge, if he had ever seen a rehabilitated man, here he was. Edgar Smith, member of Mensa, author of two best-selling books.

2. Just short of five years later, one of the attorneys telephones. He has received a report that Edgar Smith is wanted in San Diego, California, for "atrocious assault," kidnapping, and attempted murder. A young woman, her week's forlorn salary in her handbag, is dragged into a car by a man who announces that he wants her money. She resists and he plunges a six-inch knife into her, narrowly missing vital organs. She is a tiger, thrusts her two feet through the windshield, lunges against the wheel of the car, which lurches now off to the side of the road.

Desperately she maneuvers to open the door, and spills out in sight of a half-dozen pedestrians who take the number of the license plate of the car that careens screechingly off. The car is registered in the name of Mrs. Edgar Smith. The woman recovers in the hospital, is shown a picture, and identifies her assailant as: Edgar Smith.

3. The telephone rings in my office, and my secretary, Miss Bronson, answers—like all of us around the shop, an old enthusiast in the Smith cause. It is Edgar Smith, calling from Las Vegas, "Is Bill there?" He had been hiding in and around New York for a week, not disclosing his whereabouts to anyone. He had promised his mother he would fly directly to San Diego, give himself up. Now, he tells Miss Bronson, he has been mugged, and has lost all his money; would I call him? She telephones me in Albuquerque, and I telephone the FBI. Within fifteen minutes Edgar Smith, napping in his hotel room, is picked up. My next two calls are to his mother and his wife, to tell them what I did.

4. What are my "comments"? Why, I believe now that he was guilty of the first crime. There is no mechanism as yet perfected that will establish beyond question a person's guilt or innocence. There will be guilty people freed this year and every year. But for those who believe that the case of Edgar Smith warrants a vow to accept the ruling of a court as always definitive, it is only necessary to remind ourselves that, this year and every year, an innocent man will be convicted. Edgar Smith has done enough damage in his lifetime without underwriting the doctrine that the verdict of a court is infallible.

Edgar Smith, Act III

April 19, 1977

"EDGAR H. SMITH confessed today in open court to the murder in 1957 of Victoria Zielinski. He then pleaded guilty to kidnapping with intent to rape Lefteriya Ozbun in San Diego on October 1, 1976 . . . Edgar Smith was befriended by columnist William F. Buckley, Jr. who played a role in Smith's long fight to gain freedom from the death house he inhabited longer than any other person in U.S. history." AP, March 29, 1977.

"Dear Mr. Buckley:

"As you may recall, I am the overzealous (former) assistant prosecutor you referred to in Newark on June 8, 1971. If you will recall your comments during a taped interview on that date with WCBS newswoman Irene Cornell, you questioned my integrity and ethics because I labeled Edgar H. Smith Jr. a 'danger to society.'

"This letter is not to offer an 'I told you so,' but to suggest that you give serious consideration to offering an apology to the *living* victims of your 'friend' and *'cause célèbre,'* Mr. Smith. You should not forget that it was your perverted sense of justice which set in motion the events which eventually freed Mr. Smith to commit another violent crime.

"It is inconceivable that someone of your intelligence did not know long before December 6, 1971, that Mr. Smith was guilty. . . . You chose to make this matter a *cause célèbre* and to publicize your (and Smith's) viewpoint and his unfounded allegations against totally innocent people.

"As a journalist of considerable note you possess substantial power over which there is little check. Such a position imposes a duty of total candor, especially when you have made an error. Under the circumstances the public and the innocent victims of Mr. Smith's defamation deserve a well-published apology.—Very truly yours, Edward N. Fitzpatrick, Newark, N.J."

Dear Mr. Fitzpatrick:

1. I questioned neither your ethics nor your integrity, but the excesses to which your zeal took you when you proposed reading Edgar Smith's love letters in open court to demonstrate something or other. I am not a trained jurist or a trained psychologist. But the judge who released Smith was the former, and pronounced him "rehabilitated"; and the

psychiatrist who examined him prior to his release pronounced him unlikely to return to crime. Your position was what one might call boilerplate hostility.

2. It is hardly out of a perverted sense of justice that one interests oneself in the question whether justice was actually done. Smith's trial lawyer was convinced of his innocence, so was the private investigator. The state's case was riddled with ambiguity, and in one respect (the coroner's report) was inconsistent with Smith's guilt.

3. My power as a journalist can hardly be held responsible for a ruling, after an extensive hearing, by a district court judge that Smith had been unfairly tried, which opinion was sustained by the Supreme Court of the United States.

4. No lawyer I came across in the course of examining the circumstances believes that the Zielinski murder was properly murder in the first degree. That it was second-degree murder was also the opinion of the judge who released Smith. Fourteen and one-half years in jail falls well over on the strict side of a second-degree sentence. If I had not entered the case in the first place, and if he had been properly charged, Smith would have been out ahead of when he actually got out.

5. Your suggestion that I knew all along that he was guilty contradicts your subsequent statement that I "made an error" (if I had known he was guilty, and yet depicted him as innocent, I'd have been iniquitous, not mistaken); and is, by the way, as contemptible as the obvious pleasure you take from Smith's later pursuit of his criminal career.

Yours faithfully,
Wm. F. Buckley, Jr.

X.

At Home

The House

February 1976

WE WANTED something by the sea, which excluded my native green and beautiful Sharon, Connecticut, and within commuting distance of New York, which also excluded Sharon. My wife set out every day, at about the time I would go off to the office. We tried leaving the apartment at staggered hours, on the assumption that, that way, one of us would one day bump into our fellow-tenant Marilyn Monroe in the elevator; but we never did lay eyes on her, and about a month and thirty or forty houses later my wife approached me with some excitement. She had found it. "It" meant reasonably priced, on the water, and not further than an hour from Grand Central.

We came to it on a spring day—I remember Adlai Stevenson had announced that morning that the future of the Republic required him, after all, to accept the Democratic Presidential nomination if proffered. It was wet and cold, and the owner was not there to let us in; so I broke a tiny window, unlatched the kitchen-door bolt, and left a pleasant note of explanation.

We wandered through a house at once startlingly ugly and entirely captivating. Its immediate background was romantic. Chérie—as we refer to her—had recently been phased out, and her benefactor gave her nothing less than this squat, stolid, fifteen-room house—built sixty years earlier in an unsuccessful flight from Victorian excess—surrounded by beautiful trees, three acres of lawn, a four-car garage with upstairs apartment that, rented, would bring in the tax. The furnishings were startling. I remember mostly chairs, and pink plastic orchids on black wallpaper, and a total of six books—all of them *Reader's Digest* condensations. There was a bar full of shimmering mirrors and neon lights. There

403

must have been chairs there to seat everyone in the county who voted for Adlai Stevenson.

Few things hit me instinctively; and I was deeply rooted, along with my nine brothers and sisters, practically all of whom settled in or near Sharon. But I knew that I would never want to live anywhere else; and so it was with my wife, who was now three thousand miles away from her family home in Vancouver, Canada.

I called my father, who authorized me to liquidate capital; and in two weeks we had the closing—after the bankers had poked the furnace, and had found nothing flimsy in the old stucco walls, and a check for $65,000 had passed hands; and a little while later I got a $25,000 mortgage from an insurance company, at the eyebrow-raising interest rate of 4⅜ percent—twice the highest rate recommended by Lord Keynes, whose dicta on such subjects my classmates at Yale had received as revelation, poor darlings.

There was a transformation. Several, in fact. One watches, and says very little, when the lady of the house is pursuing a vision. There was a fairly orthodox phase, consummated in splendid taste; and I was happy. But soon she began to stir again; and, during the cultural revolution of the Sixties, our haven was not unaffected. One day she presented me the new room—tactfully executed during my prolonged absence from the country. It is much better to be presented with a *fait accompli*. The mind reeled. I thought of the Château at Blois, with its eclectic styles, and the one room—some famous Frenchman (as usual, the wrong one) was murdered there—full of colored spangles and dark and wine-colored bric-a-brac and ornate parquetry. It was the dining room, and its appeal had the at-onceness that Clement Greenberg celebrates as the unique attribute of art.

There was no stopping her. The sun-room soon became the bordello the Shah couldn't afford. Then the living room, a kind of Haitian concentrate. Self-respect required me, at one point a couple of years ago, to insist on a room of my own—a music room, featuring a beautiful harpsichord and the worst keyboard artist since Harry Truman. I got as far as the windows and the paintings (they are all by the fine Raymond de Botton); but She took over, which is why the room—framing the garden, a slender treetrunk trained like a geisha girl from childhood to give pleasure; the largest wild apple tree *our* treeman has ever seen; and, out there, Long Island Sound, with as many moods as those ersatz fountains the big hotels are constructing, with the Teamster Aeolus who will blow you up a storm, or whisper the sea into kitten-like placidity by turning the pressure gauges—is correspondingly beautiful on the inside. There, in the winter, the fireplace alight, a proper musician performing live or on record, you can see what the pilgrims saw, as if under glass, and understand the compulsion to Thanksgiving.

The neighborhood is wonderful. There has been, to be sure, a touch of Peyton Place in the seven or eight houses that occupy the point; but, although everyone is friendly, no one is importunate. In twenty-four years, we have been out to dinner not more than three times. That is true hospitality. Life is totally informal, though some of that will now have to go. A week or so after acquiring the house, we lost the keys to it; but it didn't seem to matter since nobody had ever heard of a burglar in the area. Until two weeks ago. A couple of them (by the evidence) found their way in, and helped themselves to three generations of silver, two apples, and one box of peanut brittle, which they pried out of a postal package—thus Federalizing their little transgression. If, after they are caught, convicted, and sentenced, they should choose to come back for another course, they will find a house as penetrable as a jewelry store at midnight.

I understand the territorial imperative. I have been (roughly) everywhere. Here is where I find, increasingly, I want to be. With Her. God knows what She will come up with next, maybe (but I don't believe it) a Warhol room. But ingenious though she is, she could never succeed in defacing that house. She has only made it more desirable, and anybody who tries to take it from me should be warned that, in addition to a mad wife, I have three mad dogs, and lots and lotsa ammunition.

The Cook

November 10, 1976

SHORTLY AFTER I was snatched from the arms of my mother to go fight in the world war to liberate Poland, I found myself doing duty in the mess hall at Camp Wheeler, Georgia, when the company commander, accompanied by sycophantic aides with polished gold bars, paid a state visit to the chef to report the findings of the Inspector General, on what it is that affects the morale of America's fighting men. In order, (1) The food he eats. (2) Mail from home. (3) Periodic furloughs.

I was very surprised. I lived for those letters from home, and had not yet tasted the joys of a furlough. But food? My attention had simply never turned to the subject. I remembered dimly that the food at school in England was bad, at home good, at prep school in Millbrook, New York, tolerable, in the Army about what one would expect which, if served with ketchup, which it always was, was also tolerable. This, then, was my intellectual introduction to the importance of good food. I was an opsimath. Others come to an appreciation of food early.

Much later I heard about the suicide at a boys' school in England, in the Twenties. At the inquest convened by a flustered headmaster, he addressed the student body: "Did anyone present," he asked, "have any idea what might have been the tragic cause of Jones's suicide?" Lord Harlech, then eight years old, raised his hand. "Could it have been the food, sir?" *He* knew that food was a matter of life and death. Even at that age.

When I married, it was to a beautiful young woman who knew as much about cooking as Congress knows about husbandry. But she craved good food, and was entirely instrumental in her approach to the problem of her ignorance. Chesterton was asked what single volume would he take with him to a desert island. He replied, "Dobson's Guide to Shipbuilding." Of course. And, in the little house in Hamden,

Connecticut, while I marshaled the case of God and man against Yale, Pat sat on a high stool, turning the pages of cookbooks.

I had two functions during that era. The first was to turn off the pressure cooker when the sound rang out, while Pat would hide under the staircase, assuming a fetal position, resignedly awaiting the explosion, and, as resignedly, her impending widowhood. The second was to taste what she ate. Taste it no matter what. A dear friend, dining with us one evening, made the mistake of taking her chocolate mousse to his lips and also swallowing it. He noticed that I brought it to my lips, only to set it, surreptitiously, down again—like Nixon handling the strong stuff in Moscow. "Bill," my friend said, "you're not pulling your oar."

It was hard, but not for very long. In a matter of months, her art flowered. And, little by little, her friends acclaimed her kitchen as a joy-stop.

Her inclination is French. Pure French. Other cuisines she tolerates, now and again even celebrates, the Chinese a mysterious exception. Here are her hard biases. There must be a first course, and it must not be routine. Not fair simply to serve melon, or a canned soup. The only first course she will serve pristine is smoked salmon or caviar, lightly embellished. She has ten or fifteen openers. My favorite is (I am unskilled at describing these things) a red caviar, mixed in onion, and sour cream, and herbs, in inscrutable, symbiotic combinations: served on fried toast, with, say, a Gewurztraminer. Another I remember is a greenish pea soup, cold, with lots of seasoning and (so help me) apple slices. On this course several years ago Daniel Patrick Moynihan became almost speechless (unhappily, not entirely so: he was in town to sell me and my colleagues on the virtues of the Family Assistance Plan) with pleasure, demanding the recipe. This my Pat forgot to furnish him, and one week later my conscience woke me, so I got it from Pat, and telegraphed it to Patrick at the White House, where—I have ever since assumed—it reposes with a cryptographer in the special prosecutor's office, as the putative marching orders for Watergate, rendered, however, in apparently impenetrable code.

Then comes fish—served very, very plain, like gold. Or

(with a nod to Italy) a risotto: I do not know why it tastes as it tastes. What is it that brings on the knowledge of the animating ingredient? I know an eccentric and hugely talented painter who inclines to blue and was asked at his gallery by Helen Hokinson: "Sir, why do you use so much blue paint?" He rose up on his toes, and gave the only appropriate answer. "Madam, blue paint is *cheaper!*" I wonder, is butter cheaper? It is certainly critical.

Or, there is veal (important, cut down on the butter; sear it, as the British said to the executioners at Rouen). About the vegetables, the most important point (how nobly our omniscient friend Nika Hazelton has dwelled on the point in her articles and books)—they must be fresh. Then, depending on the species, the appropriate sauce. My Michelangelo has not, incredibly, yet mastered a plain French salad dressing—I suspect it is her thralldom to lemon. She advised the cook on my schooner to stock the boat with lemon for a week's cruise for six people, and he produced a dozen lemons. The boat was stopped as abruptly as if we had sighted Niagara Falls 100 feet ahead, and she sent my son Christopher out on the dinghy for 100 more. Lamb, beef, chicken, moussaka . . . with the fish and the meat, always potatoes. She doesn't like fried potatoes, so she makes them listlessly. Not so the other varieties, which appear permeated with something or other that makes even self-consciously thin men ask for more. To go, at our house it is the rule, with a non-pricey red wine. (To buy very good wine nowadays requires only money. To serve it to your guests is a sign of fatigue. Vintage wine should be bought only as presents *for* your friends, and drunk, in private, only as presents *from* your friends.)

And for dessert—always fruit and cheese, more or less there, like finger-bowls, even if only to be seen, and not experienced. But usually a creation, pears, say, with one of those bittersweet yellow sauces. Or chocolate mousse (no longer is it necessary to pull one's oar). Baklava (beware the Greeks bearing gifts). Pecan pie (with a light, liqueured cream). A strawberry tarte (with creme fraîche). And, after the meal, the antiseptic restorative; superstrong coffee. If it is evening, she offers liqueurs. Did you ever have Willième, with bittersweet chocolate, or ginger? Try it on your next furlough when, after all, you do not need any letters from home, so that all those pleasures decocted by the Inspector General are subsumed in that meal, the deprivation of which, in the opinion of a precocious future diplomat in Her Majesty's Service, drove a little boy to fatal despair. Indeed we do not live by bread alone. But the defeat of Manichaeanism deserves celebrating. Once, even twice a day. My Patsy will never cease to pull her oar.

The American Look

April 1978

WHEN, HAVING no idea where I was going, I sat down to write my first novel, it suddenly occurred to me that it would need a protagonist. The alternative of trying to persuade Doubleday that I might create a new art form and write a novel about *nobody* struck me as unprofitable; and so, by the end of the day, I had created Blackford Oakes. And lo, there have been those, the feature editor of this journal included, who have denominated him distinctively American; and the editor asks now that I should say a few words about "the American look." I do so only on the understanding that I reject the very notion of quintessentiality. It is a concept that runs into itself, like F. P. Adams's remark that the average American is a little above average. The reason you cannot have the quintessential American is the very same reason you cannot have a quintessential apple pie, or indeed anything composed of ingredients. In composites, there has got to be an arrangement of attributes and no such arrangement can project one quality to the point of distorting others. This is true even in the matter of physical beauty. An absolutely perfect nose has the effect of satellizing the other features of a human face, and a beautiful face is a comprehensive achievement.

So anyway, Blackford Oakes is not the quintessential American, but I fancy he *is* distinctively American, and the first feature of the distinctively American male is, I think, spontaneity. A kind of freshness born of curiosity and enterprise and wit. Would you believe that three days after meeting her, Blackford Oakes was in bed with the Queen of England? (Not, I hasten to elucidate, the incumbent: Blackford Oakes, as the distinctive American, is a young man of taste, who sleeps only with fictitious queens, thereby avoiding international incidents.) There is something wonderfully American, it struck me, about bedding down a British queen: a kind of arrant but lovable presumption. But always on the understanding that it is done decorously, and that there is no aftertaste of the gigolo in the encounter. I remember, even now with some trepidation, when my first novel, *Saving the Queen*, came out in the British edition. The first questioner at the press conference in London was, no less, the editor of *The Economist*, and he said with, I thought, a quite un-British lack of circumspection: "Mr. Buckley, would you like to sleep with the Queen?" Now, such a question poses quite awful responsibilities. There being a most conspicuous incumbent, one could hardly wrinkle up one's nose as if the question evoked the vision of an evening with Queen Victoria on her Diamond Jubilee. The American with taste has to guard against a lack of gallantry, so that the first order of business becomes the assertion of an emancipating perspective which leads Queen Elizabeth II gently out of the room before she is embarrassed. This was accomplished by saying, just a little sleepily, as Blackford Oakes would have done, "Which queen?"—and then quickly, before the interrogator could lug his monarch back into the smoker—"Judging from historical experience, I would need to consult my lawyer before risking an affair with just *any* British queen." The American male must be tactful, and tact consists mostly in changing the subject without its appearing that you have done so as a rebuke.

Blackford Oakes appears at age twenty-three, so I stuck him in Yale, which gave me the advantage of being able to write about a familiar few acres and, I suppose, Blackford Oakes emerged with a few characteristics associated in the literature, with Yale men. Like what? Principally, I think, self-confidence; a certain worldliness that is neither bookish nor in any sense of the word anti-intellectual. Blackford Oakes is an engineer by training, and his non-royal girl friend is studying for her Ph.D. and doing her doctorate on Jane Austen. *She* is not expected to show any curiosity about how to build bridges. The American look wears offhandedly its special proficiencies: If one is a lawyer, one does not go about sounding like Oliver Wendell Holmes, any more than Charles Lindbergh went about sounding like Charles Lindbergh. But Blackford quite rightly shows a certain curiosity about Jane Austen, and probably has read (actually, reread: one never *reads* Jane Austen, one *rereads* her) *Pride and Prejudice.*

Blackford Oakes is physically handsome. Here, I took something of a chance. I decided not only to make him routinely good-looking but to make him startlingly so. I don't mean startling in the sense that, let us say, Elizabeth Taylor is startlingly beautiful. It is hard to imagine a male counterpart for pulchritude. An extremely handsome man is not the *equivalent* of an extremely beautiful woman, he is the *complement*; and that is very important to bear in mind in probing the American look which is not, for example, the same as the Italian look. So that when I decided that Blackford Oakes should be startlingly handsome, it was required that he be that in a distinctively American way, and what does that mean? Well, it doesn't mean you look like Mickey Rooney, obviously. But it doesn't mean you look like Tyrone Power, either.

I think the startlingly handsome American male is made so not by the regularity of his features, however necessary that regularity may be, but by the special quality of his expression. It has to be for this reason that, flipping past the male models exhibited in the advertising sections of the New York *Times* or *Esquire*, one never finds oneself pausing to think: that man is startlingly handsome. But such an impression is taken away, from time to time, from a personal encounter, or even from a candid photo. And the American look, in the startlingly handsome man, requires: animation, tempered by a certain shyness, a reserve.

I thought of Billy Budd. I have long since forgotten how Melville actually described him, but he communicated that Budd was startlingly handsome. Looks aside, Budd's distinctiveness was not that of Blackford Oakes. Billy Budd is practically an eponym for innocence, purity. Oakes, though far removed from jadedness, is worldly.

Billy Budd, alas, is humorless. Correction: not *alas*. "Do not go about as a demagogue, encouraging triangles to break out of the prison of their three sides," G. K. Chesterton warned us, because if you succeed, ". . . its life comes to a lamentable end." Give Billy Budd a sense of humor and he shatters in front of you into thousands of little pieces. Blackford Oakes doesn't go about like Wilfred Sheed's protagonist in *Transatlantic Blues* or John Gregory Dunne's in *True Confessions* being hilariously mordant. The American look here is a leavened sarcasm.

Escalate sarcasm and you break through the clouds into the ice-cold of nihilism, and that is my last word on the American look. The American must—*believe*. However discreetly. Blackford Oakes believes. He tends to divulge his beliefs in a kind of slouchy, oblique way. But, at the margin, he is, well—an American with American predilections and he knows, as with the clothes he wears so casually, that he is snug as such; that, like his easygoing sweater and trousers, they . . . fit him. As do the ideals, and even most of the practices, of his country.

XI.

Education

God and Man at Yale: Twenty-five Years Later

1977

I WAS STILL familiar with the arguments of *God and Man at Yale* when Henry Regnery, its original publisher, asked whether I would furnish a fresh introduction to a re-issue of it. But I had not seen the book since I finally closed its covers, six months after its publication in the fall of 1951. It had caused a most fearful row and required me over a period of several months to spend considerable time re-reading what I had written, sometimes to check what I remembered having said against a reviewer's rendition of it; sometimes to reassure myself on one or another point. The prospect of re-reading it a quarter-century later, in order to write this introduction, was uninviting.

Granted, my reluctance was mostly for stylistic reasons. I was twenty-four when I wrote the book, freshly married, living in a suburb of New Haven and teaching a course in beginning Spanish at Yale University. I had help, notably from Frank Chodorov, the gentle, elderly anarchist, friend and disciple of Albert Jay Nock, pamphleteer, editor, founder of the Intercollegiate Society of Individualists, a fine essayist whose thought turned on a single spit: all the reasons why one should be distrustful of state activity, round and round, and round again. And help, also, from Willmoore Kendall, at that time a tenured associate professor of political science at Yale, on leave of absence in Washington, where he worked for an army think tank ("Every time I ask Yale for a leave of absence," he once remarked, "I find it insultingly cooperative").

Kendall had greatly influenced me as an undergraduate. He was a conservative all right, but invariably he gave the impression that he was being a conservative because he was surrounded by liberals; that he'd have been a revolutionist if that had been required in order to be socially disruptive.

Those were the days when the Hiss-Chambers case broke, when Senator McCarthy was first heard from, when the leaders of the Communist Party were prosecuted at Foley Square and sentenced to jail for violating the Smith Act. That conviction greatly incensed Kendall's colleagues, and a meeting of the faculty was called for the special purpose of discussing this outrage on civil liberties and framing appropriate articles of indignation. Kendall listened for two hours and then raised his hand to recite an exchange he had had that morning with the colored janitor who cleaned the fellows' suites at Pierson College.

"Is it true, professor"—Kendall, with his Oklahoma drawl, idiosyncratically Oxfordized while he studied as a Rhodes scholar in England, imitated the janitor—"Is it true, professor, dat dere's people in New York City who want to . . . destroy the guvamint of the United States?"

"Yes, Oliver, that is true," Willmoore had replied.

"Well, why don't we lock 'em up?"

That insight, Kendall informed his colleagues, reflected more political wisdom than he had heard from the entire faculty of Yale's political science department since the meeting began. Thus did Kendall make his way through Yale, endearing himself on all occasions.

Kendall was a genius of sorts, and his posthumous reputation continues to grow; but not very long after this book was published he proposed to Yale that the matter of their mutual incompatibility be settled by Yale's buying up his contract, which Yale elatedly agreed to do, paying more than forty thousand dollars to relieve itself of his alien presence. Willmoore Kendall went over the manuscript of *God and Man at Yale* and, as a matter of fact, was responsible for the provocative arrangement of a pair of sentences that got me into more trouble than any others in the book. Since any collusion or suspected collusion in this book was deemed a form of high treason at Yale, I have always believed that the inhospitable treatment of Kendall (after all, there were other eccentrics at Yale who survived) may in part have traced to his suspected association with it and to his very public friendship with me (he became a founding senior editor of *National Review* while still at Yale).

You see, the rumors that the book was being written had got around. They caused considerable consternation at Woodbridge Hall, which is Yale's White House. Yale had a brand new president, A. Whitney Griswold, and he had not yet acquired the savoir faire of high office (when the controversy raged, Dwight Macdonald would comment that Yale's authorities "reacted with all the grace and agility of an elephant cornered by a mouse"—but more on that later). I remember, while doing the research, making an appointment with a professor of economics who privately deplored the hot collectivist turn taken by the economics faculty after the war. At Yale—at least this was so when I was there—the relation between faculty and students (properly speaking I was no longer a student, having graduated in the spring) is wonderfully genial, though (again, this is how it *was*) there was no confusing who was the professor, who the student. I told him I was there to collect information about the left turn taken in the instruction of economics, and he reacted as a Soviet bureaucrat might have when questioned by a young KGB investigator on the putative heterodoxy of Josef Stalin. He told me, maintaining civility by his fingernails, that he would simply *not* discuss the subject with me in any way.

It was not so, however, in the research dealing with the treatment of religion at Yale, perhaps because I ambushed my Protestant friends. I asked the then president of Dwight Hall, the Protestant student organization, if he would bring together the chaplain and the half-dozen persons, staff and undergraduate, centrally concerned with religion to hear one afternoon my chapter on religion at Yale. Everyone came. I read them the chapter that appears in this book— save only the paragraph concerning Yale's chaplain, the Reverend Sidney Lovett. (I did not want to express even the tenderest criticism of him in his presence.) Three or four suggestions of a minor kind were made by members of the audience, and these corrections I entered. I wish I had recorded the episode in the book, because a great deal was made of the alleged singularity of my criticisms and of the distinctiveness of my position as a Roman Catholic. All that could have been difficult for the critics to say if they had known that the chapter had been read out verbatim to the half-dozen Protestant officials most intimately informed about the religious life of Yale, all of whom had acknowledged the validity of my findings, while dissociating themselves from my prescriptions.

I sent the completed manuscript to Henry Regnery in Chicago in April, and he instantly accepted it for publication. I had waited until then formally to apprise the president, Mr. Griswold, of the forthcoming event. We had crossed paths, never swords, several times while I was undergraduate chairman of the *Yale Daily News*. The conversation on the telephone was reserved, but not heated. He thanked me for the civility of a formal notification, told me he knew that I was at work on such a book, that he respected my right to make my views known. I was grateful that he did not ask to see a copy of the manuscript, as I knew there would be eternal wrangling on this point or the other.

But a week or so later I had a telephone call from an elderly tycoon with a huge opinion of himself. William Rogers Coe is mentioned in the book. He advised me that he knew about the manuscript and had splendid tidings for me: namely, I could safely withdraw the book because he, Mr. Coe, had got the private assurance of President Griswold that great reforms at Yale were under way and that conservative principles were in the ascendancy: so why bother to publish a book that would merely stir things up? I gasped at the blend of naïveté and effrontery. But although I had observed the phenomenon I was not yet as conversant as I would quickly become with the ease with which rich and vain men are manipulated by skillful educators. As a matter of fact, men who are not particularly rich or vain are pretty easy to manipulate also.

I did attempt to make one point in a correspondence with Mr. Coe that especially bears repeating. It is this, that a very recent graduate is not only supremely qualified, but uniquely qualified, to write about the ideological impact of an education he has experienced. I was asked recently whether I would "update" this book, to which the answer was very easy: this book cannot be updated, at least not by me. I could only undertake this if I were suddenly thirty years younger, slipped past the Admissions Committee of Yale University in a red wig, enrolled in the courses that serve as ideological pressure points; if I listened to the conversation of students and faculty, participated in the debates, read the college paper every day, read the textbooks, heard the classroom inflections, compared notes with other students in other courses. For years and years after this book came out I would receive letters from Yale alumni asking for an authoritative account of "how the situation at Yale is now." After about three or four years I wrote that I was incompetent to give such an account. I am as incompetent to judge Yale education today as most of the critics who reviewed this book were incompetent to correct me when I judged it twenty-five years ago. Only the man who makes the voyage can speak truly about it. I knew that most of my own classmates would disagree with me on any number of matters, most especially on my prescriptions. But at another level I'd have been surprised to find disagreement. Dwight Macdonald was among the few who spotted the point, though I don't think in his piece for the *Reporter* on the controversy he gave it quite the emphasis it deserved. But he did say, ". . . Nor does Buckley claim any sizable following among the undergraduates. They have discussed his book intensively—and critically. Richard Coulson ('52) notes in the *Yale Alumni* Magazine that 'it is a greater topic of serious and casual conversation than any philosophical or educational question that has been debated in quite a few years. . . .' In contrast to many of their elders the majority has not been blinded with surprise or carried away with rage at either Buckley or the Corporation by his claim that individualism, religion and capitalism are not being propounded strongly both in and out of the classroom. The undergraduate feels that this particular observation is correct."

Well then, if this is so, why republish *God and Man at Yale* in 1977, if it tells the story of Yale in 1950? The question is fair. I suppose a sufficient reason for republishing it is that the publisher has experienced a demand for it. Not, obviously, from people who desire to know the current ideological complexion at Yale—they will have to probe for an answer to that question elsewhere—but by whoever it is who is curious to know how one student, a Christian conservative, experienced and reacted to a postwar education at Yale University, and wants to read the document that caused such a huge fuss; and those who are curious—the purpose of this introduction, I suppose—about what, a quarter-century later, the author might have to say (if anything) about his original contentions, and the reaction to them. I do have some thoughts about the arguments of this book (which I have re-read with great embarrassment at the immaturity of my expression—I wish Messrs. Chodorov and Kendall had used more blue pencil) and about the sociology of the educational controversy. It is extremely interesting how people react to the telling of the truth. We all know that, but should not tire of learning even more about it. But the problems raised by *God and Man at Yale* are most definitely with us yet. Some of the predictions made in it have already been realized. Some of the questions are still open. Some of the arguments appear antiquarian; others fresh, even urgent.

First, something on the matter of definitions. Several critics, notably McGeorge Bundy (whose scathing article-length review in the *Atlantic Monthly* was adopted unofficially by Yale as its showcase defense), objected to the looseness of the terms on which I relied. Throughout the book I used a term briefly fashionable after the war, commonplace at the turn of the century, which however now has ebbed out of most polemical intercourse. It is "individualism." I have mentioned Chodorov's Intercollegiate Society of Individualists. Well, about ten years ago even that society changed its name (to Intercollegiate Studies Institute). The term *individualism* was once used as the antonym of "collectivism." Today the preference is for more individuated terms. We hear now about the *private sector*. About *free market* solutions, or approaches. "Individualism" has moved toward its philosophic home—it always had a metaphysical usage. One would expect to hear the word nowadays from disciples of Ayn Rand, or Murray Rothbard; Neo-Spenserians. In any case, if I were rewriting the book I would in most cases reject it in preference for a broader (e.g., "conservative") or narrower term (e.g., "monetarist"). Even so, though it is unfashionable, "individualism" is not, I think, misleading as it here appears.

Now it was very widely alleged, in the course of criticizing the book's terminology, that the position of the authors of the economics texts cited here was misrepresented. For instance, Frank Ashburn, reviewing *Gamay* (the publisher's useful abbreviation in office correspondence) in the *Saturday Review*, wrote: "One economist took the trouble to extract quotations out of context from the same volumes Mr. Buckley used so freely, with the result that the texts seemed the last testaments of the robber barons." That statement puzzles me as much today as when I first read it. After all, on page 49 I had written, "All of these textbook authors take some pains to assure the student that they have in mind the 'strengthening' of the free enterprise system. Not one of them, I am certain, would call himself a socialist or even a confirmed collectivist. Witness, for example, [Theodore] Morgan's eulogy: [in *Income and Employment*]." I went on to quote Morgan:

> It is our general assumption that government should not do anything which individuals or voluntary associations can more efficiently do for themselves (page 184) . . . capitalist, or dominantly free-enterprise economies, have succeeded very well in the Western World in raising tremendously the volume of production (page 176). . . . Obviously, the American public does not want a nationalized economy or a totalitarian unity. We want to give up no segment of our area of freedom unless there is clear justification (page 177) . . . there are both economic and noneconomic reasons for preserving a dominantly wide area of free enterprise (page 193). . . .

It is hard to understand how any critic, laboring the point that I had suppressed professions of allegiance to the free enterprise system by the authors under scrutiny, could do so persuasively in the face of the plain language quoted above. The technique of associating oneself for institutional convenience with a general position but disparaging it wherever it is engaged in wars or skirmishes along its frontiers is as old as the wisecrack about the man and woman who got on so splendidly during their married life, having arrived at a covenant that she would settle minor disagreements, he major: "We have never had a major disagreement," the hus-

band ruminates. In this textbook Mr. Morgan, having professed his devotion to the private sector, went on to call for
"diminishing the inequality of income and wealth," specifically for a tax of 75 to 99 percent on incomes over one hundred thousand dollars; the elimination of the exemption for
capital gains; confiscatory taxes on inheritance "aimed at the
goal of ending transmissions of hereditary fortunes"; the nationalization of monopolies, the universalization of social security coverage; family allowances from the government;
and government guarantee of full employment. The preferences of this economist would even in 1977 be viewed as left
of center. In 1950 they were very far to the left of anything
the Democratic Party was calling for. To suggest, as Mr. Ashburn and others did, that there was distortion in representing such as Morgan as "collectivist" is, simply, astonishing;
but at another level it is consistent with the public percep-
tions. Frank Ashburn was a trustee of Yale when he wrote.
Yale University was thought of (and still is, though to a lesser
extent) as a "citadel of conservatism" (*Time* magazine's
phrase). Therefore what emerges to the myth-preserver as
principally relevant is less the left-salients in a book like Morgan's, than the obeisances to orthodoxy. Very well. But who's
misleading whom?

Now other reviewers graduated their criticism from
misrepresentation to misunderstanding. These would stress
that economics is a scientific discipline; that Keynes (for instance) could no more be called a left-wing economist than
Buckminster Fuller could be called a collectivist architect.

Philip Kurland, writing in the *Northwestern Law Review*,
was emphatic on the point. He quotes with some relish a
statement by the author of another book reviewed in *Gamay*,
Professor Lorie Tarshis. "A word must be said, before we begin our analysis, about the political implications of the
Keynesian theory. This is necessary because there is so much
misinformation on the subject. The truth is simple. The
Keynesian theory no more supports the New Deal stand or
the Republican stand than do the newest data on atomic
fission. This does not mean that the Keynesian theory cannot
be used by supporters of either political party; for it can be,
and if it is properly used, it should be. The theory of employ-

ment we are going to study is simply an attempt to account for variations in the level of employment in a capitalist economy. It is possible, as we shall see later, to frame either the Republican or the Democratic economic dogma in terms of the theory."

This point, variously stated, was not infrequently made by reviewers. But, in fact, by the end of the 1940s the analysis of John Maynard Keynes was the enthusiastic ideological engine of the New Economics. There is documented evidence that Keynes himself was unhappy about the lengths to which "Keynesians" were going, presumably under his scientific auspices. Kurland, via Tarshis, was telling us in 1951 that Keynes was all technician. As a matter of fact even that is in dispute. It is not disputed that Keynes formulated an analytical vocabulary for addressing certain kinds of economic problems, and the universalization of his vocaulary is as much a fait accompli as the universalization of Freud. But there is continuing dispute over what it is to be "a Keynesian." A long series was published in the Sixties in *Encounter* magazine under the title, "Are We All Keynesians Now?" One contributor to that series—to demonstrate the confusion—maintained that one could not properly qualify as a "Keynesian" unless one believed that the apparatus of the government should be used to maintain low interest rates. Others argued that Keynes had higher—indeed much higher—priorities. Richard Nixon, early in his second term, made the statement, "We are all Keynesians now." Even in 1973 that statement shocked the orthodox. For a Republican to have said such a thing in 1950 is inconceivable—as inconceivable, to quote Professor John Kenneth Galbraith, as to have said "We are all Marxists." Whatever a Keynesian was, at least he was the archenemy of the balanced budget, the watermark of conservative economic thought.

It is especially significant that anti-Keynesian analyses of some gravity had been published at the time the class of 1950 graduated from Yale University. These were both technical and political. But the work of Robbins, Mises, Hutt, Anderson, Röpke—to mention a few—was not called to the attention of students of economics. The operative assumption was that the business cycle was the result of an organic deficiency in the market system and that interventionism was the only cure. We know now that the factor of the money supply looms larger in causing contraction and expansion than anyone surmised at the time. The texts reviewed in *Gamay* were, I am saying, heavily ideological, and "Keynesian" was the correct idiomatic word to use to describe economists who inclined to interventionist solutions for economic problems and, while at it, social problems as well.

I do not mean to give the impression that critics were united in their disdain of my analysis of economic education at Yale. Max Eastman, who had himself written books on socialist theory, was amusingly impatient, in his obstinate atheism, with the chapter on religion ("For my part, I fail to see why God cannot take care of Himself at Yale, or even for that matter at Harvard. To me it is ridiculous to see little, two-legged fanatics running around the earth fighting and arguing in behalf of a Deity whom they profess to consider omnipotent"). But he was forthrightly enthusiastic about the economics section: "His second chapter, Individualism at Yale, is by contrast entirely mature. And it is devastating." There were others, schooled in economics, who applauded the chapter, e.g., Felix Morley, Henry Hazlitt, John Davenport, Garret Garrett, and C. P. Ives.

Max Eastman's dichotomization brings up the heated reaction to a book that professes concurrently a concern over the ascendancy of religious skepticism and political statism. I spoke earlier about a set of sentences that many critics found especially galling. When I saw the suggested formulation, written out on the margin of my manuscript in Willmoore Kendall's bold green script, I suspected it would cause difficulty. But there was a nice rhetorical resonance and an intrinsic, almost nonchalant suggestion of an exciting symbiosis, so I let pass: *"I believe that the duel between Christianity and atheism is the most important in the world. I further believe that the struggle between individualism and collectivism is the same struggle reproduced on another level."* The words "the same struggle reproduced on another level" were not originally my own. In the prolonged defense of the book I did not renounce them, in part out of loyalty to my mentor, in part, no doubt, because it would have proved embarrassing to disavow a formulation published over one's signature, never mind its provenance. But in part also because I was tickled by the audacity of the sally and not unamused by the sputtering outrage of its critics.

They were, no doubt, particularly spurred on to lambaste the suggested nexus by their knowledge of its popularity in certain Christian-conservative circles, my favorite of them being the American Council of Christian Laymen in Madison, Wisconsin, which quoted the two sentences in its publication and then sighed, "No Solomon or Confucius or other wise man of the ages ever spoke or wrote truer words than the sentence just quoted." It was the very first time I had been compared to Solomon *or* Confucius.

The widespread objection was not only on the point that to suggest an affinity between the eschatological prospects of heaven and hell and the correct role of the state in achieving full employment was something on the order of blasphemy. It was fueled by the ideological conviction of many Christian modernists that the road to Christianity on earth lies through the Federal Government. Although these criticisms flowed in copiously from Protestant quarters, they were on the whole most bitter in the fashionable Catholic journals; and indeed my being a Catholic itself became something of an issue.

McGeorge Bundy, in his main-event review in the *Atlantic*, wrote directly on the point:

"Most remarkable of all, Mr. Buckley, who urges a return to what he considers to be Yale's true religious tradition, at no point says one word of the fact that he himself is an ardent Roman Catholic. In view of the pronounced and well-recognized difference between Protestant and Catholic views on education in America, and in view of Yale's Protestant history, it seems strange for any Roman Catholic to undertake to speak for the Yale religious tradition. . . . It is stranger still for Mr. Buckley to venture his prescription with no word or hint to show his special allegiance."

On this point Dwight Macdonald commented: "Buckley is indeed a Catholic, and an ardent one. But, oddly enough, this fact is irrelevant, since his book defines Christianity in Protestant terms, and his economics are Calvinist rather than Catholic. One of the wryest twists in the whole comedy is that the Catholic press has almost unanimously damned Buckley's economic views."

Macdonald exaggerated, but not entirely. "He quite unwittingly succeeds in contravening Catholic moral doctrine as applied to economics and politics on almost every topic he takes up," the Jesuits' *America* had editorialized, concluding, "Mr. Buckley's own social philosophy is almost as obnoxious to a well-instructed Catholic as the assaults on religion he rightly condemns." (Who is flirting with the nexus now?) *Commonweal*, the Catholic layman's journal of opinion, was right in there. "The nature of Mr. Buckley's heresies were pointed out again in the Catholic press, but apparently the young man remains unmoved. He continues to peddle his anti-papal economics without any noticeable changes often under the auspices of Catholics. . . ." Father Higgins, the labor priest, objected heatedly to my "attempt to identify the heresy of economic individualism with Catholic or Christian doctrine."

I am obliged to concede, at this distance, that, the attacks from the Catholics quite apart, it is probably true that there was a pretty distinct anti-Catholic animus in some of the criticism of this book. The Reverend Henry Sloane Coffin, former head of the Union Theological Seminary, former chairman of the Educational Policy Committee of Yale, former trustee of the Corporation, chairman of a committee commissioned by the Yale Corporation to investigate my charges about Yale education without ever acknowledging them (see below), was so incautious as to write to an alumnus who had questioned Coffin about my book, "Mr. Buckley's book is really a misrepresentation and [is] distorted by his Roman Catholic point of view. Yale is a Puritan and Protestant institution by its heritage and he should have attended Fordham or some similar institution."

Now there are three strands to the Catholic point. The first has to do with the allegedly distinctive Catholic definition of Christianity; the second with the allegedly distinctive Catholic understanding of the role of the university; and the third, most simply stated, was ad hominem, i.e., an attempt to suggest that by "concealing" my Catholicism I told the discerning reader a great deal about my deficient character and, derivatively, about the invalidity of my criticisms and arguments.

Taking the third point first, a semantic advantage was instantly achieved by those who spoke of my having "concealed" my Catholicism. By not advertising it—so ran the planted axiom—I was concealing it. Inasmuch as, on writing the book, I saw nothing in the least distinctively Catholic about the points I made, I had thought it irrelevant to advert to my Catholicism. Even as I was criticized for "concealing" my Catholicism, I could have been criticized had I identified myself as a Catholic on the grounds that I had "dragged in" my Catholicism as if it were relevant.

But see, for instance, Professor Fred Rodell (of the Yale Law School) writing in the *Progressive*, probably (though there are close runners-up—Arthur Schlesinger in the New York *Post*, Vern Countryman in the *Yale Law Journal*, Herman Liebert in the St. Louis *Post Dispatch*, Theodore Greene in the *Yale Daily News*, Frank Ashburn in the *Saturday Review*) the most acidulous review of the lot. ". . . most Catholics would resent both the un-Christian arrogance of his presentation and, particularly, his deliberate concealment—throughout the entire foreword, text, and appendices of a highly personalized book—of his very relevant church affiliation." Ah, the sweet uses of rhetoric. "No mention" of Catholicism elides to "concealment" of Catholicism elides to "deliberate concealment'" (a tautology, by the way). That my affiliation was "very relevant" spared Mr. Rodell the pains of having to explain its relevance. By the same token would it have been relevant for a reviewer of a book by Fred Rodell on the *Supreme Court and Freedom of Religion* to accuse the author of "deliberate concealment" of the "very relevant" fact that his name used to be Fred Rodelheim, and that his interpretation of the Freedom Clause was tainted in virtue of his lifetime's concealment of his having been born Jewish? That would have gone down—quite properly—as anti-Semitism.

If one pauses to think about it, it is difficult to be at once an "ardent" Catholic, as everyone kept saying I was, and to "conceal" one's Catholicism (unless one worships furiously and furtively). The only place in the book in which I might unobtrusively have said that I am a Catholic is on page 31 where I mention an Inter-Faith Conference held in the spring of 1949 sponsored by Dwight Hall (Protestant), St. Thomas More (Catholic), and the Hillel Foundation (Jewish). I was the Catholic co-chairman of that conference, which is hardly the way to go about concealing one's affiliation. But even to have mentioned in this book that I had been co-chairman would have been irrelevant, perhaps even vainglorious. Should I have mentioned that I was the son of a wealthy father, in order to explain a prejudice in favor of capitalism?

With respect to the second point, I accepted as the operative definition of "Christianity" (see page 8) that of the World Council of Churches, supplemented by a definition of Dr. Reinhold Niebuhr—an organization, and an individual, never accused of being closet Catholics.

As to the remaining point, namely the purpose of education, it is hard to know what the Reverend Henry Sloane Coffin had in mind when he suggested that Yale's "Puritan and Protestant heritage" was responsible for a "distortion" that grew inevitably out of my Roman Catholicism, or McGeorge Bundy when he referred to the well-recognized difference between Protestant and Catholic views on education in America. I am aware of no difference, celebrated or obscure, with reference to the purpose of a *secular college*, about which I was writing. Yale was indeed founded as a Protestant institution, but the bearing of that datum on this book underscores rather than subverts its thesis. The man who was president of Yale while I was there said in his inaugural address, "I call on all members of the faculty, as members of a thinking body, freely to recognize the tremendous validity and power of the teachings of Christ in our life-and-death struggle against the force of selfish materialism." That wasn't Pope Pius IX talking. And, later, President Charles Seymour said, "Yale was dedicated to the training of spiritual leaders. We betray our trust if we fail to explore the various ways in which the youth who come to us may learn to appreciate spiritual values, whether by the example of our own lives or through the cogency of our philosophical arguments. The simple and direct way is through the maintenance and upbuilding of the Christian religion as a vital part of univer-

sity life." Maybe Charles Seymour should have been made
president of Fordham.

I have mentioned that the reaction to the publication of
Gamay was quite startling. Louis Filler wrote in the *New England Quarterly*: "This book is a phenomenon of our time. It
could hardly have been written ten years ago, at least for
general circulation." He meant by that that no one ten years
earlier a) was particularly alarmed by, or interested in, ideological trends in higher education; and that therefore b) nobody would have bothered to read a book that examined
those themes, let alone one that focused on a single college.

So that the book's success as an attention-getter first surprised, then amazed. It was infuriating to the hostile critics
that a man as eminent as John Chamberlain should have consented to write the introduction to it, and indeed Fred Rodell
held him personally responsible for the notoriety of the
book. ("It was doubtless the fact of a John Chamberlain introduction that lent the book, from the start, the aura of importance and respectability. . . .") But it was too late to ignore it. *Life* magazine did an editorial (cautious interest in
the book's theme), *Time* and *Newsweek* ran news stories; the
Saturday Review, a double review; and after a while there
were reviews and news stories about the reviews and news
stories. The critic Selden Rodman, although he disagreed
with the book and its conclusions, had said of it in the *Saturday Review*, "[Mr. Buckley] writes with clarity, a sobriety, and
an intellectual honesty that would be noteworthy if it came
from a college president." (Compare Herman Liebert, from
the staff of the Yale Library, writing for the St. Louis *Post Dispatch*: ". . . the book is a series of fanatically emotional attacks on a few professors who dare to approach religion and
politics objectively." Note that collectivist economics and ag-
nostic philosophy suddenly became the "objective" approaches. That they were so considered at Yale was of course
the gravamen of the book which this critic, in his fustian, was
witless to recognize.) Oh, yes, Fred Rodell: "I deem it irresponsible in a scholar like Selden Rodman to dignify the
book as 'important' and 'thought-provoking.' "Max Eastman

had written, in the *American Mercury,* "He names names, and quotes quotes, and conducts himself, in general, with a disrespect for his teachers that is charming and stimulating in a high degree. . . . This perhaps is the best feature of his book, certainly the most American in the old style—its arrant intellectual courage." (From the encephalophonic Mr. Rodell, his voice hoarse: ". . . I deem it irresponsible, in a scholar like Max Eastman, to shower the book with adulatory adjectives. . . .")

And so on, for months and months. Official Yale took no official position but was very busy at every level. The *Yale Daily News* ran analyses of the book by six professors, only one of whom (William Wimsatt) found anything remotely commendable about the book. The series was introduced by an editorial of which a specimen sentence was "When the Buckley book has succeeded in turning the stomachs of its readers and lining up Yale men categorically on the side of that great 'hoax' academic freedom, Bill Buckley will, as Professor Greene suggests, have performed a great service to Yale."

In the *Yale Alumni* Magazine the book was treated with caution, but I was offhandedly coupled with a notorious and wealthy old crank called George Gundelfinger, a gentleman who had gone off his rocker a generation earlier and periodically drowned the campus with nervous exhalations of his arcane philosophy, which heralded as the key to the full life a kind of platonic masturbation ("sublimate pumping" he called it). Copies of McGeorge Bundy's review were sent out to questioning alumni. Meanwhile, in the trustees' room, a plan had been devised to commission an inquiry by a committee of eight alumni into "the intellectual and spiritual welfare of the university, the students, and its faculty." The chairman, as mentioned, was Henry Sloane Coffin. And among its members was Irving Olds, then chairman of the board of United States Steel Corporation, thus effecting representation for God and man. The committee was surreptitiously set up during the summer, in anticipation of *Gamay's* appearance in the fall, but its clear function of unsaying what this book said was acknowledged even in the news stories.

Yale didn't have an easy time of it. Too many people knew

instinctively that the central charges of the book were correct, whatever the inflections distinctive to Yale. Felix Morley, formerly president of Haverford College, had written in *Barrons*, "[Buckley's] arguments must be taken seriously. As he suggests, and as this reviewer from personal knowledge of scores of American colleges can confirm, the indictment is equally applicable to many of our privately endowed institutions of higher learning. Mr. Buckley, says John Chamberlain in the latter's foreword, is incontestably right about the educational drift of modern times." It is confirmation of Morley's generalization that, twenty-five years later, references to religion and politics that were then eyebrow-raising seem utterly bland: almost conservative, in a way. What is unthinkable in the current scene isn't that an economics teacher should come out for a 100 percent excess profits tax, or that a teacher of sociology should mock religion. What is unthinkable today is an inaugural address by a president of a major university containing such passages as I have quoted from Charles Seymour.

So that Yale had that problem—that most people suspected that heterodoxy was rampant—and an additional problem which it needed to handle most deftly (and, on the whole, did). I made the suggestion in this book that the alumni of Yale play a greater role in directing the course of Yale education. That they proceed to govern the university, through their representatives, even as the people govern the country through theirs. This suggestion had a most startling effect. Yale's challenge has always been to flatter its alumni while making certain they should continue impotent.

The purpose of a Yale education, never mind the strictures of this book, can hardly be to turn out a race of idiots. But one would have thought that was what Yale precisely engages in. Walking out of the Huntington Hotel in Pasadena during the hottest days of the controversy, I espied the Reverend Henry Sloane Coffin walking in. I introduced myself. He greeted me stiffly, and then said, as he resumed his way into the hotel, "Why do you want to turn Yale education over to a bunch of boobs?" Since Mr. Coffin had been chairman of the Educational Policy Committee of the Corporation, it struck me that if indeed the alumni were boobs he bore a considerable procreative responsibility. Certainly his contempt for Yale's demonstrated failure was far greater than my alarm at its potential failure.

He was not alone.

Bruce Barton, the anti-New Dealer at whose partial expense President Roosevelt had composed the rollicking taunt, "Martin, Barton and Fish," saw the need for reform. But by *alumni*? "As for Mr. Buckley's cure—letting the alumni dictate the teaching—what could be more terrifying? Are these noisy, perennial sophomores, who dress up in silly costumes and get drunk at reunions, who spend their thousands of dollars buying halfbacks and quarterbacks, and following the Big Blue Team—are they to be the nation's mental mentors?" I really had had no idea the contempt in which "alumni" qua alumni were so generally held.

My notion, as elaborated in the book, was that alumni would concern themselves with the purpose of a university; that, if mind and conscience led them to the conclusion, they would not only be free, but compelled, to decide that certain values should be encouraged, others discouraged. That, necessarily, this would give them, through their representatives, the right to judicious hiring and firing, precisely with the end in mind of furthering broad philosophical objectives and cultivating certain ideas—through the exposure of the undergraduate body to (President Seymour's phrase) cogent philosophical arguments.

There are many grounds for disapproving the proposal of alumni control. But the description, by some critics, of the state of affairs I sought led me to question my own sanity and then, finding it in good order, to question that of my critics. Consider the near-terminal pain of Frank Ashburn as he closed his long piece for the *Saturday Review*:

"The book is one which has the glow and appeal of a fiery cross on a hillside at night. There will undoubtedly be robed figures who gather to it, but the hoods will not be academic. They will cover the face."

Gee whiz. Now it is important to remember that Frank Ashburn is a very nice man. He is, moreover, quite intelligent. He founded a successful boys' preparatory school, Brooks School, and, years later, in his capacity as headmaster, he invited me to address the student body, proffering the customary fee. And I did, arriving without my hood; and, to the extent it is possible to do so under less than clinical conditions, I probed about a bit, and Frank Ashburn was to all appearances entirely normal. But that's the kind of thing *Gamay* did to people, especially people close to Yale. I did mention that Frank Ashburn was a trustee?

I must not let the point go, because one *has* to ask oneself *why* it is that supervision of the general direction of undergraduate instruction is so instinctively repugnant to nonjuveniles. I do not know whether Robert Hatch, who wrote for the *New Republic*, is a Yale graduate, but in terms of horror registered he might as well have been. He took pains, in his review, to try to explain what, in fact, I was *really* up to with my bizarre proposals. "It is astonishing," he wrote, "on the assumption that Buckley is well-meaning, that he has not realized that the methods he proposes for his alma mater are precisely those employed in Italy, Germany, and Russia. An elite shall establish the truth by ukase and no basic disagreement shall be tolerated."

It really wasn't all that astonishing that I did not spot the similarities in the methods I proposed and those of the Fascists, Nazis, and Communists, because there are no similarities. My book made it plain that alumni direction could be tolerated only over the college of which they were uniquely the constituents; that alumni of institutions that sought different ends should be equally free to pursue them. Moreover, the ideals I sought to serve were those that no authoritarian society would regard as other than seditious, namely, the ideals of a minimalist state, and deference to a transcendent order.

But the notion that the proposals were subversive was jubilantly contagious. Four months after the publication of *Gamay*, Chad Walsh was writing in the *Saturday Review*: "What Mr. Buckley really proposes is that the alumni of Yale should turn themselves into a politburo, and control the campus exactly as the Kremlin controls the intellectual life of Russia." "Exactly," in the sense used here, can only be understood to mean "analogously." Obviously there are no "exact" parallels between a state directing all education and enforcing a political orthodoxy and the constituency of discrete educational institutions, within a free and pluralist society, directing the education of its own educational enterprise. Indeed, so obviously is it inexact to draw the parallel, the heretical thought suggests itself that conventional limitations on alumni are closer to the authoritarian model. A free association, within a free society, shaping an educational institution toward its own purpose, is practicing a freedom which totalitarian societies would never permit it to do. An obvious example would be a German university under Hitler which prescribed that its faculty, in the relevant disciplines, should preach racial toleration and racial equality; or, in the Bolshevik model, a constituency backing a university that, athwart the political orthodoxy, insisted on preaching the ideals of freedom and pluralism.

I find it painful, at this remove, to make points so obvious. But if *Gamay* is to be republished, it must surely be in part for the purpose of allowing us to examine specimens, however wilted, of the political literature of yesteryear; and to wonder what was the madness that seized so many people of such considerable reputation; and to wonder further that such profound misinterpretations were not more widely disavowed. Were these people lefties?—shrewdly protecting their positions by theoretical incantations? Yes, one supposes, in some cases. But surely not in others: Frank Ashburn was an Establishment figure, in lockstep with the Zeitgeist, who probably shed a wistful tear or two in private over some of the departed virtues at Yale. *They* are the enigma. The left was of course especially scornful. When, fifteen years later, a number of our colleges and universities were given over to the thousand blooms of the youth revolution, which demanded that colleges be "relevant"—i.e., that they become arms depots for the anti-Vietnam war—many of the same people who sharpened their teeth on *Gamay* were preternaturally silent.

Michael Harrington was in those days a socialist and a Christian. He would in due course repeal the laws of progress by reaffirming the one faith and renouncing the second. He wrote his review for Dorothy Day's *Catholic Worker*: "The frightening thing is that Mr. Buckley is not yet realistic enough for fascism. Mr. Buckley's aims can only be secured by fascist methods—coercion in favor of capitalists—a realistic conclusion which Mr. Buckley's five years in New Haven did not educate him to make." Neither five years' education in New Haven nor twenty-five years' education outside New Haven. The case for capitalism is stronger in 1977 than in 1950, having profited in the interim from the empirical failures of socialism, as from the scholarly accreditation of the presumptions of the free market. Besides which, the word "fascism" loses its pungency when it is used to mean, pure and simple, the exercise of authority. Mr. Harrington, even then, was flirting with heresy, which would become his succubus.

Authority is licitly and illicitly acquired by the democratic canon; and, once acquired, is then licitly and illicitly exercised. The "authority" to apprehend, try, and punish a lawbreaker is licitly acquired in the democratic circumstances of a society which, after popular consultation, makes its own laws, prescribes its own judicial procedures, and stipulates its own punishments—all subject to the rule of law. The line between licit and illicit authority in a secular society is, however, elusive, though it is generally acknowledged in the Judeo-Christian world that there is such a line, most resonantly affirmed by Christ's distinction between Caesar and God. It is an unusual experience for a libertarian to be catechized by a socialist on the theme of the dangers of coercion. Harrington's oxymoronic formulation—"coercion in favor of capitalists"—reminds us of the fashionable jargon in the commodity markets of the left (alas, not greatly changed). His sentence is on the order of "coercive freedom," or "the slavery of the bill of rights." Unless a "fascist method" can be distinguished from a plain old "method" by which the will of the entrepreneurial unit prevails over the will of the individual resolved subversively to gainsay that will, then paradoxically you are left without the freedom of the collectivity. The interdiction of that modest freedom on the grand piano Mr.

Harrington is used to thumping in his full-throated crusade
for state socialism is not only inconsistent, it is positively un-
seemly.

It is worth pursuing the matter yet one step further, I
think, in order to notice the review by T. M. Greene. Professor Greene was a considerable character on the Yale campus.
I think he was the most quintessentially liberal man I ever
came upon, outside the pages of Randall Jarrell's *Pictures
from an Institution*. As master of the largest residential college
at Yale (Silliman), he one day issued an order, in the interest
of decorum, requiring students who ate dinner in the dining
room to wear coats and ties. He was dismayed by the trickle
of criticism, and very soon indignantly repealed his own order, apologizing for his lapse into dirigisme. He taught, as an
explicit Christian, a course in the philosophy of religion
which was widely attended; but I remarked that in the opinion of his students he was engaged, really, in reteaching ethics, not religion. (There's nothing against teaching ethics, but
of course it isn't exactly the same thing.)

His reaction to *Gamay*, as published in the *Yale Daily News*,
fairly took one's breath away. He fondled the word "fascist"
as though he had come up with a Dead Sea Scroll vouch-
safing the key word to the understanding of *God and Man at
Yale*. In a few sentences he used the term thrice. "Mr. Buckley has done Yale a great service" (how I would tire of this
pedestrian rhetorical device), "and he may well do the cause
of liberal education in America an even greater service, by
stating the fascist alternative to liberalism. This fascist thesis . . . This . . . pure fascism . . . What more could Hitler, Mussolini, or Stalin ask for . . . ? (They asked for, and
got, a great deal more.)

What survives, from such stuff as this, is ne-plus-ultra relativism, idiot nihilism. "What is required," Professor Greene
spoke, "is more, not less tolerance—not the tolerance of
indifference, but the tolerance of honest respect for divergent convictions and the determination of all that such divergent opinions be heard without administrative censorship. I
try my best in the classroom to expound and defend my
faith, when it is relevant, as honestly and persuasively as I
can. But I can do so only because many of my colleagues are

expounding and defending their contrasting faiths, or skep-
ticisms, as openly and honestly as I am mine."

A professor of *philosophy!* Question: What is the (1) ethical,
(2) pragmatic or (3) epistemological argument for *requiring*
continued tolerance of ideas whose discrediting it is the purpose of education to effect? What ethical code (in the Bible?
in Plato? Kant? Hume?) requires "honest respect" for any divergent conviction? Even John Stuart Mill did not ask more
than that a question be not considered as closed so long as
any one man adhered to it; he did not require that that man,
flourishing the map of a flat world, be seated in a chair of
science at Yale. And this is to say nothing about the flamboy-
ant contrast between Professor Greene's call to toleration in
all circumstances and the toleration *he* showed to the book he
was reviewing. An honest respect by him for my divergent
conviction would have been an arresting application at once
of his theoretical and charitable convictions.

The sleeper, in that issue of the *Yale Daily News*, was William Wimsatt. The late Professor Wimsatt, the renowned
critic and teacher, was . . . a Catholic! Not an uppity Catholic. He was, simply, known by the cognoscenti to be one, and
his friends found that charming. But under the circumstances, the pressure on Professor Wimsatt to Tom must
have been very nearly unbearable, and his conciliatory motions must be weighted charitably under the circumstances.
He denounced *Gamay* as "impudent," inasmuch as its author
"used the entree and confidential advantage of a student and
alumnus to publicize so widely both embarrassing personali-
ties and problems of policy which are internal to the relation
between administrative officers and alumni." A so-so point
which, it happens, I dealt with in the book itself, in my discussion of the emasculating hold the Yale administration exercises over its alumni; but, in a sense, also a point gainsaid
by the universal interest provoked by the book, which interest focused not on its gossip value involving any one or more
professors (only three of the hundred reviews I have reread
bother even to mention by name any individual professor
named in the book).

Protected by such rhetorical cover, Professor Wimsatt
went on to say some very interesting things. He began, for in-

stance, by suavely blowing the whole Coffin-Bundy-Dwight Hall-Yale position about religion at Yale. "The prevailing secularism of the university is palpable," wrote Professor Wimsatt matter-of-factly. That's what I said. But lest that should shock, he added, What-else-is-new? "What else did Mr. Buckley expect when he elected to come here?" He went on to say, in effect, that a "modern" university cannot orient itself other than to fashion. "What would he expect of any modern American university large enough to be the representative of the culture in which he has lived all his life?"

Mr. Wimsatt is here carefully avoiding the point. Obviously a modern, acquiescent, college will tend not to buck the Zeitgeist. This begs the question whether under certain circumstances it might do so; and certainly begs the question whether idealistically active alumni are entitled to apply pressure on it to do so.

But, despite himself, Professor Wimsatt was getting hotter and hotter. "It is more fundamental to ask . . . what is actually right, and how far any individual may in good conscience tolerate or assist the teaching of what he firmly believes wrong. If I knew that a professor were teaching the Baconian heresy about Shakespeare, I should think it a pity. If I knew that a professor were preaching genocide, I should think it a duty, if I were able, to prevent him—even though his views were being adequately refuted in the next classroom." That buzz saw ran right through the analysis of Professor Greene, adjacent on the page, leaving it bobbing and weaving in death agony. But nobody noticed. "As Mr. Buckley so earnestly pleads, it is indeed very far from being a fact that the truth, in such matters of value, is bound 'to emerge victorious'. It would be easy to name several doctrines, not only genocide but the less violent forms of racism, for instance, or an ethics of pre-marital sexual experiment— which the present administration of no university in this country would tolerate." (From the 25th Reunion Yearbook of the Yale Class of 1950, published in 1975, Questionnaire #13: "Are you in favor of or opposed to: . . . People living together out of wedlock? Oppose, 42%. Favor, 43%.") Although Professor Wimsatt was hardly quotable as an endorser of *Gamay*, the passages here reproduced take you exactly as far as I go in every theoretical point. Everything else he said was in the nature of social shock absorption.

It is worth it, before making a final comment on the grander points involved, to climb out of the polemical fever swamps and look with a little detachment on the purely economic question. When I wrote this book, there were reviewers who defended the factual generalities, indeed went so far as to say the points I made were obvious. Yale's teachings were distinct from Yale's preachings—"this rudimentary fact of life," Dwight Macdonald commented, "Buckley is rude enough to dwell on for 240 pages." On the other hand, very few reviewers (certainly not Macdonald) were prepared to associate themselves with my prescriptions—though some of them acknowledged nervously that any way you look at it there was a paradox in the circumstance of alumni agitatedly supporting the cultivation of values different from their own. I think it safe to say that no fully integrated member of the intellectual community associated himself with my position on academic freedom. In March of this year Irving Kristol, a professor, editor, author, philosopher of unassailable academic and intellectual standing, included in a casual essay in his regular series for the *Wall Street Journal* (which space he shares with such other scholars as Robert Nisbet and Arthur Schlesinger, Jr.) the comment:

"Business men or corporations do not have any obligation to give money to institutions whose views or attitudes they disapprove of. It's absurd to insist otherwise—yet this absurdity is consistently set forth in the name of 'academic freedom.'" The prose is an improvement on my own in *God and Man at Yale*, but the point is identical. Yet no one rose to say of Professor Kristol that he should be wearing a hood and that he was introducing fascism to American education.

Indeed the educational establishment, although it rose to smite my book hip and thigh, has since then tended to find it more useful to take the advice of that generic class of prudent lawyers who counsel their clients to say "No comment." Even now I rub my eyes in amazement at the silence given to events—historical, sociological, and even judicial—that tend to confirm and reconfirm the factual claims of my book, and to give support to its theoretical arguments. There was, for instance, the A. P. Smith case of 1953 (*A. P. Smith Manufacturing Company* v. *Barlow*). I should like to be able to refer to it as the "celebrated A. P. Smith case." But it is not celebrated at all. It is unknown.

What happened was that a New Jersey manufacturer of valves and hydrants made a gift of $1,500 to Princeton University, and a group of minority stockholders sued, saying in effect, What does Princeton University have to do with the fortunes of the A. P. Smith Company? The case was tried and most vigorously defended, with star witnesses moving in and out of the witness stand. Not because of the $1,500, obviously, but because the precedent was deemed very important.

Well, Princeton and the management of the A. P. Smith Company won. Two courts, the superior court of New Jersey and the Supreme Court of that state on appeal, affirmed the corporate validity of the gift. Why then is the case not more greatly celebrated?

Because the price of victory was academic freedom as commonly understood. The A. P. Smith Company, in its defense brief, took the position that by giving money to Princeton it was advancing its corporate purposes strictly defined. The defense brief said: "The Smith Company turned to philanthropy not for the sake of philanthropy but for the sake of selling more valves and hydrants." *How's that again?*

But there was no recorded objection from representatives of Princeton University. Expert witnesses were called. One of them was: Irving Olds. Our old friend! Chairman of the board of United States Steel! Mr. Olds testified soberly on the stand that "our American institutions of higher learning can and do perform a service of tremendous importance to the corporations of this and other states, through acquainting their students with the facts about different economic theories and ideologies. With the good educational facilities provided by these institutions, the courses of instruction will and do lead the student body to recognize the virtues and achievements of our well-proven economic system; and, on the other hand, to discover the faults and weaknesses of an arbitrary, government-directed and controlled system of production and distribution."

That testimony by Mr. Olds was given approximately on the first anniversary of the release of the report of the Yale committee to investigate the charges leveled in this book, and Mr. Olds had then put his signature on a document that said:

"A university does not take sides in the questions that are discussed in its halls. The business of a university is to educate, not to indoctrinate its students. In the ideal university all sides of any issue are presented as impartially and as forcefully as possible. This is Yale's policy." Now the only course in comparative economic systems being taught at Yale at that time is described in this book. The professor who taught it proclaimed himself an ardent socialist in the British tradition, and defended the socialist alternative to the free market system, which one would suppose is not the system that, in the understanding of A. P. Smith, the lower court, the higher court, and Irving Olds, promotes the "selling of more valves and hydrants."

The worst was yet to be. The lower court, in authorizing the gift, ruled: "It is the youth of today which also furnishes tomorrow's leaders in economics and in government, thereby erecting a strong breastwork against any onslaught from hostile forces which would change our way of life either in respect of private enterprise or democratic self-government. The proofs before me are abundant that Princeton emphasizes by precept and indoctrination [*precept and indoctrination!*] the principles which are very vital to the preservation of our democratic system of business and government. . . . I cannot conceive of any greater benefit to corporations in this country than to build, and continue to build, respect for and adherence to a system of free enterprise and democratic government, the serious impairment of either of which may well spell the destruction of all corporate enterprise." I cannot think of a more excruciatingly embarrassing victory in Princeton's history.

Dumb judge? I invite you to find a denunciation of him by an official of Princeton University. The decision was appealed and went on to the Supreme Court of New Jersey where *another* dumb judge affirmed the lower court's decision, and made it all worse. Because *he* reminded the "objecting stockholders" that they had "not disputed any of the foregoing testimony" asserting the service Princeton is performing in behalf of free market economy; and the court reminded them, paternalistically, that "more and more they [private corporations] have come to recognize that their salvation rests upon a sound economic and social environment which in turn rests in no insignificant part upon free and vigorous non-governmental institutions of learning." Princeton didn't take its $1,500 and go hang itself, but one can imagine the gloom in the paneled office where they all met to open that judicial valentine.

The educators were saying, in response to this book, that college is a cultural sanctuary from the commerce of life. That such concessions as periodically were made by university officials were purely rhetorical—President Seymour, enjoining the faculty to cultivate the doctrines of Christ at inaugural ceremonies; Princeton deans, nodding their heads acquiescently when the court upholds a financial award on the ground that Princeton is "by precept and indoctrination" committed to spreading the gospel of free enterprise. Actually, they were saying, no interference is possible. All ideas must start out equal. (All ideas *are* equal!) To make demands on a college is totalitarian, fascist, communist, condemned by all men of understanding, reaching back to Thomas Jefferson. How widely he was used during the controversy! "Subject opinion to coercion," Philip Kurland quoted him; "whom will you make your inquisitors? Fallible men; men governed by bad passions, by private as well as public reasons. And why subject it to coercion? To produce uniformity. But is uniformity of opinion desirable? No more than of face and stature . . . difference of opinion is advantageous." And, of course, who would disagree that men are fallible? But does that mean we can rely, at the margin, other than on men? On whom was Jefferson relying for remedies when in 1821 he wrote to General Breckinridge to complain of "seminaries [where] our sons [are] imbibing opinions and principles in discord with those of their own country." Did

Jefferson wish to do something about it? Or was he describing only a situation which could not be corrected, because men are fallible, dominated by passion. No. Jefferson continued, "This canker is eating on the vitals of our existence, and if not arrested at once, will be beyond remedy." If not arrested by whom? Surely not the state. We would all agree on this? Not quite all. The state would prove to have its uses. President Seymour warned urgently and repeatedly against accepting federal aid to education on the grounds that it would bring federal interference. President Seymour retired in 1950. In the succeeding generation major private universities became totally dependent on federal funds. Remove the federal subsidy to Yale (35 percent), or to Harvard (25 percent), or to MIT (65 percent) and what would happen to them? The notion of mere trustees influencing the choice of textbooks was—and is—thought scandalous: by the same people who, calling such interference fascism, backed, or were indifferent to, legislation which twenty-five years later would permit the attorney general of the United States (ironically, a former college president, in a Republican administration, executing laws passed by a Democratic Congress) to pry out of a thoroughly private association—the American Institute of Real Estate Appraisers—the promise to destroy a textbook called *The Appraisal of Real Estate,* in which appraisers are advised that the ethnic composition of a neighborhood in fact influences the value of real estate. Under the proposed consent decree, the Institute agrees to strike from the present (sixth) edition of its textbook all the improper language. Specific textbook revisions have been prepared. These changes "will be included in the seventh edition of the text" not later than September 5, 1978. Sixty days after the decree is entered, the Institute "will commence a review of all booklets, manuals, monographs, guides, lexicons, and . . . other instructional material published under its auspices" to assure that they too conform with the text revisions. And they called fascistic a summons to free citizens freely associated, exercising no judicial or legislative power, to communicate their ideals at a private college through the appropriate selection of texts and teachers.

*   *   *

"Unless the great concepts which have been traditional to the Western world are rooted in a reasoned view of the universe and man's place in it, and unless this reasoned view contains in its orbit a place for the spirit, man is left in our day with archaic weapons unsuited for the problems of the present." I don't know who wrote that sentence, which appeared in an editorial in the Boston *Pilot*, but I know I wish I had written it because with great economy of expression it says, really, everything my book sought to say. It leaves unsaid only this. Is there a role for the non-academician in formulating that "reasoned view"? Or if not that, in catalyzing that "reasoned view"? Or if not that, in providing genial ground in which to cultivate that "reasoned view"? It is on this point that I declare myself, a generation after the event, on the side of the university with a mission.

In recent months I have been asked by representatives of Yale University to make a public declaration urging contributions to the university's capital fund. I dealt with the first such communication most tactfully, uttering an evasion, stuttering off like a member of the Drones Club. It did not work. A second request came in. I had, this time, to say No, but I begged off giving the reasons why. A third request came in, and there was then nothing to do—I was backed up against the wall: my correspondent had never learned Machiavelli's axiom that you should not cut off the enemy's line of retreat.

I have always held in high esteem the genial tradition, and I hope it is something other than sentimentality that inclines me to believe that one of the reasons I was so happy at Yale was that that geniality is—forget, and forgive, the intemperances necessarily recorded here—as natural to Yale as laughter is to Dublin, song to Milan, or angst to the *New York Review of Books*. Mostly I prefer nowadays to contend with the slogan, rather than with the man who hoists it. But sometimes there are no alternatives (in particular as the anthropomorphization of public life proceeds—you do not talk about the Democratic Party, you talk about Kennedy, Johnson, Carter). So, in my third communication, I answered directly.

"In the ideal university all sides of any issue are presented as impartially and as forcefully as possible." This was Official

Yale's answer to *Gamay*. In a world governed by compromise, in which opportunism can be virtuous—such a world as our own—I am obliged to confess: I would probably settle for such an arrangement. A truly balanced curriculum, in which as much time, by professors as talented as their counterparts, in courses as critical as the others, were given to demonstrating the cogency of the arguments for God and man. This book establishes that nothing like that balance obtained twenty-five years ago. But the allocation of ideological and philosophical commitments aside, I cannot come to terms with a university that accepts the philosophical proposition that it is there for the purpose of presenting "all sides" of "any issue" as impartially and as forcefully as possible. That will not do, for the reasons Professor Wimsatt gave.

And so I was driven to write, in what I swore until I was seduced to write this essay would be my last exchange on the Yale question. And what I said was:

"What's the problem? Why doesn't Yale donate itself to the State of Connecticut?"

The mechanical problem, as it happens, is virtually nonexistent. There is a thing called the Yale Corporation. It literally "owns" Yale. If the trustees of Yale were to vote tomorrow to give "Yale" to the State of Connecticut, there would be lots of amazement and thunderstorms of indignation—and no recourse. Obviously the State of Connecticut would accept the gift. We are talking about several hundred million dollars of real property, and half-billion or so in endowments.

What then would happen?

To tell the truth, I don't know that anything much would happen. Obviously there would be changes at the corporate level. Instead of fourteen trustees, eight of them elected by their predecessors the balance by the alumni, there would, presumably, be fourteen (or more, or less) trustees named by the Governor of Connecticut (who is already *ex officio* a trustee), and confirmed by the state legislature. Would these be a scurvy lot? That is hard to say. If you look at the board of trustees of the University of California you would not find a significant difference in the profile of its membership and that of Yale today. The University of California, particularly in recent days, has its share of flower children; but, lo, so does Yale.

What else would be different? Standards of admission?

Why? The University of California at Berkeley is as hard to get into as Yale. A state university can be "elitist" and get away with it provided there are other universities within the system that will accept the less gifted students.

The curriculum would be less varied?

I don't think that would necessarily follow. There is a luxurious offering at Yale of courses in the recondite byways of human knowledge, wonderful to behold. But—that is also true of the University of California.

Excellence of faculty? But the University of California has the highest concentration of Nobel Prize winners in the country. It is simply no longer true that the most gifted scholars insist on joining the faculties of privately run universities. As for the maintenance of a Yale tradition within the faculty, the incidence of Yale-educated members continues to decline, consistent with the de-traditionalization of Yale.

What about the quality of undergraduate instruction?

There are a lot of complaints about the mega-university, large lecture courses, graduate-student instruction. But these complaints are also increasingly lodged against Yale and Harvard as well as Berkeley, and as the economic noose tightens, economizing at the expense of the student is likelier at private colleges, whose resources are limited, than at the public universities, whose resources are less limited.

The quality of undergraduate life? Why should it be affected? Yale has insisted it can show no genealogical preferences—neither would the State of Connecticut; neither, of course, does Berkeley. Would state ownership interfere with undergraduate social life? How? There is only a single fraternity surviving in Yale; there are dozens in many state colleges. Yale's senior societies are unique, but they are privately owned; and, in any case, their survival (so heatedly opposed, for instance, by the recent chaplain of Yale, among others) would hardly be the pivotal justification for withholding the gift of Yale to the State of Connecticut.

And consider the advantages! Yale's painful annual deficit is a mere added calorie in the paunch of Connecticut's deficit. Those who desire to contribute to Yale to promote specific activities within Yale could continue to do so, even as there are private endowments at Berkeley.

And—the most interesting point of all, I think—what, in the absence of specific objections, are the philosophical objections? The sense of the swingers in the social science faculty even twenty-five years ago was to prefer the public sector over the private sector. I cannot think what arguments most of the distinguished teachers mentioned in this book would use to oppose in principle turning Yale over to the public sector.

Now, having said all that, let me say that I know why Yale shouldn't be turned over to the state. Because there are great historical presumptions that from time to time the interests of the state and those of civilization will bifurcate, and unless there is independence, the cause of civilization is neglected. Individual professors can raise their fists and cry out against the howling of the storm; but professors so inclined are resident alike at Berkeley, as at New Haven. The critical difference is the corporate sense of mission. At Berkeley that sense of mission is as diffuse and inchoate—and unspecified and unspecifiable—as the resolute pluralism of California society. At the private college, the sense of mission is distinguishing. It is, however, strangled by what goes under the presumptuous designation of academic freedom. It is a terrible loss, the loss of the sense of mission. It makes the private university, sad to say, incoherent; and that is what I was trying to say when, two months out of Yale, I sat down to write this book.

XII.

Sport

We Learned to Ski

November 9, 1975

"EFFICIENT SKIING requires us to stand flat on both skis and to be able to roll over each ski (edge it) to the same angle. To do that most of us need to some varying degree to have wedges of plastic or metal between boot and ski to compensate for our natural stance."

If you do not ski, or aspire to, this passage is as arresting as a resolution of the General Assembly of the United Nations. If you do ski, it is quite simply electrifying. It is as if you picked up a tax aid book somewhere that had in it the casual comment: "If on completing your income tax return you will remember to add the number 2X 37 08 after your name, you may, by the working of an obscure provision of the law, cut your income tax in half."

I exaggerate? I have skied every winter for twenty-one winters, in every country except maybe Guatemala. I take lessons these days from the grandchildren of those who first taught me. *And I never heard of wedges before.* Apparently this is not a coincidence, either of a conspiracy by my teachers to keep the goose unsteady on his feet the better to lay more eggs; or of an eccentric tone-deafness on the matter of the wedges. "Most resorts have barely heard of wedges, and they are almost universally ignored in textbooks on skiing."

What is also ignored in textbooks on skiing is usable material on how to ski. I leafed through a number of them years ago, and can report that, in twenty years, no skier has said to me: "*There* is a book on skiing you must read." The reason is that the textbooks are almost universally the product of expert skiers who, while trying to demonstrate their knowledge of skiing, succeed only in demonstrating their incapacity to communicate that knowledge. Commonly, their faults are either a jargon that quickly leaves the reader with the feeling that he has stumbled into a graduate school seminar conducted in German; or else a complex of instructions that leaves the reader feeling entirely helpless.

"Remember, while holding out your hip uphill, to exert downhill pressure with your ankles, forward pressure on the balls of your feet, while maintaining a slightly oblique inclination, pointing roughly at 10:30 o'clock (Amundsen and Clark, concededly, would say 11 o'clock, though we respectfully disagree) along the axis of your shoulders, making certain that your seat is parallel to your skis, notwithstanding any hip motion, or the necessity to keep your downhill arm balanced relaxedly at right angles (Masterson and Leif would, concededly, prefer an angle of 100 degrees) to the fall line." Whether such instructions are delivered in writing by ski teachers or orally by them, those are the moments—more so by far than any physical misadventure—when the mind turns to beach life. Messrs. Evans, Jackman and Ottaway have now given us an alternative, and I am not surprised to learn that it is a best-seller in Great Britain.

The temptation always in pedagogy is to communicate everything you know. The instinct is born of a combination of vanity and magnanimity. I do not know whether the authors in fact know more than they tell us about the morphology of skiing, but if they do, I most heartily congratulate them on their restraint in keeping to themselves material entirely unnecessary to the attainment of the skill to which so many of us aspire: how to ski competently, safely and gracefully. They satisfy only the normal curiosity, and in doing so they take care first to provoke that curiosity. "The secret of the turning ski is the 'side' cut of the ski." The secret! Everybody loves a secret. They then tell you something easily graspable by non-mechanical minds, but stop well short of the frontier of physics—again, whether out of ignorance or editorial instinct one knows not, being content to express either gratitude, or admiration, as called for.

The book is full of fascinating information, neatly and readably brought together. They even think, toward the end, to remind us to have a look at the mountains while skiing. And, at the beginning, to console ourselves with the extraordinary statistic that the average skier needs medical help after 200 days of skiing, and 400 days of not skiing—it is only twice as dangerous to slide down the mountain on two narrow planks of wood, as to walk your dog in Scarsdale. The concern by the authors for safety leads them to implore us, at one point in the book describing how we should test our safety bindings, to "Please do that." They succeed, moreover, in giving the impression that they and we are learning jointly, and develop an almost confessional intimacy as we move along. "This was our commonest fault," they tell us in the chapter on how to handle a mogul. You are tempted to call them up to recite your particular problems. Stylistic lapses are so rare as to make one suspect they are the responsibility of a wayward editor. (I decline to believe that Messrs. Evans, Jackman and Ottaway were responsible for the subhead, "Is your traverse a travesty?")

The authors are not ski teachers. Indeed, Mr. Evans did not begin to ski until he was forty. He is the editor of *The Sunday Times* of London. The other two gentlemen, also late starters as skiers, are his associates, as are the illustrators, who, in a perfectly spliced volume, make vivid what the authors are talking about through the use of photographs, sketches and red ink. It is a masterful job of pedagogy, and St. Martin's is hereby congratulated on bringing the book out at $12.95. It required that they reproduce photographically the English text, with the mildly annoying national idiosyncrasies ("ski-ing"). But, after all, the English invented not only the language but, for all intents and purposes, the sport; and they have certainly cornered the market now in an instructional manual that, although it will need to be brought up to date from time to time to keep pace with improvements in ski technology and hardware, is unlikely to be improved on in the lifetime of its authors.

Learning to Fly

September 1977

I HAD NO FEAR of flying when I matriculated at Yale but a very considerable fear of my father's learning that I had taken up a sport that, in 1946, he was unprepared to concede was anything more than rank technological presumption, fit only for daredevils. It turned out that several of my co-conspirators had fathers with similar prejudices, so that when our little syndicate was formed, we all agreed that communications to each other on the subject of our surreptitious hobby would go forward discreetly, lest they be intercepted. During the Christmas holidays, it was my duty to send out the accrued bills from the little grass-strip airport at Bethany where we lodged *Alexander's Horse* (as we called the little Ercoupe), and I realized, envelope in hand, I could not remember whether T. Leroy Morgan, one of the six partners, was a junior. With a name like that, I felt he must surely be a junior—was there any other excuse? On the other hand, if I wrote "Jr." after this name and my friend was in fact the "III," then his father would open the letter. I assumed his father must be formidable, since who else would live at One Quincy Street, Chevy Chase, Maryland?

So, to play it safe, I addressed the letter to: "T. Leroy Morgan—the one who goes to Yale, One Quincy Street, Chevy Chase, Maryland." It happened that, at the breakfast table distributing the mail among the family, Mr. Morgan *père* displayed an imperious curiosity about the contents of a letter so manifestly intended to be seen only by his son.

I will contract the suspense and say that in no time at all, the word passed around a circle of fathers, reaching my own. Whenever my father was faced with rank transgression by any of his ten children, he replied to it in one of two ways, sometimes both. His first line of attack would be to announce that the child could not afford whatever it was my father disapproved. He tried that for an entire year in his running war against cigarettes, but the effect was ruined when we all saw

The Grapes of Wrath and Henry Fonda, between heaves of hunger, kept smoking. His second line of attack would be to ignore the delinquency, pretending it simply did not exist. Thus one of my brothers, who hated to practice the piano, was relieved from ever having to play it again by the simple expedient of being held up by my father in public discussions of the matter as the most exemplary pianist in the family.

I received a brisk memorandum (his reproachful communications were normally rendered in that mode) advising me that he had "learned" that I was "flying an airplane" at college, and that the distractions to my academic career quite apart, I clearly could not afford such an extravagance. One didn't argue with Father, who in any case would never return to the subject except in a vague, sarcastic way. Three years later, he would write my prospective father-in-law, "You will find it very easy to entertain Bill when he visits you. You need only provide him with a horse, a yacht or an airplane."

And so for the few months of our joint venture, we continued to pass around the bills, like tablets in pre-Christian Rome. They were not, by current standards, frightening. Our capital was $1,800—$300 apiece. We paid that exactly for the second-hand airplane. We decided, after getting quotations from the insurance companies, to insure ourselves, subject to a $300 deductible payable by the offending partner. Anyone using the plane would pay his own gas, oil and instructor. All capital improvements would have to be approved unanimously. Anybody could sell his one-sixth interest to anyone at any time. Reservations to use the airplane would be filed with the secretary of the *Yale Daily News.* These, we satisfied ourselves, were surely the most informal articles of association in modern history, though I suppose it is appropriate to add that the association was one of the briefest in history.

I was off to a very bad start. My experience was akin to arriving at a casino for the first time at age twenty and winning a dozen straight passes at the crap table. When Bob Kraut, my instructor—a dour, hungry ex-army pilot, ex-mechanic, owner of the starveling little airport, who would sell you anything from a new airplane to a Milky Way—took me up for an hour's instruction, I could not believe how easy it all was. I remember it to this day: check the oil, check the gas, turn your wheel and check ailerons, pull and check elevator. Run your engine at 1,500 rpm, check one magneto, then the second, then back to both. Then gun her up to 2,250. Then exercise the knob that said "carburetor heat." Then head into the wind (or as close as possible at the single-strip field), push the throttle all the way forward, roll down the strip, when you reach sixty miles per hour ease the wheel back, and after the plane lifts off, push the wheel forward to level until you reach eighty mph. Then adjust your trim tab to maintain a speed of eighty mph. Rise to 600 feet on your course, then turn left until you get to 800 feet. Then do anything you want.

Landing? Go back to approximately where you were when you hit 800 feet and proceed downwind twice the length of the field while descending to 600 feet. Then turn left descending to 400 feet. (I forgot something: you should pull out your carburetor heat when you begin your descent.) Then turn in toward the field, reducing your throttle to idling speed, coast down, glance sideways—which helps perspective—don't let your speed fall under eighty mph till you are over the field, then keep easing the wheel back until your tires touch down, at which point *immediately* set your nosewheel right down; Ercoupes, you see, had no separate rudders, the wheel incorporating that function—a nice advantage except that you cannot cope easily with crosswind landings.

The first lesson consumed an hour, the second a half hour, and that very night I was speaking to a forlorn junior who had been a pilot during the war and grieved greatly that he could not be the following day at dinner with his inamorata in Boston. Why could he not? Because his car wasn't working, and no train would get him up in time, since he could not leave until after lunch. I found myself saying, as though I were P. G. Wodehouse himself, "Why my dear friend, grieve no more. I shall fly you to Boston."

It was all very well for my friend, who with 2,000 hours' flying, navigated us expertly to Boston, landed the airplane and waved me a happy good-bye. I was left at Boston Airport, headed back to Bethany, Connecticut, never having so-loed and having flown a total of three times.

Well, the only thing to do was to proceed. I remembered that the plane came equipped with a radio of sorts and that my friend had exchanged arcane observations and senti-ments with the tower coming in, so as I sashayed to the end of the runway, I flipped the switch—and found myself tuned in to an episode of "Life Can Be Beautiful." I truly didn't know how to account for this, and I remember even thinking fleetingly that when the traffic was light, perhaps the tower entertained area traffic by wiring it in to the controller's fa-vorite program. This bizarre thought I managed to over-come, but it was too late to stop and fiddle with a radio I hadn't been instructed in the use of, so I went through my lit-tle motions, looked about to see that I wasn't in anybody's way, and zoomed off.

I was flying not exactly contentedly that bright autumn day. I felt a little lonely, and a little apprehensive, though I did not know exactly why. I was past Providence, Rhode Is-land, when suddenly my heart began to ice up as I recog-nized that either I was quickly going blind or the sun was go-ing down. I looked at my watch. We should have another hour and a half of light! Ah so, except that I had neglected to account for the switch overnight away from daylight saving time. I had put forward my watch dutifully at about mid-night, but today I thought in terms of light until about 7 P.M., same as yesterday. I looked at the air chart, so awfully clut-tered and concentrated by comparison with those lovely, de-scriptive, onomatopoeic ocean charts you can read as easily as a comic book. I discerned that the New York, New Haven & Hartford railroad tracks passed within a few hundred yards of the airport at Groton. I descended, lower and lower, as the white began to fade, as from an overexposed negative soaking up developing solution. By the time I reached Gro-ton, I was flying at 100 feet, and when I spotted the lights on the runway for the airfield, I was as grateful as if, coming up from the asphyxiative depths, I had reached oxygen.

I approached the field, did the ritual turns and landed without difficulty—my first, exhilarating solo landing; my first night landing; on the whole, the culmination of my most egregious stupidity. But there we were: plane and pilot, intact. I hitchhiked to the station, waited for a train, and by 10 o'clock was sitting at a bar in New Haven, chatting with my roommate about this and that. I never gave, a thought to Mr. Kraut.

I have been awakened by angry voices, but by none to equal Robert Kraut's the following morning. While hauling the plane from the hangar, an assistant at the airfield had overheard me conversing excitedly with my friend on my impending solo flight from Boston to New York. In the internalizing tradition of New England, he had said nothing to me about my projected violation of the law. But he spoke to his boss about it later in the afternoon, who exploded with rage and apprehension. Kraut called the tower at Boston, which told of an Ercoupe having landed and then taken off at 4:07, without communication with the tower. Kraut calculated that I would arrive in the Bethany area in total darkness and thereupon began frantically collecting friends and passersby, who ringed the field with their headlights, providing a workmanlike illumination of a country strip. Then they waited. And waited. Finally, at about 10, Kraut knew I must be out of fuel and, therefore, on the ground somewhere other than at Bethany. Whether alive or dead, no one could say, but at least, Kraut growled into the telephone, he had the pleasure of *hoping* I was dead. *Why hadn't I called him?* I explained, lamely, that I did not know he even knew about my flight let alone that he thought to provide for my safe return. He consoled himself by itemizing lasciviously all the extra charges he intended to put on my bill for his exertions and those of his friends, which charges the executive committee of *Alexander's Horse* Associates voted unanimously and without extensive discussion would be paid exclusively by me.

I got my clearance to solo; and, twenty flying hours later, my license to fly other people. I am compelled to admit that I cheated a little in logging those twenty hours, giving the odd half-hour's flight in the benefit of the doubt, listing it at one hour, and I feel bad about this. But I did achieve a limited proficiency, and I would often go out to the field and take up a friend for a jaunty half-hour or so in my little silver monoplane, though I never felt confident enough to do any serious cross-country work, having no serviceable radio.

I remember two experiences before the final episode. In the early spring I invited aboard a classmate, a seasoned navy veteran pilot. We roared off the lumpy field under an overcast that the mechanic on duty assured us was 1,200 feet high. It wasn't. The Bethany airport is 700 feet above sea level, and at 1,000 feet, we were entirely enveloped in cloud. I had never experienced such a thing, and the sensation was terrifying, robbing you, in an instant, of all the relevant coordinates of normal life, including any sense of what is up and down. We would need, I calculated, to maintain altitude and fly south until we figured ourselves well over Long Island Sound. Then turn east and descend steadily, until we broke out unencumbered by New England foothills; then crawl over to the New Haven airport, which is at sea level. I willingly gave over the controls to my friend Ray, who assumed them with great competence as we began our maneuver. Then suddenly there was a hole in the clouds, and he dove for it, swooping into the Bethany strip, landing not more than three minutes after our departure. I stayed scared after that one and resolved never again to risk flying in overcast.

Then there was the bright spring day with the lazy-summer temperature. My exams, it happened, were banked during the first two days of a ten-day exam period. In between I did not sleep but did take Benzedrine. Walking out of the final exam at five the second afternoon, numb with fatigue and elation, I was wild with liberty, and I knew I must stretch my limbs in the sky. So I drove out to Bethany, pulled out *Alexander's Horse* and zoomed off by myself, heading toward downtown New Haven and climbing to 4,000 invigorating feet. There I fell asleep.

I have ever since understood what they mean when they write about the titanic intellectual-muscular energy required to keep one's eyes open when they are set on closing. What happened was that the drug had suddenly worn off, and the biological imperative was asserting itself with vindictive adamance. It was, curiously, only after I landed that I found it relatively easy to summon the adrenalin to stay awake for long enough to make it back to my bedroom. In the tortured fifteen minutes in the air, my eyes closed a dozen times between the moment I discovered myself asleep and the moment I landed. It is safer to learn these things about the human body aboard a sailboat than an airplane. Boats can be dangerous, but they don't often sink when you go to sleep at the wheel.

My final flight, like so many others, was propelled by a certain mental fog. My best friend at Yale became engaged to my favorite sister. All my siblings had met Brent, save my poor sister Maureen, cloistered at the Ethel Walker School, in Simsbury, Connecticut. I would instantly remedy that, and I wrote my sister, age fifteen, telling her to send a map of the huge lawn that rolls out from the school (which I had many times seen while attending various graduations of older sisters). It arrived by return mail—on all accounts the most nonchalant map in the history of cartography. At the east end, she had drawn vertical lines marked "trees." Running parallel from the top and bottom of that line to the west were two more lines, also marked "trees." At the extreme left end of the paper she had marked "main schoolhouse." Armed with that map and my future brother-in-law, I set out on a bright spring afternoon for Simsbury, which was about an hour's flight away.

I found the school and flew around it a couple of times with a creeping agitation. My sister having advised her classmates of my impending arrival, the entire school was out on the lawn, and, when they spotted us, their great cheer reached us through the roar of the little engine. The trees at the east side happened to be the tallest trees this side of the California redwoods. I buzzed them a time or two. Could they really be *that* tall? I estimated them at a couple hundred feet. That meant I would have to come over them, then drop very sharply, because a normal landing approach would have had me three-quarters down the length of the lawn before touch-down. "Well," I said to my stoical friend, "what do you say?" Fortunately, he knew nothing about flying.

I was terribly proud of the way I executed it all, and I wished Mr. Kraut had been there to admire the deftness with which I managed to sink down after skimming the treetops,

SPORT 461

touching down on the lawn as though it were an eggshell. I looked triumphantly over to Brent as our speed reduced to thirty mph. The very next glimpse I had of him was, so to speak, upsidedownsideways. We hit a drainage ditch, unmarked by my sister, that traversed the lawn. The problem now was quite straightforward. The aircraft was nosed down absolutely vertical into the ditch, into which we had perfect visibility. We were held by our seat belts, without which our heads would be playing the role of our feet. We were there at least a full minute before the girls came. I am not sure I recall the conversation exactly, but it was on the order of:

"Are we alive?"

"I think so."

"What happened?"

"Ditch."

"Why did you run into it?"

"Very funny."

"Well, why didn't you fly over it?"

"We had landed. We were just braking down."

But the girls, with high good humor, giggles and exertion, managed to pry us out. We dusted ourselves off outside the vertical plane, attempted languidly to assert our dignity, and were greeted most politely by the headmistress, who said she had tea ready in anticipation of our arrival. We walked sedately up the lawn to her living room, accompanied by Maureen and two roommates. The talk was of spring, Yale, summer plans, the Attlee Government and General MacArthur, but Maureen and her friends would, every now and then, emit uncontainable giggles, which we manfully ignored. It all went moderately well under the circumstances until the knock on the door. An assistant to the headmistress arrived, to ask whether her guests had any use for—"this," and she held forth *Alexander's Horse*'s propeller or, rather, most of the propeller. I told her thank you very much, but broken propellers were not of any particular use to anyone, and she was free to discard it.

Eventually we left, having arranged by telephone with Mr. Kraut to come and fetch the corpse at his convenience. We returned to New Haven by bus. Brent, who had a good book along, did not seem terribly surprised, even after I assured him that most of my airplane rides out of Bethany were round trips.

Oh, the sadness of the ending. The plane was barely restored when, during a lesson, one of my partners was pleased by hearing his instructor say as they approached the strip for a landing, "You're hot!" My friend figured, in the idiom of the day, that this meant he was proceeding splendidly, so he nosed the ship on down, crashing it quite completely. As he later explained, what reason did he have to know that, in the jargon of the trade, to say you were "hot" meant, "You're going too fast"? He had a point. The estimate to repair *Alexander's Horse* was an uncanny $1,800—exactly what we had paid for it. Mournfully, we decided to let her rest, selling the carcass for $100. Father was right, as usual. I couldn't afford to fly.

At Sea

August 1976

I HAVE HAD the curious career of sailing since I was thirteen but having sailed only four times other than as captain of the vessel I was on. Except for reading about it, I am somewhat ignorant of how other captains and their crews behave. The first of the four exceptions was aboard my own boat, in my first ocean race, the Vineyard Race, from Stamford to the lightship off Martha's Vineyard and back—260 miles, over a three-day weekend in 1955. My experience had been only on lakes and, after buying *The Panic*—a forty-four-foot steel cutter, and my first ocean boat—a couple of weeks of poking about on Long Island Sound before signing on for the race. I asked a friend of vast experience to serve as skipper, and he agreed. He had raced at sea all his life, and during that weekend I learned much about starting tactics, racing strategy, flag protocol, current and drift anticipation, and weight distribution; and about the importance to me of the skipper's having a relentless, if tough-minded, good humor.

The next spring, having resolved to make the glamorous Bermuda Race, I looked again for a skipper. I was still too inexperienced to be my own captain, and had not yet taught myself celestial navigation. A young banker was recommended, but he withdrew late in the spring after detecting an insuperable incompatibility between us. My friend of the Vineyard Race (he was himself committed to another vessel) suggested an old sailing partner from St. Louis, who turned out to be agreeable and competent, and I also brought on the phlegmatic, genial, super-competent Mike Mitchell, who was then my insurance agent and is now running the motel and yacht marina at Christmas Cove, Maine. And all went well, if that can be said about any ocean passage.

It was five years before I sailed under another skipper. This was at the invitation of Mike Mitchell, who was acting as first mate on a gorgeous thoroughbred in an afternoon race on Long Island Sound. The owner-skipper, altogether civil on shore, became the legendary tyrant on board, and yelled orders as though he were Ahab espying the whale at last. These orders came out in a complex, largely incoherent tangle, omnidirectionally beamed to his eight subjects—including one sixteen-year-old, whom he addressed only as "Boy!" All this commotion seemed especially incongruous in an afternoon of winds so lazy they nearly fell asleep in the sun. At one point, I walked over to the windward side to slacken a snagged genoa sheet, and the skipper exploded with imprecations to the effect that I had fatally unbalanced the boat. I looked sidewise at Mike Mitchell, who returned me a Yankee smile, part pain, part amusement, part cunning—Mike sold insurance to the old tyrant. It was worse that every time he spoke he proved he knew less about sailing than any of the eight of us. Less, even, than Boy! One leaves such people alone. Permanently.

Ten years after that, I was invited to sail in an overnight race with my hero. My hero was William Snaith, whose book *Across the Western Ocean* I had read with near-idolatrous pleasure. We knew each other only slightly, and when, expan-

sively, he asked me at a friend's house one night if I would
like to navigate for him the following weekend, I accepted,
with trepidation. It was as if Toscanini had invited me to take
the concertmaster's chair at his concert the following weekend. I would be sailing, for the first time, on a boat every
member of whose crew could be expected to be a finished
ocean racer. I recognized, when I was introduced to them,
two of Snaith's sons and a regular sailing companion, described in Snaith's book. The mood struck at the outset was a
kind of short, competent civility irradiating from the volatile,
brilliant skipper. Before it was over, the rhetoric had developed into a surrealistic, sustained hostility, mostly between
the skipper and his older son, spokesman for the crew, which
I understood to be metaphorical in nature, but which once or
twice flirted toward a stridency that froze my blood. Such
rhetoric, I take it, is accepted as entirely routine aboard
many happy vessels, but I was already too old to adapt to that
kind of thing. Besides, even if I could succeed in breaking a
lifetime habit and substituting billingsgate for my normal
hearty command, laced only with a little genial sarcasm when
its absence would clearly disappoint, perhaps even confuse, I
would so surprise my companions that they would either
walk off or send in their resignations on reaching home.

Your companions on board are a crucial consideration.
For me, there is one no-further-questions-asked disqualifer:
personal rudeness of any sort—and rudeness includes any
sign of impatience. (The exception: the captain, or the
helmsman, shouting out impatiently the need for a snatch
block, a flashlight, a Scotch-and-soda.) I know of a yacht that
raced across the Atlantic, everyone aboard a perfect gentleman but inexperienced in the absoluteness of the law of
proper shipboard behavior. And so it happened that a few
days out, A watch made a rather provocative entry in the log
respecting the inferior achievements of B watch during the
antecedent tour of duty. B watch fired back in its own entry
four hours later. After twenty-two days, arriving at Santan-
der, Spain, the four members of A watch and the four members of B watch got off the boat with their gear, and from
that moment on no member of either watch ever addressed a

single word to a member of the other, even when they were all cozily back in New York, or whatever.

Aboard a yacht, the resonance of bad humor shatters everything that the entire experience is designed to bring you—like an alarm clock going off in Carnegie Hall. I remember years ago resolving never again to invite to race with me one friend for the simple sin, on his day as breakfast cook, of responding to a request from the cockpit to pass the honey with "Can't you just wait a minute!" On board, the protocol is that anyone will do anything for anyone—the perfect crucible for the Golden Rule. "While you're below, would you bring me up some foul-weather gear [my sunglasses] [my book] [an aspirin]?" is the operative social convention aboard a sailing boat. It was pushed to its limit one day by a famous yacht designer when his eighteen-year-old son slipped down the companionway to visit the head, leaving the father and six companions at the wheel: "John? While you're below, would you cook dinner?"

I engaged once in a polemic with Norris Hoyt, a veteran seaman who taught English to fortunate students at St. George's School, in Newport, and is now retired. He took public issue with me over a complaint I had published against the creeping professionalization of sailing. In pointing out the mysterious inexactitude of specialized knowledge about a boat and its accessories, I gave as only one of many examples the demonstrated inadequacy of foul-weather gear advertised as competent to keep a man dry at sea. With great huff, Mr. Hoyt (whom I subsequently discovered to be a most engaging and undogmatic man) replied in a published article that he had made numerous transatlantic crossings in his life, and that he had not once—not *once*—been either cold or wet. Now, you must understand the gravity of this kind of boast in the amateur community I write of. It is—simply—*unbelievable.*

In his article, Mr. Hoyt gave a step-by-step account of just how he handles the problem of dressing for the cold and the wet. His methods remind me of my trip to the Antarctic, before which I submitted to a technician's lecture on how to keep warm. I walked away from the lecture with a trunk-load of clothes supplied by the United States Navy which, when I donned them, left me entirely comfortable in temperatures that brushed up against fifty below zero. But I must add that it could not have taken the Queen of England as long to dress for her Coronation as it took me to put on my costume in the mornings I was in the Antarctic; and it is a wonder that Mr. Hoyt has any time to devote to watch duty after preparing himself for it. But let us leave the point moot and agree to say modestly: You *can* keep warm on a boat, but the preparations necessary for doing so vitiate, substantially, the pleasure of the day's sail.

On the matter of keeping dry, I remain, perforce, a skeptic. My brother-in-law Austin Taylor, who is called Firpo, believes in attacking problems head on, and he designed his own foul-weather gear for our first race to Bermuda. It was the grandest and most elaborate piece of gear I have ever seen, not less imposing for its responsibility of keeping dry 250 pounds of human flesh. It had rubber gloves with shock-cord belts, all-directional zippers, seamless balaclavas—everything except, perhaps, a catheter tube. The first hard wave that tore into *The Panic's* cockpit left Firpo totally drenched and, on top of that, facing twenty minutes of disassembly before he could dry his bare skin. A sailing companion who had observed with awe the design and engineering of the ultimate foul-weather suit comforted Firpo with a practical suggestion for the next trip: "You must go to a garage, strip, and have yourself vulcanized."

I have done a lot of racing—on a lake as a boy, and at sea on *The Panic* and its successor, *Suzy Wong*, a forty-foot yawl. Since 1972, my sailing has all been cruising, mostly aboard *Cyrano*, a sixty-foot schooner I bought in 1968, but I am not absolutely sure that if *Suzy* and I had developed into a highly successful racing combination I wouldn't be out there racing still. Though the estrangement from racing came gradually, I think I can trace the seeds of it to 1965. I disappeared surreptitiously from the campaign for mayor of New York in order to participate in the race from Marblehead, Massachusetts, to Halifax, Nova Scotia, which I had roughly the same chance of winning. Though it was a rough ride, my crew— Peter Starr, my (young) old friend, who began sailing with me twenty-one years ago, when he was thirteen; Reginald Stoops, my plastics-engineer buddy; Evan Galbraith, my classmate, lawyer, banker, and splendid companion; and two friends with whom I now raced more or less regularly— managed *Suzy* well. We made no significant errors in seamanship or navigation or strategy, but when we finally slipped across the finish line there was only a single boat that hadn't yet come in. (It was F. Lee Bailey's. He told me later that on learning I had beaten him he deserted ocean racing and bought a jet airplane. I comforted him by telling him that at least he had effected an economy.) By contrast, in the very first race to Bermuda on *The Panic*, we had done quite creditably, halfway in our class.

Suzy, although she was designed by Sparkman & Stephens, which is like saying about a violin that it was made by Stradivarius, could never live up to her theoretical rating—that is, her rating under something called the Rule. The first comprehensive Rule was formulated by the Cruising Club of America in the mid-1930's; there are now other Rules, formulated by other sailing organizations, but yachtsmen speak simply of "the Rule." The Rule is designed to make all vessels that compete in an ocean race theoretically equal in speed by imposing graduated handicaps. These are calculated by such compounded anfractuosities that nowadays only a half-dozen men even affect to understand the Rule, and no one can give you your rating without feeding all the relevant factors into a computer—not just any computer but a monster type bunkered somewhere on Long Island for the purpose of guiding missiles to Mars and giving yachtsmen their ratings. The original idea of the Rule was to keep ocean racing from being only a rich man's sport. It is still such a sport, substantially, but certainly not so much so as it would have been in the absence of the Rule. The first handicaps imposed under the Rule were designed to discourage the idea that every yachtsman had to own two boats—one to race in, the other to be comfortable in. Fifty years ago, it was assumed that a very narrow-hulled boat would easily beat a boat with a beamy hull. Since narrow hulls make for uncomfortable living quarters, the very rich had begun the practice of racing in their sleek, thin boats, after which ordeal their second boats, tubby and comfortable, would rescue them from asceticism.

Other factors crept in as the Rule grew in complexity: for instance, the desirable balance between safety and speed. In order to support a mast on which you have run up a huge stretch of canvas whose purpose is to trap the wind and convert its force into forward motion, you must relieve it of unbearable strain. The cables that reach from the head of the mast fore and aft (they are called, respectively, the headstay and the backstay) present no problem. The angle going up from the bow and the stern will be sufficiently acute to give the mast fore and aft stability. But the two cables that go to the beams ends of a boat (they are called shrouds) are something else. Exaggerate the problem. Suppose your responsibility is to secure a thousand-foot-high radio tower. If you ran wires from the top of the tower to points not more than six feet away from the base, you would have shrouds that ran very nearly parallel to the tower itself, providing practically no additional support. Accordingly, the closer to the base of the tower the shrouds are fastened, the heavier they have to be. At the other extreme, if you were permitted to go out, say, 500 feet from the base on either side to rivet down the shrouds, you would end with an equilateral triangle of sorts, and the shrouds would head up from the ground to the top at a comfortable angle of sixty degrees, permitting relatively light cable. So it is on a boat. The wider the beam, the easier it is to provide stability for the mast, with a light cable. The slimmer the beam, conversely, the more difficult the matter of stability, and the greater the need for heavy cable; and, ultimately—since something has to give if you keep narrowing the beam—you will have to shorten the mast. The Rule penalizes masts according to their length.

Every two years or so, the Rule is changed, mostly to frustrate the loop-holer, the Rule-beater. One inventive yachtsman discovered that *his* handicap was decreased much more than his speed by his simply eliminating his mainsail. By a single modification in the Rule, a hundred million dollars of racing boat can be anachronized. Nowadays, a successful racing boat is a tangle of expensive mechanisms designed to beat the Rule. *Suzy*, with her noble teak, is probably too heavy to have profited even from radical surgery. We raced her in 1971, in the annual race from Stamford to Martha's Vineyard and back. Once again, boat and crew were in nearly perfect sync, and once again we trailed the fleet. So in due course I retired her from regular campaigning, though I would still race her, if I got around to it, for the fun of it, which was mostly why I raced her and *The Panic* all those years—my point being that an ocean race is really a test of yourself and your crew, that there are too many variables to permit one to conclude that this vessel or crew is superior to that other vessel or crew.

There are, of course, considerable differences between racing and cruising. Normally, a cruise is conceived as a daytime sail from one harbor to another. You arrive late in the afternoon, drop anchor, swim, hike, have a drink, cook and eat dinner, and then perhaps play cards, simply talk, or address yourself to an especially recalcitrant part of the boat's equipment which you neglected during the day. Everyone eventually turns in, sleeps soundly, wakes up rested. The whole of the ship's complement is up, and down, together.

So is it in the daytime race as well. It is when you sail over distances requiring shifts in crew that the nature of the experience radically changes. When you race, you need more men on watch: at least three (in a boat up to fifty feet long), and if you need to perform intricate work, such as jibing the spinnaker or reefing the mainsail, you generally wake up a fourth. When you cruise, you don't, in serene circumstances, need more than two men on watch. This means that in overnight cruising you are on duty less than half the time. To go on duty for four hours, then off duty for eight hours, is manifestly more relaxing than to go back on duty after only four hours off. Moreover, since under such arrangements you have roughly sixteen hours of leisure to deploy, there is more time to be gregarious, to read, to attend to miscellaneous projects.

That is one difference between cruising and racing—important, but not really the principal difference. During a race, when the wind is very light—two or three knots—you itch with frustration, and tread carefully as you go back and forth on deck lest you upset the delicately weighted list of the boat, calculated to expose the sails most seductively to the anemic wind. In gale force, you struggle to keep hoisted the maximum serviceable canvas, driving the boat through discomfort as fast as you can make it go without blowing out the sails or generating counterproductive nose dives into the sea or heeling over so far as to neutralize the top area of your sail. If you are working in the wind—that is, if you are zigzagging toward your objective, because it lies ahead of you in the same direction whence blows the wind—you strap in the sails ("close-hauled"), and the boat heels over, making its way over and under breaking waves, which periodically roar down the deck and inundate you, your sandwich, and, occasionally, your spirits. There is the single objective: to get there as fast as possible.

When you cruise and the wind roars, you reef, or even lower, a sail that is inimical to your special purposes. It does not matter to you that during that night you will travel seventy miles instead of seventy-five. And anyway, over the long haul—over stretches of sea in which all sorts of conditions are met—you will get where you are going as soon as the racer, because you will use engine power during the slack stretches. Although there is no reason to emasculate a sailing boat when cruising, and no way to assure comfort—in very heavy weather a boat racing and a boat cruising will behave almost identically—there are times when little concessions, made at the sacrifice of speed, give you a margin of comfort you are denied in a race: dousing your genoa jib (the largest) and putting up the No. 2 at midnight if it is getting rough; leaving off the fisherman in a schooner or the mizzen staysail in a yawl; leaving the reef tucked in for an extra hour when the wind lightens, instead of shaking it out the moment you think the boat is capable of taking the extra strain.

Mike Mitchell used to sail with an old friend, the owner of a racing boat, and the friend's freshly taken wife. The wife was unshakable in her belief that there was no reason at all for a sailboat to right itself after being knocked on its side, with the result that whenever the boat heeled over sharply

she would don her life preserver, recite her prayers, and prepare to abandon ship—a comprehensively distracting performance in a Sunday afternoon's race. Mike's friend finally
took his wife to a psychiatrist for help. The psychiatrist, himself a sailor, prescribed for her one of those roly-poly dolls
that little children amuse themselves with. They knock it
down, only to see it bounce up again. It is Wimpy-like in
shape, with, instead of feet, a sealed bowl full of bird shot.
Even if you tilt the head right down on the floor, the weight
of the bird shot easily overcomes the light weight of the head,
rolling the doll back on its feet. Thus, the doctor explained, a
sailboat. If you have ten thousand pounds of lead (exactly
what we had on *The Panic*) at the bottom of six feet of keel
(the depth of ours), and the boat is pushed over on its
(rounded) side, then you have 60,000 pounds of pressure
agitating to right that boat. Meanwhile, since the boat's mast,
in the hypothesis, is now parallel to the water, or almost parallel, the sails have obviously lost the air power that knocked
the boat over. Accordingly, with 60,000 pounds insisting on
rectitude vs. zero pounds insisting on distortion, the boat will
right.

When the woman heard this explanation, she asked, "Why
do some boats sink, then?"

"Other factors," her husband snapped.

This woman's opinion of sailboats was shared by my wife,
Pat, but I was able to persuade Pat early in our cruising career (she resolutely refused to race), even without the roly-
poly doll, that a sailboat *will* right itself. Nevertheless, the second day out on *The Panic* I noticed a two-inch section of that
omnipresent plastic tape from which you punch out labels
and the like. It was pegged to the circumference of the boat's
inclinometer, a four-dollar piece of hardware you tack on the
cockpit bulkhead. The inclinometer has a pendulum that in-
dicates, on an arc, the angle of the boat's heel at any given
moment. Opposite the twenty-five-degree point on the scale
was the tape, reading "PATSY GETS OFF."

For *years*, I whispered in Pat's ear the safety features of
oceangoing sailboats. I even told her that, in a sense, the
smaller the boat, the *greater* the safety—as a cork bobbing on
the water is indestructible, whereas a destroyer clearly isn't.

That was a mistake; thereafter, she rejoiced at any opportunity to lavish on her friends my implied preference for riding out a storm on a cork instead of on the Queen Elizabeth. In my flying days, before we were married, and before I learned to say "I'm going to do it anyway," I tried telling her that gliders, which I had recently cultivated, were actually safer than airplanes with engines, because something could go wrong with an engine but the glider depended only on gravity and updrafts. That became another of her favorites, and she has several times suggested, with radiant scorn, and in disgustingly appreciative company, that I should communicate my insight to Pan American, which by doing away with its engines would increase its safety record and save a lot of money.

And, it is true, I háve had a few unpleasant experiences at sea—one or two of them with her aboard.

My first misadventure happened in the spring of my second year at the Millbrook School. I was sixteen. Four years earlier, in 1938, my father had transported two of my sisters and me, much against our will, to boarding school in England for a year. I had detected a bargaining position, and asked my father if, on my return from England, he would give me a sailboat. He was better than his word, giving me not only a sailboat but a sailing instructor, who spent the summer with me. The boat was a seventeen-foot Barracuda-class sloop, and I kept it at Lake Wononskopomuc, about seven miles from our home in Sharon, Connecticut. The lake, which is also known as Lakeville Lake, is very beautiful, about one square mile, spring fed, surrounded by high, wooded hills. It then had two landmarks. At one end was the Hotchkiss School. At the other, Wanda Landowska.

All summer for three summers, we raced three days a week, twice each day, a ragtag fleet of six boats, each of different design. The dictator of the fleet was a retired martinet who had served in some nautical capacity during the First World War and never got over it. He rejoiced at any infraction of the rules, because it permitted him to schedule, at his lakeside cottage, a court-martial of sorts, which he conducted with great gravity, managing nearly full attendance by the primitively effective expedient of giving all the boat-owners a great deal of whiskey to drink, to help them endure the discipline of his ruling, which, after much exegesis, he would eventually divulge. The five other boat-owners ranged in age from twenty-five to fifty; I was thirteen that first summer, and I had never before (nor have I since) devoted myself so completely to any single enterprise. Seventy-five races a summer for three summers may strike some as a few races too many. It struck me as too few races by far, and I would go to bed Tuesday and Friday and Saturday nights in delirious anticipation of the next day's drama on the water, waking early to see how the wind was blowing. My boat, *Sweet Isolation* (I named it in honor of my father's political preferences in 1939), did very well in all but the lightest and the heaviest airs. Two of the three summers that I raced, I won the trophy for scoring the most points. The trophy had been donated by the Lakeville Community Chest—cost, retail, $12.50—and I still have it.

It was well before the racing season, a cold spring day early in May. I took out for an afternoon's sail my sister Patricia, her English tutor, Cecilia Reilly, and a classmate from Millbrook, David Cates. A sudden puff swept down from the surrounding hills, and we capsized. It was not unusual to capsize in the lake; it was more a nuisance than an event. A motorboat would tow you to shore, and you would bail out the boat and relaunch her. Though the water was cold, it wasn't paralyzingly cold. But after we had been clinging to the boat for a few minutes it dawned on us that a) there were no other boats in sight; b) we were exactly in mid-lake, and therefore were unlikely to be spotted; c) we had only two life preservers on board; and d) Miss Reilly did not know how to swim, and David Cates not at all well.

I decided to leave Patricia (Trish) in charge of the boat. She and David could stay afloat by hanging on to it. Miss Reilly must don one life preserver. I would set out with the other and swim the half-mile to the Hotchkiss School and get help. A hundred yards along the way, I abandoned the life preserver, which was slowing me down. A hundred yards farther, I abandoned my shoes, socks, and pants. When I finally reached shore, I was bitterly cold, and frightened about the condition of the crew. I rushed up the huge lawn that slopes up from the Hotchkiss boathouse, spotted a door in the nearest building, and opened it, interrupting a full faculty meeting of the Hotchkiss School, presided over by a legendary and terrifying headmaster—learned, austere, caustic, and widely known for his impatience with schoolboyism. Shivering in my dripping shorts and T-shirt, I had trouble making sense, but the Duke, as they called the headmaster, calmly emitted a cluster of instructions, which resulted simultaneously in a motorboat's being dispatched to the middle of the lake, my being led off to the infirmary, and a telephone call's being placed to my parents. That night, it was all the subject of great excitement. As is almost always the case, the shock came a little later. David Cates, Trish told me—and he eventually admitted it—could not have held out much longer.

Five eventful years after that, I took *Sweet Isolation* on a trailer, with Trish, my sister Jane, and Richard O'Neill, who would be my roommate at Yale when we matriculated the following month, for a weekend of sailing off Edgartown. During those five years, I had graduated from prep school, done a half year at the National University of Mexico, undergone basic training in the infantry, attended officers training school, and served as platoon leader in infantry basic-training centers, while Richie, a resident of Lakeville, a graduate of the Hotchkiss School, and a boyhood friend, had fought in the war in Europe. We all felt terribly grownup until, the first evening, the waitress refused to serve the grizzled veterans a beer. Our driver's licenses betrayed us as being just short of twenty-one; only Jane, freshly graduated from Smith at twenty-two, could order from the bar. After dinner, we took a ride around the harbor in the Edgartown Yacht Club launch, which we boarded as though we were on our way to our own yacht. The New York Yacht Club fleet was in, and I had never before seen a fleet of oceangoing boats. I looked about me with admiration and envy: the trim, exquisitely maintained boats, ranging in size from thirty-five to seventy-two feet, with owners and crew comfortably aboard, chatting, drinking, washing the dinner dishes; the little anchor lights almost perfectly integrated with the stars above;

the moon highlighting the crosscurrents of the harbor. I was still unhooked by the lure of blue-water sailing, but I sensed that night that sometime, years away—exactly nine years, it proved—I would be back in the harbor, boarding my own boat.

It was blowing hard the next day, and the Yacht Club had its own race going, out in the Sound. We boarded our lunch, launched my little open boat, and set out downwind, along Chappaquiddick. A mile out, the mainmast suddenly lurched crookedly aft. The headstay had parted at the turnbuckle, and the foot of the mast, unsecured, slipped proportionately forward along the boat's bottom. The mainsail had to come down, and as I loosed the halyard, Trish reached for it, slipped, and fell into the sea. She was quickly separated from us as we went ineluctably downwind. I reached for a heavy prewar outboard motor and seated it with difficulty on the transom mount, and quickly threaded the starting cord. I pulled it once, twice, ten times. By now, Trish was barely visible astern. We could not tack our way back to her without rerigging the headstay, and that required straightening the mast. Richie tried starting the motor. My heart beat in an agony of frustration. Then, with great poise, a launch suddenly materialized, and a moment later we could see Trish being hauled out of the water. The launch then came to us, threw out a line, and towed us back into the harbor. Everyone was talking when we were reunited at the dock, and I was cursing the defective turnbuckle and the outboard motor. Exhausted, we trudged back to our hotel. Late in the afternoon, I returned alone to attend to the boat, which was sitting now in a boatyard; and, concealed behind its hull, I wept, hysterical at the thought of what had nearly happened. I had very nearly drowned my sister. It was, to use the word formally, a trauma. It haunted me into my twenties. I rehearsed a thousand times what I should have done. It was as simple as instantly—by reflex action—tossing out a life preserver. *The moment someone goes overboard.* It sounds axiomatic. But at sea in an emergency very little is axiomatic that you have not silently drilled yourself to do—like steering in the direction of a skid when you're driving in the snow. Man overboard is the greatest single menace of the sea.

It cannot exactly be classified as a misadventure of the per-ils-of-the-sea variety when your ship sinks and nobody is in it, but it is the kind of thing that creates apprehension in people like Pat, and even in people unlike Pat. Two months before my first Bermuda Race, in 1956, the switchboard operator at my office told me my boatyard, in Stamford, was calling. (I have, by the way, long since discovered how you get through on the telephone to yachtsmen who are otherwise unap-proachable people. You simply tell the operator you are call-ing from the boatyard. No yachtsman in the history of the world has ever been too busy to talk to his boatyard.) It was Eva Swann, a secretary at the boatyard.

"Mr. Buckley, I'm afraid I have some bad news." She was clearly on edge.

"What is it, Miss Swann?"

"*The Panic* sank."

"Sank?"

It transpired that, going down to the dock that morning, the yardmen had seen in the space previously occupied by a forty-four-foot steel cutter only fifty feet of mast, rising straight—indeed, proudly, one supposes—out of the water. Everything stopped, and the whole force of the yard was mo-bilized to pump out the boat and bring her, slowly, to the sur-face. The damage was unspeakable. When the seawater reached the level of the batteries, the acid was drawn out. Since the hull was made of steel, the entire boat was convert-ed into a huge galvanic field, so to speak, which corrosively began to gnaw away at the wiring, reducing it in a few hours to copper filigree.

Miss Swann having prepared me, she put me on to William Muzzio, the volatile, peppery, omnicompetent owner of the yard. We would need, he said, new wiring throughout, a re-built engine, a new generator, all new upholstery, a new ra-dio direction finder, a new radiotelephone. He was sure the sails had survived—they had been quickly washed in fresh water. The gas and water tanks would survive, he thought. He did not know whether all that work could be completed in time for the Bermuda Race, but he would make every effort.

"What happened?" I managed to ask.

"I don't know," he said. "We checked all the sea cocks. They're O.K."

If Mr. Muzzio didn't know what happened, it was unlikely that anyone would know; but, even as the work began, I found it endlessly disconcerting that the boat, sitting jauntily at dock one night, three days after it had last been sailed, should simply . . . sink. There is something less than an unquenchable intellectual curiosity among professional boat people. The insurance company had to pay out $10,000 to put *The Panic* right, but the company's inspector would not engage in anything like an exhaustive discussion of what might have been the cause of it all, though Stamford does not lie within the perimeter of the Bermuda Triangle, where One Isn't Supposed to Ask What Happened. The reason there are so many mysteries at sea is that nobody bothers to try to solve them. This particular mystery was solved, quite accidentally, under circumstances more hectic than the sedentary, regal sinking in the womb of Muzzio Brothers Yacht Yard.

It happened more than a year after my family had rechristened my boat *The Ti-panic*, and we were racing from Annapolis to Newport. All night long, we had tacked against a relentless southerly, fighting our way down the Chesapeake. At ten in the morning, I was off duty and sound asleep, with Mike Mitchell at the wheel, when Reggie woke me. In his calm way, he told me to look down at the floorboards. They were underwater. I jumped up, tore up the floorboards, and saw a mass of water overflowing the bilges and rushing up into the lockers with every leeward roll of the ship. Reggie and I could feel no water coming into the boat from the engine water-cooling system or from the stuffing box. A quick investigation of the sea cocks showed them to be in good order. Two crew members were mobilized to work the big hand pump. Working steadily, they only just managed to keep pace with the leak. I raced back to the cockpit, and Reggie, Mike, and I conferred. The water is shallow in the Chesapeake, and in the southern section there are stretches of mud and sand at depths of two feet. We decided that the only thing to do was to head for a sand shoal and beach *The*

Panic before she sank from under us. Moving to the wheel, I took a bearing, bore off the wind, and headed for shallow water about a mile away while Mike jumped into the bilges to have his own look. Seven or eight minutes later, he ambled up, a smile on his face and a beer in his hand. "Let's get back on course," he said. "I found the trouble."

The electric bilge pump, which Reggie had switched on before waking me, was, of course, the first mechanism I had checked, and it had been humming away industriously, though its capacity was insufficient to keep up with the flow of water coming into the boat. But Mike, unsatisfied, had unscrewed the hose from the pump, thinking that perhaps the rubber impeller had burned and that if he replaced it we might get some relief. He found that the pump was working fine, except that instead of drawing water from the boat into the sea it was drawing water from the sea into the boat. Astonished, he turned the switch off, then on again—and suddenly the flow of water was in the right direction. In a minute or two, he could see the water level receding.

Here was the mystery solved. An electric pump sucks water from the bilges and forces it up a hose, which becomes a copper pipe that rises above the water level outside the boat. The pipe elbows around, and the water falls by gravity down the pipe and out to sea through an open sea cock. We could now easily reconstruct what had happened. A piece of mud or sponge or whatever had been sucked up from the bilge and was rising under pressure up the pipe just at the moment, sometime during the night, when a crew member checked the bilges and, finding them dry, turned off the pump. There the foreign matter lodged, beneath sea level, like a cork, sustaining the weight of the water above it. In due course, the cork began to dissolve, and the dammed waterfall poured into the bilges—creating suction sufficient to bring a continuous flow of water up from the sea to the elbow. And now, by the law that specifies that water will seek its own level, Chesapeake Bay was happily filling up the cavity in the hull of *The Panic*. And, of course, the more water we took in, the lower the boat sank, guaranteeing a disparity in water level until our boat's decks were level with the sea. At that point, water would cease flowing into our bilges—a point of only academic comfort, since the boat would now sink like a full bathtub. When Reggie turned the electric pump on, the impeller was set in motion, but the pressure of the water flowing down redirected the innocent pump's energies, which now added mechanical pressure to the gravitational pressure bringing seawater into the boat. It was instantly clear what had caused *The Panic* to sink the year before. But on that occasion it had taken two and a half days for the clot in the pipe to disintegrate. It was simplicity itself to guard against a recurrence of the problem. We merely ripped out a tiny section from the pipe that moved down to the sea cock, so that if a reverse flow were started it would abort at that air hole.

End of problem. But there is always the scar left, causing you to wonder: How many other causes are there, potentially, for boats suddenly to drown?

Three months after every Bermuda Race and every Annapolis-Newport Race, which are run in alternate years, comes the last of the season's major offshore races, the annual Vineyard Race, in which I made my debut in 1955. The next year, I was the skipper. We had rounded the lightship and were headed for the finish line at Stamford, 130 miles almost due west. Mike was at the tiller when I went below to sleep. The spinnaker was flying, under a stiff northeasterly, the fog was pearly thick, and we posted a member of the crew forward to listen hard, away from the distractions of cockpit talk and grinding winches, while every few minutes we sounded our own foghorn, and occasionally looked up at the radar reflector, designed to attract maximum attention on the radar screens of the big boats. I slept fitfully until I was summoned to relieve Mike, near midnight. Mike, always the competitor, was very excited. *"See over there?"* he said, pointing ahead. I could make out a few lights through the fog—a stern light, a masthead light, and perhaps a flashlight. "We're overhauling that poor bastard!" Mike exulted, handing me the tiller. He stepped up from the cockpit to experience from the deck the special pleasure of sliding by a competitor. Mike was right. We were getting closer and closer. I checked the compass—dead on the course I had stipulated. I eased the bow the slightest bit up, to make certain we would be comfortably to windward of the boat. Then came the screech, the ricocheting crunch of steel bouncing over rocks, and, in a moment, motionlessness. There is nothing to match the motionlessness of running solidly aground. It is as if concrete had suddenly hardened around you. Now that we were no longer moving downwind at eight knots, the wind on our backs was eight knots stronger. A hundred yards away was the boat we were pursuing, now plainly visible: two forlorn street lights, one mile north of Point Judith, Rhode Island. We were two miles off course.

I looked down at the compass in dismay. Even now, it pointed us in the direction I had charted. But there was urgent work to be done. Already, Reggie had the tide tables out. He told us that we were one hour and a half past low tide, and that the water would be high just before five in the morning. We called Peter Starr, who was fourteen years old and was asleep in the forecastle, but there was no rousing him. We pulled up a hundred yards of chain past his ear, and two hundred yards of line, and he heard nothing. The boat's steel hull ground away on the rocks, and he heard nothing. We eased our heaviest anchor into the dinghy, and rowed out a hundred yards astern. After attaching our nylon mooring line to the anchor, we dropped it into the water, rowed back, and attached the end of the line to a bridle that we rigged from one to the other of our heavy genoa winches, which were situated across from each other above the cockpit. Now we had a harness of sorts, allowing us to apply simultaneous pressure on both winches. Thus prepared, we began working the boat aft, using also the reverse power of the engine at full r.p.m. We succeeded in moving about five yards, but then we came on something like an underwater stone wall, over which, under the careening force of eight knots, *The Panic* had leaped. She was not about to leap back over, even at the urging of a couple of No. 4 winches. We finally stopped, and I cut the motor.

It was the moment to call the Coast Guard. To my astonishment, the Coast Guard Station at Point Judith, which was almost within hailing distance, acknowledged our distress call immediately. After a considerable conference at the other end, we were informed that we lay in waters so pock-marked with rocky shoals that no Coast Guard vessel could approach us to bring help without endangering itself. The officer recommended that we wait until the next day and get a barge from Newport to float us out. We were not in any personal danger, the Coast Guard reminded us—all we had to do to start life afresh would be to abandon ship and walk to the beach. And, of course, wake up Peter.

There was nothing to do except to make a massive effort at exactly high tide. To lighten the boat, we emptied our water tanks. (We had 120 gallons, which at about eight pounds per gallon is a lot of weight.) Then I noticed that the spotlight was weakening, and decided to put a fresh battery in it, to be ready for the big effort at four-thirty, but I couldn't find one in with the flashlight batteries. Mike poked around. "Here it is," he said, opening the binnacle box. I removed the battery. "Do that again," Reggie said, "and look at the compass." The battery removed, the compass changed its heading eleven degrees.

We made it, but it was close. If the wind had been from the southeast, we would not have had the protection of the peninsula opposite, and the waves during the night would have battered the boat to pieces. A wooden boat would probably not have survived. As it was, the damage to the keel and rudder was extensive.

I thought we could conceal this episode from our families without any problem at all, and it was agreed all the way around. There was theoretically no need to conceal it from Peter, who was entirely unaware of it, waking relaxed at about seven. I would simply say that we had withdrawn from the race because our spinnaker had blown out and there was no substitute. In the early afternoon, we stumbled into a marina in New London and docked. I went to the telephone and reached Pat, who was visiting her parents in Vancouver, three thousand miles away. Her first words were peremptory: "What time did you get off the rocks?" At least she said it before listening to a vivid narrative about the decomposition of the spinnaker.

I could not tease out of her the source of her intelligence until, home from her visit, she finally broke down, with great relish. She had been at a cocktail party while her father, at home, listened to the evening news on the radio. It must have been a very slow night, because the last item was to the effect that the Coast Guard in Boston had reported that the cutter *Panic*, owned by the writer William F. Buckley, Jr., was on the rocks off Point Judith, Rhode Island. My father-in-law was a heavy man, of decisive mien and habit. He dispatched the chauffeur for his daughter, authorizing him only to instruct her that she was to return instantly to the house. There, with much solemnity, he gave her the news, and soon the Royal Canadian Navy in Ottawa was on the telephone to the Coast Guard in Boston, which relayed back a conversation with the Coast Guard in Point Judith to the effect that nothing more had been heard from *The Panic* but there was no reason to fear for the safety of the crew. Mike's father had heard the same broadcast, and welcomed his son home with a new drink, "Point Judith Scotch" (on the rocks).

A misadventure. It taught me not only to inspect the compass area from time to time for magnetic distractions but never to rely on a compass alone, if there was an alternative to doing so, in a fog anywhere near land. The radio direction finder, trained on Point Judith, would have alerted us to a deteriorating situation. There were, of course, months and years ahead of us to improvise on Mike's calling enthusiastic attention to boats we were about to overtake.

The most illuminating experience I have had at sea was in October of 1958. Pat's brother Firpo and I (we were co-owners) resolved to cruise *The Panic* to Bermuda, leave it there during the winter, and charter it by the day in the spring to tourists who desired a cruise in Bermudian waters. We yanked Peter out of school and assembled a crew—fine fellows all, but undistinguished as seamen, through no fault of theirs. I picked the fifteenth of October to set out, because, on the one hand, we wanted weather as warm as possible, and, on the other hand, we wanted to be on the safe side of the hurricane period. The Defense Mapping Agency Hydrographic Center puts out a chart for every month of every year on which are tracked the major storms and the paths they traveled the same month during the preceding ten (or more) years. Our chart showed only one storm of hurricane strength in the general area after the fifteenth of October, and it had done its mischief comfortably to the east of Bermuda.

After three or four of the most beautiful days of sailing I can remember—crisp, cool days, with the wind steady from the southeast, the Kenyon (speedometer) never reading below eight knots, the moon at night framed by clouds, providing us with a kind of private, silvery superhighway, New York–Bermuda, Non-Stop, Reserved for *The Panic*—we hit a most awful storm. It came on us suddenly. It had been building doggedly but moving slowly, and now it began to run. We had an anemometer on board, and at midnight it clocked winds of seventy knots; anything over sixty-five is hurricane speed. Late in the afternoon, when it was blowing about fifty knots, I decided to heave to. I had never done it before, but this clearly was the time to see what the maneuver would do for us, so I gave Firpo the tiller and, with Peter, went forward, took down the No. 3 jib, and replaced it with the storm jib, which we led back through a snatch block to the windward genoa winch. We had already prepared the storm trysail on the track to the side of the mast, like a spare train, ready, when we pulled the switch, to run up the mainmast. Now we pulled down the reefed mainsail and ran up the storm trysail. The storm trysail is what they call "loose footed," which is to say that the foot (i.e., the bottom side of the triangle), like the forward sails, is not fastened to any boom, and air can spill out between the sail and the main boom, to which only its clew (i.e., the corner farthest aft) is fastened. We pulled the mainsheet as tight as possible, flattening the sail. Then I took the tiller and shoved it over as far as I could to leeward. The boat edged up into the wind, without the strength to come about but with enough to cause the jib, even though it was led aback, to luff: there was too much pressure aft. I could move the rudder back a little from its extreme hard-left position or I could slightly ease the mainsheet. I tried the tiller, and now the effect was eerie. The boat came to virtually a dead stop, both sails hard. I looked about me in triumph. We could have played a game of checkers in the cockpit, except that the checkers would have blown away.

I took a piece of line and made a becket, securing the tiller in place—about as complicated as tying a shoelace.

Here is what happens when you heave to. To begin with, you hoist enough canvas (made out of the toughest material) to dominate the boat's movement but not enough to challenge the storm's machismo. Less sail than the two storm sails there isn't. If the wind is too strong to allow you to keep even them up, then you do something most appropriately named. You "run." Downwind. Always in a bad storm your objective is to reduce your speed in the water. *Pace* Pat, the bobbing-cork idea. Bear in mind that the wind does not distinguish between an obstacle made of canvas and one made of steel or wood, so even if you run, without so much as a handkerchief hoisted, you are still—as far as the wind is concerned—an obstacle, which is the square measurement of everything that lies above the water and is exposed to the wind. Enough of an obstacle, in very strong wind, to generate dangerous forward speeds. High speeds are dangerous because there is no practical means of synchronizing your movements and those of the waves, which are always irregular and sometimes very erratic; if you are running at, say, eight knots, you will soon find the bow of the boat submarining into the bosom of a huge wave, which causes great havoc. In such situations, some boats can even pitchpole—that is, do a vertical somersault, the mainmast, for a moment or two, pointing down like a surrealistic fin centerboard, and the keel pointing up, like the dorsal fin of a whale. People have survived pitchpoling, but no mast has done so. One must assume that there are people who have *not* survived pitchpoling—survival, by the way, is likelier in a centerboard boat than in a keelboat. (*The Panic* is a keelboat.) Short of pitchpoling, there is the dangerous yaw, the bow digging into the water, the stern bouncing off, leaving your beam for the wind and waves to work on.

How, then, if you are running, do you keep down the speed of the boat? By trailing lines (the easiest way); each line is an anchor of sorts, and you can keep tying them together so as to form a huge bight. By trailing a sea anchor, which is like a large canvas parachute designed to brake the boat's motion by dragging underwater (and is sheer hell to retrieve). By using reverse engine power. Moreover, you can let the boat travel backward, if your boat is the kind that does that more comfortably—that is, trail your lines forward and haul up into the wind. But beware the rudder. Sudden backward movements with the rudder off center can wrench and disable it. It is better, of course, for the great breakers to attack you from the bow of the boat than from the stern, because they will be partly dissipated by the cabin trunk before reaching you. You can, when things have come to such a pass, put a can of oil in a bag filled with rags, punch a couple of holes in the can with an ice pick, and trail it from a point on the boat as far forward as possible—in the case of a boat like *Cyrano*, off the twelve-foot-long bowsprit. The instant slick of the oil is said to prevent most waves from breaking under its umbrella, at the center of which is you. I have never had to run, or use oil.

When maneuvering to heave to, you are fine-tuning right-left oscillations in the heading of a boat to the point of rendering them nugatory. The wind catches the little trysail aft, and, because the tiller is held over to leeward, or away from the wind, the boat's bow swings up into the wind. But no sooner has it done that than it exposes the forward sail, the jib, to the wind. Because the jib has been led aback—that is, fastened not to leeward, where it belongs, but to windward—you reach out for the wind, catching it before you are headed directly into it. The wind's force is now trapped by the jib, propelling the bow back to leeward. But the moment it has moved a mere matter of inches, the aftersail has again caught the wind, reversing the swing. A well-balanced boat, perfectly tuned, will heave to in such a way as to make the oscillations imperceptible. The wind is quite simply stymied, and you have become like the cork. There *is* forward motion (otherwise your rudder would be inoperative); but we are talking about two knots or so.

It was eerie primarily because of the contrast. The noise of the wind tearing through the shrouds and the lifelines was a continual howl. The waves rose and fell a dozen feet above our heads, and we rose and fell, but the waves did not break over us. The canvas dodger over the companionway protected totally the faces of the two men who nestled at that end of the cockpit, and it occurred to me that there was no reason for three men to stay on watch. There was nothing to do except sit there and wait it out, so we ate something and went through the night. I rested with some apprehension, always alert to the sibilant wind and roaring seas, and wondered what could possibly go wrong, and what I would do in the chaos if something did.

Nothing did go wrong. But the next morning, at about eleven, I made a mistake. The wind had abated slightly. It was back to fifty knots, and I was growing restless. We were pointed southwest, and Bermuda lay southeast. I thought that we should try to resume course and get the boat moving again by sailing with the wind abeam under storm jib alone, making at least a little progress toward our destination. So I loosed the becket and took the tiller in hand, and ordered the storm trysail brought down. The windward jib sheet was eased inch by inch and the strain taken on the leeward sheet. It was in tight when I said, "Here we go," and brought the tiller up, to take the bow downwind. We suffered an instant knockdown. (A knockdown is when the boat suddenly goes from vertical to horizontal, or nearly horizontal.) Generally, they hit you when your boat is practically at a standstill. If you are moving along, a sudden gust of wind will cause you to heel over, but the forward movement of your boat absorbs the suddenness of the blast, distributing it among keel, sails, and rudder.

I did not believe that *The Panic* could be made to suffer a knockdown when it was flying only a storm jib. But it did— one so severe that we were on our side, and a huge wave from abeam bulldozed into us, wrenching the entire binnacle from its mount on the cockpit floor and heaving it over toward the sea. Peter lurched out and grabbed it a second before it fell into the ocean, his torso stretched over the lifeline. Firpo grabbed him by the belt of his slicker, and kept him, and the binnacle, from going over. I yelled to loose the jib sheet, but it was almost immediately unnecessary. We were righting on our own steam, the sixty thousand pounds of pressure on the keel asserting themselves, roly-poly-doll-wise. The cockpit was half underwater when we loosed the jib sheet well out, and within minutes we were making five knots toward Bermuda.

What I especially remember about the next six hours is the size of the waves. The wind kept abating, but the waves, as if sullen at the wind's default, grew proportionately hilly, then mountainous. They rose thirty feet high. But *The Panic* was untroubled, and in due course we had up our reefed mainsail, and then our No. 3 jib. At noon, the sun was briefly out, and I snatched a latitude and established our position as on a line that ran seventy miles north of Bermuda. The trouble was, I did not have any close idea of our longitude, and the sun wasn't out in the afternoon to permit me a running fix. Our radio direction finder began picking up a commercial station in Bermuda, and the crew was lighthearted in anticipation of arriving perhaps a little bit after midnight. The off watch declined its privileges, preferring to stay up now to the end. At about 6 P.M., a Bermuda patrol boat cruised up to us in the ebbing light. I shouted out, "Give me a course to Gibb's Hill!" A sailor shouted back, "A hundred and twenty degrees!" I was putting the information on the chart (Bermuda has to be approached with extreme care; it is like a starfish of coral reefs) when Firpo told me to come up and look at the extraordinary horizon. It certainly was extraordinary. We were completely surrounded by low, low clouds, not much higher than a steamer, black as pitch. The wind was suddenly gone. The skies grew grayer as the light faded, and the black noose began to tighten, and I felt a sudden touch of air in my face, cold, undecided. I gave orders to bring down *all* sails. Something was going to hit us immediately from somewhere. In five minutes, the storm was back; and, laboriously, once again we hove to. The wind was not as heavy as before, but it rained now from time to time—hard, passionate rain—and the direction of the boat kept changing as the storm danced around us. No one slept.

The next day was gray and lumpy, and now the serious question was *Where were we?* Miraculously, the sun appeared at about noon for exactly as long as it takes to get a single sight, and I put us at forty miles north of Bermuda—but, once again, longitude uncertain. Around 7 P.M., I noticed that the crew was demoralized. No one would eat. The dishes were piled up from the last three meals. There was no conversation, no unnecessary motion. I had encountered such a scene once before, in the infantry, when a company of soldiers completing their basic training was ordered to storm a hill to seize imaginary enemy installations. It was noon, the temperature a hundred and ten degrees. At midnight the night before, the trainees had been made to crawl on their bellies under barbed wire and tracer ammunition, only to be awakened at 2 A.M. for a forced march. They started up the hill, and then, as if rehearsed, they all stopped and sat down. Nothing mutinous. They simply could not move on. Discipline was out of the question. Our shrewd battalion commander was called in by walkie-talkie. He looked at the men only briefly, then dispatched four trucks from the base, loaded the men into them, and took them to a lake, where they swam.

A crew member slightly more.alert than the others came back from the emergency storeroom with two large tins of hardtack. I reached into the tangle beside the icebox and got out a bottle of port. Hardtack looks like dog biscuits, but tastes slightly better, I think. Port goes well with hardtack. Soon everyone had a glass of port and was munching a biscuit. And beginning to talk. I said there was no point in trying to make progress under sail that night. We could not approach Bermuda without a more specific idea of where Bermuda was, because of the shoals. Under the circumstances, we would set only a No. 3 jib for stability, and more or less hold our own on an easterly course. Two men would stay up, but only for two-hour watches. The others would sleep.

The next morning, the recovery was complete. It was a brilliant blue day, and we spotted a cruise ship, obviously headed toward Bermuda. In a few hours, I had a running fix, showing that the storms had taken us forty miles west of Bermuda. We began to slog against the easterly, tacking, tacking. At 4 P.M., a Coast Guard plane buzzed down and recorded our sail number. At seven, we saw Gibb's Hill Light. (The radio direction finder was forty degrees off calibration.) Still there were five hours of tacking left to do before, a few minutes past midnight, we rounded the shoal area, easing, exhausted, into St. George's Harbour—seven days out of New York.

The radiotelephone had not worked. My wife's anxiety had mounted, and telephone calls between her and her mother in Vancouver had grown in frequency. That very morning, her mother had acted. She had telephoned Pat and announced calmly, imperiously, "Tell the Coast Guard to go out and find them. And to send *me* the bill." The airplane, that afternoon, had done its duty.

One night on *Suzy*, with Pat aboard, I proposed to cross the St. John River's Reversing Falls, at St. John, New Brunswick. I resist as somehow extraneous the temptation to describe the river, which is surely the most beautiful in the world. The subject of this story is the Reversing Falls. What you have on the one hand is the Bay of Fundy, with its famous gargantuan tide fall—forty feet is typical in the upper reaches of the bay. Enough power rushing in and out twice a day that if it could be harnessed it would generate electricity to light the world, or so they say. And what you have on the other hand is a 400-mile-long river, flowing through Maine and New Brunswick, with a tide fall of a few inches, which debouches into the bay. When the tide is out, the St. John River is falling into the bay, and the transitional mile between the river and the bay looks something like the runway to Niagara Falls. No boat could survive in those rapids for a moment; indeed, they are so spectacularly scary that tourists come from all over just to sit and stare. When the tide is in, the bay is pouring into the river, and the transitional mile between the river and the bay looks exactly the same as usual—except that the rapids are running in the opposite direction. Do not ask why, but it happens that three hours and fifty minutes after low tide, and two hours and twenty-five minutes after high tide, the Bay of Fundy and the St. John River fight each other to an ironic standstill, and then the water is as smooth as a skating rink. For ten minutes. That is when you power across.

Pat begged us to wait until the morning to make the crossing, but we cooed her into a resigned silence, marked time with a lengthy gourmet dinner, and took off at two minutes after eleven. We were two minutes early. I do not know whether our watches were off or whether through some inexplicable miscalculation we had taken the time from the wrong table. Reggie, as had been arranged, was below, leaning over the navigation table atop the icebox, to feed me quick-fire navigational instructions. But the current scooped us up, and while Reggie was intoning calmly, "Keep at two hundred and ninety-five degrees for exactly four minutes, toward the fixed white light," I was headed at twenty degrees toward an Esso gas station, which I would smash into in about two minutes. When the current is taking you faster than your engine drives you, the rudder has little effect. Reggie, crouched over his magnifying glass, and intent on his assignment, was saying things like "On your right, you should be seeing a flashing green approximately abeam." Meanwhile, a mass of yellow-gray foam surged toward us, like sea lava about to overtake us. It proved to be the discharge of pulp deposits from a mill that lets it all go just as the tide begins to turn. We were within a hundred yards of the gas station when, gradually, like the feeling that creeps back into your hands after a frostbite, the rudder began to respond. The equilibrium was finally upon us, and the amphibious operation against Esso Petroleum was aborted. The lessons are too obvious to expatiate upon. I have, in fact, wondered why the city of St. John does not indulge itself in a navigational light that turns green from red when the precious ten minutes begin. Perhaps it has to provide an occasional wreck to maintain tourist interest.

These are highlights from experiences of my own and of boats I have sailed. I have read a lot, and listened a lot, and doubt whether many seasoned ocean sailors would disagree with the following propositions:

(1) The chances of a well-rigged, well-sailed, well-constructed boat's going down in the open sea (you are safer there than near land) by reason of ocean conditions are so small in the safer latitudes in the safer months that you should not become obsessed with the question of physical survival. On the other hand, you must make emergency arrangements.

(2) The gravest danger is man overboard.

(3) There is one other very grave danger, and that is fire. Astonishingly, the race from Newport to Bermuda, which

has been conducted every second year for more than fifty years, has brought death by drowning to only a single human being. Several boats have been destroyed on the rocks around Bermuda, but the crews have always been saved. The exception was a member of the crew of a large yacht in which a fire got out of control. The distress signal was caught by another craft, which powered in to render assistance. One by one, the refugees jumped aboard. One man slipped and fell into the sea in between the boats and drowned immediately. On *Cyrano,* we maintain two large and two small fire extinguishers, handily placed. A diesel engine is indispensable to one's peace of mind, since gasoline is so combustible. We also have automatic circuit breakers, which isolate short circuits. Needless to say, the gas cylinders for the stove are stowed on deck.

On our last long ocean cruise, Reggie agreed to serve as chairman, of sorts, of a safety committee. We pooled our knowledge, and decided to gear up for two kinds of emergencies. There is a third kind, but you needn't bother about it: a whale eats you, or a steamer runs you down in a storm. We defined as Emergency A any development that would result in *Cyrano's* sinking within two minutes—the whale barges into you, let us say, or you hit an iceberg. Hanging on the davits was our unsinkable Boston whaler. It was packed with emergency food and water for ten people for ten days. It could be lowered into the water in about fifteen seconds. Sheathed knives, to be used to cut any lines that might foul, were strapped alongside. Forward of the cockpit-cabin area we kept a twelve-man life raft, neatly tucked into a small barrel, and packed with food, medicine, flares, and a radio that had the strength to emit for seventeen hours emergency signals to overpassing aircraft. Also, it was equipped with a kind of Arabian tent, to protect us against the sun's rays. The raft would be inflated immediately on hitting the water, and one hundred feet of light line would keep it attached to *Cyrano.* (I know personally of two shipwrecks in which a life raft was thrown overboard with no thought given to what would happen to it. What happened in both cases was that the raft drifted out to sea and was of no use to anyone. A raft should always be tied to the boat.) The right-hand locker next to *Cyra-*

no's steering wheel was filled exclusively with life preservers. To each were attached a waterproof flashlight, a whistle, and a package of dye marker (a substance that, once you puncture its plastic container with your teeth, dissolves and colors the sea red).

We would work in pre-stipulated pairs, one senior partner, one junior. In Emergency A, only the whaler, the life preservers (tied loosely to one another, and jointly to the boat), and the twelve-man raft would be unloaded. Each crew member was then to jump overboard, swim to the life preservers and don one, and swim either to the whaler or to the life raft.

In Emergency B, we would know that the boat was going down but that we had five or more minutes. The life preservers would be donned first in this case. The captain would work until the last minute giving our position and a distress signal on-the radio's emergency band. Two additional, eight-man rafts, tucked into cavities just beyond the pillows of the berths in the cockpit section, would be hauled out, inflated, and trailed alongside. We would fill them with as many supplies as we had time to gather together. In a raging sea, schematic arrangements of this sort are sheer fantasy, and you simply do what you can. But in a moderate sea, losing ground against, say, fire or an uncontrollable leak, you have time even to remember the corkscrew.

"Peter," I said late on a white summer afternoon about fifteen years ago to Peter Starr, "let's face it. Someday we'll have to sail across the Atlantic." We were walking about the mossy rocks that surround York Harbor, Maine, getting some exercise after a long day's sail from Gloucester, before returning to *The Panic* in the Hansel-and-Gretel harbor for dinner. Peter agreed. It wasn't until June of last year that I finally undertook the cruise across the Atlantic, on *Cyrano*, and Peter wasn't with me; he had to withdraw at the last moment, because of a business emergency. On board, in addition to a professional crew of three, were my son, Christopher; Christopher's friend Daniel Merritt; Evan Galbraith; Reggie; and my sister-in-law Kathleen Finucane, who is called Bill. We sailed from Miami to Bermuda to the Azores to Marbella, Spain.

You *never* set out on time for a cruise, even with fifteen months' notice, but Danny, with his invincible optimism, told me that the boat would be ready to sail forty-eight hours early. At the appointed hour, however, the loran (long-range navigation) was suddenly not working; the radar was not working; and the new automatic pilot was not finally installed.

One wonders just how much expertise an ocean sailor can genuinely rely on—"expertise" being a word that is precisely used by a total of about twenty people. I pause to define it as meaning a body of operative knowledge. It isn't synonymous with *expertness.* One cannot be an expert except in a field in which there is something to be expert in—i.e., in which there is expertise. A radar technician can be expert only insofar as there is room for expertness. Beyond that, he is extemporizing. It is, of course, one thing if a particular product is defective, or is defectively installed, and another if that product presumes to standards that it is not scientifically justified in presuming to. The gentleman who (eventually) installed our automatic pilot effected an installation that came apart during that day's midnight watch; Danny put it back together, using bolts rather than screws, and *his* installation held. But not the pilot, which suddenly stopped working when the professional crew started the return voyage. Six thousand miles without the automatic pilot. There are grounds for believing the installer sloppy, or inexpert, in installation, but the machine's breaking down after one month suggests defective design; or else there is a mystery. Mysteries abound at sea. I had an autopilot on *Suzy* that worked with exquisite precision for three years. One day, it stopped working, and I assumed the necessity of getting spare parts, or even of replacing whole units. In the course of four years, six technicians, three boatyards, and, finally, the personal mechanic for the president of the manufacturing company tried to make it work again. (At this point, every component unit had been replaced.) It never did; never has. Come see.

The gentleman who looked at the radar in Miami succeeded in decocting from it only the faintest signal, eclipsed in less than a day at sea. A gentleman in Bermuda tried to fix it and couldn't. A gentleman in Marbella fixed it for $600—twenty-five percent of the original cost of the instrument—and it lasted about a week. Now, this is a Japanese machine about which it is boasted that there are six completely discrete and replaceable components, so that the problem is supposed to be as simple as identifying the delinquent part, throwing it away, and inserting the new part. That turns out to be hogwash. One doesn't know whether it is intentional or inadvertent hogwash. Perhaps there is a man in Japan who, with his little tool kit, could have set the radar right in minutes. The question seriously arises whether that man's skills are thaumaturgic rather than mechanical. Or is he an artist? Artistic jury rigs are feats of individual achievement but one cannot deduce from them an expertise that sustains them.

Before we left Miami, a gentleman exhorted me there and then to buy a brand-new loran, with the latest gee-whizz digital scanners, which seek out the two relevant transmitting loran stations and their slave stations and track them automatically and continuously, giving you second-by-second fixes, which you then plot on your chart. I was persuaded, and bought. The new loran set stopped working about thirty minutes after we left Miami; was not revived even after a half hour's telephone conversation at sea between Reggie and an expert who gave minute instructions; and did not work even after a replacement unit was installed in Bermuda.

So it went; so it almost always goes. There are problems that beset what one might call middle-sized boats. The big boats have on board their engineer and electrician, who can fix or replace almost anything that goes wrong. The very small boats don't have radar or loran or automatic pilots. *Cyrano* is in the class between, and perhaps it is for that reason that there is an insufficient expertise to provide reliable electrical or electronic systems for her, though it must be observed that the little commercial fishing boats use the same kind of radar and loran that is offered to the sailboats—with, however, the significant difference that such boats are always operating under power, and their instruments no doubt adjust to, or are designed to adjust to, regular operation, rather than the episodic operation of the sailor anxious to conserve his electrical power.

ATLANTIC CRUISE JOURNAL, MAY 30TH: Peter's withdrawal left us short one qualified watch captain, so my idea of four hours on, eight hours off will have to yield a little on the side of rigor. Every other cycle the watch captains will get only four hours off between watches. I have made up watch rosters for years, and sometimes they're like the inside of a Swiss clock. Racing, a crew member is on duty half the day. I use the Scandinavian system, 4-4-4-6-6. The six-hour periods fall between eight and two and between two and eight, during the daylight hours. That gives everybody one longish sleep a day. Breaking up the day into five parts means that you repeat a watch only every forty-eight hours. Nothing is drearier than to come on board and learn that you are on duty every single night from midnight to four. I have tried on this cruise to devise a system that will keep mixing us up, so that every watch captain (Danny, Reggie, myself, and the professional captain, Philip Campagna) will alternate with the watch assistants, Christopher, Van, Aunty Bill. Campagna and Van are out there now, having relieved Bill and me.

The wind is steady from the southeast, getting lighter. We ended by powering a little and clutching in the automatic pilot. Lighter, ocean-racing sailboats now use, almost as a matter of course, autopilots that are governed by the wind. They are designed to maintain a boat's heading at a constant angle off the wind. The disadvantage is that they necessarily redirect the boat when the wind changes, and this may happen when you are asleep. If you instruct a wind-vaned autopilot to keep you headed ninety degrees off the wind (let us say), you could conceivably wake in the morning to find yourself going back home, if the wind changed direction by 180 degrees. The wind-powered autopilots were developed primarily for the single-handed ocean racer, and a gentleman who won the transatlantic race several years ago records that his own model was so marvelously successful that his hands were on the tiller for a total of only twenty minutes from Southampton to Newport—twenty-eight days.

Other boats, such as *Cyrano,* use autopilots operated by power. These have the obvious disadvantage of consuming power, offset by the advantage of maintaining a steady compass course irrespective of a) whether there is any wind at all and b) where the wind is coming from. They operate through a compass of their own, which, once set, sends out electrical impulses that keep the wheel turning in the proper direction to maintain the stipulated course. They require a little mothering, but are splendid mechanical achievements.

JUNE 2ND: The sun was bright, but we were without wind and had to power the whole day long. At noon, we stopped and swam. Christopher, the .222-magnum cocked, sat on the cabin deck, prepared to fire at any shark attracted to our flailings. Aunty Bill decorously stayed below, so that we could do without swimming trunks. If the Atlantic is polluted, it is polluted elsewhere than at Latitude 31, Longitude 79, where the water is a cobalt blue and accepts as confidently as trained dolphins accept their dollops of fish the traditional beer can you throw over the side, to marvel at its endless visibility as it sinks into ocean water unmurked by the detritus of civilization. There is a great fuss this season about the danger of sharks, thanks substantially to the best-selling scare story on the subject. There are, of course, sharks everywhere in the oceans, even as there are rats everywhere on land. Ten years ago, I took lessons off the Virgin Islands in the use of scuba gear, and during one underwater session my instructor, using a graphite pencil on a slate, wrote "Hammerhead shark" and pointed to an object floating about thirty feet away, apparently as contented as a cow, and more or less looking at us, but without any trace of greed that an amateur could detect. I followed my instructor along as he went on scribbling on his underwater palimpsest, describing the underwater population, which for the most part was harmless, but not entirely. There were several barracuda and one moray eel. On surfacing, he told me that the experience was altogether normal, though spotting a moray eel was "a bit lucky," and that the key to a serene relationship with sharks was simply this: Bear it in mind that they are so dumb you can neither anticipate nor outwit them. Accordingly, you play the statis-

tics, which are vastly reassuring. Avoid swimming in tandem
with outflowing garbage—which one would tend to avoid doing for reasons entirely independent of the fear of sharks.
Don't swim if any part of your body is bleeding. If you swim
at night, enter the water gradually rather than splashily. And
look forward to a ripe old age, limbs intact. I respond joyful-
ly to almost any permissive franchise, and have never since
given a thought to the danger of sharks—a serenity I have
not communicated to Christopher, who in guarding the ram-
parts visualizes the enemy and loses his appetite for disport-
ing in enemy territory. The swim was very refreshing, and
the lunch tasted better, and we were less depressed by the
absence of wind.

JUNE 5TH: More properly, June 6th. Because we tied up at
2:50 A.M. at St. George's Harbour. Early this morning, the
wind almost directly behind us, the gollywobbler up, we conducted a pool: At what time would we spot the light from
Gibb's Hill? It is a powerful beacon, with a twenty-six-mile ra-
dius. Before the construction of the lighthouse, during the
high days of Bermuda's role as a way station to Virginia and
points south, hundreds of ships foundered on the treacher-
ous rocks here, it is said. Even now, Reggie's schoolmate
Teddy Tucker devotes himself full time to locating wrecks
and salvaging 300-year-old cargo. He has found gold and silver and jewels, including a famous emerald crucifix, but
mostly such stuff as lead and copper.

I picked 8:15 P.M. for the landfall, and bets were taken
ranging from 6:30 P.M. to midnight. At noon, after the sun
sight, I decreed that our watches should move forward by
one hour. When the light at Gibb's Hill was spotted, at 8:10
P.M., just off the port bow, where it should have been, we
were catapulted into a great legal controversy. Danny et absolutely al. v. WFB. Danny had "bought" 7:15 P.M., and insisted that since the bets were made this morning, before our
watches were moved forward, he had clearly won the pool. I
took the position that we were betting that morning on what
would be the time on our wristwatches at the moment of the
landfall. Van, as a graduate of the Harvard Law School, was
consulted by Danny, and I suspect that this appeal to his van-

ity suborned him to find, after appropriate deliberation, for the plaintiffs. The matter was economically moot at this point, since Christopher, Aunty Bill, Reggie, and Van had already paid over their dollar bills to Danny. I reluctantly gave my dollar to Danny, sniffing something about the dangers of ochlocracy. "What's that?" he asked. I told him it was the only kind of government that would find for *him* in a dispute with *me*. Reggie then proposed a loser's toast, to my navigation—a toast I acknowledged with a graceful speech minimizing the complexity of my achievement. We were all in high spirits.

There is an underappreciated phenomenon at sea in a small boat. This is the exasperating length of time it takes after spotting a major beacon to pull in to the wharf. The tendency on seeing the light is to think the trip over. It took us almost seven hours, even at eight knots, to get in (against a tide of about one and a half knots). These long hours are anticlimactic, and it is sensible to dampen the spirit of celebration. On making a landfall, the crew usually (except in a race) breaks out the bottle. If there is still six hours' sailing to do, that can make for a very wet landfall. Van, experienced in these matters, retired to his cabin to read a book. The boys eventually peeled off and went to sleep. Having given everyone advice, I failed to heed it myself—I cannot be wrenched from the wheel between a landfall and arrival. Coming into St. George's is a spooky experience: one flows in through a deep but very narrow cut that becomes visible only as you become convinced that you are headed right into a hill. The placid lights of seventeenth-century St. George's were suddenly before us, and for the first time in six days the ocean swells were suspended, and we crossed the harbor to the slip as if skating over ice.

JUNE 14TH: We've been gone fifteen days from Miami, and we have 1,100 miles to go before reaching Horta, the westernmost port in the Azores. It isn't hot, just warm. When we have a long stretch under straight power, I wonder about motors. I received from Pat osmotically a most preposterous superstition, which I have never quite been able to shake; namely, that motors should "rest." I have talked the matter over with Reggie, who knows everything, and he once reminded me that the Perkins 150 we have on board is identical to the motor widely used by the little shrimp boats that go out for two or three weeks at a time without any sail whatever, except, perhaps, a little steadying sail to put up when the winds are very bad. Theoretically, you can use a motor forever if only you will keep it perfectly lubricated. That means (in our case) stopping and checking the oil every twenty-four hours, and changing it every hundred hours. The filters need to be changed more often. They collect the glop that would otherwise assault the cylinders. You are supposed to get almost perpetual use from a good, sturdy diesel, but you don't, of course—although, I am assured, if you don't get 7,000 hours out of the Perkins, you are neglecting your motor. That's 5,600 miles.

Early in the afternoon, a cargo vessel passed a mile or so behind us, heading northeast. Captain Campagna "spoke" her. To "speak" a ship means to establish communication with it at sea. The captain routinely asked her where she was headed (Amsterdam) and what her position was (she gave it). This intelligence was relayed to me, and I advised the plebes that the ship was in fact five or six miles south of the position she took herself to be at. This aroused great gales of parricidal laughter, in which Danny joined and, finally, Van, leaving me only Bill, who thought it an inescapable deduction that if someone was mistaken in calculating our joint position, it was the ship's navigator, and not her brother-in-law. I volunteered to rub the nose of any skeptic in the evidence of my sun sight and the dead reckoning of the mere hour and a half that had elapsed, but, I told them, since this would require that they exert themselves intellectually, I knew I was safe in making the challenge. Christopher and Danny *love* that sort of thing, and I happen to know that they are, with whoops of surreptitious laughter, planning revenge.

JUNE 15TH: We had our first big storm today, and hove to. I had never hove *Cyrano* to before. Captain Campagna favored running, but I elected not to, and as we struggled in the screech and wet to lead the two staysails aback, as tight as drums, I remembered prayerfully the representations of the sailmakers that these sails would stand up against the greatest stress. We would soon find out, because the wind was fifty knots, gusting well over that, and apparently building, like the seas. The spray came in off the starboard bow, and then one monstrous wave—though not of the size of one that hit us later, after we had resumed sailing—which caught me while I was forward with the sails. It is unsettling to meditate that one wave of that kind weighs many more tons than the thirty the boat weighs. After the storm trysail was up, I took the wheel from Danny to make the adjustments. *Cyrano,* not being a racing boat, responds less quickly than *The Panic* did, so I felt the necessity for a little rudder control. Otherwise, the oscillations that enable a boat to heave to successfully would probably have been a little too widely separated, making for distinct lurches first to leeward, then to windward. I gave the engine 800 rpm, which in a smooth surface would mean about four knots of speed. Then I began turning the wheel to starboard. (It requires nine turns to move the rudder hard over to the opposite position.) At about six turns, with that much engine, the vessel walked into the magical equilibrium that is the ecstasy of the boat successfully hove to. It was fine to look about at the drenched, wind-blasted, anxious faces of Christopher and Danny, Captain Campagna and Van, and, in the cockpit, Aunty Bill as, suddenly, *Cyrano* acted as if we had crossed the Reversing Falls into a lake. The wind and the noise, the howling and the waves seemed to mount in resentment of our insulation.

Three hours later, the worst was over—the wind, clearly abating, down now to about forty knots. So we eased off on the windward sheets; picked up the slack to leeward, first of the mainstaysail and then of the forestaysail; and—remembering the knockdown of fifteen years ago—let them luff as we turned decisively downwind until the air engaged them, and only then made an upwind adjustment toward the heading on which we had been sailing before the storm hit.

We ate dinner buffet-style—silent, mostly, but strangely exhilarated, and close to each other after an annealing experience. I halved the watches—two hours of duty seemed enough under the circumstances—and at 2 A.M. rose to take my own, with Van. By then, the genoa could come into service again. Christopher and Danny had experimented with it at my suggestion, then checked with me for the O.K. to douse it. No telling where we were, so I decided to put the boat on autopilot and, with Van prepared to take notes and clutching the chronometer, try to get a Polaris sight—for the stars had grumpily come out, giving us a horizon of abnormal clarity. I mounted to the top of the cockpit cabin with two safety belts, to make a sort of gimbal for me: one belt to keep me from lurching sidewise into the sea, the other to keep me from lurching off the roof. I positioned myself and, for a fleeting moment, got both Polaris and the horizon tentatively in the sextant mirror, when the mainstaysail boom banged against my head, and a spout of ocean water from a rogue wave balling the jack on my leeward topside drowned the sextant in salt. My job then became to clean the sextant quickly—salt water will corrode the mirrors in a few hours. Never mind the navigation: I'll figure out tomorrow where in hell the storm took us. After cleaning the sextant, and with the boat still under autopilot and making nine knots under sail, I sat for the balance of the hour forward with Van. From the area in front of the cabin you saw on the stampeding seas a kinetic fleck of red from the port running light, green to starboard, and a touch of white ahead, reflecting the forward light. The sails were snugged in and powerful, working in overdrive, leaving the boat almost erect as it tore through the ocean. The stars began to assert themselves, while a bottle of wine, secured by the boom vang between us, emptied slowly as we paid mute tribute to *Cyrano,* her builder, her designer, and the architect of the whole grand situation.

On the twenty-ninth, I decided, on impulse, to change course by twenty-five degrees, so that, at an expense of a mere ten to fifteen miles extra voyaging, we could lay eyes on the tip of Portugal that day, rather than head directly for Gibraltar. The crew approved, and at 1702 on the twenty-ninth we heard Christopher's excited voice from the crow's nest. "Land ho!"—Cape St. Vincent. Odd, but any other formulation than the traditional one would have seemed, somehow, affected, irreverent.

That night, sailing at hull speed in the Bay of Cádiz, anticipating Gibraltar late the following afternoon and Marbella before midnight, both Bill and Reggie approached me, separately, to inform me in whispers that the boys had, *sponte sua*, organized a Captain's Dinner. Bill, musing, added that she could not remember ever before, in all her life, "thirty days without tension." It was our last night, seated about the dining table: music; dumpy little low-gravity candles scattered about the chart table, shining through red, blue, green, and yellow glass; the gas lamp in mid-table; and the gourmet meal, beginning with a can of caviar, and champagne bought in Miami by Danny and Christopher. The meal was extensive and imaginative. "I decided to brighten up the dessert," Danny wrote in his journal, "with two huge sparklers I bought in Miami for just this occasion." The sparklers were explosively effective, and startling, and probably there had not been such elation in these waters since the Battle of Trafalgar.

Index

Acheson, Dean, 160
Adams, F.P., 409
Adams, John, 109, 356
Afghanistan, 237
Africa, 60–62, 160, 240–41, 254, 271
AFTRA, 374
Age of Discontinuity, The (Drucker), 26
Age of Uncertainty, The (Galbraith), 348–49
Airborne (Buckley), 379–80
Al Smith Dinner, 112–14
Alcoholics Anonymous, 299–300
Alexander, Shana, 35
Alexander's Horse (plane), 454–62
Alinsky, Saul, 271
Allen, Gary, 379
Amalrik, Andrei, 37, 257
America (magazine), 426
American Civil Liberties Union (ACLU), 283–85, 389–90
American Council of Christian Laymen, 425
American Institute of Real Estate Appraisers, 443
American Spectator, The, 23–25
American Tradition, The: A Gallery of Rogues (Greenway), 188–90
Americans for Democratic Action, 147
Amin, Idi, 43–45, 241
Anderson, Jack, 109, 329
Anglican Church, 288, 289
Angola, 58
Annapolis-Newport Race, 477–79
Annenberg, Walter, 78
Antigone, 358–60
Apollo-Soyuz mission, 47–49
Arab-African bloc, 253
Arab nations, 222, 252–53
Argentina, 61, 266–70, 305
Argentina Yacht Club, 269
Army, United States, 210
Arnoni, M. S., 163

Artists' Union (Soviet Union), 258
Ashburn, Frank, 421, 422, 427, 432–34
Asia, 61, 62, 87, 239
Associated Press, 283
Astaire, Fred, 193
Astor, Lady, 265
Austen, Jane, 411
Australia, 275
Australian Consolidated Press, 162
Austria, 275

Baker, Howard, 96
Baldwin, Colleen, 364
Ball, George W., 30–32, 204, 205
Barney's Men's Clothing Store, 318–20
Barton, Bruce, 432
Bauer, Peter, 236
Bay of Pigs invasion (1961), 70, 119, 120, 132–35
Becker, Carl, 356
Beckmann, George, 182
Beethoven, Ludwig van, 358–59
Belgian colonists, 254
Belgium, 275
Benn, Tony, 245–47
Berlin, 111
Bermuda Race, 463, 466, 479, 490–91
Bernstein, Carl, 124
Biddle, Eric, Jr., 64
Bilderbergers, 344
Blanco, Hugo, 41–42
Bolivia, 67
Borges, Jorge Luis, 268–69
Boston Globe, 161, 163
Boston Pilot, 444
Boys in the Band, The (play), 317
Bozell, Brent, 153
Brennan, William J., Jr., 315
Brewster, Kingman, 220–22
Brezhnev, Leonid, 310
Bring on the Empty Horses (Niven), 190–94

Brittan, Samuel, 249
Brown, Dee, 189
Brown, Gen. George S., 110–11
Brown, Jerry, 86
Brown, John, 282
Brown, Robert McAfee, 235–37
Browne, Robert E. ("Bob"), 351
Bruce-Briggs, B., 207–9
Bryant, Anita, 317, 318
Buchanan, Patrick, 229
Buckley, Christopher, 492, 495–97,
    499–501
Buckley, James, 93–95, 108–9, 174–76,
    213, 366
Buckley, Jane, 474
Buckley, John, 224
Buckley, Maureen, 460–62
Buckley, Pat, 403–9, 471–72, 481–82,
    489–90, 498–99
Buckley, Patricia (Trish), 473–75
Buckley, Priscilla, 341, 342, 344
Buckley, Reid, 328
Bundy, McGeorge, 420, 425, 428, 430
Bunker, Ellsworth, 229
Burgess, Anthony, 177, 244
Burke, Edmund, 27
Burnham, James, 52, 230, 255
Butz, Earl, 104–6

California, 210, 211
California, University of, 445–46
Callaghan, James, 248
Calley, Lt. William, 268
Cambodia, 44–47
Camp of the Saints, The (Raspail), 255
Campagna, Philip, 495, 499
Canada, 275
Capellanus, Andreas, 190
Capote, Truman, 120–21
Carter, Hodding, III, 102
Carter, Jimmy, 36–39, 56, 57, 59, 80,
    101, 102, 106, 107, 110, 112–13,
    128–29, 167, 218, 219, 222, 223,
    230, 237–39, 248, 286, 344–45,
    385, 386
Castro, Fidel, 66, 67, 231, 264–66
Cates, David, 473–74
Central Intelligence Agency (CIA),
    63–67, 72, 119, 120, 133, 134,
    328–29
Cervantes, Maria, 296–97
Chalfont, Lord, 58
Chamberlain, John, 429, 431

Chambers, Whittaker, 24, 53, 141–43,
    147
Chaplin, Charlie, 193
Chase, Mary Ellen, 326
Cheever, John, 316, 317
Chesterton, G. K., 225, 406, 412
Chiang Ch'ing, 182
Chicago, 387–89
Chile, 234
China, 34, 58, 61, 87–88, 128, 144–45,
    154, 182–83, 239, 272–74
Chinese Shadows (Leys), 272–74
Chodorov, Frank, 415, 420
Chou En-lai, 181–83, 272
Christianity, 286, 287, 289, 313, 424,
    425, 428–29
Christiansen, Greg, 377
Christie, Agatha, 330
Church, Frank, 106
Church of England, 288, 289
Churchill, Sir Winston, 272
Civil Rights Congress, 148, 149
Civil Service Commission, 64–65
Civil Service Loyalty Review Board, 144
Clark, Ramsey, 44
Clemensen, Douglas C., 359
Cleveland, James C., 366–67
Coe, William Rogers, 418
Coffin, Rev. Henry Sloane, 426, 428,
    430–32
Colman, Ronald, 193
Colson, Charles, 118, 131
Common Market, 245
Commonweal (magazine), 426
Communist Party (U.S.), 160, 170
Company, The (Ehrlichman), 117–21
Condition Humaine, La (Malraux), 24
Congress, U.S., 32
Connally, John, 91, 96–97
Connecticut, 176
Conservative Intellectual Movement in
    America since 1945, The (Nash), 23
Convention on the Prevention and
    Punishment of the Crime of
    Genocide, 43–45
Cooke, Terence Cardinal, 114
Cooper, Jeff, 339
Costikyan, Edward, 386
Coulson, Richard, 419
Council on Foreign Relations, 379
Countryman, Vern, 427
Cousins, Norman, 291
Cromie, Robert, 326

Cronkite, Walter, 97
Cuba, 264–66.
    See also Bay of Pigs invasion
Cuban missile crisis (1962), 162
Cuernavaca, Bishop of, 183
Culhane, Chuck, 352–53
Cultural and Scientific Conference for
    World Peace, 147
Cultural Revolution, Chinese, 272
Cuomo, Mario, 391–93
Cyrano (schooner), 466, 485, 491–92,
    494, 499–502
Czechoslovakia, 160, 168

Dane, Clemence, 193
Davenport, John, 424
Davies, John Paton, 144
Davis, Angela, 51
Davis, Elizabeth Gould, 189
Day in the Life of Ivan Denisovich, A
    (Solzhenitsyn), 24
Day of the Jackal, The (Kraft), 70
Dean, John, 106, 117
Declaration on Human Rights, 54
Deep Throat (film), 314–16
De Gaulle, Charles, 70, 322
De Laurentiis, Dino, 74
Democracy and Education (Dewey), 26
Democratic National Convention
    (1968), 168–69
Democratic National Convention
    (1976), 165–67, 170–71
Democratic Platform (1976), 86–89
Denmark, 244, 275, 303
De Voto, Bernard, 219
DeWalt, Father M. M., S.J., 361–63
Dewey, John, 26, 145–46, 154
Dinah Shore Show, 324–25
Dolder Grand Hotel (Zurich), 274
Dole, Robert, 100
Dominican Republic, 133
Donaldson, Sam, 91
Douglas, Paul, 311
Douglas-Home, Sir Alec, 37
Drucker, Peter F., 26
Dukakis, Michael, 179
Dulles, John Foster, 144
Dunaway, Faye, 72, 73

Eastern Europe, 37, 106, 107, 154, 168
Eastman, Max, 424, 429–30
Echeverría, Luis, 256

Educational Exchange (newsletter), 343
Edwards, Jonathan, 83
Egypt, 232
Ehrlichman, John, 70, 117–21, 386
Eisenhower, Dwight D., 98, 129, 131,
    132, 157
Ellsberg, Daniel, 130
Emerson, Gloria, 35–36
Encounter (magazine), 423
England, 29, 203, 208, 242, 245, 246,
    248, 250. See also Great Britain
Eric H. Biddle, Jr. v. The United States of
    America, 65
ERP (Argentinian revolutionary group),
    267, 268
Europe, 241, 255, 274–76.
    See also Eastern Europe
Evans, Harold, 452, 453
Execution Eve (Buckley), 326–27

Fadiman, Clifton, 294
Fagan, Richard, 41
Fairbanks, Douglas, 191, 193
Falconer (Cheever), 316
Falk, Richard, 41
Farber, Barry, 326, 391
Farley, James, 112
Farrago, Ladislas, 68
Federal Bureau of Investigation, 65–69,
    120, 179–81
Federal Power Commission v. East Ohio
    Gas Co., 377
Feuer, Lewis, 178
Filler, Louis, 429
Finucane, Kathleen (Aunty Bill),
    492–93, 495, 496
"Firing Line" (television program), 308,
    309, 373, 374
First Circle (Solzhenitsyn), 24
Fitzgerald, F. Scott, 193
Fitzpatrick, Edward N., 398
Floto, Charles, 355
Flynn, Errol, 193, 314
Fontaine, Roger, 229
Ford, Betty, 300–3
Ford, Gerald, 49–51, 54, 61, 77–79,
    91–96, 100–3, 105–7, 113, 161, 163,
    177, 301, 312, 344, 345
Ford, Susan, 301
Foxes' Union, The (Kilpatrick), 194–96
France, 29, 255, 256, 275
Francis, Arlene, 326
Franck, Thomas M., 203–5

Franco, Generalisimo Francisco, 60, 255–56, 267
Freud, Sigmund, 209
Friedan, Betty, 316–17
Friedman, Milton J., 200
Friendly, Alfred, 157, 162
Fritchey, Clayton, 157
Fromm, "Squeaky," 262n
Frost, David, 126–31
Frye, Alton, 92
Fulbright, J. William, 62
Future That Doesn't Work, The (Tyrrell, Jr., ed.), 249

Gable, Clark, 193
Galbraith, Evan (Van), 492, 495, 497–501
Galbraith, John Kenneth, 57, 112, 231, 276, 322–23, 348–50, 372, 423, 467
Garbo, Greta, 193
Garrett, Garret, 424
Genocide Convention, 43–45
George-Brown, Lord, 247
Germany, 256. See also West Germany
Gilmore, Gary Mark, 389
Giscard d'Estaing, Valery, 37
Glazer, Nathan, 140, 145, 392
Glenn, John, 165
God and Man at Yale (Buckley), 24, 415–47
Goering, Hermann, 391
Goldman, Eric, 153
Goldwater, Barry, 97, 98, 165
Gorky, Maxim, 262
Gouzenko, Igor, 157–58
Graham, Katherine, 125
Grant, Cary, 191
Great Britain, 160, 203, 222, 242–50, 256, 275–76
See also England
Greece, 140–41, 233
Greene, Theodore M., 427, 436–38
Greenway, John, 188–90, 338, 339
Greer, Germaine, 141
Griswold, A. Whitney, 417, 418
Groueff, Stephane, 46
Gulag Archipelago, The (Solzhenitsyn), 24
Gundelfinger, George, 430

Halperin, Morton, 124–25
Hammett, Dashiell, 147–50

Harlech, Lord, 406
Harrington, Michael, 41, 69–70, 434–36
Hart, Jeffrey, 350
Hatch, Robert, 433
Hayden, Tom, 41
Hayek, Friedrich, 103
Hays, Wayne, 312
Hazelton, Nika, 408
Hazlitt, Henry, 424
Healey, Denis, 246, 248–49, 275–76
Heifetz, Milton, 290, 292
Hellman, Lillian, 139–52, 156
Helms, Richard, 117, 119, 120
Helsinki Agreement, 39
Helsinki Conference, 37
Henry Regnery Company, 50
Herlihy, John M., 340
Hersey, John, 143
Hersh, Sy, 371
Hess, Karl, 365, 366
Higgins, Father George, 426
Hiss, Alger, 142–44, 179
Hitler, Adolf, 29, 181, 183, 256
Hogan, Robert F., 355
Holbrooke, Richard, 45–46
Hollywood, 190–94
Hollywood Ten, 155–56
Hook, Sidney, 26, 156
Hoover, J. Edgar, 65–67, 120, 180–81
Hopkins, Miriam, 193
House of Commons, 248
House Unamerican Activities Committee, 143, 150
Howe, Irving, 145, 151
Hoyt, Norris, 465–66
Hughes, Paul, 157–58
Huk Communist insurgents, 187
Human Rights Commission, 238
Humphrey, Hubert H., 82, 163–74, 183, 184, 312
Hunt, Howard, 118, 119
Hutchins, Robert, 155

IBM, 54
Income and Employment (Morgan), 421
Ingersoll, Robert, 89
Ingerson-Rand, 54
Institute for Pacific Relations, 144
Internal Security Committee, 157, 161
Intercollegiate Society of Individualists (later Intercollegiate Studies Institute), 420
Internal Revenue Service, 149, 150

International Ocean Sailing Race, 269
Inveighing We Will Go (Buckley),
    377–78
Israel, 87, 110–11, 222, 250–53, 364–65
Ives, C. P., 424

Jackman, Brian, 452, 453
Jackson, Henry, 91
Jackson Amendment, 54–55
Japan, 185–87, 208, 275
Japanese-Americans, 208
Javits, Jacob, 97–98
Jay, Peter, 249
Jefferson, Thomas, 109, 156, 356,
    442–43
Jews, 282
John, Elton, 295–97, 379
John F. Kennedy Memorial Hospital v.
    Heston, 291
Johnson, Lady Bird, 225
Johnson, Lyndon B., 65, 119–21, 127,
    168, 169, 224, 225
Jones, Donald, 376
Jordan, Barbara, 96, 165, 166

Kama River plant, 53–57
Kazan, Elia, 141–42, 147
Kempton, Murray, 139, 142, 148–49
Kendall, Willmoore, 238, 415–16, 420,
    424
Kennedy, Edward M. (Ted), 201–3
Kennedy, John F., 63, 71, 119, 121, 127,
    132–35, 162–63
Kenner, Hugh, 360–61, 368–69
Kenya, 253
Keynes, Sir John M., 275, 337, 347–48,
    422–23
Khmer Rouge, 44–46
Khrushchev, Nikita S., 234
Kidder, Jerome, 385–86
Kilpatrick, James Jackson, 194–96, 281
Kilpatrick, Marie, 195
King, Rev. Martin Luther, Jr., 65–69
Kissinger, Henry, 32–34, 41, 51–53, 60,
    86, 100, 117, 121, 124–25, 129, 251,
    271, 325
Klay, Andor C., 358–59
Koch, Edward, 41–43, 143, 176, 366,
    367, 391–93
Koenig, Murray, 385
Koestler, Arthur, 147
Korean War, 140, 201
Kraft, Joe, 70

Kramer, Hilton, 145, 151
Kraut, Robert, 455, 458
Kristol, Irving, 439
Krokodil (magazine), 243
Kurland, Philip, 422, 442
Kutcher, James, 149
Kuwait, 275
Kuznetsov, Anatoly, 146

La Opinión (newspaper), 270
Labor Party (Great Britain), 247, 249,
    250
La Rochefoucauld, 302
Lasky, Melvin, 145
Latin America, 61, 62
Lattimore, Owen, 144–45, 155
Lehmann-Haupt, Christopher, 363
Leningrad, 259–63
Lens, Sidney, 41
Leonard, John, 154–55
Letherman, Lawrence, 180–81
Lewis, Anthony, 371
Lewis, C. S., 62
Leys, Simon, 272–74
Liberia, 237, 271
Libert, Herman, 427, 429
Libya, 275
Liddy, G. Gordon, 156
Life (magazine), 429
Lincoln, Abraham, 31–32
Lindsay, John V., 99
Lippmann, Walter, 153
Little, Brown, & Company, 152
Lodge, Henry Cabot, 105
Lofton, John, 34–36, 370
Lopez Rega, José, 267
Louisville Courier-Journal (newspaper),
    158
Love in the Ruins (Percy), 52
Lovett, Rev. Sidney, 417
Luce, Clare Boothe, 160, 286, 380
Lumumba, Patrice, 66

MacArthur, Charles, 193
MacArthur, Gen. Douglas, 110
McCain, Adm. John, 229, 232
McCarthy, Joseph, 144, 152–61
McCarthy, Mary, 147
McCarthy Committee, 141, 157
McCarthyism, 139–63
McCloskey, Robert J., 41
Macdonald, Dwight, 147, 417, 419,
    425–26, 439

McFadden, Jim, 351
McGinnis, Joe, 323, 326
McGovern, George, 88, 169–70
McGrath, Most Rev. Marcos, 266
Macmillan, Harold, 242–45
Madden, Sandra J., 379
Maddox, Lester, 170
Malraux, André, 24
Mankiewicz, Frank, 266
Manlove, Murl J., 360
Mao Tse-tung, 128, 181, 182, 272
Marcos, Ferdinand, 186–88
Martins de Hoz, 269
Marx, Karl, 349
Massachusetts, 179
Massachusetts Bar Association, 179
Matis, Stasnley, 353–54
Matthews, Rives, 337
Meadows, Edward, 347–48
Medvedev, Zhores, 262
Melville, Herman, 412
Mencken, Henry, 214
Merritt, Daniel (Danny), 492, 493, 495,
    497–98, 502
Mexico, 217
Meyer, Elsie, 341–44
Meyer, Frank, 341–44
Meyer, John, 341
Michael, Franz, 182
Michener, James, 87
Middle East, 87.
    See also Arab nations; Organization of
    Petroleum Exporting Countries
Mill, John Stuart, 437
Miller, Col. Fred W., 355–56
Mitchell, Mike, 463, 477–79, 481, 482
Mobutu, Sese Seko, 253
Mondale, Walter F., 90, 110
Monday (newsletter), 34
Montgomery, Robert, 193
Montoneros, 266–68
Moore, Bishop Paul, Jr., 288, 317
Morgan, Theodore, 421
Morley, Felix, 424, 431
Mormons, 312–13
Morritt, Michael R., 364
Moscow, 257–59
Mount, Ferdinand, 249–50
Moynihan, Daniel Patrick, 108, 109,
    210–11, 213, 305, 392, 407
Muskie, Edmund, 166
Muzzio, William, 476–77

Nabokov, Dmitri, 362
Nabokov, Vera, 361–63
Nabokov, Vladimir, 318, 322, 361–63
Naipaul, V. S., 253–54
Nash, George, 25
Nathan, Robert, 192
National Council of Teachers of English
    (NCTE), 293–95, 355
National Review (magazine), 157, 158,
    241, 337–81
NBC, 154–56
Nehru, Jawaharlal, 234
Nepal, 237
Nessen, Ron, 78
Netherlands, the, 275
New York (magazine), 33
New York City, 175–76, 211, 288, 394
New York Daily Mirror, 162
New York Daily News, 162
New York Herald Tribune, 162
New York Post, 158
New York State, 176, 210, 211, 394
New York Times, 34–36, 85–86, 98, 241,
    281, 317
New York Times v. Sullivan, 205
New York Yacht Club, 474
New Yorker, The, 63–65
New Republic, The, 33
Newsweek, 429
Nicholas, Czar, 263
Nicholas and Alexandria, palace of, 263
Nicholson, Sir Harold, 304
Niebuhr, Reinhold, 428
1984 (Orwell), 24
Niven, David, 190–94
Nixon, Richard M., 32, 33, 50, 52,
    77–79, 91, 98, 102, 103, 105,
    117–31, 141, 170, 229, 326, 423
Nock, Albert Jay, 304
North Vietnam, 29–30, 33, 35–36, 44,
    130
Norway, 275
Numann, Noelle, 304–5
Nuremberg trials (1945–46), 43

Okes, Blackford (fictional character),
    409–12
Olds, Irving, 430, 440–41
O'Neill, Eugene, Jr., 343
O'Neill, Richard, 474, 475
Ophus, Jan, 372–73
Organization of African Unity, 252–53

Organization of Petroleum Exporting Countries (OPEC), 222
Orwell, George, 52, 274
Osborne, John, 33
Ottaway, Mark, 452, 453

Palestinians, 252
Panama Canal, 229–35
Panic, The (cutter), 462, 466, 467, 469, 471, 476–84, 486, 487
Paris, Treaty of (1973), 32, 33
Parr, George, 225
Patolichev, Nikolai, 55
Patton, George, Jr., 189–90
Paul VI, Pope, 255
Pauling, Linus, 161–63
Pavlovich, Bill, 378
Peking, 273
Percy, Walker, 52, 325
Pérez, Carlos Andrés, 183–85
Perón, Isabella, 267
Perón, Juan D., 267, 269
Peter and Paul fortress (Leningrad), 262
Philippines, 186–88, 233
Phillips, William, 145, 151
Pike, Douglas, 35
Pius XII, Pope, 286, 290
Poland, 106, 107, 234
Pollack, Sydney, 72, 73
Ponchaud, Father François, 45
Power, Tyrone, 193
Pravda (newspaper), 39, 40
Prickman, Louis E., 380
Princeton University, 440–42
Progressive Party, 25, 147
Protestantism, 282, 285–86.
  See also Christianity
Pullman Company, 54

Quinlan, Karen Ann, 290, 291

Rabin, Yitzhak, 252
Rachmaninoff, Sergei, 327–28
Raspail, Jean, 255
Rather, Dan, 375, 376
Rauh, Joseph L., Jr., 157
Rayburn, Sam, 368
Reagan, Ronald, 52, 91–94, 97–101, 229, 232–34
Redford, Robert, 71–74
Reed, Clarke, 92

Reems, Harry, 314, 315
Reeves, Richard, 77–79, 83, 131
Regnery, Henry, 50, 415, 418
Rehyansky, Joseph A., 338
Reilly, Cecilia, 473
Republican Party, 97–101, 171
Reston, James, 87, 371–72
Resignation in Protest (Weisband and Franck, eds.), 203–5
Reynolds, Jack, 181–83
Rhodesia, 62, 271
Ricardo, David, 349
Rickenbacker, Bill, 352
Right to Die, The (Heifetz), 290, 292
Rinfret, Pierre, 347
Rio de Janeiro airport, 276–77
Ripon Society, 98
Robbins, Harold, 316–18
Robeson, Paul, 149, 159–61
Robinson, David, 346–47
Roche, John P., 339
Rockefeller, Nelson D., 97, 203–4
Rodell, Fred, 427, 429, 430
Rodman, Selden, 429
Roe v. *Wade,* 302
Rogers, Will, 74
Roman Catholic Church (Catholicism), 285, 286, 288, 425–28
Roosevelt, Franklin D., 103–4, 127, 269
Roosevelt, Theodore, 232
Rosenbaum, Richard, 93
Rovere, Richard, 152–54, 157
Rowan, Carl, 67–69, 159
Royal Commission on the Vulgarization of the Book of Common Prayer, 289
Rubinstein, Arthur, 327
Ruesthe, A., 340
Rumania, 107
Rumsfeld, Donald, 78
Rusk, Dean, 204
Russell, Lord Bertrand, 155
Russell, Francis, 179–81
Russia (pre-revolutionary), 263, 264. *See also* Soviet Union
Russian people, 278
Russians, The (Smith), 261

Sacco and Vanzetti case, 179–81
Sakharov, Andrei, 257, 262
Salas, Luis, 224–25
Salazar, Antonio de Oliveira, 60

SALT I, 40
SALT II, 39
SALT treaties, 230
Samphan, Khieu, 46
Sanders, George, 193
Saudi Arabia, 222
Saving the Queen (Buckley), 328, 380, 410
Say's Law, 348
Scandinavia, 28
Schindler, Rabbi Alexander, 111
Schlesinger, Arthur, Jr., 132–35, 145, 153, 204, 209, 427
Schmidt, Helmut, 37
Scorpio, E. M., 379
Scott, George C., 322
Scoundrel Time (Hellman), 139–52, 156
Scrabble, Virginia, 194–96
Security Council, United Nations, 230
Service, John Stewart, 144
Sevareid, Eric, 176–78, 373–75
Seymour, Charles, 428, 432, 442, 443
Shantung, 273–74
Sharp, Eliot H., 364–65
Shipler, David, 54
Shore, Dinah, 324–25
Shostakovich, Dmitri, 147
Shure, Leonard, 358
Silver, Charles, 113
Simon, William, 310, 311
Singleton, Donald, 385
Slattery, William J., 370–71
Smith, A. P., 440
Smith, Edgar, 395–99
Smith, Hedrick, 261, 278
Smith, Ian, 241, 271
Snaith, William, 463–64
Snerd, Mortimer, 147
Sobran, Joe, 346
Socialist Party (Great Britain), 247
Socialist Workers Party, 149
Solzhenitsyn, Aleksandr, 24–25, 49–51, 55, 58, 139, 247, 262, 272
Sophocles, 359
Soustelle, Jacques, 270–71
South Africa, 62, 270–72
South Korea, 111
South Vietnam, 28–34, 44, 131, 170, 224
Southeast Asia, 60, 61, 239
Soviet bloc, 236
Soviet Constitution of 1936, 39
Soviet Union, 26, 29, 34, 37–40, 50–51,
    53–60, 70, 74, 81, 129, 130, 144–47, 152, 154, 156, 159, 160, 162, 168, 182, 230, 239, 257–64
Soyuz-Apollo mission, 47–49
Spain, 233, 255–56
Spock, Benjamin, 41
Stalin, Joseph (Stalinism), 145–47, 151, 152, 154, 156, 160, 265
Stang, Alan, 344
Starr, Peter, 467, 480, 482, 486, 492
State, Department of, 41, 60, 144, 182
Stein, Gertrude, 368–69
Stevenson, Adlai, III, 213
Stewart, James, 319
Stigler, George, 348–50
Stoessel, Walter J., Jr., 345n
Strauss, Robert, 171
Suez Canal, 232
Suicide of the West (Burnham), 52, 255
Sullivan, Sean E., 377
Supreme Court, U.S., 215, 225, 283, 302, 315, 377, 399. See also specific cases
Suzy Wong (yawl), 466-69, 493
Swann, Eva, 476
Sweden, 250, 275
Sweeney, Paul, 373
Sweet Isolation (boat), 473
Switzerland, 208, 244, 274–75
Symbionese Liberation Army, 268

Taft, Robert A., 24
Taft, William Howard, 232
"Tail Gunner Joe" (television special), 154–56
Taiwan, 87–88, 128–29
Tarshis, Lorie, 422, 423
Taylor, Austin (Firpo), 466, 482, 483, 486, 487
Taylor, George, 182
terHorst, Jerry, 105
Thatcher, Margaret, 248–50, 309, 350
Thieu, Nguyen Van, 29–33
Third World, 236–37
Tho, Le Duc, 130
Thornhill, Arthur, 152
Three Days of the Condor (film), 71
Tibet, 237
Time (magazine), 159, 161, 285, 429
Timmons, Ronald, 385–86
"Today" show, 322, 323, 332
Torrijos, Gen. Omar Herrera, 231, 234

Tragedy in Dedham (Russell), 179–81
Transkei, 270–71
Trilling, Diana, 141, 152
Trilling, Lionel, 141
Trotsky, Leon, 149
Truman, Harry S, 110, 127, 131, 140, 162
Trumbo, Dalton, 156
Tucker, Teddy, 497
Turkey, 140–41, 233
Tydings Committee, 155
Tyler, Tom, III, 340
Tyrrell, E. Emmett, Jr., 249

Uganda, 43–45
United Nations, 234, 237–39, 241–42, 253, 254
United Nations Covenants, 39
United States Committee for Justice to Latin American Political Prisoners, 41
United States Information Agency, 50–51
Up from Liberalism (Buckley), 381
U.S.A. Institute, 59

Van den Haag, Ernest, 221
Vanocur, Sander, 35
Venezuela, 183–85, 278
Viasa airline, 276–78
Viator, James, 356
Videla, Gen. Jorge Rafael, 267–69
Vietnam, 38, 44.
  See also North Vietnam; South Vietnam
Vietnam War, 28–36, 87, 130–31, 168–69, 203–5, 210, 229, 325
Village Voice, The (weekly), 105
Vincent, John Carter, 144
Vineyard Race, 462–63, 479
Von Dreele, William H., 344
Von Hoffman, Nicholas, 123
Voyles, Joseph, 376

Wakefield, Dan, 328

Waldorf Conference, 147
Wall Street Journal, 162
Wallace, George, 165, 170, 385
Wallace, Henry, 25, 107, 146–47, 154, 160
Wallen, Charles, Jr., 360
Walsh, Chad, 433
Watch on the Rhine (Hellman), 146
Watergate affair, 117–35, 214–15
Waugh, Evelyn, 153–54
Wechsler, James, 141
Weisband, Edward, 203–5
West Germany, 250, 275, 303
Westinghouse, 54
Weyand, Fred, 180–81
Wheeler, Tim, 352
White, Theodore (Teddy), 123, 141, 373–75
Will, George, 229–30, 342
Williamson, Chilton, 376–77
Wills, Gary, 128, 140, 142, 147
Wilson, Edmund, 149
Wilson, Harold, 245–47
Wilson, Woodrow, 109
Wimsatt, William, 430, 437–39, 445
Winston, Henry, 59
Woodward, Bob, 124
World Council of Churches, 235, 428
World Telegram and Sun, 162
World War II, 186–87
Worsthorne, Peregrine, 37
Wright, H. G., 346
Wurf, Jerry, 166

Yale Alumni magazine, 430
Yale Corporation, 445
Yale *Daily News,* 418, 430
Yale University, 25.
  See also God and Man at Yale
Young, Andrew, 44, 240–42
Young Socialists (Great Britain), 247–48
Yugoslavia, 107

Zaire, 253–54
Zumwalt, Adm. Bud, 229